T0274313

an Atlanta Story

SIMON & SCHUSTER PAPERBACKS

NEW YORK LONDON TORONTO SYDNEY NEW DELHI

RAP CAPITAL

JOE COSCARELLI

Simon & Schuster Paperbacks
An Imprint of Simon & Schuster, Inc.
1230 Avenue of the Americas
New York, NY 10020

First Simon & Schuster trade paperback edition October 2023

SIMON & SCHUSTER PAPERBACKS and colophon are registered trademarks of Simon & Schuster, Inc.

For information about special discounts for bulk purchases, please contact Simon & Schuster Special Sales at 1-866-506-1949 or business@simonandschuster.com.

The Simon & Schuster Speakers Bureau can bring authors to your live event. For more information or to book an event, contact the Simon & Schuster Speakers Bureau at 1-866-248-3049 or visit our website at www.simonspeakers.com.

Interior design by Carly Loman

Manufactured in the United States of America

1 3 5 7 9 10 8 6 4 2

Library of Congress Cataloging-in-Publication Data is available.

ISBN 978-1-9821-0788-8
ISBN 978-1-9821-0789-5 (pbk)
ISBN 978-1-9821-0790-1 (ebook)

And if this is the fault of America, how dire a danger lies before a new land and a new city, lest Atlanta, stooping for mere gold, shall find that gold accursed!

—W. E. B. Du Bois, "Of the Wings of Atalanta," 1903

Fuck 'em! We ball.

—Curtis Snow, *Snow on tha Bluff*, 2012

CONTENTS

PART III

RAP CAPITAL

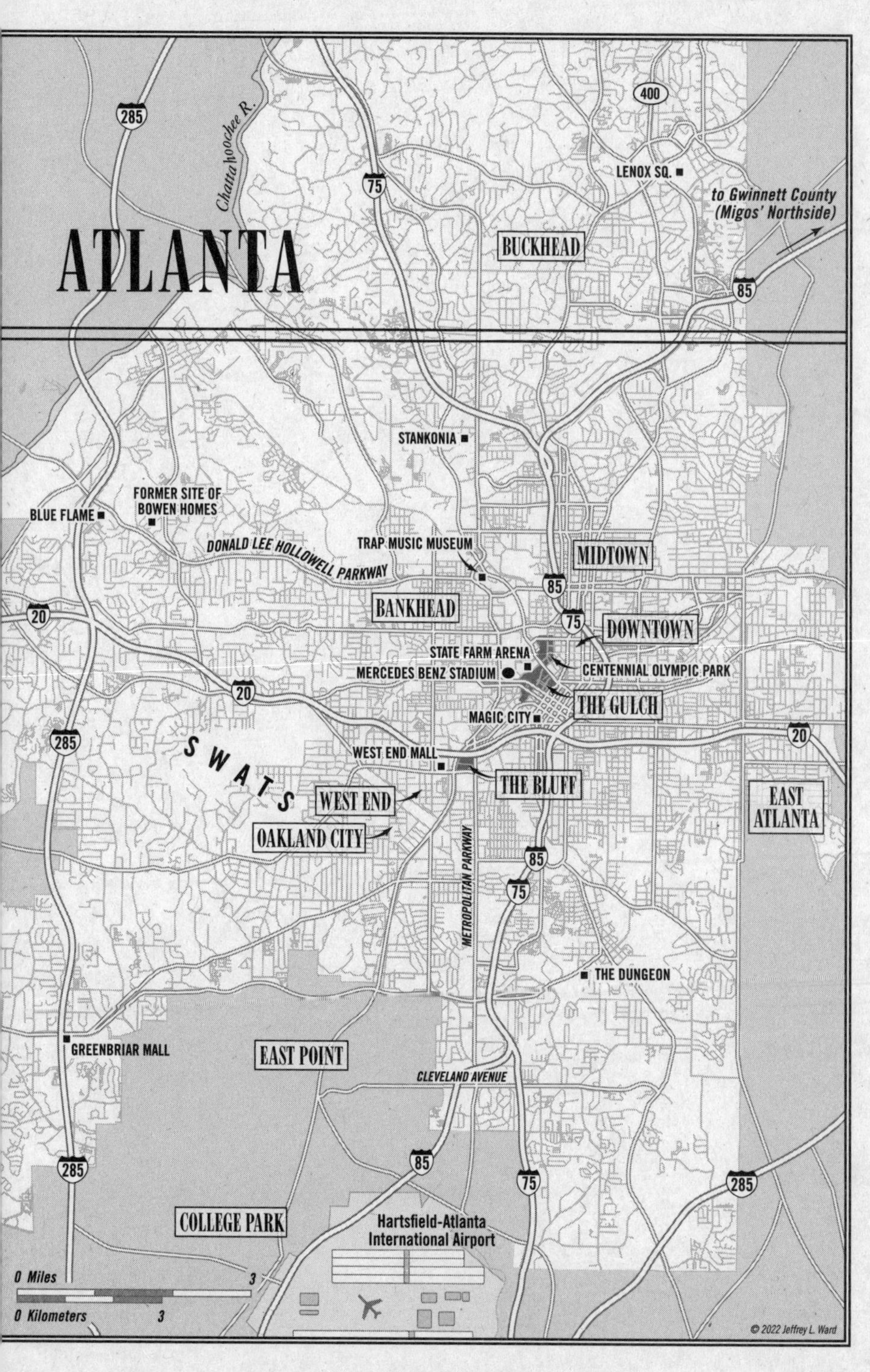
ATLANTA
285
Chattahoochee R.
400
LENOX SQ.
75
to Gwinnett County
(Migos' Northside)
BUCKHEAD
85
STANKONIA
FORMER SITE OF
BOWEN HOMES
BLUE FLAME
TRAP MUSIC MUSEUM
DONALD LEE HOLLOWELL PARKWAY
MIDTOWN
BANKHEAD
20
DOWNTOWN
STATE FARM ARENA
MERCEDES BENZ STADIUM
CENTENNIAL OLYMPIC PARK
THE GULCH
MAGIC CITY
SWATS
WEST END MALL
THE BLUFF
WEST END
EAST
ATLANTA
OAKLAND CITY
METROPOLITAN PARKWAY
THE DUNGEON
GREENBRIAR MALL
EAST POINT
CLEVELAND AVENUE
COLLEGE PARK
Hartsfield-Atlanta
International Airport
0 Miles 3
0 Kilometers 3
© 2022 Jeffrey L. Ward

INTRODUCTION

DOMINIQUE JONES WAS NEVER EXPECTING A REVOLUTION. HE wasn't even supposed to be a rapper, let alone an activist. But in Atlanta, Georgia, in the summer of 2020, the man known as Lil Baby wasn't left with much of a choice.

Early that June, as he marched down Mitchell Street, west of downtown, Baby raised his fist in the air, mirroring the more seasoned protesters, and he joined them in their chants of "No justice, no peace!" Skinny and loping, the rapper was discreet as could be, save for the cameras following his every step, dressed in a plain black T-shirt and matching snapback, no chains, and a bulbous white medical mask obscuring most of his newly famous face.

"This is what matters," Lil Baby leaned over and told his guide for the day, an ambitious local city councilman. About an hour in, when a white business owner on the route passed out bottles of water to the group, Baby handed him $500.

Days after the protest, the Southwest Atlanta native, only three years into an unlikely music career, would see his biggest album yet hit number one on the *Billboard* chart for a second time—and in the weeks that followed, a third, fourth and fifth. But even as a millionaire on the rise, Lil Baby wasn't that far removed from his days at the mercy of white corrections officers, or the cops who had thrown him into a room with no cameras to remind him who was in charge. The year prior to the demonstrations, Baby, already a budding star, had been removed from a sports car in evening traffic and pushed face-first into the Atlanta pavement to be handcuffed for speeding.

So as another summer of Black Lives Matter uprisings took shape around the country, the urgent response to months (years, decades, centuries) of consequence-less killings of Black people—Ahmaud Arbery, Breonna Taylor and George Floyd Jr. recently among them—Baby felt personally obligated to take to the streets of his hometown during the global COVID-19 pandemic. He needed to confront what had long been his reality, especially before rap helped rescue him from a chaotic world of guns and drug dealing that had already sent him to prison once.

Still, this wasn't his comfort zone. Generally reserved and content to keep his head down, Baby did not consider himself a role model or a particularly political person. When it came to hip-hop, he hadn't exactly grown up on Public Enemy or N.W.A. He was twenty-five; even the local philosopher-gods in Goodie Mob and OutKast were a bit before his time. He didn't much look up to artists anyway. "Money is the only fucking option," went the thesis statement of his first-ever single.

Yet within a year after the protests, Lil Baby would be at the White House with George Floyd's family, meeting with Joe Biden, Kamala Harris and Nancy Pelosi about policing and criminal justice reform. Because whether he'd planned it or not, Baby had become a leader, the culmination of nearly three decades of Atlanta rap—and specifically the Southern subgenre known as trap music, which revolved around the blaring sun of the drug trade—from Raheem the Dream, MC Shy D and Kilo Ali through Gucci Mane, TI and Young Jeezy, not to mention untold other innovators, both recognized and disregarded along the way. Their work grew from struggle, from racism, from pain, from impossibility, and it worked on two crucial levels: for those who felt it, lived it, needed it, and for those who wanted to dabble in the ups and downs, if only from afar. Their experiences—Baby's experience—growing up rough in the city of Atlanta had somehow become national youth culture, their music the dominant lens through which a neglected humanity was partially understood, all while serving as America's principal artistic illustration of both crushing poverty and absurd, unexpected wealth.

A convicted felon raised by a single mother on government assistance, Baby detailed in his jittery music just how amazing and awful it could feel simultaneously to make it out of such insurmountable circumstances. His very existence was a political statement. But his music up to then—wordy, rich, wrenching and bass heavy—was, according to his fans, the perfect soundtrack for reckless driving or basketball highlight montages, not protests. Baby's motivational street anthems sometimes sounded like they were being played in fast-forward, like he had too many things to say at once, and they had been filled lately with jabbing boasts about wearing so much diamond jewelry that it all tangled together, about buying floor seats at Madison Square Garden and standing up to cheer not because he cared about the game, but just to show off his wares. More than anything else, Baby's music was autobiographical, full of details that may have felt insignificant to anyone outside of his family or closest friends—allusions to illicit business on Sparks Street, near-miss shootouts, the hustlers who helped him and the women who wanted to. This was the stuff, like the songs of his Atlanta forebears, that was so potent, so original, so honest, well stylized and alluringly transgressive that it had become a worldwide touchstone, in spite of being grounded in discrete places and plights that were otherwise often ignored.

Like his predecessors, Lil Baby blended an oral tradition of neighborhood dope-boy mythology with melodic, ominous synth-and-808-driven beats to create a constantly evolving sound that, in a wholly unexpected development given its serrated edges, had ended up a go-to mode for much of music, white or Black, by the late 2010s. Lady Gaga, Beyoncé, Miley Cyrus and Ariana Grande mined trap's rhythms and its slang; Super Bowl commercials tapped its talent; and suburban teenagers everywhere adhered to its sleek and loud designer dress code. Like the essence of jazz, rock, disco, techno and so on, the source code was always Black, but the applications were widespread and only sometimes came with acknowledgment—trap was being borrowed, sampled, looted, diluted, hoarded, disparaged and hailed all at once. Years after the statement had already become a fact, a T-shirt announcing ATLANTA INFLUENCES EVERYTHING became a defiant, wearable meme.

But as the culture reporter and critic Rodney Carmichael wrote in 2016, "To be an ATLien means being simultaneously fetishized and stigmatized in much the same way America outwardly loves Black culture but inwardly loathes Black life."

Lil Baby knew this dichotomy in his bones as he marched on that summer day. In fact, he had already recorded a new song to that effect, inspired by the unmistakable moment he was living through. What most who saw Baby protesting didn't know at first was that his participation was also doubling as research—and as a music video shoot—for the biggest swerve in his brief career so far.

At midnight on June 12, 2020, Lil Baby released "The Bigger Picture." Immediately hailed as an essential Black Lives Matter protest anthem—and with the promise that its proceeds would support the movement—the song was tidy and timely on the surface. But it was most striking upon closer listen in its stream-of-consciousness ambivalence, its inability to stay simple. "It's bigger than Black and white," Baby rapped. "It's a problem with the whole way of life."

Across three unwieldy verses, Baby declined to sublimate the uncouth complexities of his own experiences, celebrating a new car and an old friend who just beat a murder charge before declaring, "I find it crazy the police'll shoot you and know that you dead, but still tell you to freeze." This was the whole story, still unfolding, not a neat narrative. "I can't lie like I don't rap about killing and dope, but I'm telling my young'ns to vote," he rattled off, his unpredictable candor making his bursts of compassion and critique land harder.

In the same song, Baby refused to condemn all cops; encouraged Black gun ownership out of necessity; vowed to never testify in court; and admitted to running at the first flash of blue lights. He sounded exhausted and angry and alive. Eventually, "The Bigger Picture" would be streamed hundreds of millions of times, reaching number three on the *Billboard* singles chart and earning Baby two Grammy nominations, plus a double-platinum plaque. But first, the night after the song's release, it happened again, as Baby must have known that it would. This time, it was at home.

Outside of a Wendy's in South Atlanta, Rayshard Brooks, an unarmed twenty-seven-year-old Black father of four, spent more than thirty minutes speaking calmly with two white police officers before taking off on foot with one of their Tasers as they attempted to handcuff him for having driven drunk. Seconds later, Garrett Rolfe of the Atlanta Police Department fired his service weapon three times, hitting Brooks twice from behind.

"I got him," the officer said, according to the prosecutors who later charged him with murder. As had become routine, the killing was caught on tape.

The next night, the Wendy's was burned down as the protests in Atlanta intensified. A few weeks later, on the Fourth of July, near the same cursed site, an eight-year-old Black girl was shot and killed in the runoff mayhem. It would be a bloody summer in Atlanta, and the city ended the year with 157 homicides on record, the most in more than two decades.

Lil Baby, coming from where he did, could not avoid being affected directly by the tragedy that continued to surround him, even as a rap star. Not everyone would make it out from where he had, a relentless reality that was underlined again and again in 2020. It was also the best year of his life. In Baby's Atlanta, an imperfect place and a cradle of culture, he was, at least for the moment, a hero.

In the beginning, it was Terminus.

Originally founded as the endpoint of the Western and Atlantic Railroad, long before the tangled mess of spaghetti highways and the construction of the busiest airport in America, the city that would become Atlanta had its roots in transportation. A blue city in a red state, a Black metropolis in a white country, an energized urban center with a small-town vibe in the slow-moving, spread-out South, Atlanta has always been a place of collision: the screwed-up, salvaged result of a violent history, from General Sherman's Civil War march of flames to the murderous race riots of 1906, from the plague of Jim Crow lynchings to the burial of its assassinated native son, Martin Luther King Jr.

W. E. B. Du Bois, the Black sociologist and future cofounder of the NAACP, wrote in 1903 that Atlanta was "south of the North, yet north of the South"—and also a land full of "vulgar money-getters." Across decades and centuries, the city has been "a bastion of both white supremacy and Black autonomy," according to one historian, and pretty much always "on the brink of either tremendous rebirth or inexorable decline," in the words of another. It was the first place in the United States to build public housing, shunting poor Black residents into overcrowded, underfunded slums over the course of fifty-plus years. And then it was one of the earliest places to unceremoniously tear that housing down, pushing those struggling families even further to the fringes in hopes of stamping out crime and hosting the 1996 Olympic Games.

Through many rounds of upheaval, Atlanta has made itself both incredibly diverse and unbelievably segregated—"a 60 percent Black city that floats in a sea of white suburbia whose inhabitants desperately avoid contact with the untouchables," as the journalist Robert Scheer wrote in 1978, not knowing how true that statement would remain more than four decades later. It's the kind of town where a Black mayor could be voted in by a Black majority while a white minority keeps 95 percent of the local wealth, where the civil rights movement was birthed only to see segregation get worse by 1980 than it was in 1940, following generation after generation of white flight. When a serial killer began terrorizing Black Atlantans in 1979, murdering their children with enough brazenness to fuel a dozen modern true-crime specials, it took sustained pressure from Black mothers before anyone else would pay attention.

At the same time, Atlanta's Black Mecca status has been well earned in the eyes of so many, sprouting as it did from a strong network of historically Black colleges, universities, churches and businesses that have their roots in the ugliest periods of American history. At the start of the Civil War, Atlanta was home to fewer than 10,000 people, but it had quadrupled in size in the ten years prior and would continue to grow exponentially in the decades after. Today, the metropolitan area is home to more than two million Black people—substantially more than Chicago, Washington, DC, Philadelphia or Houston, and second in the nation only to New York, which is three times more populous. By proportion, that makes Atlanta easily the Blackest major metro area in the country, even as the city itself is becoming whiter. In 2018, *Forbes* called Atlanta the best place in America for Black people economically (tied with DC), while political victories in 2020 and 2021 had Democrats promising an altogether new Georgia, thanks largely to a diverse Atlanta and its suburbs.

Again and again, the city has been held up as a steadfast beacon for the New South and the New America, with shining historical examples like Sweet Auburn, the Black commercial district of the early twentieth century that sprung up after the race riots. But in line with the jaggedness of its history, Atlanta has also long relied on myth, superficial shine and Band-Aids to cover its historical wounds and ongoing afflictions. It branded itself as "the City Too Busy to Hate" in the 1960s, when there was still plenty of time for racial animus, and often falls back on the same kind of sloganeering today as rampant inequality festers and Republican backlash to progressive gains earns comparisons to the voter disenfranchisement of Jim Crow. Some have still ventured so far as to call the city Wakanda. (*Black Panther* was filmed in town.)

Yet across its successes and its struggles, Atlanta and its Black residents in particular have proven time and again to be resolute, resourceful and experimental, continually pushing boundaries in politics, business and culture—especially, since the end of the twentieth century, in music.

Raheem. Shy D. Kilo. Jermaine Dupri. Big Gipp. Khujo. T-mo. CeeLo. Big Rube. Cool Breeze. Big Boi. André 3000. Killer Mike. Ludacris. Pastor Troy. TI. Jeezy. Gucci Mane. Shawty Lo. Fabo. Lil Jon. Crime Mob. Baby D. OJ da Juiceman. Soulja Boy. B.o.B. Waka Flocka Flame. Young Dro. Travis Porter. Rocko. Rich Kidz. 2 Chainz. Trouble. Bankroll Fresh. Future. Migos. iLoveMakonnen. 21 Savage. Rich Homie Quan. Young Thug. Playboi Carti. Gunna. Lil Nas X. Lil Baby.

All of those men—and they have tended to be overwhelmingly men—have had Atlanta and its outskirts in common on their way to making some of the most impactful, commercially successful and influential music of the last thirty-plus years. (Even Kanye West, the son of a pioneering Black photographer at the *Atlanta Journal-Constitution* and a Clark Atlanta University English professor, shares these roots.) Many from the city have become international celebrities, many more only footnotes or building blocks. But this colorful lineage has changed the course of not only hip-hop but culture writ large, tearing through fashion, sports, television, film and, of course, the internet.

Flowering wildly in just enough isolation, unbound by the claustrophobia of city blocks or strict tradition, Atlanta's rap music is the result of having the freedom to unfurl until the strictures of the American South start to suffocate—and then pushing further. When Ralph Ellison, in describing Richard Wright's *Black Boy*, compared the book to the blues, he called that earlier form of Black Southern sound "an impulse to keep the painful details and episodes of a brutal experience alive in one's aching consciousness, to finger its jagged grain, and to transcend it, not by the consolation of philosophy, but by squeezing from it a near-tragic, near-comic lyricism." That tradition lives on in this music, even as it is stripped for parts. But increasingly—thanks to technology and an insatiable market always hungry for glimpses of so-called authentic Blackness—the most uncompromising of Atlanta artists have been afforded the opportunity to spread outside the city limits. The radio, Spotify, YouTube and Hollywood alike are replete with, as Ellison wrote, "the paradoxical, almost surreal image of a black boy singing lustily as he probes his own grievous wound."

None of this was a foregone conclusion. For as long as rap music has been considered by region, artists from the South have been discounted, demeaned and overlooked, dubbed ignorant or inaccessible, overly simplistic or vulgar or simply too country, in line with broader prejudices against people—and especially Black people—from below the Mason-Dixon Line. In 1990, when *Spin* magazine published an infographic detailing rap scenes around the United States, it called Atlanta's "basically the same as Miami's," with one label executive complaining about demo tapes "marred by funny sounding accents and pronunciation" and concluding: "It's just not happening yet."

Even in the two-plus decades since OutKast released its 1994 debut *Southernplayalisticadillacmuzik* and declared, with rightful defensiveness, "The South got something to say," for a national audience, the disrespect continued. *Hip Hop Is Dead*, the 2006 album by Nas, was widely assumed to be targeting the ascendant Southern rap of the time, like crunk and snap music; in a promotional skit starring Nick Cannon in blackface and bling, Nas warned of "ridiculous dances, ignorant behavior, and general buffoonery" that would lead to "hip-hop's permanent annihilation." Three years later, Jay-Z rapped, "My raps don't have melodies," on "D.O.A. (Death of Auto-Tune)," again framing the North as the arbiter of hip-hop authenticity.

But both men lost their misguided battles. Artists from Atlanta and across its neighboring states have continued to innovate, lyrically and sonically, breathing new life into the genre—often using those derided Auto-Tuned melodies, South-specific language and, yes, dances, even as "mumble rap" became a twenty-first-century pejorative for a new, outré style of Atlanta hip-hop.

The paths of these artists, laid bare in Atlanta, represent the modern American dream—to make it out of poverty and obscurity to renown and riches—and also the American nightmare, as young Black men wrestle generational curses, crippled school systems, incarceration and racism on the way to an improbable destination atop art and commerce. And while the winners may have once seemed like unicorns who somehow reached this pinnacle, these generations (and micro-generations) of local rappers have routinely exploded the expectations of what a young Black man from little or nothing could hope to achieve in the broader American consciousness. Largely through music, the city has become a conveyor belt of exceptions.

That so much of this contradictory cultural history happened in the birthplace of Uncle Remus and Spike Lee, *Gone with the Wind* and Freaknik, is not a coincidence. It could only have been Atlanta. The Black defiance on display, too, can be traced to the city's beginnings and its forefathers, like the twelve-year-old R. R. Wright, who, when asked in 1868 by the commissioner of the Freedmen's Bureau what he should tell the children in the North about their Southern counterparts, replied, "Tell them we are rising."

Geographically, Atlanta is nothing if not a textbook example of urban sprawl. A collection of small towns, suburbs and "neighborhood planning units"—with endless strip malls, shopping centers, industrial parks, cul-de-sacs and tract houses—the metropolitan area pretends to be one big thing. But each section—often referred to in the city as Zones 1 through 6, in line with their respective police patrol areas—comes with its own customs, lingo and issues, many of which overlap, but all of which originated somewhere specific.

It's largely thanks to Atlanta's alternating history of oppression and opportunity that the city has been carved up into its current shape and form. In literal terms, it is a wobbly oval of juxtaposed worlds outlined by a man-made border—Interstate 285, known as the Perimeter or the Beltway. ITP (inside the Perimeter) represents everything within the asphalt circle, mostly Fulton and a little bit of DeKalb, two of the five core counties of the expansive metropolitan area. OTP (outside the Perimeter) sit the infinite suburbs—Marietta, Jonesboro, Lawrenceville, etc.—in the counties of Cobb, Clayton and Gwinnett, plus the remainder of the other two. To arrive at Hartsfield-Jackson Atlanta International Airport and start driving, which most do—because public transit, too, has been strangled by the invisible boundaries and dividing lines of racism—is to be smacked in the face with the full extent of that sprawl: some eight thousand square miles (about the size of New Jersey), including three separate business districts (downtown, Midtown, Buckhead), where every third street is called Peachtree and you may never learn if they ever connect.

The highways are so wide, crowded and plentiful that they can't help but feel like landmarks, with I-285 swelling from eight to twelve lanes at its widest, most chaotic junction. From Exit 1 (East Point) near the airport, one can follow the Perimeter clockwise around income brackets and ways of life, from the majority-Black southwest through Smyrna, Sandy Springs and so on, and end up edging against the whiter suburbs to the north and east, then back down around to Decatur and College Park.

Like Miami, Houston and Los Angeles, Atlanta doesn't feel much like a big city in most places. Its downtown skyline hardly matters. Instead, because there was no water or mountains hemming it in, the town bulged outward, always with a careful eye on which areas were getting too Black or not white enough, with adjustments made accordingly by the elite.

Off the highways, the defining visual feature of Atlanta is its foliage. Known as the City in a Forest, the place includes vast blankets of green overgrown kudzu that fills in the gaps between an encyclopedia's worth of trees, creating a canopy that makes the word "urban"—with its connotations of grit and gray and glass—feel entirely inapt. The dogwoods bloom thick and plump, the towering maples go screaming orange, the pines sit on stilts and the oaks have seen it all. It's not getting more plentiful, but the greenery still feels infinite—magnolias, cedars, crape myrtles, sweetgums, elms, crabapples, river birches, hickories—and it's this ocean of trees that makes every Atlanta neighborhood feel apart from every other one, and also kind of sleepy and quaint.

Yet rap music comes out of every crevice. In the neighborhoods more likely to come up in songs than in guidebooks—places often referred to using street names as synecdoche, like Bouldercrest, Cascade, Candler, Cleveland and Jonesboro—the living is low-density, with loose residential subdivisions creating self-contained villages with hyperlocal hierarchies on quiet streets, in backyards, empty lots, gas stations and corner stores. Single-family homes sit low to the ground and back beyond long driveways, with porches or pillars behind wild shrubbery.

Like "OTP or ITP," "house or apartment" is another consequential Atlanta divide. Off the interstate, squat clusters of low-income, cheaply paneled concrete or brick apartment buildings represent a quintessential local vista. Usually two or three floors each, tucked back away from a wooded road, these apartments tend to have plentiful parking, concrete staircases with a gap between every step and a seen-better-days basketball hoop that functions as a gathering point for kids and their bikes and the older guys who just want to put up a shot or two. Once meant to replace the demolished Atlanta housing projects, the apartments have been imbued with elements of those projects' mythologies, and also their risks. Today, these little worlds of potential are blanketed in security cameras that are purposefully prominent instead of hidden, requiring groups of weed smokers or other mischief-makers to slip around corners into darkened zones, which are never that hard to find. These complexes have names that feel machine-generated for maximum suburban banality: Avalon Ridge, Heritage Station, Auburn Glenn, Trestletree Village or any similar innocuous Mad Lib—Something Courts, Pines, Towers, Estates or Commons. The reality is often far bleaker.

But those who grew up in these spaces, away from Atlanta's shiny side—its Fortune 500 companies, like Delta, Coca-Cola and the Home Depot—are the ones who carry the history and traditions of the city's disenfranchised and its cast-offs, mostly over beats. In the decades since Atlanta first put itself on the cultural map with homegrown music, its residents have exploited the city's societal and geographic idiosyncrasies to build an affordable and close-knit hip-hop infrastructure that rivals that of New York or LA in impact—and with maybe more originality.

What follows in this book is not a comprehensive history of Atlanta, its culture, its sounds or even trap music—deserving projects that could and should fill several volumes. Instead, it is a zoomed-in portrait of a modern music scene and its direct antecedents, an examination of a small slice of a world with major reverberations. The story touches on events from the late 1970s to 2021 but centers on the years 2013 to 2020, a transitional moment in the music business and popular culture. Like Seattle grunge in the 1990s, London post-punk in the 1980s, Laurel Canyon folk in the 1970s or Detroit soul and R&B in the 1960s, Atlanta rap in the 2010s was the result of overlapping, tight circles of friends, families and rivals who took what their surroundings forced upon them and turned it into art, money and, sometimes, salvation.

Having spent much of the last decade in and out of Atlanta, including four years of dedicated reporting for this project—resulting in more than one hundred interviews across dozens of hours at recording studios, clubs, offices, block parties and on immersive ride-alongs—I have encountered many of the big names at the center of this network. But I have also learned the stories of the lesser-seen connectors, the grunt workers, the mothers, the DJs, the dealers, the prospects and the also-rans, who are equally important to the equation. From Bankhead to Buckhead, mansions to trap houses, office buildings to strip clubs, Atlanta is defined by its rap music. But the flashy and fast-paced world has rarely been seen below surface level as a collection not of superheroes and villains, cartoons and caricatures, but flawed and inspired individuals all trying to get a piece of what everybody else seems to be having.

Atlanta's music entrepreneurs once saw a blueprint in the old-fashioned local record labels like Ichiban, LaFace and So So Def. But a revamped industry—newly reliant on social media followers and invisible digital streams instead of CDs, cassettes and records—has led in recent years to an unprecedented gold rush, one that makes previous attempts to call Atlanta the new Motown seem premature. Streaming music, an alien concept just a decade ago—except to the rappers and fans who built the thriving underground economy of online mixtapes—now represents more than 80 percent of the action in the US record business, which recorded $12.2 billion in revenue in 2020, after being left for dead post-Napster. That change in format revealed what was long obvious to those paying attention: rap is the engine of most American youth trends, the genre firmly at the mainstream center of popular music and culture.

Throughout this new era, Atlanta in particular has undergone near-continuous rolling tremors of creative renaissance, as executives from near and far scour the city's neighborhoods for fresh songs and new stars. This effort has only intensified since 2017, when a trio known as Migos from northeast of the city topped the *Billboard* chart with "Bad and Boujee," an ode to cooking crack in style. The music of the 2010s, a crossroads turned victory lap for the industry, can largely be traced through Atlanta's world-beating wins—and its losses.

No local organization has proved a more reliable talent incubator or hitmaker during this period than the company called Quality Control Music. Founded in 2013 by the veteran rap manager Kevin Lee and his partner Pierre Thomas, a deep-pocketed investor with a spottier résumé, the label became, during the course of my reporting, the gold standard for a creative enterprise in Atlanta. Local and corporate-backed, familial and all business, Quality Control built upon the success of Migos, its first act, by tapping into what Atlanta had to offer over and over again, merging the city's street life and experimental impulses to feed the world more of what it has been demanding for decades, or even centuries: melodic tales of drugs and violence, sex and luxury—subjects all the more enticing, controversial and unsettling to American audiences when delivered by Black voices.

This book tells partly of that label's origins, its obstacles and its personalities—including the three Migos, Lil Baby and his partner in early rap ambivalence, a man known as Marlo—but also its influence and influences. Because Quality Control did not appear out of nowhere, and it does not exist in a vacuum. As they thrived, other Atlanta labels, crews and studio collectives—Freebandz, YSL, Slaughter Gang, Street Execs, LVRN, Think It's a Game—were on competing journeys, each inspiring imitators. Within and beyond these circles are countless individuals for whom rap is a business and a passion, a tie to street life and a raft away from it, and each of their contributions is crucial to what is known simply, in a show of its power and its reach, as *the culture*. Across Atlanta's recording studios, clubs, lounges, boutiques, traps and boardrooms, rap dreams are powering umpteen overlapping economies and are as likely to convince a teenager to stop selling drugs as to start; to make a poor man rich or a poor man poorer; to keep someone in jail or out of it. In artistic, commercial and human terms, Atlanta rap represents the most consequential musical ecosystem of this century so far. These are the stories of some of the people who make it tick, and the city that made them that way. Because Atlanta influences everything.

PART I

I.

PULLING TOGETHER

WAYNE WILLIAMS WANTED TO MAKE IT IN THE MUSIC BUSINESS. A self-proclaimed studio hand, audio engineer, talent scout and manager, Williams, who wore the flashy-patterned, wide-collared shirts of his time, was not handsome or talented enough to be a star himself. But he worked for years to assemble a group—dubbed Gemini, after his own astrological sign—that he hoped would stack up against the Jackson 5.

It was the 1970s in Atlanta, a burgeoning Black creative paradise in spite of itself. Maynard Jackson, the city's first Black mayor, had empowered a nascent music scene with the 1974 creation of the Bureau of Cultural Affairs, and it seemed to be working: Curtis Mayfield moved South for more inspiration after writing most of the *Super Fly* soundtrack in the city, while the Georgia-raised James Brown's variety show *Future Shock*—a wobbly *Soul Train* rip-off broadcast by the nascent mogul Ted Turner's first "superstation"—was being filmed in town. Something big was beginning, and Wayne Williams wanted in.

Born on May 27, 1958, and raised on Atlanta's historically Black West Side, he had long been known as a prodigy. The only child of schoolteachers, Williams taught himself as a boy how to wire electronics, founding his own neighborhood radio station, WRAP, from his family's tiny brick home. By the time he was hitting puberty, the station had evolved into something professional—its young mastermind set up transmitting equipment atop a local public housing project—and Williams was featured, sitting at the control board, in *Jet* magazine. "By then I was also thinking about how to make some money," he recalled, revealing the heart of his ambition at a time of great growth, and growing pains, for Black creatives in the South.

As an adult, Williams was slight at five foot five inches, with blemished and scarred skin, a squarish Afro and aviator eyeglasses that could seem either nebbishy or cool, depending on whose face they framed. It was safe to say he lacked any speck of glamour. But by the early 1980s, as a Georgia State dropout, he had turned his attention to circulating leaflets at local community centers and schools, auditioning kids for a chance to hit it big in music under his tutelage. A hustler with a sheen of professionalism, having registered companies with names like Nova and Omega Entertainment before ever releasing a note of recorded music, Williams would fake it for as long as possible, talking a big game and working whatever connections he could muster to little end. Eventually, after attempting to help their son follow his show-business aspirations, Williams's supportive parents would be forced to file for bankruptcy.

Williams had visited the city's recording studios with potential talent for years, leaving with hours of tape that no one would ever hear, another wannabe hoping to score on somebody else's shine. Then, late one spring night in 1981, his star search came to an abrupt, anticlimactic end that was also the seed of an international news event. Against all odds, Williams was the main attraction.

Near 3 a.m. on a Friday, he was driving in his family's white 1970 Chevrolet station wagon over the Chattahoochee River, through Northwest Atlanta, when he was pulled over following the sound of a splash below. For weeks, Atlanta police and the FBI had been staking out the area, with the city on edge over the disappearance of numerous Black children, and when they stopped Williams, he said, "I know this must be about those boys." In a baseball cap and glasses, he told the officers that he was just looking for a pay phone to confirm an audition the next morning with an entertainer named Cheryl Johnson. But the authorities never found a Cheryl Johnson. Two days later, the naked body of a twenty-seven-year-old man washed up in the area. Not long after, Williams was charged with the murder of Nathaniel Cater.

For the better part of two years, beginning in the summer of 1979, Black Atlanta had been gripped with fear over a child killer. That the first body the authorities sought to tie to Williams through dog hair and carpet fibers was a grown man—as was the second, Jimmy Ray Payne—was but a technical inconvenience for law enforcement. In Williams, they had found a sore thumb, decidedly provincial, who happened to spend a lot of time around children under the guise of work.

Later, at trial, prosecutors would argue that Williams, a bachelor who lived with his parents, was gay and a pedophile. He maintained his innocence. Yet no less than James Baldwin, who covered the case for *Playboy* and eventually in a book, *The Evidence of Things Not Seen*, referred to Williams as an "odd creature"—"a spoiled, lost and vindictive child." Baldwin described the suspect's aura as "terrifying," though the author, like many Black people who followed the case, remained skeptical about the scope of Williams's overall guilt.

"Atlanta at the time was in a panic," Williams said later from prison, after being convicted of killing the two adults and sentenced to life for each, effectively closing the other cases that involved more than twenty missing children. "They wanted any suspect that they could find," he said. "And let's just be honest: It had to be a Black person, because if it had been a white suspect, Atlanta probably would have gone up in flames."

Debate over the real killer's race—and why he could only be Black, or, alternatively, only be white—persisted for decades, and even today. Most agree that Williams, with his odd manner and a career going nowhere, was probably a murderer of some kind, though maybe not at the scale for which he was scapegoated. But at the time, a former business associate was able to put any larger questions of culpability aside, instead framing the alleged child killer as an Atlanta striver through and through.

"Whether he's guilty of these crimes or not," the acquaintance told the *New York Times*, "Wayne has won. He has always wanted attention, and he's got it."

* * *

Jeffrey Lamar Mathis, the fifth boy and sixth child to go missing, was ten when he disappeared in March of 1980. His body—all four feet eight inches and seventy-one pounds of it—was discovered by FBI agents and their cadaver dogs in a briar patch almost a year later. Due to the time passed, the boy's body had badly decomposed, and the cause of death could not be determined. He was identified by his dental records. (The spelling of Mathis's first name varies widely in the public record, from FBI files to news accounts, a detail perhaps indicative of the level of attention paid to the case.)

In a school photo from the time, Mathis wore a green and orange T-shirt meant to resemble a child-sized football jersey, its sleeves and collar ringed in white. His smile was sly and slightly crooked. Known as sharp-witted, tough and independent, he was exactly the type of Black boy to be unfairly explained away as a lost cause, incapable of being protected or reined in. Mathis's mother, Willie Mae, worked as a maid while raising six children. His father, William, a security guard at a cemetery, had been murdered on the job during a robbery years earlier. At the time of the disappearances, and in the decades since, the media—and Williams himself—portrayed the victims of the Atlanta Child Murders, as the killings came to be known, as hustlers and runaways, street kids from broken homes (or "drop shots," in the suspect's dated terminology) with no curfews or coddling.

CNN had launched right as the story was heating up in the summer of 1980, becoming the first twenty-four-hour news network, a crown-jewel-to-be of Ted Turner's Atlanta-based Turner Broadcasting System. Mayor Maynard Jackson was in his second of three terms. But the city's ever-simmering class divide, among Black Atlantans in particular, was apparent in both the depiction of the victims and the inattention their families and neighbors felt as children vanished, one by one, for more than a year before most took notice. A lack of coordination among law-enforcement agencies would be blamed for the scattered response, although those from the affected neighborhoods saw only neglect. In the midst of rising panic over the missing children, an explosion occurred at the day care center in the Bowen Homes projects, also on Atlanta's West Side, killing four kids and a teacher. Speculation that the incidents were connected—and that there was a white supremacist onslaught afoot—couldn't help but follow. (The explosion was later blamed on a faulty boiler.) Around the same time, the city's Chamber of Commerce started using the slogan "Let's Keep Pulling Together, Atlanta."

Mathis's mother helped to found the Committee to Stop Children's Murders, a plainly confrontational name for a victims' advocacy group that just wanted the police to stay in touch. In addition to courting law-enforcement resources, the mothers' group also sought to fight the impression, advanced by Mayor Jackson's "silly press statements," that all of the missing were "street urchins who come from broken homes and families on welfare," as the *New York Times* put it. "They pointed out that several of the murdered children were in gifted-student programs in their schools and that most of them were trying to earn money honestly"—running neighborhood errands, for instance—"and that many of the families were working people and not on welfare." Eventually, the activist mothers of the missing were threatened with criminal and civil misconduct charges for shoddy fundraising—mistakes they said they made due to a lack of experience.

For Mayor Jackson, who sought to portray Atlanta as a beacon of opportunity and progressivism in the post-civil-rights New South, the deaths of poor Black children was at the very least an inconvenience for his selling of Atlanta as a "cultural and commercial haven," the historian Maurice J. Hobson wrote in *The Legend of the Black Mecca*. The murders and disappearances even spurred neighborhood vigilantes to mobilize in the spirit of the Black Panther Party for Self-Defense. (When New York City's own vigilantes, the Guardian Angels, paid a visit to Atlanta to offer their services, they "left the city bewildered by the fact that guns could be purchased at grocery stores.") And yet it wasn't until this slice of Black Atlanta was already vibrating with terror and anger—with certain children no longer allowed to play outside and a citywide curfew in effect—that an FBI task force was assigned to the case. President

Ronald Reagan appointed Vice President George H. W. Bush to coordinate federal and local efforts, but the anguish of those grieving mothers barely registered until the stain of inaction was too ugly to ignore.

In the fall of 1980, Jackson posed before news cameras in a three-piece suit, with two uniformed cops behind him, displaying sloppy piles of small bills—ones, fives, tens—representing a $100,000 reward for information about the murders. Skeptics said the photograph "resembled Boss Hog counting his money," and Muhammad Ali, outraged at the ongoing emergency and perhaps embarrassed by the small sum, donated $400,000 more. A few months later, celebrities provided a momentary spotlight and reprieve for the city. Frank Sinatra and Sammy Davis Jr. headlined a benefit concert at the Atlanta Civic Center, raising $148,000 for an investigation that was by then costing the city approximately a quarter million dollars per month. The Atlanta-based Coca-Cola Company gave $25,000; Burt Reynolds, who had taken to shooting movies in town, threw in $10,000. "We use humor, music and talent as a weapon to fight evil," Davis told the press, though Baldwin referred to the event as "buck-dancing on the graves" of the young victims. Atlanta, he wrote, was "for a season, a kind of grotesque Disneyland."

Little of this belated attention would trickle down to Jeffery Mathis's family, some three weeks removed from the loss of their hope but no closer to real closure. Years later, when some files from the investigation were unsealed, Willie Mae Mathis was still searching for answers. "The parents don't know what happened to our children," she said. "The police didn't tell us anything."

For Baldwin, the carnage of those years was tied to the area's broader history, dismantling the fantasy that Atlanta, only one hundred years on from slavery, represented any sort of sanctuary. The children of Atlanta "are also the heirs, it is worth remembering, of the distilled and dreadful bitterness of the blood-soaked and sovereign state of Georgia," he wrote. "There is absolutely nothing new in this city, this state or this nation about dead black male bodies floating, finally, to the surface of the river." The killings would come to represent an unmistakable psychic gash on top of a deeper historical wound.

This was the backdrop against which Atlanta rap was born, and the sounds, words and beats that would come to define the city bore more than a trace of the chaos and pain the murders caused in the Black community. André Benjamin and Antwan Patton, eventually known as OutKast's André 3000 and Big Boi, were four years old when the first children disappeared. Jermaine Dupri, the mastermind behind So So Def Recordings, was six. Young Jeezy and 2 Chainz were toddlers. TI and Gucci Mane were right behind them. All were of Atlanta and raised among the paranoia, the skepticism of institutions and the two-sided coin of parenting options—shelter versus exposure to the cold world—only exacerbated here. "The music, storytelling, folklore, and culture that emerge from the poor and marginalized communities of Atlanta—what we call 'trap'—are built on the generational, psychological, linguistic, and ideological roots that grew from the traumas of the Atlanta Child Murders," wrote Dr. Joycelyn Wilson, a professor of cultural studies who has used hip-hop to teach social justice.

Keisha Lance Bottoms, who was elected mayor of Atlanta in 2017 with the support of many from the city's rap elite, was in elementary school during the killings. She, too, has recalled the constant warnings from adults that going outside alone left her vulnerable. In 2019, Bottoms, another product of the West Side (with an R&B singer father, no less), announced that she was reopening the cold cases that had been swept up or buried in Williams's conviction. Her administration hoped to use DNA technology to "help bring some peace to the families who for so long have felt like they were forgotten." The scars, four decades later, had only barely faded.

Yet the renewed recent interest—including a podcast, *Atlanta Monster*, along with an HBO documentary and a Wayne Williams plotline that nodded to Mathis on Netflix's serial-killer show *Mindhunter*—only served to again stoke the uncertainty and jitters that continue to surround all aspects of the disappearances and murders. (The claims unearthed later from Charles T. Sanders—an Atlanta white supremacist with ties to the Ku Klux Klan and once a suspect in the case—that the KKK was responsible and that the killer had "wiped out a thousand future generations of n——s," did not help the healing.) But whether Williams was the right—or only—man, the lack of real resolution in the case, with its interwoven threads of racial violence, bureaucratic neglect and the intra-Black class divide, would be felt acutely not just by those who experienced the murders directly but by many generations after.

Lashon Farley, a slight local girl from a strict Baptist family, knew Jeff Mathis as the class clown. They shared a fifth-grade homeroom at J. C. Harris Elementary School, a place, like so many in Atlanta, filled with Black people and named for a white man—in this case Joel Chandler Harris, the folklorist and early appropriator of African American culture known for his Br'er Rabbit and Uncle Remus stories. The two-story brick school was located in their West End neighborhood, not far from where Williams was raised, an area that had once been an upper-class white suburb but was 86 percent Black by 1976, following waves of white flight.

Lashon had known Jeff since kindergarten, and she considered him one of her best friends. Earlier on the day of his disappearance, she recalled nearly forty years later, the boy had been paddled by the kids' teacher, with the FBI noting in its investigation that Mathis had fought with a classmate. Seeing him punished was Lashon's final memory of Jeff. Around 7 p.m. that Monday, he was sent down the road by his mother to the Star Service Station on Gordon Street for cigarettes, a dollar in hand. The last anyone saw of him, the boy was getting into a blue vehicle.

The next morning, their teacher sat the class down and told them what most had likely already heard: Jeff had not returned home after his evening errand. "Everything was just solemn," Lashon said, and the euphemisms deployed in the company of children were all but worthless, his eventual fate inevitable. "At that point"—even as a kid—"you kind of knew." The neighborhood theorizing was unavoidable. "It had to be somebody that he trusted," Lashon, now an adult with grandchildren of her own, considered. "And he didn't trust anybody."

Most of Lashon's family had lived in the West End, a quiet middle-class neighborhood, for years, and even in a budding capital, the crimes were decidedly local, close at hand. "The crazy part was, we knew Wayne Williams," she said. He had interned at an advertising agency where one of her aunts worked. Mathis's mother knew the Williams family, too, and she would keep running into them at the grocery store. As a result of this proximity, the ambient terror of the killings would not soon fade, casting a pall over Lashon's adolescence, as it would for so many Black children of that era in Atlanta. "It took me a long time to get over it," she said.

Yet it was only later that Lashon Farley realized how directly she could trace that foundational thread of her life through the decades to the kind of daughter, wife and mother she would become. Though she couldn't have known it—and never would have expected it at the time—the choices she made as a result of her upbringing, shaped as it was by the horrors that happened nearby, would come to alter the path of Atlanta rap history.

2.

A FEW GOOD MEN

ALREADY A SCRAWNY INDOOR KID BY NATURE, ONE FOR BOOKS AND crossword puzzles, Lashon would spend the rest of her preteen years, after Wayne Williams, in the quiet bubble of her own nerdiness and enforced domesticity. Her parents had recently separated, but family members congregated around her grandparents' home, known as "the big house," on Inman Street in the West End, and Lashon was expected to stay close. Her sister Laraina, less than two years her junior, was by default Lashon's best friend and confidante, and would remain so into adulthood. Lashon was a Girl Scout. When she grew up, she wanted to be a heart surgeon.

Like many in the area, Lashon's family remained unconvinced by the official story of Williams's victim count, even after he was arrested and convicted. They conceded that maybe he was a damaged weirdo, responsible for a couple of killings, but the whole operation—boys and girls, prepubescent children and young adults? "In their hearts, they didn't believe they had the right person," Lashon said. The panicked authorities "were just looking for something to grasp and hold on to."

As a result of these inklings, the practical strictures that had been imposed on the lives of some West Side children because of Williams did not relent much after his capture. "We definitely couldn't go anywhere," Lashon recalled. "We could hardly go out and play, and we weren't even really allowed to before that. But after, we never gonna have a childhood." *You know they didn't get the real killer, right?* the adults told Lashon and her sister. *Y'all still going to play right here.*

"At some point, we gotta have a life, too!" Lashon pleaded. But it would be years before she was allowed to stray.

When she was sixteen, after relentless begging and extended negotiations, Lashon's mother finally started to ease up, and she was allowed to attend some teenage gatherings—but only with her little sister by her side, an effective handicap on the way to true freedom. Bringing home a boyfriend remained out of the question. So when it came time to graduate from high school, Lashon's requirements for what came next included *space from her parents* and *access to men* near the top of the list. She'd made good grades, but her mother couldn't afford college and suggested the armed forces instead. "I weighed ninety-seven pounds soaking wet—what military am I going to?" Lashon scoffed. "Then I got to thinking about it . . ."

Financially, enlistment made sense. The money started coming in as soon as you signed up, and travel would be required. After boot camp, the military was mostly just a regular job—"a seven-to-four job, not even nine to five"—and with added stability on top of it. At eighteen, clutching a slip that cleared her for service despite her being underweight, Lashon shipped off to Parris Island, South Carolina, for Marine Corps basic training.

She cried every night for the first month. Then a hairline fracture in her hip—the kind of injury that could be expected when a stick figure with no history of physical activity was suddenly carrying a hundred-pound pack and a rifle for ten miles—set her back. Twelve weeks of training turned into twenty-four. Aviation logistics school in Fort Eustis, Virginia, came next. Lashon missed Atlanta.

But everything was worth it when she got to Japan.

Lashon's father worked for Delta, fixing planes for the Atlanta institution that helped to make the city a worldly concern, so she'd done some traveling already, taking first-class summer trips to California, Oklahoma and Texas. But her deployment orders said Okinawa, and that was something different. She'd never been out of the country, and she spoke no Japanese. Yet it was there, on a tiny island stuffed with US military personnel, that a once-cosseted young Black woman from Atlanta would blossom. Despite being molded for maximum toughness, female soldiers at the time were still expected to uphold certain beauty standards—hair and lipstick done daily, etiquette classes included—and Lashon leaned into her femininity for the first time, finally surrounded by eligible partners and no parents.

"The Marine Corps was looking for a few good men and so was I," Lashon cackled, looking back. "The ratio of men to women over there was ridiculous—like twenty men to every woman. That was a plus! And you never got a chance to spend your money, because they were always in competition."

The drinking age, crucially, was eighteen. "All there was to do was club and drink, club and drink, maybe see a movie. But basically just partying and drinking, partying and drinking." One local cocktail called the Purple Haze was said to be laced with opium, leading to a rash of soldiers with failed drug tests. But few found themselves discouraged.

In this version of Okinawa, it wasn't long before Lashon, now nineteen and living it up, got pregnant for the first time. Uncertain of how to handle it, she was spared a decision when she suffered a miscarriage during a typhoon and had to be whisked an hour away to the proper facilities by Humvee, water and blood sloshing everywhere. But even that couldn't mar her stay in Japan, which she remembers as a highlight reel of men, sushi and scuba diving. A year later, Lashon returned to the United States with the confidence of experience, and also two potential paths for the rest of her life.

It was a classic story, really: On one hand, there was Prince Charming, a serviceman she met in Okinawa who had everything accounted for back home. He came from a good Baltimore family, his father a doctor at Johns Hopkins who planned to leave his son and future daughter-in-law a well-established residence upon his impending retirement. *But who's going to clean it?* Lashon thought, uncertain in the face of a sure thing. "He had his life mapped out. That's what I didn't like, because I'm a fly-by-the-seat-of-the-pants type of girl." Moving to Japan as an unleashed teenager after a strict upbringing had brought that out of her. But they got engaged anyway.

Still, Lashon's other option lingered. Thom Jones, another fellow marine she'd collected abroad, was from Darien, Georgia, south of

Savannah—"a little small country town where he was the shit." A big fish in barely a puddle. "There ain't nothing like a country boy," Lashon said. "Cool, laid-back . . .

"But he was a ho then. I should've known."

What happened next was predictable, like the fate of so many nice guys. "You hear it in the back of your head, but you just gotta see for yourself," Lashon said. "You hear that voice saying, *No no no no*, but something about you—you defy it." Someone else's swagger can happen to a person.

The overly stable fiancé was stationed in South Carolina, but Lashon was working in Jacksonville, one state to the north, right alongside her bad boy Thom. Weekend visits from the good man were one thing, but temptation was right there, every day, a piece of her Okinawa adventures everlasting. "I was stuck with him, so it was bound to happen," she said. "I ended up getting pregnant."

Even then, the prince wouldn't go away so easily, and he told Lashon that he was prepared to push through it—the wedding, the house, even raising another man's child. *Why struggle?* Lashon considered. "His parents didn't have a problem with it. He didn't even have a problem with it!" Everything could've been different.

But the pull of uncertainty proved impossible to ignore for someone who'd never really rebelled before. "Quite naturally, I didn't go for the straight and narrow," Lashon said. "Engaged to the straight and narrow, but got pregnant by the cricket."

"And that's how it began . . ."

3.

JUST MULTIPLY

If there was a Big Bang for Atlanta rap, it probably happened during Freaknik.

Late to the party when it came to innovations in Black music, especially given its stature as an early Southern center and driver of civil rights, the city of Atlanta did not play much of a role in the first booms of hip-hop. Up north, Kool Herc and company's Jamaica-to-the-Bronx connection brought DJ and sound system culture to the urban doorstep of 1970s funk, creating a clash that would ripple outward from New York indefinitely. Meanwhile, Nashville was synonymous with country music—a genre, like most, that had Black in its DNA—and Memphis molded the blues. New Orleans owned jazz. Even in Miami, so far south that it ceased really being the South, a tradition of soul and R&B studios, early dirty-rap parodies and high-pulse party music were quicker to take off. Atlanta needed to play catch-up.

What the city did have to build on was a thriving Black power structure—including politicians engaged with the arts. And thanks to its network of HBCUs, dense clusters of upwardly mobile young people were coming to Atlanta throughout the 1990s, ready to show out, spend money and dance when they weren't busy getting ahead. What they needed was a soundtrack.

These were the days of big perms, gold hoop earrings, shrinking jean shorts, oversized jerseys, thick gold rope chains and low-sitting, wide-bodied vehicles. But it was rap, in all its splintered forms, that would be Freaknik's animating life force, and the collision of the two would leave the city ever changed. The music that grew from this period melded influences from the North, South and West, befitting Atlanta's geography and its status as a transportation hub. By the time the annual Black college spring break bacchanalia crested and crashed later in the decade, Freaknik had shined an unprecedented spotlight onto a rapidly evolving, suddenly lucrative local culture.

Among the hordes drawn to Atlanta to carve out a piece for themselves during this time was an unassuming Midwesterner and blooming business mind named Kevin Lee. Despite his low-key mien and partiality to more esoteric forms of dance music, Lee would go on to shape at least four waves of Atlanta rap to come. But first, like so many of his generation and station, Lee came to Atlanta to party.

Freaknik might as well have been an Atlanta recruitment convention. A former high school quarterback from Indianapolis, Indiana—not exactly a cultural center—Lee was attending Saint Augustine's University (then Saint Augustine's College), a tiny HBCU in North Carolina with fewer than one thousand students. In Atlanta, his entire college class of 1993 could probably fit on a single street corner. Whenever he visited, business of all sorts appeared to be booming.

Lee made his first Freaknik pilgrimage around 1992, and he spent the next few years chasing that high. The club scene in Atlanta was like nothing he'd ever experienced, well worth the hundreds of miles he and his friends routinely drove from Indianapolis on the weekends, rushing back to get to class on time. At Atlanta Live, Club 559, Club 112 and more, a who's who of DJs each filled a niche, spinning different flavors of local and national hip-hop, booty shake, soul, R&B and dance music. One Friday night in 1994, Lee even caught a performance by an up-and-comer known as Biggie Smalls. Not yet an icon, the Notorious BIG was on a joint tour with his Bad Boy Records labelmate Craig Mack, whose "Flava in Ya Ear" was the New York record of the moment. Thanks to the national headliners, there were women everywhere—enough to convince Lee and his friends to come back to the same club the next night. But the second time they pulled up to the Warehouse downtown, the vibe had shifted from only twenty-four hours earlier. The line was still down the street, filled with the usual clusters of young men in the day's baggy fashions, but it was leading to a different entrance than the previous evening. Just about all of the women were absent.

"Straight on Friday, gay on Saturday—we had never seen anything like it," Lee recalled decades later. The club that had just hosted a Bad Boy showcase had transformed completely for the party known as Tracks on Saturday, a throwback to the house nights from when the Warehouse was called the Phoenix in the early 1980s.

Right there in the heart of the South, Atlanta might as well have been another planet. But for someone like Lee, the city's every quirk was another potential asset to be seized, and it was clear there was more than enough to go around for anyone who bothered to show up.

FREAKNIK'S EXACT HISTORY remains contested, but most agree that it began near the Atlanta University Center in the early 1980s as a picnic—hence the portmanteau, which combined visions of a wholesome family outing with a youthful descriptor and hot dance of the moment. (Both Chic's 1978 hit "Le Freak" and Rick James's "Super Freak" from 1981 were influences.) Sponsored at first by the DC Metro Club, college kids from the DMV area, the gathering was meant to bring together students at the neighboring historically Black schools who weren't returning home or hitting the beach over the spring holiday. According to Sharon Toomer, then a Spelman student and one of Freaknik's founders, the first edition attracted about fifty people, who barbecued chicken and listened to Parliament-Funkadelic and go-go music, the DC-specific funk spinoff. "It was very innocent," Toomer told the *Atlanta Journal-Constitution*.

More often spelled Freaknic (or Freak-nic) at the time, the party began in Midtown's Piedmont Park, northeast of downtown, and John A. White Park, further to the southwest, largely escaping notice by the white mainstream and even some Black locals for the better part of a decade. But it grew every year, becoming a word-of-mouth sensation among students at Morehouse, Spelman and Clark Atlanta University, as well as connected schools throughout the South. By the midnineties, the weeklong party became a pilgrimage and rite of passage, and the crowds could not be contained. Freaknik took on a closing *k*, as well as a reputation as a carnival of dancing, drinking, sex, drugs, music and traffic. In 1994, attendance at the loosely organized event was estimated around 200,000, with spillover touching every mall, patch of grass and interstate in the area. In what may be the enduring image of Freaknik, cars at a standstill became mobile stages, sometimes as far north as the tony neighborhood of Buckhead, with women dancing out of windows or convertible tops, and men climbing onto seats and roofs to catch a panoramic view and pass a bottle, a blunt or an affirmation. The animated T-shirts and hats sold roadside were sought-after souvenirs (and now thrift-store gems), with slogans like "They told us not to come, but we came anyway—Atlanta Freaknic will never die, just multiply."

It didn't take long before the city government was itching to shut the whole thing down. They cited often-racialized claims of looting, indecent exposure, sexual assault and general rowdiness. But whereas some saw mayhem, budding entrepreneurs in the entertainment industry were busy making the most of Freaknik's captive audience. Up until that point, Atlanta had been a cultural powder keg waiting for a full-scale detonation. Freaknik would become the match.

Decades earlier, the government in and around Atlanta may have, however inadvertently, helped to set the stage for this explosion—a pattern that would repeat itself often over the years as the city's social and political policies, or lack thereof, fueled the ascendence of the arts, including local rap culture. In 1973, Georgia governor Jimmy Carter had created the Film, Video and Music Office, marketing the state as fertile creative ground and a filming location for Hollywood productions. Mayor Jackson's Bureau of Cultural Affairs also supported artists with grants and free concerts in public parks. By 1975, the nascent entertainment scene would get a personal touch from another well-connected figure: Bunnie Jackson, Maynard's wife and Atlanta's First Lady, who wanted to start a public relations firm.

FirstClass Inc.—cofounded with Hank Aaron's wife, Billye Aaron, and others—began by giving tours of Black Atlanta to out-of-town convention-goers. But it soon turned its energy toward PR, thanks to the social reach of its principals. Despite knowing little about the music industry going in, Bunnie would become a go-to promoter for acts like Lena Horne and the Jackson 5 in Atlanta, realizing along the way that she could land a record deal for an unknown group on the strength of her name and connections alone. Bunnie and Maynard divorced in 1976, and when she stopped taking alimony from her ex-husband, she had the music business to thank.

With her innate knack for dealmaking, Bunnie quickly stretched beyond PR and promotion, serving as manager for the R&B and funk group the SOS Band, whose platinum single "Take Your Time (Do It Right)" was written in her basement. She also crossed paths with acts like Cameo, a New York funk band that moved south, and Jimmy Jam & Terry Lewis, producers who would help shape the Atlanta sounds of TLC and Usher, plus Janet Jackson, Prince, Mariah Carey and more. From Bunnie's blooming 1980s network, it was a straight line to future Atlanta rap royalty: the former First Lady married Ray Ransom of another local funk group called Brick, and she personally sent the band's road manager—a North Carolina native named Michael Mauldin—to study at Atlanta Technical College.

Mauldin had a son who was known to attend rehearsals and take it all in, a kid many expected to follow his father into the family business. By the age of ten, Jermaine Mauldin had already danced onstage with Diana Ross. At twelve, he appeared with a Jheri curl, popping and locking in a jean vest and fingerless white gloves, in the music video for the rap group Whodini's "Freaks Come Out at Night." Raised in College Park, across Atlanta's southwestern border, Jermaine quickly became known as something of an industry prodigy, expanding his dancer's portfolio amid puberty to become a talent scout, DJ, producer and early mixtape hawker.

At some point—in a father-son plot to play down the younger Mauldin's musical pedigree—the teenager dropped his dad's name in favor of his middle one and started going by Jermaine Dupri. And it was Dupri—

along with a crop of fellow producer-executives like LA Reid, Babyface and Dallas Austin—who would help lay the groundwork for the modern rap and R&B business in Atlanta. (Mauldin, meanwhile, wasn't the only Atlanta funk patriarch molding the future: Brick's front man and saxophonist, Jimmy Brown, also had a musically inclined son, Patrick, known as Sleepy. Sleepy Brown would bring his funk and soul DNA to the hip-hop production trio Organized Noize, the early architects of OutKast's sound, along with Rico Wade and Ray Murray.)

Before founding So So Def Recordings in 1993, Dupri hit upon his first major success when he discovered two thirteen-year-olds at the Greenbriar Mall, then a go-to spot for kids from the SWATS (for "Southwest Atlanta, Too Strong"), an area covering the neighborhoods and suburbs of Cascade, the West End, College Park and East Point. In an age-old showbiz tale that would become even more common among Atlanta's future rap stars, the boys Dupri found weren't exactly musicians at first—he could work that part out later. The important thing was that they had a vibe.

"They didn't sing, they didn't rap, they didn't do nothing. But they looked very hip—they just had the look," Dupri once said. "I just watched them and said, 'These kids could be stars.'"

With their clothes turned backward as an attention-grabbing gag, the duo became Kris Kross, a multiplatinum rap act for kids that established Dupri's golden touch, certifying him in the minds of music executives from New York and Los Angeles. A writer, producer and manager for the group, Dupri was still just nineteen. Atlanta, too, was only getting started.

NEARLY TWO DECADES later, Dupri explained that growing up in Atlanta in the late eighties had instilled in him a certain fearlessness as a young Black man that could transcend upbringings, from his own relative privilege to someone like Rico Wade's lack of it. "I don't think Martin Luther King could've been from no other city besides Atlanta," he said. "Because it's no intimidation in this city. I was never intimidated by nobody white. Nothing. Nothing that they did. I ain't never been intimidated by nobody white—period. Ever. If I seen somebody white that got a big-ass house, I'm saying to myself, 'I'm gonna get that same shit. I'mma get more cars than they got.'

"You go to other cities and it's a white section. Ain't no white section in Atlanta. If it's some big-ass houses over there, and ten white people live there, you can best believe there's two or three Black people in that same neighborhood, I swear to God.

"Am I lying?" Dupri asked Wade.

The demure Organized Noize producer shook his head. Despite his influence and commercial track record, including smashes like TLC's "Waterfalls" and En Vogue's "Don't Let Go (Love)," Wade carried not a trace of his counterpart's celebrity aura. The two men had gathered that day to reminisce in the studios of Atlanta's V-103, 103.3 FM ("the People's Station"), at the invitation of the DJ Greg Street. A Mississippi native, fishing enthusiast and Southern radio legend—*It's 6 o'clock, time for Greg Street to rock*—Street had spun across Alabama and Texas before settling in Atlanta in 1995, the prime Freaknik years.

"I seen Rico go up in people's office and say shit that you would never expect he was supposed to say," Dupri went on. "But he wasn't intimidated, and he felt a certain way about his music and his sound and he got what he wanted. That's something that's deep-rooted in this city."

For Wade, such confidence grew from the dueling prominence of two kinds of Black Atlantans he witnessed moving through the world while growing up in the SWATS: the big-time dope dealers and the big-time politicians, including Mayor Jackson and his successors Andrew Young and Shirley Franklin. "To see Black people who were established doing something, even though you might not want to take that path—I don't think none of us wanted to be politicians—it still was cool to know that we had some people who meant something," Wade said. That nearness to variations on Black power helped to fuel the music.

As Dupri and Wade were establishing themselves, other seeds of the professionalized music industry that Bunnie Jackson had planted earlier were springing up as well. Antonio Reid and Kenneth Edmonds, better known as LA and Babyface, a duo inspired by Jimmy Jam & Terry Lewis, created LaFace Records in 1989 as a joint venture with Clive Davis's Arista, giving Atlanta a major-label presence. Reid told *Ebony* magazine that he had chosen to raise his family and establish his business there because it was a "Black city with strong Black politicians."

There were also the beginnings of a local independent boom that leaned toward harder hip-hop than the R&B and pop-rap fare coming from early LaFace (TLC, Toni Braxton) and Dupri's So So Def (Kris Kross, Xscape, Da Brat). Bass music, a.k.a. booty shake or booty bass, had bubbled up from Miami and defined the Atlanta underground—including the plentiful strip clubs—for years. Florida's parallel to New York's early hip-hop, Miami bass was designed to be felt as much as heard, and it came from a DJ culture that soundtracked parties in public parks, skating rinks and school dances—places usually humid and near enough to the beach to result in the gradual loss of clothing.

When Freaknik took off, "booty-shake music was still the biggest sound," Dupri explained. "They didn't dance to slow rap music in the strip club. It was all fast—Raheem the Dream, Success-n-Effect, Kilo, Shy D—these guys were like Run-DMC out here."

MC Shy D, whom many credit as the first rapper to make noise out of Atlanta, was actually from the Bronx, where he grew up a few buildings down from his not-quite-blood-cousin, hip-hop pioneer Afrika Bambaataa. Later, he connected Atlanta directly to Florida by signing to Luke Records, the company founded by the bass legend and 2 Live Crew leader Luther Campbell. But Shy D also repped his adopted hometown on records like "Atlanta—That's Where I Stay," and Dupri would eventually repay the favor in his attempt at a city theme song, "Welcome to Atlanta," where he rapped, "If you was ridin', you was bumping to homie Shy D."

In the transitional moment of the early nineties, the Atlanta-based Ichiban Records, which initially released soul albums by Curtis Mayfield and Clarence Carter, also turned to bass music. Before TI and Shawty

Lo, Bankhead and its Bowen Homes projects were represented by Kilo Ali, who recorded for Ichiban and its bass imprint Wrap Records. (Ali had come to Ichiban from Arvis Records, another progenitor of Georgia hip-hop that helped develop Raheem the Dream, a fellow Atlanta bass pioneer.) Ali found success with upbeat sex-and-party records like "Dunkey Kong," which helped spread an early, pre-viral dance sensation from Atlanta in the form of the Bankhead Bounce—a shoulder-shimmying move that Michael Jackson even brought to the MTV stage in 1995. But Ali had also experimented with more socially conscious hip-hop on tracks like "America Has a Problem 'Cocaine,'" from 1990, a spiritual predecessor to groups like Goodie Mob and OutKast.

None of this music had much in common sonically with the Atlanta sound to come, at least upon first listen. But along with introducing a cast of creators that would carry through—sturdy branches on the unwieldy Atlanta family tree—certain musical and lyrical ideas reveal themselves in flashes. Ichiban, probably best known for the white rapper Vanilla Ice, also brought the world proto-trap music in the form of Decatur's Ghetto Mafia, a duo that ran its obvious West Coast gangster rap influence—big synths, gun talk, law-enforcement antagonism—through the countrified filter of groups like UGK, from Port Arthur, Texas, and 8Ball & MJG of Memphis, Tennessee. This more lyrical and aggressive form of Southern street rap would be threaded through later acts like Baby D and Hitman Sammy Sam of Big Oomp Records.

Though important in Atlanta, these guys weren't exactly burning up the charts. Dupri, though, always had designs on a wider audience beyond the streets, the clubs and the rest of the Southern underground. "Even today, my records don't have super slang and they don't really sound hella country," Dupri told the journalist Roni Sarig in his history of Southern hip-hop, *Third Coast*. "I just didn't want to be stagnated as just a Southern artist. I want people to say my name the same way in New York as they say it in California. When you go too South, they got a section for you, like a smoking section in the airport."

With radio-and-MTV-ready slickness on one side—sans too much obvious Southernness—and the rougher edges of booty shake and burgeoning gangster rap on the other, Atlanta needed a great unifier to make its name nationally. Dupri would sometimes try to bridge the gap himself. Beginning in 1996, his *So So Def Bass All Stars* compilations—put together with the help of a local DJ turned A&R executive, Jonathan Smith, a.k.a. Lil Jon—featured songs like Playa Poncho's "Whatz Up, Whatz Up" alongside Ghost Town DJs' "My Boo," which combined a booty-shake beat with pop–R&B hooks. But no one did more to legitimize Atlanta, artistically and commercially, than OutKast.

André Benjamin and Antwan Patton met as teenagers attending Tri-Cities High School in East Point. One day in 1991, when the two were sophomores, they ran into each other while window shopping at the upscale Lenox Square mall in Buckhead and bonded on the MARTA train ride back home to the SWATS. Both had catholic taste beyond their years—A Tribe Called Quest, Das EFX and De La Soul, but also Gil Scott-Heron, Sly Stone and Kate Bush—and an overarching bohemian sensibility that set them apart from their peers. They could also rap—*fast*—in an intricate style that wasn't exactly dominant or popular locally.

In 1992, Rico Wade invited the promising teenage best friends to the Dungeon, the makeshift basement recording studio where his Organized Noize production trio was trying to get off the ground. Organized Noize had initially worked in a storage room at Jellybeans, the influential Southwest Atlanta skating rink that had by then seen better days. But in yet another link between Atlanta's Black power structure and its youthful innovators, the city's police chief at the time, Eldrin Bell, was a family friend of the Wades and had helped them find a house at 1907 Lakewood Terrace with an unfinished, subterranean room perfect for making music. Hence, the Dungeon.

Before the mainstream-shifting Afro-futurism, the Grammy Awards, "Miss Jackson" and "Hey Ya!," OutKast was just another upstart trying to get noticed by the budding Atlanta music industry. Organized Noize already had a line into LaFace—having helped form TLC by scouting would-be stars across the city's rich talent show circuit—but the hit-chasing LA Reid was skeptical of straight-up Southern rap as an investment. For a tryout that the group saw as sabotage, Reid agreed to include a song by OutKast on the label's 1993 Christmas album.

But "Player's Ball," OutKast's debut single, was so undeniably distinct, packing in plenty of Southern sauce and slang, plus a West Coast funk influence and a vague enough premise—"Ain't no Christmas in the ghetto," as Wade put it—that the track transcended the holiday season. With a proudly local video directed by a young Puff Daddy, "Player's Ball" would go on to hit number one on the *Billboard* Hot Rap Songs chart and stay there for six weeks.

OutKast may not have been the first rappers to come out of Atlanta, but they were the most *Atlanta*. Big Rube, the voice-of-God spoken-word specialist from the Dungeon Family collective, credited the duo with highlighting—and revitalizing—entire neighborhoods on their side of town. "It represented all our asses," Rube said in *Third Coast*. "You could literally drive around listening to it and find some shit, because motherfuckers were talking street names. Look at Campbellton Road—it was dying down, there wasn't no business. Then OutKast came out bigupping Campbellton Road, talking about Club Illusions, and next thing you know Club Illusions is packed every week, and there's more people coming over to Campbellton Road to get their hair done, get something to eat."

OutKast also stood apart, then and forevermore, in its chameleonic ability to be a little bit of everything: fans of the North, but Southern raised; failed hustlers—having flunked out of stealing cars and selling dope—and not really pimps, but knowledgeable-enough slick-talkers; educated and sociopolitically inclined, but with an ear for adrenaline shots of willful ignorance. There was nothing like them before, certainly nothing after, and Atlanta would not be Atlanta without them.

The success of "Player's Ball" earned OutKast a debut album, *Southernplayalisticadillacmuzik*, released on LaFace in April of 1994. It was right on time. By then, Atlanta's rap sound was beginning to perfectly triangulate the influence from its Northern, Southern and Western hip-hop counterparts. On top of a psychedelic funk and soul foundation, the city was melding the urgent energy that had grown from New York, adding elements of the flashy and dance-centric Miami bass movement and throwing in plenty of the gangster rap acuity that had spread from N.W.A's Los Angeles through Houston, Memphis and New Orleans, where Master P's No Limit label and Cash Money Records were budding as indie empires peddling raw street music.

Everything came together at Freaknik, as the competing rap labels of the moment blanketed the city with flyers and free stuff, filming music videos among the crowds and hoping their artists' mere presence could cause a scene. OutKast's debut album had a perfect launchpad when the weather turned warm that spring, and a street team hit the Freaknik crowds with marketing manna: a sampler of songs packaged with promotional dice and incense, the two sides of OutKast (and Atlanta) in the palm of everyone's hand. "We made these packets and passed them out so everyone went back home and had our sounds," André said. "That's how OutKast got around the country."

Jermaine Dupri, too, knew a marketing opportunity when he saw it. "So So Def as the soundtrack of Freaknik—that was my goal," he once explained. The more in-your-face, the better. "It was the beginning of 'flexing,' in every kind of way. The birth of riding around with your system blasting, with TVs in your car. All of that stuff came from people wanting to be seen at Freaknik."

By the time spring break '96 rolled around, "it was just *stupid*," Dupri recalled, back in the studio at V-103. That year, he flew into Atlanta once the Freaknik festivities were already under way and he rode MARTA from the airport to near Piedmont Park, going semi-undercover in his own kingdom. "It felt like Disney World," he said. "There was so many people in the streets, I was walking around like, *I can't believe it.* Crazy. I'm talking about crazy. *Craaaaaazy.*

"It meant everything to the city. For a minute, people didn't actually pay attention to Atlanta culture—even people that actually lived here didn't pay much attention to it. Atlanta wanted to be New York, Atlanta wanted to be LA—all the cities that were getting respect. But it wasn't happening.

"Then," he said, "we had our own thing."

Freaknik itself wouldn't last much longer, though there would be repeated attempts to revitalize the established brand name later. With the 1996 Olympic Games starting that summer in Atlanta, not long after spring break, the city had to prove that it could deal with turned-up college kids before the rest of the world descended. Stifled by an increased police presence and literal roadblocks, as mandated by Bill Campbell, Atlanta's third Black mayor after Jackson and Young, Freaknik faltered. By 1999, it was all but dead.

Still, the event had made its lasting dent. More than just the home of an isolated annual party, Atlanta had become a year-round destination with an unmatched nightlife—including about forty functioning strip clubs—among the young Black elite that had been flocking to the city. From Michael Jordan to MC Hammer, movie stars, musicians and athletes fell in love with the people, the sounds, the history and the weather. The flash of local icons like Dominique Wilkins, the Atlanta Hawks star, and Deion Sanders, who played for both the Braves and the Falcons at the same time, would bring even more pop-cultural cachet—and help to birth Atlanta's rap swag (tangles of chains, bright patterns, designer sunglasses, Louis Vuitton man-bags). Floored by how far their money went down south compared to places like Los Angeles or New York, a generation of new Black millionaires and aspirants, including stars of the moment like Keith Sweat, Teddy Riley and Bobby Brown, snapped up expansive real estate and moved to town. (Brown's Bosstown studios, where OutKast recorded its early music when it outgrew the Dungeon, would eventually become Stankonia.) No matter where you were from originally, there was nowhere hotter to be, and to succeed, for any young Black striver with a taste for glamour.

That was Kevin Lee. For an ambitious music lover with formative connections to the streets, there was a cosmic pull toward the youthful edginess of Atlanta, as if every highway exit were paved with platinum.

Lee's mother, who raised him alone, had a steady job while he was growing up in Indianapolis, but he still came from a tough neighborhood, and he knew its struggles and its intricacies—savvy that would serve him well in the city—even as he remained mostly on the periphery. He also knew that in the world he came from, the periphery was never very far from the action, and he would end up with the scars on his leg to prove it.

At school in Raleigh, Lee studied economics. He was also a good enough basketball player to score a scholarship, playing a few years of Division II ball as a proud Falcon. But his senior year at Saint Augustine's, Lee was visiting with some drug dealer friends at an inopportune moment when he ended up on the wrong side of a shotgun blast, ending his athletic and academic career. He spent five months in the hospital recovering and another six in a wheelchair, learning to walk again.

Fortunately, Lee was already a better party promoter than an athlete. His late-night "two-to-sixes"—known for their exclusive locked-door policy—were as much of a draw as there could be in a town like Raleigh, some four hundred miles from the Black Mecca. Having established himself on a small scale in entertainment already, Lee knew he had the beginnings of a business vision when he left school and returned home to Indianapolis to heal.

There, with a group of old friends, he would create his first record label, coming up with a generic name (Universal Stars), renting an office and divvying up tasks among a few too many people—entertainment law, A&R talent-searching, marketing, production. For Lee, it was a good start at delegating and connecting the dots. But the label never got around to releasing any music. Indianapolis just wasn't the place to make things happen. But Lee had another idea.

One of the friends he often drove with down to Atlanta was a big-time hustler who would eventually be sentenced to life in prison on RICO charges. That guy's local "connect" was originally from the Bay Area, but his crew had invaded the rising Southern city with its eyes on a new hustle, and Lee liked to link with them whenever he was in town.

"I grew up around drugs, I grew up in this shit," Lee said. "But seeing these young boys driving Benzes—twenty, twenty-one years old—I was like, *What the fuck? Them boys are down here doing it!*

"*And they not selling drugs, they doing music!?*" He almost couldn't believe it.

Having outgrown Indiana, Lee knew where he needed to be to make something happen. In fact, he couldn't get Atlanta out of his head. Over and over again, Kevin Lee told himself, *I gotta get back there.*

4.

THE BABY BOY

IN 1990, AHEAD OF HER TWENTY-FIRST BIRTHDAY, LASHON FARLEY opted for a shotgun wedding to the lovable scoundrel Thom Jones at a North Carolina courthouse.

The couple welcomed a daughter, Deja, soon after, but hardly spent six months under one roof as a happy family. Thom cheated often, and recklessly, Lashon said, fathering another child outside of his marriage within a few years. Distance played a role, too, as Thom became a military officer assigned to stints in Texas and Virginia—and also a "pompous asshole," but one who could still pop back up and charm Lashon at the right moments.

A second daughter, Shayla, came next for the hot-and-cold couple. But by then, Lashon had left North Carolina and returned to Atlanta, once again seeking out the protective bubble of her own family. Thom went back to Japan; Lashon took a job at the post office, where she started at about $12 an hour. "Still poverty," she said.

They definitely weren't *together*-together the last time it happened. Thom, back in town however briefly, was watching the girls while Lashon worked. "Of course, me being a woman, I wasn't really seeing anybody, and it was just one of those days," she said. They fell into that old pattern.

After the deed was done, Thom was on his way. But Lashon called him almost immediately with the inkling of big news.

"I'm pregnant."

"How you know?"

"Oh, I know."

Lashon chuckled at the memory. "Sure enough . . ." And that was that. "Me and their daddy, we never got back together," she said. "That was our last time."

Lashon thought hard about ending the pregnancy. She was a pragmatist when it came to romance, a child of divorce lacking any fairy-tale delusions. "I knew I didn't want to be married to him. We adults. It's not a movie—things happen, and you get past it. End of story." Single mom, three kids—it wouldn't be easy. She made the appointment to have an abortion.

But when the time came for the procedure, Lashon couldn't follow through. "I had paid for it and everything," she said. Thom, who had sent the money and was deferring to her wishes, had a feeling that she wouldn't.

Well, I got two already, Lashon decided. *What's one more?*

But a boy was not the same, not even close—not this one, at least. Dominique Armani Jones was born December 3, 1994, after a hellish pregnancy that included two months of bed rest for his mother. It didn't get much easier from there.

From the start, Dominique was *fast*, rip-roaring to go, go, go—to experience everything, all the time. More. Now. Again. He was always one step ahead, learning, plotting. But he was also coddled, a classic Southern mama's boy. Lashon had sworn that after two kids she was done with breastfeeding. "He's getting a bottle," she told her mother. Famous last words.

"Three years old, he was still hunting me down"—attached at the tit. "I would be holding him, and if somebody even looked like they were coming to get him, he'd be wrapping his legs around my waist." But that didn't last; it rarely does.

Dominique showed early signs of focus, order and attention. As a toddler, he was already folding laundry and helping his mother clean up around the house. "I would walk in the kitchen, he'd be straightening out the refrigerator—three years old," Lashon said.

Once, when Dominique was about four, she bought him a pair of inline skates. But before his mother had gotten a chance to teach him how to use them, or at least hold his hand for balance, the preschooler had mastered his glide, tricks and all. "I look up, and he's out there skating backward," Lashon said. "He looks at it, he sees it, and he can do it."

Dominique also listened intently, revealing himself as a sponge for language. Before he could read, he was already quoting the Bible. Lashon and her family were Primitive Baptists—the kind of old-school, clapping-and-stomping Baptists who still washed feet and feasted on a communal dinner after church—and although they did not worship every Sunday, they went enough that it was part of them. Given its geographic primacy, Atlanta had long been a destination for pastors and elders across the South, and Dominique, the precocious boy who could spit the Word back at them, became known as something of a local attraction.

"They would always look for him—'Where's the young man that always gets so excited at church?' Every time they came to town, they'd be looking for him—'Where the little preacher man?'" He was destined for the job, the church folk told Lashon—a vessel for a message, God-sent.

In those days, Lashon was still working nights at the post office, so her stepfather would watch Dominique and his sisters overnight. In the mornings, the boy wouldn't let the old man leave until he could bend his ear with scripture. *God told me to tell you this*, Dominique would insist, sitting his granddaddy down for an improvised sermon. Lashon had never seen anything like it, until Dominique did it again. The boy had soul, and then he had music.

One day while driving, Lashon and her sister were listening to the radio when a song by the local rapper Kilo Ali came on. "Turn it up a little bit," Dominique, still a toddler, demanded from his car seat. He took in the sounds for a moment, before he hollered again toward the adults. "Turn it down now," he said, considering what'd he heard.

"That's Kilo Ali?" Dominique asked, apparently knowing full well. "I went to school with him."

Lashon and her sister could only exchange glances. Dominique had never been to school a day in his life, and certainly not with an adult rapper from the nearby projects. "What's your comeback after that?" Lashon recalled. "We was *blowed*."

For a time, Dominique stayed close enough, despite his curiosity and the pull of the world just beyond the West End neighborhood where his family had its sturdy roots. His father rarely came around, but he also rarely promised to, leaving Dominique little room for disappointment. There were no Christmas assurances, no birthdays waiting in the driveway for an adventure that never came. Instead, Lashon and her Inman Street matriarchy stepped up, carrying most of the emotional and financial load—mother, aunts, sisters, grandmother. But amid the feminine energy, Lashon also noticed her young son developing his rascally streak—disrobing his sisters' Barbie dolls in the bathtub, for instance. *This boy's going to be something else*, she told herself even then.

At first, Dominique and his sisters attended a Black-run private school, learning Spanish and chess alongside math, science and English. They thrived. Then money got tighter.

In the wide, cold waters of public school, Lashon's little boy turned a bit more daring, and he flourished socially. At Brown Middle School, Dominique won Mr. Sixth Grade, appearing almost a full head shorter than his female counterpart, even with a crown on.

The kind of adolescent for whom most things came naturally, Dominique was physically gifted as well. He tried football and ran some track, but sports couldn't hold his attention. Always slim and never tall, he wasn't growing into any kind of athlete anyway. Sometimes that choice gets made for you. Besides, he was happier chasing more anarchic thrills, wrestling with friends in the yard or doing backflips off the roof.

None of which is to say Dominique did not have a will to win. It was that competitive edge—with victories increasingly measured with age in financial and material gains—that would pull him outside among the older kids and into the bordering Atlanta neighborhoods that gave him a bit more of a frisson than his own.

He was still prepubescent when his grandfather taught him the basics of gambling with a couple of dice. Initially, Lashon bristled—she had always been told that a cousin of hers was fatally stabbed over a dice game. But as a bonding experience for Dominique and his most prominent male role model, games like cee-lo seemed harmless enough. The boy already liked to wear coveralls just like the old man, and rolling dice brought them even closer. But gambling also gave Dominique entree into new worlds, like the local parks and apartment complexes where the grown guys did their thing.

Like so many of those who would become his most loyal compatriots—brothers and business partners in ventures illicit and otherwise—Dominique met his best friend through dice. Ced was a small but sturdy figure with an always-stern face. But before they were an inseparable pair, the two were rivals, at least when it came to gambling. In their first encounter, Dominique, who was maybe—*maybe*—in sixth grade at the time, beat Ced, a teenager some five years his senior, out of $1,200 in a street game.

"At twelve years old!" Ced recalled later in an Atlanta recording studio, his watchful eyes constantly darting up toward the live feed of security cameras. "Next day I'm looking for him like, where's that lil n—— at who just got off the school bus. He came back dead fresh on me! Pocket full of money. Twelve years old!"

It wasn't long before word started to get around about the little guy who just might win the shoes off your feet. "He was fourteen, fifteen, taking the money of people twice his age," Lashon said. "But I knew it would come back and cause trouble. Men don't like to lose things."

Soon, Dominique started missing his curfew. One night, he came home with a broken elbow. "After that, I said, 'That's grown people's business. Do you know how serious a dice game is?' " Lashon recalled.

But Dominique, never inclined to show much fear, swore playing the odds was all in good fun. *At least he's mathematically inclined*, Lashon reasoned. And even though it kept her up at night, she always knew where she was likely to find him: down at the park, huddled in a rowdy semicircle, probably shooting craps with crumpled dollar bills at his feet.

It was the combination of Dominique's penchant for loitering outside at all hours with guys nearly twice his age and Lashon's irrepressible maternal instincts that would give the kid his nickname. Again and again, there was Lashon, pulling up in the hood looking for her little one, who hadn't answered his cell phone or shown up for school, or dinner, or curfew. On top of everything, Dominique was messy, liable to leave his garbage everywhere and fall asleep where he shouldn't—"typical little baby shit," as he said later. The guys, as they do, got to teasing. Lucky roller or not, he was nothing more than a mama's boy—a child being tugged home by the ear.

And so it stuck: Lil Baby, the fearless gambler with a wide grin, a sliver of space in the center of his smile, a deep dimple on his right cheek, a puffed-out chest and a mother who just wouldn't leave him all the way alone. "Uh-huh," Lashon told her son's friendly tormenters. "You wish your mama would be checking on you!"

Gambling was, in effect, Lil Baby's first real job, his introduction to the quick money that would endear him to what is known, in and around Atlanta, but also universally and without much variation, as *the streets*—or, to Baby and his cohort, with their indefatigable Atlanta accents and always-evolving slang, the *skreets*. A singular entity, threading invisibly through disparate neighborhoods on almost every side of town—and with matching parallels in most every American city—the streets were the subterranean layer under Atlanta's network of higher learning, its office parks and corporate headquarters, its civil rights landmarks and its McMansions. The streets were where a young kid could learn some things his mother might prefer he'd never known—a self-contained economy, a bazaar of wares, an endless pool of opportunity, betrayal, lust and, potentially, a life sentence. And it was through Lil Baby's love affair with the streets that he, a young Black man in a city like Atlanta, met another constant presence in his life: the police, known around town simply as *12*—as in, *Fuck 12*—a perpetual counterweight to the pull of the block.

The first call in what would become an unfortunate tradition between mother and son came from Dominique himself. He was around fifteen. "Mom, me and my friends were walking through the park and a police officer stopped us and said he was going to lock us up," Dominique told his mother, the officer by his side.

"What were y'all doing?" Lashon asked, already knowing the answer.

"We were playing with some dice . . ."

"Oh, so you were gambling?"

The officer said he would let them go with a warning. No one involved expected it to stick.

By then, Dominique's mother had changed jobs, moving from the post office to the Fulton County Courthouse, where she worked as a cleaner. Such proximity to the law would come in handy later. But even with steady employment, some government assistance and occasional contributions from a boyfriend, Lashon struggled to keep her son shielded from all he wanted and what came with it. An allowance could never compare to the amounts changing hands every day outside.

"Him being my only boy, I always knew I had to step it up with him," Lashon said. "I would get paid and give him two hundred dollars, but two hundred dollars is nothing to a gambler when you're coming home with twelve hundred dollars."

Homework wasn't holding her son back either. Before dropping out in tenth grade, Dominique did a tour of Atlanta's public and alternative schools, succeeding and sabotaging himself equally along the way. First, he was kicked out of Tri-Cities High in East Point, where André and Big had created OutKast. Booker T. Washington, the first public high school for African Americans in Georgia, just north of the West End, couldn't contain him either. Fights, flirting, skipping class, small-time candy-selling scams—Dominique did it all. At least one adult said his adolescent hell-raising made them want to quit teaching entirely.

One year at Washington, Dominique missed sixty days of school before his mother was even alerted. "Because guess what?" Lashon said. "He was passing. He would go, do the work and leave." Teachers would rather give Dominique an open-ended hall pass than have him banging a drumbeat on the desk, goofing off and causing trouble with his classmates. His mother assumed ADHD, but he was never diagnosed.

No matter where Lashon put him, Dominique would turn back up where the money was—either in Oakland City, the nearby neighborhood where his friends lived, or at the West End mall, where the girls and clothes and potential customers were. And she could see how things were trending: the less Dominique went to school, the less he needed it, based on the amount of money he apparently had coming in.

Still, it was easier to imagine him as nothing more than a dice player until all the signs said otherwise. For a while, Dominique took some care to hide what his mother assumed were his ill-gotten gains, but that didn't last long. The point, after all, was to show them off. Eventually, Lashon started noticing "little slick shit" around the house—new shoes, new clothes, all beyond her means.

Cleaning up after someone also comes with clues. One day while tending to Dominique's room, Lashon discovered some numbers carved into the underside of a wooden table. Even if she had wanted to try, the exact combination of figures etched there was impossible to explain away innocently. They could only have been one thing: weights and prices.

"What a nick is, what an ounce is—he had scratched it under the table," she said. This was homework of another sort, a beginner's guide to a next-level hustle. "I called him in there and I said, 'Well, what are these numbers?'" Of course, she had a pretty good idea already. "I hadn't been out of the game that long," Lashon said.

She was left, then, with an impossible choice. But Lashon's initial instinct to smother her only son the way she'd been smothered by her parents was not only futile, it felt borderline cruel—a single mother's desperate helplessness in the face of her son's ambitions, regardless of their wider wisdom.

She knew Dominique was bright, self-possessed and excelling at the things he was putting his mind to, be they what they were. It was partially due to his ability to squeeze success from any circumstance, Lashon realized, that her leash for Dominique had gradually gotten longer and longer, until she realized she was no longer holding it at all.

"I began to feel sorry for him," she said. "At first, I didn't let him do nothing or go nowhere. But I felt guilty for keeping him in, 'cause he a boy—they supposed to get out, do stuff, have friends. I don't know if that was because of my childhood—sheltered because of the Wayne Williams thing. But I knew that boys, once they get out there, they get out there."

She'd always be in his corner. But Lashon knew that by the time he was sixteen, Dominique—her Lil Baby—was essentially on his own. "I just want you to know, it's a lot of stuff come with these streets," she told him. "When you make the decision to get in them, know that it's consequences for being out there.

"You my child, I love you dearly. I would love to keep you safe and spoil you and give you everything that your heart desires. But I'm not in the situation to do it. Really no parent is, unless you're some billionaires. So your greatest lessons you're going to learn are going to be in the streets. But always hear my voice: *I know you know right from wrong*. And I'm going to leave it at that."

"I prayed about it," she said, "and I let him go."

5·

"CALL ME COACH"

KEVIN LEE PACKED HIS BAGS FOR ATLANTA NOT LONG AFTER THE 1996 Olympics, where the domestic terrorist and antiabortion zealot Eric Robert Rudolph planted a pipe bomb in a downtown park, killing one person and injuring more than one hundred.

The thousands of Black Atlantans displaced by the long bureaucratic push for the games—including the many homeless people locked up for the occasion—were not the real threat, it turned out. But the political and cultural dissonance in the city surrounding its international showcase was feeding its rap sound at a particularly electric moment, and now Lee could feel it firsthand. By the beginning of 1997, he was a full-time resident.

In Lee's mind, there was nowhere else to be in the South at that moment if making it in rap music was the idea, and for someone who saw himself as a future mogul, it was the only thing that mattered. He had a feel for the city already after years of visits, and maybe his HBCU connections would come in handy.

But while Atlanta was hospitable by nature, it was also a notoriously insular town, where what neighborhood you grew up in and who you knew were probably more important than your résumé, and so they weren't exactly handing out jobs in the local music business to outsiders. For a time, Lee supported himself as a special education teacher at Tri-Cities High School, where he rocked a short beard, a puffy twist-out and colorfully patterned bohemian shirts. At night, he hung around the studios that had popped up during Atlanta's first music boom, hoping to soak up whatever he could.

After doubling down on local rap, LaFace Records was running the city. In the fall of 1995, OutKast's Dungeon cousins in Goodie Mob had released *Soul Food*, a dense, genre-hopping album with an explicitly political bent, again broadening the boundaries for Atlanta rappers. OutKast, the label's other breakout rap group, was also increasingly out there and experimental, following up *Southernplayalisticadillacmuzik* with the spacier *ATLiens* a few weeks after the spotlight of the Olympics lifted, and bringing attention right back to town, albeit a different side. "Elevators (Me & You)," a woozy, downbeat single that recounted the group's story so far—and featured Dré, still a few years from renaming himself André 3000, wearing a turban in its music video—would become the group's most successful song to date despite its bold eccentricities, topping the rap songs chart and hitting number 12 on the *Billboard* Hot 100, just under "Macarena" and hits by Jewel and Alanis Morissette. *Aquemini*, OutKast's even heavier third album, wouldn't be far behind, and it somehow sold even better than its predecessor by going further afield and extraterrestrial, partly over the duo's own intricate, self-produced beats, like the bluesy, country-fried stomp of "Rosa Parks."

For someone like Lee, whose taste skewed beyond straightforward hip-hop and who was known to wear a turban of his own, the unlikely international success of Goodie Mob and OutKast was yet another reason to appreciate Atlanta. "They rapped about substance and culture and shit that was going on in the South. But they still rapped about the trap," said Lee later, detailing the early days of his relationship with what he called "the Blackest city in America" as it evolved from infatuation and intrigue toward something more like true love. "It was a moment that can't be done again."

As a child, Lee had gone with his mother to visit a friend of hers in Harlem, and he saw firsthand the way Black culture could bubble up in local communities and eventually change the world. In Indianapolis, Lee's mother and grandmother worked at the RCA Records pressing plant, which thrived from 1939 until 1987, and he developed an ear for new sounds, having been raised on R&B and jazz, but also early hip-hop records like "King Tim III (Personality Jock)" by the Fatback Band and the Sugarhill Gang's "Rapper's Delight." When one of Lee's closest friends growing up was gifted two turntables, the boys took to spending all of their money on vinyl. A cousin of Lee's was a DJ and helped to encourage this new obsession. As a teenager, Lee also broadened his adventurous sonic palette with road trips to Chicago, where house music was developing throughout the 1980s.

One thing that house and early hip-hop had in common, a genetic link that originated right in Lee's formative years, was the importance of the drum machine—specifically the cult-favorite Roland TR-808, which would become the backbone for most of Atlanta rap. Dismissed at first because it did not sound anything like a real drum set, the 808 launched in 1980 and was discontinued by Roland soon after due to a lack of sales. But the machine's unnatural hits, clicks, thwacks and booms would nonetheless go on to provide the rhythms for an absurd amount of disparate electronic music, from Yellow Magic Orchestra and Detroit techno to Miami bass and Marvin Gaye's "Sexual Healing," plus Bambaataa's "Planet Rock," MC Shy D's "Rapp Will Never Die" and so on. Thanks to the short shelf life of the original, the drum machines could be found cheap on the secondary market—perfect for bedroom amateurs—and eventually the 808's sounds were reproduced digitally, making them available to just about everyone who needed some kick. Like the New York hip-hop originators and booty-shake pioneers, the architects of trap music would have access to a simple but infinitely tweakable tool kit.

While LaFace and So So Def were dominating, Lee was in the background building up the next generation, as Atlanta's take on bass music continued morphing into something more assertive, in line with innovations from Master P's No Limit Records in New Orleans and the borderline gothic gangsters of Memphis's Three 6 Mafia. In 1997, Atlanta's Jonathan Smith—the wild dude with the big screams and smiles who DJ-ed clubs and A&R–ed the *Bass All Stars* compilations for Jermaine Dupri—began releasing his own music under the name Lil Jon. His debut album, *Get Crunk, Who U Wit: Da Album*, introduced his group the East Side Boyz and helped to stack another building block on a growing

Southern subgenre: crunk, known for its hectic 808 claps and hyped-up chants, reminiscent of Miami bass, in shout-along songs with simple prompts, like "Cut Up" and "Shake Your Booty."

Not long before the turn of the century, Lee found his own crunk evangelist, someone who could war cry and growl with the best of them. The guy could also really rap. A down-home character with a big beard and long dreads, Pastor Troy was born in Fairburn, outside of Southwest Atlanta, to a drill-sergeant-turned-pastor father, so barking was in his blood. Troy went to college in Augusta, and by the time he returned to the Atlanta area, he was building an underground name.

Lee met Troy around the time he was learning an invaluable music-business lesson that resonated in the city and beyond: if you wanted to start an independent record label—a.k.a. a money pit—you needed someone with a separate steady income stream who was ready to blow serious cash. For Lee, that ultimately unwise investor was a professional basketball player—Alan Henderson of the Atlanta Hawks, an old friend who played high school ball in Indianapolis. While in the NBA, Henderson started a little company called Hendu Entertainment and he hired Lee, who had ears above all else, as an A&R man like Lil Jon was for Dupri—an on-the-ground talent scout for stars and songs.

The Hendu label went nowhere, producing little music of note. But they were early to Pastor Troy, who would become Lee's first real management client and a legitimate Atlanta legend, immortalizing the *We rea-dy, we rea-dy!* chant that still echoes through local gatherings today, from clubs to graduations, on his defining 1998 single "No Mo Play in GA."

With Lee as his artistic shepherd, the rapper barraged Atlanta with gravel, grime and clever marketing tricks, like free church fans to promote his group the Congregation. "Pastor Troy really introduced street music to the city," Lee once said, citing the rapper's "crazy-ass, wild energy." And while Troy's national profile would prove short-lived, he represented a crucial artistic step in the city as a direct predecessor to pure-adrenaline Atlanta artists like Waka Flocka Flame, and even the drill music that would follow from Chicago, London and Brooklyn. Troy also helped to amplify the drug-music boom already on its way, rapping lines like, "I make the ghetto my lobby, make they habit my hobby / Bought a little Arm & Hammer, cook it, sell, then copy."

But it was Lee's next major client who would officially knight him as a macher in local circles and really make the trap house an Atlanta rap landmark, leaving his manager with a new nom de guerre in the process.

After splitting with Troy in the new millennium—proving that musician and manager remained one of the ficklest relationships in love or art—Lee first took on a small stable of up-and-coming producers instead. Across Atlanta's matrix of recording studios, where he had developed connections with his solid word and refined taste, Lee was working to push their beats on any rapper who would have them until he received a tip that rearranged his world.

One day like any other, a studio manager informed Lee of a potential score for his producers: There was a crew of young rappers holed up in the A-room of Dark Studios—the recording equivalent of a master bedroom—and they obviously had cash to throw around. The guys had been in there nearly a month trying to get something going. "This is a lick for you," Lee's friend said. "You can make some money."

Upon pulling up, Lee met the man holding the purse strings—a hustler known as Lil J, who had designs on becoming the next big rap CEO à la Master P. Lil J was twenty-one, a native of Hawkinsville, Georgia (population 3,280), and he had a 2001 Lexus LS 400 sitting on twenty-inch rims in the parking lot. He knew of Lee's work with Pastor Troy and seemed open to input on his would-be label. But Lil J declared firmly that he was not a rapper.

Lee immediately knew otherwise. Despite his protestations, Lil J had laid down a few cursory verses on his artists' songs, and his raspy country drawl, along with his untouchable, seen-it-all demeanor and street shine, were what stuck out to the budding talent scout in his midst. Lil J wasn't a musician yet, but there was something there to mold, and soon enough, he had a new stage name: Young Jeezy.

Lee's work with Jeezy would become a kind of formula for the manager and his artists, one that was repeated in hoods around the country, but especially in Atlanta, over and over again in the years to come. A street guy with excess swag and cash—or at least a loyal hood patron—might bristle at first at the idea of making art out of his life, but with the encouragement and ear of someone like Lee, he would come to see music as a path toward peace and prosperity that the streets could never offer. And all it took to become the manager for a guy like that was a plan, some patience and persistence. Street hustling, after all, never lasted forever. What Lee saw in Jeezy was the same raw star power that Jermaine Dupri spotted in the Kris Kross boys at the Greenbriar Mall. But with rap audiences growing more obsessed with authenticity—not to mention the production and sale of drugs, with everything that lifestyle afforded—hustlers who actually knew the game in detail came with an upper hand and stories to tell. In Atlanta, a lot of people could recognize the real thing.

After some convincing and experimentation, Lee made Young Jeezy his main project, and the pair spent years developing a sound and persona that would connect first on the streets of Atlanta and then around the world. They were in the studio every day, with Lee playing executive producer, critic, cheerleader and taskmaster as he pushed Jeezy from a reluctant MC toward full-package artistry. It was Lee's perfectionism and tendency to tell Jeezy, "Do that shit over," in the studio that helped give Lee a name that would echo across Atlanta for the next two decades, rarely in association with Duke University basketball: Coach K.

"One day he was just like, 'A'ight, Coach. You think you're my coach or something?'" Lee recalled later. He had always preferred to lie low on the sidelines and was never going to jump on the mic or in a music video like the hip-hop player-coaches of the time, Jermaine Dupri, Master P and Puff Daddy. But Lee did know the importance of branding, and with his first initial added, he made sure his new moniker stuck. "I was like, *Damn, I like that*," Lee said, deciding then and there on a new rule: "Whenever we're out, don't call me by my first name. Call me Coach."

The manager was innovating on the artist's side, as well. While the street code was typically one of silence and discretion, Coach K pressed Jeezy to rap about how he really lived his life—like, for instance, the time when Jeezy, Coach and two women popped dozens of bottles of Cristal in the club just to show up some actual famous people nearby.

For them, this was an average night out. "I remember it was like six a.m., and we were coming out the club," Coach said. "We were in the car, and I said, 'Man, you've got to start talking about this shit in your music,' and he was like, 'Nah, I can't indict myself like that, man.' I'm like, 'Dog, just be real witty, and talk about that shit in third person. Jay and them do it all the time.'"

It didn't take much prodding. In fact, Jeezy—who would go on to market himself as the Snowman in a not-so-subtle reference to his illicit product of choice—saw his reputation grow exponentially through his real-life proximity to the Black Mafia Family, or BMF, a cocaine syndicate originally from Detroit that had set up an Atlanta outpost. Around the time of Jeezy's rise, BMF had started dabbling in rap for—depending on whom you ask—bragging rights or money-laundering purposes. (Most likely both.) The organization's honcho Demetrius Flenory, better known as Big Meech, even appeared in "Air Forces," one of Jeezy's early videos, which was shot at one of the two luxury Miami hotels that BMF had rented in their entirety for an associate's birthday. With Meech backing him up, Jeezy described himself "in the club, blowing dro, throwing gang signs" with "eight bitches, ten bottles of Cris." In other words, exactly what Coach had called for—introducing Atlanta nightlife to the rest of the world with flair and a dash of danger.

To anyone who lived through it, the BMF era in Atlanta—that is, the four years before Meech and dozens of his associates faced a crushing federal indictment—was like if Cirque du Soleil put on a show scored by Jeezy in Scrooge McDuck's money pit. With dollar bills raining from the sky, it was like Freaknik on steroids, every night, if every car in traffic was a Lamborghini and there happened to be a Bengal tiger in the trunk, lounging with two strippers. And the tiger's teeth were made of gold. Those were the BMF years.

"This whole city was turned up," Coach said, struggling to find the words. "If you didn't see the show . . . It's kind of like the circus—you can't really come home and tell nobody what you seen. That four years was some of the most amazing shit I've ever experienced. The money was plentiful—*everywhere*—all the clubs was popping every night. It was a movie." More specifically, it was the movie that the now-widespread phrase *It was a movie* must be referring to.

In the minds of those who lived through it, Atlanta has never—and will never—return to the levels of extravagance that accompanied the brief BMF takeover. Federal prosecutors later estimated that the group was bringing in tens of millions of dollars a year, and nearly $300 million in total, much of it flaunted in public at Atlanta's finest establishments—Velvet Room, Club Chaos and more. Brazen doesn't even begin to describe it. There was a $500,000 music video for a song that didn't deserve it; a hip-hop and hood-celebrity magazine, *The Juice*, that helped set the tone for WorldStarHipHop and the Shade Room; and millions more spent on nightlife. For Meech's mythic thirty-sixth birthday at Compound on the West Side in 2004, the go-to Atlanta party planner Hannah Kang, a first-generation Korean American who grew up in Decatur, rented six figures' worth of exotic wildlife, including lions, tigers, zebras and an elephant. "The best times in Atlanta," Kang said. "Everyone felt rich."

From waitresses to strippers to DJs to dealers, people were making money, and therefore—outside of law enforcement—they were all thrilled. The ecstasy didn't hurt either. "Whenever there's drugs in the street, the nightlife is going to move," as Coach has explained. "When it's slow, there's a drought, the nightlife is slow as hell."

To Kang, who planned Beyoncé's twenty-first birthday at an Atlanta skating rink around the same time, those years were a blurry dream. "I feel goofy saying this shit, because it doesn't even feel real," she said. "And what's crazy about Atlanta is that I have never worked directly for any white person in the history of my career. Not once."

But BMF's biggest middle finger of defiance toward Atlanta's rank and file was also its simplest flex. In a city defined by its looping highways and interstates, there was no better way to send a message than with a billboard. And as Atlanta's music gained prominence, billboards advertising rap labels and albums in highly trafficked locations became a kind of arms race and territorial pissing match, putting hip-hop on the same level, product-wise, as Coca-Cola and Chick-fil-A. For more than a decade, Jermaine Dupri's company announced itself with its trademark Afroman logo right where I-75 and I-85 connected just north of the airport approaching downtown—ATLANTA, the sign read, HOME OF SO SO DEF RECORDINGS. But for a few years in the early 2000s, So So Def had company. On I-75 and even Peachtree Road in Buckhead, twenty-by-sixty-foot canvases announced, in a nod to *Scarface*: THE WORLD IS BMF'S.

Technically, this was an ad for a record label, BMF Entertainment, home to a single rapper—Bleu DaVinci—since the group's alliance with Jeezy was kept strictly off paper. But federal authorities investigating the crew couldn't help but take a billboard that advertised out-of-town drug dealers as a taunt. Only in Atlanta.

It was a testament to Coach K's discretion, his ability to move quietly and deliberately, that for all of the mayhem and excess surrounding the BMF era, he is not mentioned among, or even alongside, its cautionary tales. Coach knew Jeezy's connections could be beneficial from a marketing standpoint, so he played the background, working parallel to the crew, even as it created hurdles for his business. For a while, Atlanta radio wanted to keep its distance from BMF—and thus, Jeezy—lest they appear to be condoning the syndicate's behavior outside the clubs, which included, according to law enforcement, murder, kidnapping, money laundering and flooding the area with dangerous drugs.

Coach, in problem-solving mode, relied instead on another outlet for the music, building Jeezy's fan base through the mixtape circuit—an end-around to radio and labels that had evolved from unauthorized party bootlegs and DJ-led blends into a crucial underground promotional tool for rappers that would reshape Atlanta music. Borrowing from advancements being made up north by 50 Cent's G-Unit and Cam'ron's Dipset—who were turning mixtapes from grab-bag compilations into more focused artist showcases—teams like Coach's helped establish a repeatable playbook for rappers across the South, who watched Jeezy move, by some accounts, millions of CDs from trunks, flea markets, barbershops and corner stores without the active help of his record label.

Coach's neighbor at the time, an HBCU alum known as DJ Drama, was becoming the go-to guy to promote, prune and shout over a rapper's tracks (a.k.a. "hosting" a mixtape), and together, they made Jeezy's first two semiofficial releases—*Tha Streetz Iz Watchin* in 2004 and *Trap or Die* in 2005—hood favorites and modern rap classics. "Two record deals, radio still won't play me," Jeezy rapped on the intro to *Trap or Die*. "But I don't give a fuck 'cause the streets done made me."

Coach's job was to make these mixtape releases feel like events—the dawning of a new era in the city—and he knew just how to do it. "All traps closed today," announced the ubiquitous radio ad that declared *Trap or Die*'s release date a national holiday for all dealers and users.

Later, in a sign of the broader industry's cluelessness and slowness to adapt, DJ Drama's studio would be raided by a Fulton County SWAT team investigating copyright violations on behalf of the Recording Industry Association of America and some of the same corporations that were by then paying his operation for street-level promotion. The racketeering charges didn't stick, but the high-profile 2007 bust resulted in most of the operation moving online.

By then, Jeezy was already in the big leagues. His mixtape hustle culminated in the summer of 2005 with *Let's Get It: Thug Motivation 101*, a major-label debut for Def Jam, the quintessential New York–based hip-hop label, which was then being run by none other than LaFace's cofounder LA Reid. But on their way to the national mainstream, Jeezy and Coach K—who was also managing the pivotal producers Shawty Redd and Drumma Boy—had helped to create a sound that would come to define Atlanta music in the coming years.

"Man, when the rapper's rapping, you should be able to smell the dope cooking," Coach once explained, citing the work of his own beatmakers and dubbing trap "the book of the streets." He wanted Jeezy's music to be simple and booming, dark and ornate, spacious and lush. Samples were rare, a decision that could be traced back to Organized Noize's use of live and programmed original sounds as a money-saving technique. "Crack-baby beats," Coach called them. "It's like four sounds. 808s. Leave that shit open so a n—— can put his ad-libs in there! That's how we were doing it with Jeezy. He had a really slow flow, so leave the beat open. And go on the beat and pocket, but let your ad-libs be the other components of the beat!"

Ad-libs, a secondary vocal track of exclamations, onomatopoeia and underlining interjections, were the sound of a rapper reacting to his own clever lines in real time. From James Brown's grunts, snorts and *Hit me!*s to Michael Jackson's *HEEHEE*s and *OWW*s, there was a long tradition of ad-libs in Black music, dating back to spirituals, jazz and blues. But never had they been so central to a genre's appeal as they were in trap music, where the ab-libs could often be catchier and more visceral than the lyrics themselves. For Jeezy, who sounded like he smoked two packs of dynamite a day, a simple *AYYY*, *CHEAAA* or *HA-HAAA* could sound like a warrior's wail or villain's cackle, and just about every Atlanta rapper who followed would be required to come with at least one noise as distinctive. (Eventually, the South Atlanta wheeze-and-squealer Playboi Carti would build his entire sound from such mouth-made effects.)

While Jeezy was crossing over to the mainstream music industry, his rise was coinciding with the other faces that would eventually belong beside his on the Mount Rushmore of Trap—namely TI, who released his album *Trap Muzik* in 2003 (and therefore asserts ownership over the genre), and Gucci Mane, the absurdly prolific mixtape king originally from Alabama, but who was raised in East Atlanta's Zone 6.

A self-destructive iconoclast and cult figure turned mainstream celebrity, Gucci Mane's own debut album, *Trap House*, came out in 2005, rightfully giving him some share of the credit for popularizing the term that became an Atlanta sound and musical movement. Portly and menacing before he was buff and approachable with a gleaming smile of veneers, Gucci's constantly evolving flow was, as the critic Jon Caramanica wrote, "buoyant and melodic, with light comedic flourishes," and came with "a slurry intricacy that's inscrutable to old-fashioned hip-hop purists, but holds consistent thrills."

Gucci loved cars, drugs and women in all different colors, describing them with such pizzazz that it sounded like he'd found a new gear for the

English language. This was a man who once rapped the words, "Sorry, dude, I farted and it smell like calamari soup," and then proceeded to rhyme "calamari" with "gnarly" (as in, what his "white girl in Hawaii" says when she's surfing). The city's premier modern musical folk hero, Gucci Mane, even more than his better-selling contemporaries, would see his rap genes mutate across all of Atlanta's law-enforcement zones, making him probably the most influential figure in the twenty-first-century scene—a guru, a godfather, a cautionary tale and a role model all at once. Of course Coach K was partially responsible. But the connection, seemingly inevitable in retrospect, was not initially likely—and might not even have been possible to pull off for someone with any less than Coach's levels of steadiness and diplomacy. The same could be said for Gucci Mane's levels of unpredictability.

Gucci's buzz in Atlanta began around the same time Jeezy released *Tha Streetz Iz Watchin*, thanks to an unauthorized remix about robbing. In 2003, a group from the West Side called Dem Franchize Boyz had released a minimalist, bubblegummy single called "White Tee," which made crunk sound happy-go-lucky—"I hit the mall in my white tee / Oh, I think they like me"—replacing trap's digital snares with snaps (hence the micro-genre designation snap music, which reigned briefly in Atlanta through the mid-2000s). Like Jeezy, Gucci was another hustler who was reluctant to consider himself a rapper, and he put a more sinister bent on the catchy, repetitive track, changing the titular shirt color to match his tone: "I kill in my black tee / I steal in my black tee," etc. Gucci then promoted the song via unpaid performances at any dingy lounge, bar or strip club that would have him. But in an early sign of the chaos to come in his career, the rapper had already fallen out with the guys who appeared alongside him on the track by the time they shot the music video for "Black Tee." Instead, the others had a Gucci look-alike pretend to rap his verse with a black bandanna obscuring most of his face.

It was while making the rounds with "Black Tee" that Gucci met Coach at Walter's, the Atlanta shoe store and networking spot. Coach had been taken with Gucci's off-kilter odes to cooking crack, and he put the word out on the street that he wanted him to collaborate with Jeezy.

"Yo, I'm Gucci Mane," the rapper told the manager when they finally ran into each other. "I'm who you've been looking for."

Though he and Jeezy already shared a collaborator in the producer Shawty Redd, Gucci came with a secret weapon in the form of a church boy and pianist originally from the Bay Area. Born Xavier Dotson and known as Zaytoven, Gucci's favorite beatmaker would end up coauthoring the trap sound from the basement of his parents' house in the Atlanta area while attending barber college. It was one of Zaytoven's instrumentals that brought Coach, Gucci and Jeezy together, and then tore them apart.

During their first time working together, at Patchwerk, a studio founded by the Atlanta Falcons player Bob Whitfield, the rappers came up with "Icy" (sometimes called "So Icy"), using a hook by Lil Will of the Dungeon Family. The buoyant track was more pop than anything in either man's arsenal up to that point, and it immediately took off in clubs and on Atlanta radio in 2005, setting the table for their respective major record deals.

Jeezy had his BMF bona fides but nothing safely marketable, and Def Jam wanted "Icy" for his proper debut. But Gucci complicated things when he turned down $100,000 from the label for the rights to the song. Multiple attempts to settle the ownership dispute, including in-person summits with both rappers, also failed, and the situation devolved rapidly, with Jeezy allegedly relying on his BMF associations to keep the city on his side. According to Gucci, Big Meech's sway in the clubs was enough to make DJs start cutting off "Icy" before Gucci Mane's verse, leaving the rapper feeling blackballed in his own city.

Coach has said that Gucci struck first with a recorded diss track—in which he even threatened to "snatch" Jeezy's manager—but it was Jeezy who escalated things beyond repair with the song "Stay Strapped," in which he offered a $10,000 bounty to anyone who could steal the "Icy" diamond chain Gucci had made to celebrate the song's success. Gucci responded with "Round 1"—"Put a dress on, n——, you Meech's bitch"—and not long after, a man was dead.

Gucci said he fired in self-defense. It was May 10, 2005, exactly two weeks before the release of his first album, when the rapper left the Blazin' Saddles strip club with a dancer and a friend. Back at the woman's house, five guys rushed in with a set of brass knuckles and guns. During the ensuing scuffle, Gucci let off a shot, sending his attackers fleeing. One of the men, Henry Lee Clark III, or Pookie Loc, was found dead of a gunshot wound in the woods of a nearby middle school. An aspiring rapper, Pookie had reportedly been close to signing with Young Jeezy's Corporate Thugz Entertainment, and loud rumors around Atlanta linked the ambush to BMF. Jeezy denied any involvement—"Lord knows I ain't send the homie on no dummy mission," he rapped later—and the murder charges against Gucci were eventually dropped.

But it would take fifteen years and multiple tries before the two rappers, both over forty by then, could make a stilted sort of peace. In 2020, they shared the stage at Atlanta's storied Magic City strip club for a Verzuz battle of their hits and disses, revisiting the venom of their past—with Gucci going extra hard—before declaring the hatchet buried, however begrudgingly.

"I wanted to do this shit for the culture," Jeezy said that night. "I brought you here to show you the world care about what the fuck we got goin' on, because we are the culture. You feel me? Me and you. Where we came from. What we been through, n——. Us. Me and you. All these kids out here doing what the fuck they do because they saw what went on with us, dog."

He was right that Atlanta had never forgotten the deadly beef between two of its biggest homegrown stars at the exact moment of their ascendance. And it had been up to Coach K to help manage the aftermath, though not only on the side where he started.

EVEN WITH ALL they had accomplished, Coach K and Young Jeezy split by 2008. The next year, Coach was working with his former artist's blood rival.

First, however, he sulked. In a sign of the breakup's intensity and their enduring respect for each other, neither Coach nor Jeezy has ever said exactly what happened between them. But the rupture destabilized the young executive as he tried to figure out what came next, and he holed up for a while in Miami to brood.

When he returned to Atlanta, Coach, now an established presence in the local scene, let his interests take him in more unconventional directions—branching out that would prove fruitful in the long run. In addition to his deep love for dance tracks—clubs that played house music were "Kevin's world," he'd say later, "and then Coach would go to the Bounce, in Bankhead"—he always identified as something of a hipster. And in Atlanta, the home of André 3000, proud Black weirdos were plentiful and on the rise in the new millennium. While trap music was thriving throughout the aughts, MySpace had also exploded, and rap blogs and mixtape sites like DatPiff were taking the genre in a thousand directions at once. Online piracy and industry greed had helped tank the official business, with CD sales peaking in 2000 and never recovering. But free music online had never been freer, as cheap technology democratized at-home experimentation and consumption.

Before linking with Gucci Mane, Coach spent time incubating that kind of underground talent in real life, managing a collective called Hollyweerd that he saw as a mix of OutKast and the Pharcyde. He also worked with a before-his-time eccentric who went by Pregnant Boy and a female rapper named Muffy. This diverse scene was sometimes referred to as "hipster-hop"—though, fortunately, the name never took off—and it grew out of parties like Broke & Boujee and Sloppy Seconds Saturdays that started at a small club called the Royal, then owned by Coach, who imagined it as an Atlanta parallel to a Lower East Side lounge. Despite having a capacity of just 250, "all the hip kids that wasn't trapping, that's where they evolved from," Coach said. "They were internet kids—that's where the hipsters lived." It was yet another audience he would learn to reach directly, expanding rap's presence within the city.

At the same time, Coach was working, post-Jeezy, with yet another successful hustler, Rocko, who had at least one ambitious eye on the music game. After quietly collaborating with—and investing in—acts like Dem Franchize Boyz and Young Dro, Rocko turned to his own rap career, and Coach helped him negotiate a deal under LA Reid at Def Jam. But despite helping to coin the term "swag rap"—for the flossy, lightweight, MySpace-era Atlanta sound—and writing a few durable hits over the years, like "Umma Do Me" and "U.O.E.N.O.," Rocko's real lasting legacy would be bringing the world a man dubbed Future. Originally known as Meathead (and then Phuture), the rapper born Nayvadius Wilburn was yet another adopted child of the Dungeon Family discovered by Rico Wade, whom Future called his cousin. But he didn't break through to become one of Atlanta's bestselling and most influential artists until much later. Future, too, would eventually sign with Reid, the industry's top Atlanta booster—by then at Epic Records—but only after signing a much smaller, street-level deal with Rocko's label, A1 Recordings.

The contract disputes and lawsuits that followed between Rocko and Future would expose a chronic problem in many local rap scenes, where arts patronage often takes the form of cash stuffed in a duffel bag. As Coach described it, "The money came from out the black market—it came from out the streets—to build the shit." So young artists, often from bad circumstances and in need of funds, have been known to sign expansive deals with little or no lawyering for some right-now money, only to realize later—say, when a major label comes calling—how much they owe, percentage-wise, to the independent, street-level labels that helped give them their start. At some point, that money needs to be kicked back in hefty chunks of royalties or paid off entirely, leaving some artists in a maze of tangled contracts, with many expectant mouths demanding their taste. In theory, having someone like Coach K in your corner could minimize these complications.

But while Rocko was one thing, no one in Atlanta cut more of these semicasual, cash-transaction record deals than Gucci Mane. His eventual cosmic brood—which could never really be contained by an official crew or label—was like the Atlanta rap Dream Team. But in 2009, Gucci Mane himself was still the star attraction, and he had a new deal with

Warner Bros. despite having been in and out of prison and rehab, squandering the potential of his first three albums many times over. For his next go-around, he needed help making good on his pop promise. So not even five years after being charged with murdering a Young Jeezy associate, Gucci turned to Coach for help. Both men needed the reboot.

As part of his renewed chance at fame, Gucci Mane had been given his own major-label imprint, which he called 1017 Brick Squad. He surrounded himself with friends like OJ da Juiceman, a sprightly workhorse known for his yappy *aye!* ad-lib, and Waka Flocka Flame, a towering little-brother figure who was the son of a business partner and could be mistaken only for muscle. Gucci had long been managed off and on by Waka's mother, Deb Antney, and she, like everyone else in town, also did business with Coach K. With Gucci's career riding on his fourth album, *The State vs. Radric Davis*, Antney convinced her unruly charge that Coach could help them navigate the treacherous industry waters as a consultant.

Both men, understandably, had to think about it. Coach checked with his friends and partners about working with a onetime enemy, but eventually he just said, "Fuck it." Then, he proved himself to Gucci by keeping the money rolling in—the easiest way to cement one's worth as a manager and the quickest way to Gucci's heart. While on tour, the rapper would offer his new ally a bonus if they left any given town having made $100,000, and Coach would routinely line up a string of well-paid guest verses wherever they were. "We'd go into the city, do a show, pick up forty to fifty thousand dollars," Coach said. "Then we'd line up five features. We'd leave that city with a hundred thirty thousand dollars in one night." That year, Gucci would land a verse with no less than Mariah Carey.

Along the way, Coach became the most reliable presence within the hurricane that was Gucci's life. "He's really good at keeping the process moving, and not getting caught up in the nonsense," Todd Moscowitz, then the CEO of Warner Bros., once explained. "Every day, if I couldn't find Gooch, I could find Coach." That was another mark of a good manager.

In the run-up to Gucci's new album, he and Coach primed the streets (and the internet, where Gucci was catching on with Coach's hipster demographic) with an unmatched run of mixtapes—no fewer than eight throughout 2009, including three dubbed the *Cold War* series that were all released on the same day. But Gucci had also violated his probation by using drugs, and even after a stint in rehab, he was sentenced to a year in jail—a bid scheduled to start right before the release of *The State vs. Radric Davis* in December 2009. It was a testament to Coach's foresight—including shooting six music videos in advance—that the album became a success anyway, hitting number ten on *Billboard* and eventually moving 500,000 copies even at a tough time for music sales. Gucci Mane, from behind bars, still felt ubiquitous, his legend only growing.

But the ensuing years did not get any easier for the rapper, who was battling mental illness, chronic paranoia and an addiction to lean and pills, seemingly racking up as many criminal charges as he did guest spots. By January 2011, after releasing an underwhelming follow-up for Warner Bros., Gucci was in a psychiatric hospital. When he got out a few days later, he had a multicolored, three-scoop ice-cream cone tattooed across most of his right cheek. Coach was concerned, but he also saw that photos of the tattoo were burning up the internet—it was all part of the package with Gucci Mane.

As the rapper spiraled, Coach kept the mixtapes coming, even renegotiating Gucci's deal with Warner to include those not-exactly-albums—an industry precursor to the days of streaming and commercially available mixtapes, a move rappers like Drake have since employed to try new sounds and keep their fans sated in between big releases. "He had a couple more stints in jail, but we was running," Coach said.

He recalled a show in Los Angeles, after Gucci was once again released from jail—this time for allegedly pushing a woman out of his moving Hummer—that was attended by "gangbangers, hipster kids, Blacks, Mexicans, whites." "That was the first time Gucci was performing for all the little hipster kids," Coach recalled. "They were like, 'Gucci's God, man. He's the god of the trap.'"

Just like he'd done with his own nickname, Coach ran with it, branding his artist the Trap God and cementing Gucci's place for the historical record. TI had *Trap Muzik* and Jeezy did his thing, but to Coach, "Gucci was the epitome of the young boy in the hood, waking up every day in the trap." The manager also knew there was much more mileage to get out of that alluring Atlanta essence.

Coach and Gucci would part ways for good in 2013, not long before the erratic rapper went on one final rampage down Moreland Avenue in East Atlanta that ended in a police standoff and, eventually, a federal charge—possession of a firearm by a convicted felon. Using an intricate plea deal that rolled together an entire buffet of alleged crimes, the rapper was sentenced to more than three years in prison. When he did return, Gucci was fit, sober and seemingly rehabilitated. To some, his music was never the same. But before he went away, Gucci had already quite literally laid the foundation for the future of Atlanta rap, and he left a substantial portion of it under the care of Coach K.

Always an eager and unfussy collaborator who treated his studio output like faucet water—eternally, unthinkingly replenishable—Gucci had founded a recording studio near East Atlanta that might as well have been a research and development lab for the city. The Brick Factory—a drug pun on the name of a famous New York and Miami spot, the Hit Factory—had three studios, a workout room and an apartment setup, for anyone who wanted to stay and record for days at a time. Gucci's reputation for working with rising Atlanta rappers early was already established—he made the *Free Bricks* mixtape with Future in 2011—but with the Brick Factory and his starter label 1017 Brick Squad, he began incubating talent in earnest. He tended to favor those in his own image—tough-talking street guys like Young Scooter, a friend of Future's, and Peewee Longway, a crazy-eyed bowling ball of a man with a thing for tarantulas and firearms—but always with an experimental edge. Coach knew to respect Gucci's ear, and his gut: "He's such a free spirit. He knows before it hits."

But it was Peewee who first brought Young Thug to the Brick Factory. Then a beautiful, scraggly string bean with face tattoos and a mess of mangled teeth like shattered glass, Young Thug was from the south side of the city, a total stranger to Mr. East Atlanta. But after taking one look at him, Gucci repurposed the $25,000 in cash he had waiting for Peewee and gave it to Thug instead, certain he'd found a superstar. Between Thug and his next find, Gucci's instincts would define Atlanta for the years he was locked up, elevating trap music to an international, chart-topping concern and changing Coach's life—and the lives of those around him—all over again.

Zaytoven, the reserved producer-slash-barber, actually spotted the trio first, not on the streets or in an Atlanta studio, but—fittingly, it would turn out—on the internet. "There's some boys here who sound just like you and they're rapping over some beats that sound just like mine," Zaytoven told Gucci Mane in 2012, introducing him to a no-budget YouTube video for a song called "Bando" by some young guys listed as Migos. That day—after showing off the video to Scooter, Thug and Peewee—Gucci personally called the booking phone number listed in the video's online description and demanded that the three Migos come see him right away.

Like Gucci, Thug and others before them, the most Atlanta thing about the group was its stylistic defiance—an unshakable belief in its own ideas and eccentricities, which managed to seem fresh even while building on local legacies. It's remarkable looking back to see just how much of the trio's magic formula was apparent in the primordial video for "Bando," a love letter to the abandoned houses used to cook and sell drugs that employed a familiar Atlanta tool kit but sharpened it on the edge of youthful clarity and abandon.

Quavo, the de facto leader of Migos, begins the song over a dinky nursery-rhyme beat that sounds like it was made on the cheapest of Casio keyboards. "Trap, trap, trap," he offers. "Trap. Trap, trap. Trap. Whoa. Trap, trap, whoa, whoa, whoa, skrrt, skrrt, skrrt, go." Then, immediately, comes the song's chorus, bouncy but barely more melodic than its spoken intro and almost stupefyingly repetitive: "Trappin' out the house with the boards on the windows (*trap!*)," Quavo says in a monotone three times. He repeats the phrase "Trapped out the bando" six more times, seasoning each with an after-the-fact ad-lib (*bando!* or *whoo!*) that follows no discernible pattern. The song goes on, more or less like that, for four and a half minutes, until each member—first Quavo, then Offset and Takeoff—has his turn describing the art of trapping out the bando. It might as well go on forever. (The video, of course, illustrates what it might look like to trap out the bando.)

Arguably annoying and undeniably joyful, not everyone liked the song's fizzy, almost haughty simplicity. But Gucci Mane understood it right away. When the group showed up at the Brick Factory to meet him, there were only two of them. The third, Offset, was incarcerated in DeKalb County on a parole violation. In a disputed anecdote that would cause static with the group much later, Gucci Mane said the first thing he noticed about the two young men was their "fake-ass jewelry," leading him to take two gold chains from around his own neck and gift them on the spot to his would-be protégés. Gucci had also prepared $45,000 in cash for the rappers—$15,000 apiece—and he arranged in a call with Offset from jail to send his share to a lawyer. After Quavo and Takeoff left, Gucci said he noticed the necklaces they'd walked in with at the bottom of a Brick Factory trash can.

That was all it took. Migos essentially moved in, joining the Brick Factory at a vibrant moment—the early rumblings of a quake that would mark a new era in the city, with Gucci churning out mixtapes before his crash, Young Thug finding his helium-high squeak of a voice and young producers like Metro Boomin and Southside learning on the job from veterans like Zaytoven and Honorable CNOTE. Gucci dubbed the studio "some hippie commune shit."

"We locked in," Quavo recalled of those early days recording at the Brick Factory. "It wasn't no business, like you need to sign something. It was just love. No paperwork. We were just working all night, all day. He'd wake me up like, 'Quavo! Quavo! Let's do this. Let's record.'"

As the group worked tirelessly to finesse its sound, Zaytoven couldn't help but show off his find around Atlanta, likely knowing that if the group was going to blow, they'd need a guiding light beyond the erratic Gucci Mane. The producer called Coach K to gauge his gut, and Coach, intrigued and always reliant on word-of-mouth reputations, got to asking around.

"I remember hollering at some of the little hipster cats like, 'Yo, you heard of Migos?'" Coach said. "They were like, 'Fuck yeah—"Bando"!'" That was enough for him to get serious. *I'm going after these boys*, Coach decided. And he happened to have a new potential business partner he thought might be interested, as well.

6.

HARDWORKIN' MONEY

PIERRE THOMAS SOLD HIS FIRST CRACK ROCK WHEN HE WAS ABOUT ten years old.

An Atlanta native, Thomas was in the fifth grade, and he knew already that he couldn't have the things he coveted—the things some of the other kids had—unless he got them himself. He talks about coming to this realization, and then doing something about it, with the steeliness and subtle pride of someone for whom it worked out, someone confident that his struggles were worth it and that they made him maybe a bit better than the next man—a position that's easier to take once you've earned and then spent a few million dollars, only to earn even more after that. Thomas made his first million in 2010, he has said, when he was almost thirty, during a time he refers to euphemistically and often as "before music." As in, "I had money before music."

When he talks about how he started earning, even as a kid, he is not bragging exactly, and certainly not seeking sympathy for the way drugs defined his early life. He's just laying out the facts of his own industriousness and advanced maturity, and also the kind of environment that not only required but encouraged such traits. To hear him tell of such an unforgiving reality—one where a Black child would feel like it was inevitable that he was made to sell drugs before puberty—is not all that different, in its matter-of-fact tone, from hearing Warren Buffett describe how he once delivered newspapers or sold chewing gum and golf balls, saving up to buy a pinball machine that would then make the money for him by just sitting there, taking other people's coins at the barbershop. For Buffett, more money meant more pinball machines, which meant more money.

On the worst corners of Westside Atlanta, where Thomas grew up in the 1980s, it wasn't newspapers or gum, golf balls or pinball that were in high demand, but crack cocaine. Thomas's mother was addicted, and his father, in and out of prison but mostly in, preferred heroin. Thomas, in his textbook Black Atlanta twang, with which the city's name has maybe one *t* but definitely not two—says it *HAIR-on*. When his dad called to check in from time to time, he let young Pierre know that as the oldest boy, he was the man of the house now, as if he hadn't gathered that on his own already. Thomas knew full well that they were struggling to pay bills, and also to buy him sneakers and clothes. Sometimes he and his brother had to go to the neighbor's house, pot in hand, and ask for hot water so they could take a bath.

All things considered, Thomas still says that he came from a "good home." But outside on the streets of Atlanta, there were only certain possibilities available to him. There was a saying in the hood back then, when Thomas grew up, *Thirty off a hundred*, and that was how he came to selling. The older guys on the block, knowing which kids were in need and also which ones were most capable, would toss them a starter pack of ten crack rocks—the dusty little yellowish nuggets that counted to users as an affordable individual serving. This was the more extreme version of giving them a few bucks to run an errand at the store and telling them to keep the change. But this scenario came with the expectation that more money would come back quick.

From there, the kids knew what to do from watching, having grown up around buyers and pushers. "You gotta go sell the ten crack rocks for ten dollars apiece," Thomas once explained. That would bring in $100, with $70 due to the source and $30 in pure profit pocket money. "Then you gotta go flip that again," Thomas said. You buy a little more, hopefully at a decent wholesale rate, and break it down in a way that makes financial sense, stretching the substance where you can with filler, like baking soda. "You go flip that two, three times," Thomas said. "Then I could go buy them Bo Jacksons, or them Deion Sanders, or them dopeman Nikes, or whatever I was trying to get."

There's another phrase for this involuntary precociousness in Atlanta and beyond, but primarily in the South, where it makes real estate sense: *jumping off the porch.* To jump off the porch, in certain neighborhoods, is to stop being an innocent, passive observer at the hip of a mother, a father, a grandmother, a grandfather, an auntie, an uncle or an older sibling, and to get into the game with some urgency and force. You don't walk or step off the porch, you *jump.* Even by the standards of a tough area, like the West Side of Atlanta in the crack-epidemic 1980s, ten years old is early to have taken that leap. But it's not unheard of—not at all. Thomas was first locked up at age fourteen, and he's estimated that he was arrested more than a dozen times after—"jail like ten times, prison three times"—but he says as much with the same dispassion he uses to talk about selling crack.

"N——s go to jail every day out here," he said. "That's just normal shit that's happening when you in the hood."

PIERRE THOMAS CAN be an imposing presence, more grizzly bear than teddy bear, but with both in there. Everyone just calls him P and it's been that way forever, though some spell it Pee, and he's not picky. P has a big boyish face turned downward with contemplation, his close-cropped hair, jawline beard and thin mustache always tidy. Deep worry lines sit across his forehead like creek beds, and his barely-there brows accentuate intense eyes that do a lot of talking for him. But P is reserved until he isn't, prone to watching and listening and then activating with unchangeable opinions born almost always from personal experience. Otherwise, he stays quiet.

Depending on the day, P can be either cagey or disarmingly straightforward about the contours of his old life. Though he *yadda-yaddas* a lot of the in-between steps—once teasing, "Do you know what I had to do to get my first half a million dollars? I can't even tell you, but it wasn't easy"—P implies that his thirty-off-a-hundred days were pretty short-lived and that he came up quickly to larger amounts that could disappear just as fast. Sometimes, he likes to call the "before music" fund that he eventually squirreled away his "hardworkin' money." "That's what it was," he told a reporter in his early days of speaking to them at all. "Hard-workin' money. You feel what I'm saying?"

But rather than dwell on his specific hardships, P is more comfortable speaking generally about the cruel plight of being poor and Black in Atlanta, maybe only a few miles from an upwardly mobile upper-middle-class reality that, for many, never really feels like an achievable destination. "It's hard getting money out here, especially for young Black men with no education, coming from low-income areas—not a lot of opportunities," he said one afternoon in the fall of 2017, in front of a recording studio he owned—his second—the one with his boat-size Mercedes-Maybach parked out front like a shiny, road-ready eggplant.

"You see a lot of the glamour on TV, but they don't ever take them cameras down 20 West, over there on the West End, Oakland City, Mechanicsville, Bankhead, MLK. When people see Atlanta, they don't know there's a whole other side of Atlanta, and it ain't good. People out here struggling."

Insofar as people do know this other side of Atlanta, they know it through rap music. And much of that music in recent years has been brought to the world by P, though he never expected to have a role in that. Rap domination was never P's dream. To him, the dope boys were always bigger than the rappers. And the rappers weren't known then, like many are today, to be ex–dope boys, either. More often, they wanted to *be* the dope boys, or in their proximity—to dress like them, drive like them, appear on their level.

P got hip to the music game through his little brother, who wasn't all that good at it. They both appreciated the hustle of guys like Master P, Birdman and TI—"they come from the same thing we come from"—but not enough that P wanted to emulate them, at least at first. "Music was my brother's passion," P said. "I never was really into it like that."

He watched his brother sink endless hours, and also thousands of dollars, into a guy they knew, another Southwest Atlanta hustler who rapped as Gorilla Zoe. Zoe found some success, replacing Young Jeezy in the group Boyz N Da Hood after Jeezy's solo career skyrocketed, and he released an album of passable Jeezy-lite raps, *Welcome to the Zoo*, on

Puff Daddy's short-lived label Bad Boy South in 2007. But despite a few singles over the years that filled the gaps between TI, Jeezy and Lil Jon songs, Zoe's career was not one that made the guys behind him rich.

Still, P watched his brother, the original aspiring rap impresario in the family, and he learned. "He wasn't taking the proper steps to be everything he could be in it," P said. "He's still successful in other business ventures, but he had a label that wasn't really operated as a label. He didn't have an office. He had the resources and the funding to be a lot of the stuff that he wanted, but . . ." P trailed off.

He filed those mistakes away as he ran up his own hardworkin' money, taking what he made in the streets and investing it as he got older into safer pursuits than drugs or music—mostly real estate. P bought some buildings and even a daycare center. But he also kept getting arrested, building a serious rap sheet that included charges for possession with intent to distribute, aggravated assault, possession of a firearm by a convicted felon and reckless conduct, for once putting a brick through a woman's window. As late as 2009, P was in the streets heavy enough that he found himself in what he called "a real situation," deploying his trademark plain-speak that also happens to conceal a lot. He didn't go into the specifics of how this real situation developed, but he was direct about how it ended: P and his best friend Q both got shot.

"I survived," P said, "but he didn't."

That was how it went in the streets. Everyone knew the likely outcomes, to the point that they became a cliché understood inside the hood and out, one that was no less true for how often it was repeated: *You wind up either dead or in jail.* Maybe you're rich first, and then you're dead. Maybe you're rich in jail—that was something approaching a best-case scenario. But it didn't change the outcome. P had been in jail, and he'd been close to death on more than one occasion. Making money off music, long shot or not, started to look like paradise compared to those other options, especially after he watched his best friend die. If it was all a gamble, and some losses would hurt more than others, he might as well roll the dice on the least dangerous one.

"With me, I ain't have shit in the beginning. I ain't have nothing. I started with nothing," he said, rationalizing an investment that he knew from the jump was a serious risk. "I seen people before me that had money and went broke. You can try to save money—and I encourage people to save and stack money—but bills come every week. My mind state was, money going to evaporate. I don't mind gambling my money. If I win, I win. If I lose, I lose. Never know if I don't try."

As he spoke, P circled back to the same point again and again, as if it were the only destination—but also like he still needed convincing. "If I lost with it, what am I losing?" he said. "I ain't have shit from the start."

So P built a studio.

Naturally, it was in Southwest Atlanta. When he says it was on Metropolitan, the Atlanta native in him expects you to know what that means. Metropolitan Parkway, formerly known as Stewart Avenue, is a two-mile strip that runs from the neighborhood of Capitol View down into Hapeville. But less literally, it's shorthand for a red-light district so notorious—so known for its hourly motels, strip clubs, liquor stores and trailer park—that they had to literally change its name in an attempt at a rebranding. Built on the old Dixie Highway, Stewart Avenue once called to mind FJ's Tavern, "the last of the redneck biker bars" and the site of a triple murder; the Goldrush Showbar, the closest strip club to the airport; and the Alamo Plaza motel, a hot-pillow joint with the unofficial slogan *Want a date?*, where the infamous 1993 killing of a groom-to-be and his best man by a pimp during a bachelor party would eventually prove fatal for the name Stewart. By 1997, the street had a new name—Metropolitan—though it would take another decade before the newspaper started cautiously referring to the "gentrification" of the area, which still included plenty of boarded-up storefronts and vacant lots.

When P set up shop on a more residential stretch of the road, he still "bricked up all the windows, because the music game dangerous," especially on Metropolitan. The squat building, built in 1900 and without a discernible color other than ugly, was on a corner, and its façade had all the charm of an abandoned insurance office. But inside, P used his funds to make it a hospitable recording environment with top-of-the-line equipment, carpeted walls, big-screen TVs, theater seats, red leather couches and, of course, security cameras. In all, P spent about $300,000 to get the place operational.

But if starting a studio was one thing, finding artists worth recording was much harder. P's first attempt at a record company around 2010—an arrangement with his partner Dirty Dave, a rapper from Charleston—was dubbed Dirty Dollar Entertainment. But it didn't take long before the label went the way of his brother's earlier attempts in the business, losing P a ton of money and leaving him nothing much to show for it.

Unlike rolling dice or real estate, investing in music was a special kind of risk because it involved betting on the whims of another person, P explained—often someone not far from a stranger. "You gotta have some balls to invest your money into another man not knowing if it's gonna work or not—investing it into another man you don't know, you don't have no history with. That's a major gamble," he said, having experienced a quick string of failures in his early days as an executive. "I invested millions of dollars into artists that I didn't make one dime off of.

"Half a million here, four hundred thousand in this artist, three hundred thousand in this one—didn't make a dime," P ticked off, auditing in his head. "I had to eat that as a loss. The artist can keep going, but I had to eat that cost. You know how hard it is to get three, four hundred, five hundred thousand in this world today? Know what I'm saying?" Hardworkin' money went fast.

After Dirty Dollar failed to take off, P was close to cutting bait on his entire rap-empire experiment. He considered renting out the studio on Metropolitan to other suckers lighting their money on fire by trying to make it in hip-hop, or even to someone who knew what they were doing. It didn't matter much to him either way. But like any Atlanta street guy sniffing around the music business, P had crossed paths with Coach K, and he figured that if anyone might be able to help him put something together, it was the best manager in town.

Maybe Coach could take over the whole studio, keeping a steady stream of money coming in, and P would just cash the checks, he thought. Being a landlord was more like owning a pinball machine. But when P called Coach around 2013, near the end of his rope and bordering on desperation, he came with a plea that Coach had heard before—one that Coach actually knew how to assist with.

"Man, help me get out these streets," P said. "I got this studio, but I just need some help."

At that moment, Coach happened to have a plan coalescing. And P—who came with a big reputation in the streets and extra-deep pockets—was the perfect final piece. Coach sensed in his proven gut that Atlanta was at yet another moment of musical transition, with Gucci Mane locked up more often than not. So he had taken a trip to meet the young men known as Migos at the home studio they called the Bando. This particular bando—which shared its name with the song that had certain Atlanta streets buzzing, thanks to a YouTube video and word-of-mouth curiosity—was not exactly an abandoned house for cooking crack; it was the basement of Quavo's mom's home in Lawrenceville, Georgia, northeast of the city in Gwinnett County, some forty miles from the Atlanta airport. Gwinnett—or the Northside, as Migos would come to brand it in their trademark ad-libbed catchphrases—was barely even Atlanta. But it had its own reputation.

Home to the state's largest Latino population, Gwinnett had become, by 2009, a center of drug trafficking in the Southeast, with Mexican cartels gaining a foothold in strip malls and rental houses. Given Atlanta's interstates, the city was already known as a key distribution point for narcotics. But the suburbs afforded the space for things to fester. Just before the turn of the decade, a Gwinnett street called Buckingham Place, in the city of Duluth, became a cartel hot spot, and then the site of a huge federal seizure of meth. In Lawrenceville, a Mexican grocer, El Parral Carniceria y Fruteria, was revealed to be a front for selling cocaine. The Gangster Disciples, Latin Kings and other gangs thrived.

The friends who would become Migos were in high school at the time of Gwinnett's shift. At first, they rapped under the name Polo Club, since they loved to pose during the MySpace era in Ralph Lauren and Jordans. But around 2010, the trio started calling themselves Migos, which hinted at shadowy cartel connections while also serving as a nod to their slice of the Atlanta area.

When Coach visited Migos at the Bando, he had already encountered them in passing at Gucci's Brick Factory studio, where Quavo and Takeoff had spent about six weeks in an intensive rap boot camp, learning from their mercurial hero and building up a huge backlog of material. But down in Mama's basement, the scene was much more do-it-yourself, with a little computer propped precariously on a chair and a blanket covering the microphone.

The jankiness of the setup belied the quality of what the boys were obviously onto. As they played Coach hyperactive trap songs in progress like "China Town," "Hannah Montana" and "Versace," the experienced rap manager, now with a little gray in his beard, found himself having to contain the extent of his excitement, lest he—a poker-faced industry veteran—show his hand to some fresh-faced kids in Polo and starter jewelry.

Coach was tantalized by the possibility of working with a youthful rap collective. Groups were common enough in the city, but a local one had not really broken out on a national scale since OutKast. (The ADHD swag rap of Rich Kidz and the jubilant strip club anthems of Decatur's Travis Porter represented two near misses in recent Atlanta history, pre-streaming revolution.) But beyond the packaging, Coach was electrified by Migos' voices, patterns and cadences—the way its members weaved syllables into a beat, chopping up their lines into rhythmic triplets that could make percussive dents in the brains of listeners. What might've sounded irritating at first was actually their way of hooking you—vocal persistence had always been an effective musical tactic, after all. And while the trio was obviously descended from Gucci—that was clear in their vocal tones and subject matter, their playful irreverence regarding the English language—they imbued his jovial menace with even more exuberance via absurdist repetition, plus a punk spirit of chaos and directness.

Coach saw in the trio a recombination of specific elements from his past: The work ethic and wittiness of Gucci. The originality of Jeezy. The energy and ad-libs of Pastor Troy. *This shit is special*, Coach thought as he left the Bando, a burned CD in hand. He couldn't wait to show P.

7.

A NEW WAVE

BORN ON APRIL 2, 1991, QUAVIOUS KEYATE MARSHALL WAS ALWAYS the obvious Migos front man, though this was rarely, if ever, spoken out loud. The most distinctive, hookiest rapper, even as a teenager, he was a budding songwriter who could inject unpredictable bits of melody into his rhymes without trying. More important, Quavo, as he came to be known, had a glow and the easy smile of a natural heartthrob—that crucial piece for any variation on the boy band, even one based in the trap.

Quavious was an athlete before he was a rapper, starting as a quarterback for the Berkmar High School Patriots in nearby Lilburn (population 11,596—motto: "Small town, big difference"). During his senior year in 2009, his team won only one of its ten games, against an opponent with no victories. But its "spindly" quarterback ran a no-huddle offense and liked to throw the ball deep. His coach knew him as a prankster and recalled the future musician always showing up early for practice, singing in the locker room. Still, when the season ended, Quavious dropped out before graduating, drawn increasingly to rap and to the streets.

Quavo was Takeoff's uncle, despite being just three years older. Because of their closeness in age and interests, the pair grew up more like brothers, raised mostly by Quavo's mother, Edna. "She had a house full of n——s playing games, shoes off, eating all the food, and it's hard times—but she never complained," Quavo, whose father died when he was a child, told *Rolling Stone*. (*Mama!*, which became a go-to Migos exclamation, was not just an ad-lib but a tribute to her and the other matriarchs behind the group.)

Rap was mostly Takeoff's thing at first. Like his uncle, the baby of the three, born on June 18, 1994, had the name of a faraway royal—

Kirsnick Khari Ball—but he tended to hang back, observing with sleepy eyes while Quavo gleamed. As a child, Kirsnick loved wrestling, making the other boys imitate moves on the backyard trampoline, but he also put the most early hours into the craft of rapping on his way to becoming the group's most dexterous technical MC.

As nineties kids from the South—originally raised in Athens before they moved to Lawrenceville when Kirsnick was in elementary school—the boys grew up buying albums and mixtapes at the flea market, supplementing a steady stream of Tupac and Biggie with TI, OutKast, Goodie Mob and Gucci Mane. They also shared a special love for the Cash Money empire—chiefly Lil Wayne, who had become an honorary Atlanta touchstone despite being from New Orleans, collaborating widely across the region and setting more than a decade's worth of experimentalist rap trends. The Hot Boys, Lil Wayne's original foursome from childhood and one of the defining rap groups of the late nineties, had started young but never made kiddie music. That was a blueprint they could follow. Kirsnick loved the Hot Boys, and he pushed his uncle to rap alongside him after football practice.

Together as teenagers, the two performed their early songs, like "I'm Gettin Money" and "Shawty Like," as Polo Club at the local skating rink. They released their first mixtape when Quavious, who previously rapped as Crunk Boy, was in tenth grade. With matching chin-length dreads, often dyed blond or red at the ends, Takeoff and Quavo Stuntin (another early variation of his stage name) might as well have been twins—a next-generation, tougher version of Kris Kross with actual blood between them. But it was Offset who made the Migos alchemy add up, introducing a dash of cunning and unpredictability to the steady familial mix.

Kiari Kendrell Cephus, born December 14, 1991, was Quavious's year at school, and he played wide receiver at Berkmar High—when he was around. Hotheaded and intense, with panther eyes and a mischievous trademark bite of his bottom lip, Kiari was raised by his mother, Latabia, a North Carolina native, in Lawrenceville. He started hanging around Edna's house in sixth grade and took to calling the other guys his cousins, crediting them with pushing him to rap. When he was a teenager, Kiari's family lived in a nice house on a quiet street called Musical Court. But he soon turned—and then crashed—hardest into the streets, not because he didn't have a supportive and loving family at home, but because of what he identified as his own inner rage and restlessness, ingredients that with the proper outlet and tending often became ambition. He felt a driving need, in other words, to be the man.

Even after Kiari became Offset, he was always careful and adamant in explaining that he had been brought up well by his mother and stepfather, Kevin. "I don't want n——s to think I ain't never had a father figure," he said later in his Atlanta mansion's basement, pointing out Kevin, who was still part of the family despite having split with Latabia. But Offset had last seen his biological father—"my lame-ass daddy"—when he was about five years old. They didn't speak again until he was twelve. Then another decade-plus passed. "He on dope somewhere, I guess," was the most Offset would surmise.

In his father's absence, Offset made a promise to himself: he would never, ever become a deadbeat—or in his words, a "fuck n——." It just wasn't an option. "None of that shit." So when he had his first child, a son named Jordan, at the age of seventeen, a pre-Offset Kiari forged out on his own. "I was getting locked up trying to feed this n——," he said. "I was hitting licks, breaking into people's houses to bring it back."

Offset knew he was hardheaded and reckless, and he took full responsibility. "It was me," he said. "When me and my mom was getting into it, and I wasn't staying with her—seventeen, eighteen, nineteen—that was me being a knucklehead, trying to find the ropes. I started tripping. It was me. A lot of n——s be blaming their moms and shit—nah, hell nah. It was me. I was tripping. The path my mama wanted me to take, I wasn't taking it."

School never worked for him. Even as a wealthy adult, Offset held on to his skepticism about a system he knew was stacked against him and all the kids like him. "You know how many people is still in the projects with college degrees, bro?" he asked long after such concerns were directly relevant to him. "In the trenches, bro. Can't get out. That shit don't do nothing for society and them." A normal job? Didn't seem worth it.

"It's hard. It is. Especially if you're coming from poverty—even with the degrees!" This was the stuff that got Offset heated, the idea that you could do everything you're supposed to, take out student loans, and still end up behind, just where you started. "People be expecting to go to college for twelve years and get your money when you're thirtysomething. Then you start in a hole. That's what fuck a lot of people up. Some people just leave because the shit be too expensive. Then they be too backed up. It's like an eviction."

For young Kiari, a teenager with a mouth to feed and something deeper unsettled within him, even robbing felt like a surer thing than the straight and narrow, which often led back to the bottom. His mother and stepfather tried to keep him busy with anything that could hold his attention, namely, sports—baseball, basketball, football—but as he got older, he bucked the structure and hierarchy of a team, preferring to jump off the porch to make a name for himself.

Offset always was a born performer uninterested in anonymity. In a home video from 2009 that's still floating around YouTube, a baby-faced Kiari rocks a small mohawk and a single chain over his red Polo Jeans T-shirt, parked on a plastic lawn chair in a bedroom scattered with dirty clothes and beauty products. A Gucci Mane mixtape track called "Ego Trippin" plays in the background as Kiari pops and locks his upper body, rolling his chest and neck in fluid motions that are so natural as to seem unnatural. Quavo, off camera for most of it, beams at his friend's abilities.

Nearly a decade later, at her son's colossal home, Offset's mother, Latabia, would let it slip that her son was not just a bedroom dancer but a professional one—a child star who appeared around the age of eleven in videos for TLC and Whitney Houston. In "Whatchulookinat," Houston's music video from 2002 about the paparazzi, little Kiari stands out among the squad of child shutterbugs in a gray suit and bowler hat, eyes wide and busting a move. Catching herself quickly in the midst of a motherly brag, Latabia tried to backtrack on the personal disclosure, acknowledging that her son now had a certain image to portray. But he earned that reputation, too.

In 2011, not long after Migos released its first independent mixtape, *Juug Season*—a juug being any illicit means to a financial end—Offset and Quavo were arrested as part of a major gang sweep of Gangster Disciples in Gwinnett County. The charges were eventually dropped, and Quavo said later that the arrest was "just for show." But it demonstrated that the boys, now legally adults, were on the radar of local law enforcement. "We cliqued together, called ourselves Migos, started terrorizing, got in trouble," Quavo once explained. The next year, Offset would face his first felony conviction for possessing stolen property.

By then, fatherhood wasn't his only financial concern—it turned out music was expensive, as well. There was equipment needed for the Bando—about $4,000 worth from the local Guitar Center, an upgrade from when they just used the free Windows Movie Maker software to record on beats, downloadable for nothing online. Then there were DJs to grease with cash and drinks, either for hosting their mixtapes or as encouragement to play early Migos songs in the club. Most costly, however, was the general lifestyle upkeep—even a shoestring version of it. "You gotta flex," Offset explained early in Migos' ascent. "You gotta look good, bro. Especially coming from the outskirts and wanting to take over the whole Atlanta."

This was a running paradox in rap, a frustrating Chinese finger trap for so many young artists in the twenty-first century, with every moment potentially documented on social media. Hip-hop is seen by so many as a final or only chance to escape downward mobility, poverty, the streets, the mud, the trenches. But it's also an arena that necessitates flexing, showing off, being richer, better dressed and better appointed than the next guy. In most cases, you need both—to have struggled and to have overcome. But at the beginning stages of a career, the appearance of overcoming usually overlaps with the end of the struggle. In other words, you can't get on if you aren't already shining to some degree, even if the music you're making is a document of that struggle. It's faking it until you make it taken to an extreme. Yet if you're caught faking it too blatantly, that can call into question everything else you've been saying about your struggles *and* your successes. If indeed Quavo and Takeoff showed up to the Brick Factory with fake chains, as Gucci Mane claimed, it was because they felt they needed to flex to be taken seriously—to show that they didn't need Gucci as badly as he needed them. *You gotta look good, bro.*

Trying to keep up had its consequences for Offset. He appeared on the *Juug Season* mixtape and its follow-up *No Label*, released in June 2012, and in between stints in prison, he recorded some of the music that blew Coach away in the Bando. But he wasn't around as things really started to heat up for Migos, missing out on Gucci's tutelage, the rush of being pursued by well-known industry figures and other little victories, like a packed-out club singing "Bando" back to them at the *No Label* release party and all the momentum-generating appearances that came after. These were moments Offset could never get back, time he would have to make up for down the line, both mentally and technically, as a rapper. For a while, he was scared to write a chorus for the group, because it meant he would have to carry the track. He felt behind as a songwriter.

Still, Migos always made clear that they came as a package deal of three, even with one in jail, and Quavo and Takeoff turned "Free Offset" into their rallying cry in videos and on T-shirts as they built a name. Coach K was not discouraged either. After his visit to the Bando, he was confident that the boys and their rookie manager, Jerel Nance, a childhood friend and the unofficial fourth Migo, could be molded into something great, even with Offset's situation.

But Coach knew that P could be slow to get back to him, and they had no time to waste, with Gucci having already put his stamp on the group and other Atlanta street A&Rs circling Migos as the elder rapper spiraled out. Coach gave P his CD of unreleased Migos music and encouraged him to quickly give it the real Atlanta temperature check—the car test. "You need to ride to this shit," Coach said.

With Migos' nonstop exclamation points rattling his speakers around the West Side, P found himself intrigued and energized, drawn first to "the dude with the long dreads"—Takeoff—whose rapping reminded him of the Cleveland group Bone Thugs-N-Harmony, early experimenters with rap melody and the triplet flow. In his typically pithy thumbs-up-or-thumbs-down rating system, P gave Migos a simple rave: "Man, these n——s are crazy." He meant it in the best way.

The other advantage that P brought with him—other than cash, a studio and the balls to gamble—was knowing Gucci Mane. It was practically cheating. P and Gucci were best friends who called each other brothers, having met in the streets. Guys from where they're from, who carry themselves like they do, tended to cross paths, becoming either allies or enemies, or one and then the other. These two, in Atlanta parlance, turned into *partners*—not in a business sense, exactly, but more of a spiritual one.

At first, P was hesitant about pursuing Migos—he didn't want to be seen as acting out-of-pocket by encroaching on Gucci's new artists at a vulnerable moment for his friend. But with Coach's encouragement, he reached out to the rap godfather in jail.

"Bro, go get 'em," Gucci told P. "We'll figure it out."

Having learned from the best, P then stuffed a duffel bag with cash and presented it to the guys as a gesture of his commitment, financial and beyond—but especially financial. Still, he and Coach needed to feel that commitment reciprocated, knowing that they were dealing with three distinct men with discrete personalities and, potentially, disparate goals. "What's the history of groups?" Coach cautioned. "They split up." So the executives sat down to ask Migos flat-out about their chances of breaking up down the line.

The three Migos were unequivocal—they were family.

"If you give me ten years of your life, we'll make a whole lot of money, and I'll make you guys as big as you can be," Coach told them.

Let's do it, Migos said.

"The music was crazy," P said later, "but what made me really wanna go hard for them is that they packed all their clothes and moved into the studio—literally lived there, sleeping on reclining chairs and making music all day." It was, after all, a long drive from Gwinnett to Metropolitan.

Originally, the plan was for P to sign Migos to his foundering fledgling label while Coach played the role of manager as he had in the past, with Gucci's enduring cosign and input. But given Coach's experiences in the first decade-plus of his career, he knew how easily a manager could be cut out and left owning nothing. Instead, with what he and P believed was a franchise-making talent as their first artist, the two men began to seriously consider forming a new independent record label around Migos, reinvigorating P's dampened musical aspirations and Coach's career at the same time. "It all came together," Coach said. "My skills, his credibility." (A third partner, even more camera-shy than P, was Coach's right-hand man since the Jeezy days, known—barely—as Twin, and sometimes No IG Twin, for his lack of an Instagram account and dedication to the background.)

Migos also ran with a caravan of friends and hangers-on who happened to be—or at least were willing to become—aspiring artists themselves. In rap, perhaps more than any other genre or business, it is assumed, though not always with enthusiasm, that artists will bring a small boatful of associates along with them, usually as some combination of security, makeshift tour managers, next-up artists or the errand boys known as weed carriers—the guys whose job it is to keep a constant quiver of blunts rolled, and also take the possession charge if it comes to that. Many play all those roles at once. In addition to providing paying work for friends, rappers and their backers who employ this extended-circle strategy also consider it a reliable way to keep a replenishing talent pool close at hand. But for every Waka Flocka Flame, who proved himself a quick learner and worthy investment for Gucci Mane, becoming a star in his own right, there were dozens of others who sucked from the rap-game teat and gave a questionable amount in return.

A few friends of Migos had, at minimum, charisma and some discernible talent, and they would go on to round out Coach and P's first shot at a full label roster. Rappers like Rich the Kid and Skippa Da Flippa, supporting characters in the early Migos universe, would fail to stick around. But Skippa did help popularize the head-in-the-crook-of-the-arm dance move known as "the dab," which many first heard as Migos slang—"dab" being another word for "swag"—before it took over white America, with everyone from Bill Gates to Hillary Clinton dabbing left and right from 2015 to 2017. Coach and P also took on local artists like Johnny Cinco, a singing rapper who called himself "Hood Drake," and OG Maco, a wild jumping bean from Coach's hipster connections whose minimalist screamer "U Guessed It" became an early viral hit on the short-form video platform Vine. (Looking back on those lean, ragtag motley-crew days a few years later, Coach could only sound exhausted: "It was like we were running a big-ass group home.")

But Migos was, without question, the priority—the group worth really investing in. And things were moving fast. They agreed to work with Coach around February of 2013, just as Offset was sentenced to eight months in prison for his probation violation. By March, Coach and P had set up their label around the trio.

While Coach served as a public face and known ambassador for the young group, ferrying them around to his industry connections at radio stations, at clubs and in the media, P played the background and eased the young rappers' transition into professionalism with his seemingly endless access to cash and recording time. As summer approached and their movement spread across Atlanta and the internet, Migos holed up in P's studio to finish their next mixtape, the first that would come with any real backing or fan anticipation. But before the trio could debut on a larger scale, the new record label needed a name—something for the group to rep and shout with the same fervency and stickiness they did every other phrase.

P felt that Dirty Dollar had been a bad fit for a company because it was "too street," and Coach encouraged him to change it up and "make it clean," with some additional personal poignancy. P thought hard, deciding that the label's name should begin with the letter Q—a tribute to his murdered best friend and "guardian angel." Coach texted P a stream of ideas, hitting on one in particular after he pulled a scrap of paper from the pocket of some fresh jeans—a stamp of inspection that marked expensive denim: Quality Control, it said.

Coach sent P the dictionary definition of each word, and they felt apt enough. As a phrase, it was just vague enough to work. And once it was designed in a simple interlinked gold font, somewhere between the Olympic rings and the Audi logo, Quality Control Music—or QC—managed to stick.

By May, Migos had released an updated, souped-up video for "Bando," their runaway street hit, featuring Quavo and Takeoff in better clothes and designer sunglasses, with more gold chains and fatter piles of cash. In place of Offset was an army of supporters rocking their crisp "FREE OFFSET" shirts, and poster boards held triumphantly in the background advertised the trio's upcoming release: a mixtape called *YRN*, or *Young Rich N——s*, including nineteen songs and features by Gucci Mane and Soulja Boy.

The mixtape was set to come out on June 13, a few days ahead of Takeoff's nineteenth birthday, and also the Thursday before Hot 107.9's annual Birthday Bash concert that Saturday at the Philips Arena in downtown Atlanta—a local hip-hop holiday that guaranteed the presence of rap heavyweights in town. In anticipation, Quavo and Takeoff went on a promotional tear, spreading their *YRN* posters and Offset T-shirts—along with another that said TRAP in the Gap font—across Georgia, hitting a different club and radio station almost every night, from Atlanta to Decatur to Valdosta. Coach also had them cater to the more diverse constituency at Beer and Tacos, a recurring party in the city that combined the hood kids and hipsters in one sweaty mass.

But Quavo had his heart set on appearing at Birthday Bash, despite not being on the official bill, which included 2 Chainz and B.o.B. He told Coach, however hyperbolically, that he'd quit music if they couldn't perform. Why else have a known manager in your corner? It was up to Coach K to make it happen.

Across town, not long before the show, DJ Drama, the Atlanta mixtape king who had a scheduled slot at the concert to bring out a parade of special guests, was considering who he could invite that would really make the crowd react. At his Means Street Studio in the historic district of industrial warehouses northwest of downtown, Drama threw out some names: Rich Homie Quan, an Atlanta guy with a rising rap-sung hit in "Type of Way," was a sure thing. Trinidad James, the flamboyant local jester whose "All Gold Everything" had become a crossover smash, was another. And this young guy from Philadelphia named Meek Mill seemed like a safe bet. But when somebody mentioned Migos, a debate kicked off.

"You gon' disappoint me," one guy told Drama at the mere suggestion.

"Are they from here?" another wondered.

"Yes!" one out-of-towner responded insistently.

The pro-Migos enthusiast just happened to be Drake, the reigning prince of hip-hop and one of its most reliable hitmakers, who was quickly becoming a Canadian, biracial on-ramp to the pop mainstream for emerging rappers. Drake was someone who treated regional rap music like an obsessive fan, constantly scouring the internet for new sounds. So as the barbershop-style parley picked up, he asserted himself as the resident Migos expert and defender.

"Don't get it twisted, I fuck with Migos," Drake told the skeptical room. "Yo, I'm just letting you know they have a wave. I'm just letting you know."

The pop-star rapper even named some lesser-known Migos tracks from *YRN* that he already loved, like "Adios" and "Pronto," even though the tape had just come out. DJ Drama, who had seen the Migos movement growing firsthand, ultimately agreed: if Birthday Bash was the premier showcase of current Atlanta rap, then Migos had to be there.

It would be the first time that the group ever rehearsed for a show. But it was what happened backstage at Birthday Bash that would help make Migos and Quality Control unstoppable.

Quavo was eating wings when it happened, his hands slathered in sauce. But Drake, who was appearing as a special guest with 2 Chainz, didn't seem to mind as he approached the relatively unknown rappers. Just like he had at Drama's studio, Drake rattled off his favorite Migos songs like an eager fan—"Pronto," "Bando," "Chirpin"—this time to the young guys who'd actually made them.

Migos couldn't let the moment pass without taking up the multiplatinum rapper on his fandom. "We're looking at him like, *You Drake?*" Takeoff said later.

The star-struck rookies suggested making a song together, likely knowing that the promise of collaboration could be a conversational crutch among rappers, one that's often empty—like a regular person telling an acquaintance that they should catch up sometime during a chance run-in. But Drake really was a fan—and a savvy talent scout—one who was early enough that he couldn't risk missing the Migos wave. Sure enough, he texted a few days later asking for something to work with.

Coach and P assumed that Drake would jump on one of the *YRN* tracks that were already bubbling, like "China Town" or "Dennis Rodman." They sent him three options. Instead, within a few days, Drake had added a verse on "Versace," uploading his version of the song to SoundCloud exactly a week after Birthday Bash. Within days, Justin Bieber had posted a video of himself rapping along. Almost instantly, Migos had moved beyond Atlanta and was approaching the rap stratosphere.

"Versace" was like "Bando" on Red Bull and Ciroc, reveling in high luxury instead of street grime. In barely three minutes, the name of the title brand was repeated nearly two hundred times—including thirty-six in the chorus alone, which featured no other words. The rest of the lyrics were free-associative and borderline nonsensical, with references to the Illuminati, John Gotti, Tony the Tiger, an obscure Eddie Murphy character and the Disney film *The Mighty Ducks*. To this day, many find the song infuriating, though none deny that it's sticky. And whereas "Bando" merely sounded like it was produced by Gucci Mane's go-to collaborator Zaytoven, the skittering start-and-stop beat for "Versace" actually was.

The song represented a full-circle moment for the group and the producer. Zaytoven had been the one who first showed Migos' original "Bando" music video to Gucci. (Yung LA, the Atlanta rapper who showed it to the producer, only did so because he thought Zaytoven had made the beat.) But even in 2013—years after his first mainstream hit, Usher's "Papers," cowritten with Gorilla Zoe—Zaytoven was still working in a barbershop cutting hair when he wasn't defining the trap sound by making piano-based beats for Gucci and his associates. It was the success of "Versace" that finally made Zaytoven give up his nine-to-five.

But as massive as the song got in Atlanta clubs and beyond—and even with its eventual recognition by fans and critics as one of the defining rap songs of the decade—"Versace" barely hit *Billboard*, peaking at number 99 on the Hot 100 and never cracking the top 20 on the R&B/hip-hop or rap charts. Though a net gain from an attention perspective, Drake's involvement proved frustrating to Migos and Quality Control when the upstart record company failed to get the legal clearance from Drake's major label to sell the new version of the song on iTunes and other official retailers.

Coach and P saw the commercial roadblock as a kind of retribution from the larger industry that loomed over them. At the time, they were adamant about keeping Migos independent, and Quality Control believed it was being frozen out by the system for failing to sign away their prized asset. Since Drake took up so much oxygen on the track—and also put his verse first—radio and club DJs could cut the song off before Quavo, Takeoff or Offset even started rapping, leaving Migos as a footnote on its own breakout track.

In many ways, Migos was still ahead of its time in 2013, and for years after, both in sound and in business. The music industry at the time was thrashing in place, struggling to recover from the bottoming-out of the CD market. And while rap mixtapes were booming online, the major labels had not yet found a way to really profit off internet attention beyond track downloads, which favored white pop stars with more affluent audiences. Spotify had quietly debuted in the United States in 2011, but it would be a while before the service caught on. In 2012, there was a glimmer of hope when the labels saw their first rise in global music revenues since 1999. But 2013 saw another dip as revenues fell by nearly 4 percent.

At the same time, street rap was still being overlooked as a niche concern. In the year of *YRN* and "Versace," the bestselling album was by the British boy band One Direction, followed by Eminem (who had just turned forty-one) and Justin Timberlake. The biggest songs were "Blurred Lines" by Robin Thicke, which featured TI in full pop-crossover mode, and "Thrift Shop" by the white rapper Macklemore, a track that decried rap materialism. "Versace," in contrast, was brash, electric and proudly regional, the soundtrack to an underground bubbling far enough over that anyone paying attention to the swell should've seen that it could not be contained.

But Migos, if nothing else, had velocity—and, lately, its own money. The group's first summer under Quality Control was a string of weeks-long stretches with no breaks as gigs bled into press appearances and trips out of town to show up at events and meet a national media that was eager to introduce the faces behind an urgent update of the trap boom. With all that came higher prices for paid appearances, starting with club walk-throughs—the nightclub cameos that might include standing on a booth or table while the DJ plays your songs over and over again—and eventually proper concerts at colleges and ticketed venues.

All QC had to do was keep pouring gasoline on the Migos fire. In August, the trio released another mixtape, *Streets on Lock*, with Rich the Kid. September saw a shiny $100,000 video for "Versace," filmed at a rented mansion in Miami complete with Zaytoven at a grand piano, a Donatella Versace look-alike and a cheetah. There was also, for the first time, luxury product placement, including a bottle of tequila on the piano that netted the group a few thousand dollars, and the clumsy appearance of an app that Migos would later record a whole song about. (The startup, Bedloo, never took off.) In October, there was another mixtape. In December, they featured on another. Then February. Then February again. In all, Migos would have a dozen street-level releases before ever bothering with an official album.

Along the way, the group became whole again. As "Versace" crested in the fall of 2013, Offset was released from DeKalb County Jail, having served his eight months for violating probation. "I've been through it before, but that's my last go-round," he told the *Fader* in an interview upon his release. "There's money to be made, ain't no more playing. That's the old me, I threw that away." Takeoff compared Migos' situation with Offset to a game of double Dutch: "He can just jump right in."

The guys were elated to pick Offset up as a free man, with fresh piles of cash in hand for their absent brother. Coach asked right away if he wanted to head straight to the mall. But Offset had other plans.

"I wanna go to the studio," he said.

8.

HIGHLY FAVORED

After Lashon Jones resigned herself to her son Dominique's newfound teenage independence, the calls from the police station—and then the courthouse and the county jail—only became more common.

When it was burglary, Lashon held on to what hope she had in her son's character and assumed that Dominique was just a middleman, selling stolen flat-screens to family friends who were willing to look the other way on their provenance. Then there was the weed, which was harder to explain away. And the guns for protection. And the traffic stops that led those searching for the weed and guns directly to what they were expecting to find. That part, at least, could've been avoided, Lashon thought.

"I just don't get that about men, period—young guys, Black, white, Mexican, I don't care. You know you dirty! Why wouldn't you use your blinker? Why you got the music up so loud? Every time," she said. As far as the police were concerned, Dominique might as well have had a license plate that said DEALER. "It was never about the weed," his mother sighed. "It was always traffic that led to the weed."

Lashon's concerns had become more pragmatic as she came to realize the limits of her influence. Keeping Dominique from the hood entirely, inside at home on a PlayStation instead, was all but impossible without eliminating his social life and likely ruining their relationship for good. He'd long outgrown her—and therefore the effects of any old-fashioned punishment—and his father could only do so much through the phone. Lashon's boyfriends could help out, but they weren't there to parent. She mitigated the circumstances as best she could.

Lashon wouldn't just drop Dominique off in the hood willy-nilly. But when he'd swear to her that he was only going to the West End mall for a haircut—*Just an hour, Mom, I promise*—she'd reluctantly let him, only to find out far too often that he'd been locked up in half that time. By then, Lashon, like her son, was developing a rapport with the local officers on foot patrol, who knew exactly what Dominique was up to and sometimes let him slide with a warning to stay off the corner with his little hand-to-hand drug plays. Whenever she picked him up from the area, she would roll down her window to thank the cops for their patience.

Lashon also took to renting her son cars in her name, learning quickly what was required: nothing too flashy (nor too shitty), and it had to have Georgia plates—anything out of state drew more suspicion. "I knew he was doing what he was doing, but he needed a way to get around as opposed to standing still somewhere," she reasoned. "At least if you mobile, and you ain't just posted in one place, you know, like . . . I didn't condone it, but he was still my child at the end of the day."

As his profile in the streets grew, Lashon noticed Dominique becoming paranoid. He switched his rides more often and always located a compartment in each car to stash whatever needed stashing—things that sometimes, when a jam would arise, also needed to be left behind. "I be feeling so sorry for the people that rent them cars after him," Lashon said. "Every rental car that he's ever been got in, they just don't know that they've had a pistol hidden somewhere in there."

Financially, if not morally, there was now less to worry about. Dominique had started chipping in like the man of the house would. His mother realized the money was serious when she heard him going up to the attic repeatedly. Unable to quench her curiosity with assumptions, Lashon went up there one day to see the gains for herself. There, carefully rubber-banded, were stacks of dirty bills, smoothed out and meticulously arranged in patterns. "Everything had a little black rubber band. He knew if you took anything, because he might turn one hundred twenties this way, or he might turn eight tens that way, so he knows when something's missing." When Lashon, somewhat offended, confronted Dominique about his makeshift security tactic and suggested he try a safety deposit box instead, he insisted that the booby trap wasn't intended for her, but for his colleagues outside. *Well, I hope the attic never catches on fire*, she thought.

Sometimes, Dominque would disappear for days or weeks at a time. "He's always been goal-oriented," Lashon said, recalling times when her son would vow not to return home until he'd made, say, a few hundred thousand dollars for his enterprise. "He would be gone for like two, three weeks. He would come home dirty, but gon' make his money." She kept her distance and refrained from asking too many questions, but she also became the kind of accomplice that only a mother could, failing to say no when the safety of her son or his friends was at stake. Whenever one of Dominique's buddies got kicked out of their own house or just needed a place to hide, her door was always open, her table always full. "I'm cooking for them—all in there, one big happy family," she said.

Only years on did Lashon realize the extent of her involvement. Eventually, Dominique would come clean about one specific night when she'd let in a pair of boys who seemed extra desperate. They were on the run, it turned out, having potentially killed someone. "I was like, '*What!?*'" Lashon recalled. "And he said, 'You wouldn't have let them come?'

"I said, 'Yeah! But I would've liked to know the whole situation.'" That's the kind of mom she was.

By the time he was seventeen, Dominique's social reach had expanded along with his growing net worth. At his request, Lashon started dropping him off at a recording studio a bit further south than his usual stomping grounds. Inside, a rap trio had started to build a name locally with a series of mixtapes and some street-level hits that were becoming difficult to ignore. "I knew that song—'Versace, Versace'—but I couldn't stand it," Lashon said. When Dominique told her he was going on a trip to Miami with "that group the Migos," she could only laugh at the idea he knew them well enough to score an invite.

"Yes I do, Ma, yes I do!" Dominique insisted. Unbeknownst to her,

Offset had basically given his two-bedroom condo over to Dominique while the rappers were out on the road.

"There's some adults going on this trip?" Lashon asked.

He assured her that there was—a guy named P that he knew from around.

As Dominique and his friends' fortunes turned, flashiness followed, and Lashon urged the crew to keep a low profile given the source of most of their income. She knew Dominique and the Oakland City guys had started calling themselves 4 Pockets Full, or 4PF, nodding to their Zone 4 neighborhood and also their cash on hand. But Lashon kindly requested they leave certain things off Instagram, where she lurked in order to keep an eye on them. The boys listened about as often as could be expected.

But none of Dominique's new connections, or the steps he and his mother took to limit their exposure, could stop those dreaded jailhouse calls from coming while Lashon was at work. "No sooner do I clock in and start cleaning up than I see my phone ring," she said.

"'Mmhmm, I already know—they got you again.'"

"'Yes, ma'am.'"

When he got too big to sell on the sidewalk, Dominique had moved into a corner store as a kind of subletter, paying the Arab guys who owned the place to hide his weed behind the ten-cent candy. But despite being a successful enough entrepreneur, Dominique wasn't exactly a criminal mastermind. During one foot chase, he led the police back to his stash spot, where in addition to candy, they found "the weed, the scales, everything," his mother said.

"What'd I tell you?" she reminded him. "Maybe it ain't meant for you to be in the streets if you go to jail every time and nobody else do!"

Luckily, Dominique had a lifeline. Lashon's low-wage job cleaning at the county courthouse put her in close proximity to those who would be deciding her son's fate, over and over again. Even the judges knew her smiling face. She could pull some strings.

Dominique's first charge, for burglary, was expunged after his mother and her alliance of courthouse coworkers talked him into a sentence of group therapy and community service. The next time, for drugs, Dominique received first-offender status and was ordered to get his GED, which he passed easily, filling his beleaguered mother with momentary delight. "The lady with the test said, 'I hope he plan on doing something productive in his future,'" Lashon said. But during Dominique's six months of probation, he was caught up again while—what else—weaving through traffic in the Fulton County suburb of East Point.

"Everybody know you follow all the rules in East Point, Georgia!" Lashon said. "People can come from Missouri and they've heard about East Point."

Dominique, as usual, was moving dirty. Police found a handgun and some twelve pounds of weed—not exactly an amount for personal use. By this point, "he wasn't no penny-ante," his mother said. "He wasn't selling ounces—they was moving *pounds*." Lashon landed somewhere between pride and denial in the matter, convincing herself that it was only marijuana that her son and his friends were selling—never the harder stuff. "They too scared," she said. "Weed is it."

This time, even with Lashon's word to the judges now all but worthless, she still managed to score her son another break. The judge agreed to roll all of Dominique's various looming offenses together for a total sentence of three years, leaving him likely to serve about eighteen months, or two years max, including a nine-month drug program. The judge knew Dominique wasn't an addict, but she wanted him to see the effect that drugs had on other people, lest he go through life thinking selling weed was no big deal. Dominique was sent somewhere resembling a psychiatric hospital more than a prison—with dorms instead of cells and no shackles—and he was expected to attend group classes that functioned like rehab. Lashon couldn't believe his good luck. "This boy is so highly favored," she said.

But prison would come sooner than it was supposed to. According to his mother, Dominique was kicked out of the drug program after he "ran into a racist," who called him "a n——" over a piece of paper. Dominique let the slur slide at first. But back in the dorms, tensions already high, the guy took to swinging around a lock in a sock as Dominique passed by. That one didn't go well for the white guy.

The next time Lashon showed up for visitation, she got to talking to the older couple waiting behind her in line. They exchanged pleasantries and parental war stories about their difficult offspring. *Oh, our son got into a fight*, the couple told Lashon. "My son, too!" she said.

Only once they were inside the visitation area did Lashon put the pieces together. "They sitting with their son, and we start making eye contact—*oh my god*," she said. "'You didn't have to beat him like that!'" she muttered to Dominique. "Both eyes black, nose broke—he fucked him up, I'm sorry."

"It was me or him," Dominique assured her, noting that—to the other guy's credit—it had been somebody else entirely who told. "Of course it's always a snitch somewhere," Lashon said.

At that point, there was nothing more she could do. Dominique Jones, twenty years old and guilty of a drug charge, was being transferred to a maximum-security prison. Resigned to the fact that he'd run out of slaps on the wrist, Dominique wrote a letter to his mother and left it with his lawyer, along with instructions that she not read it until she got home. All Dominique could do at that point was apologize.

"I just started *boo-hoo*ing," Lashon said, letting her son know in response—truthfully—that she'd never been disappointed in him. "I would have never chose that path for you," she said, "but as much as I would love for you to do something else with your life, it's not my life—it's yours. You have to answer for everything. It's what you chose.

"That being said, it caused a lot of heartbreak," she told him. "I will miss you. And as soon as they say I can come see you, I'll be there."

Smith State Prison was about two hundred miles southeast of Atlanta, in a tiny town called Glennville, known for having plenty of three things—pecans, crickets and prisoners. Every weekend until Dominique got his hands on a contraband cell phone, Lashon would drive the three and a half hours to Glennville, leaving at 5 a.m. to maximize her visitation hours. Her baby, she knew, just needed someone to talk to, plus some change for the vending machines. Lashon would bring about fifty dollars' worth of quarters, and the pair would sit there eating prison-grade hot wings and hamburgers for hours, until she retired to a motel, passed out watching TV and woke up on Sunday morning to do it all again. It was there, in a dingy visiting room with fluorescent bulbs, that mother and son bonded as adults on the level.

"That's when he started opening up a lot," Lashon said, "talking about stuff that happened in the streets that I didn't know about. He was just spilling everything. I was like, *Hell nah! Nuh-uh—you didn't!* I got a clearer picture of what he had going on."

While incarcerated, her son's hustling also continued, thanks in part to Lashon, with Dominique becoming a go-to guy for scoring contraband inside. Circumstances be damned, no one could say that he wasn't a go-getter. And though Lashon had always helped where she could, it was while Dominique was locked up at Smith that his newly plugged-in mother became a more crucial figure in his business enterprise. Fellow inmates, too, were forced to involve their friends and family to make the shadow economy turn. First, someone on the outside—"sister, girlfriend, mama"—would make a purchase via Western Union money order. Then Lashon would make the pick-up, relaying the confirmed payment back to her son inside. Business boomed so much that the trips became a job of their own.

"I would go to Western Union about eight times a day," Lashon said. "I thought they were going to red-flag me at one point." Instead, the Western Union employees just gave her a box of slips that she could have already filled out by the time she arrived. "That boy ran me good for eighteen months," Lashon said.

It wasn't just the money orders. Dominique was also spreading cash around, having put an uncle in charge of organizing and protecting his liquid finances while he was gone, but relying on Lashon to execute his more philanthropic giving—$300 for a partner's bond here, $60 on another's commissary books there. "Heart of gold, heart of gold, heart of gold," his mother said.

Still, Lashon chose to sacrifice, declining to let Dominique pay her bills while he was gone. Her son, after all, was expecting his first child.

"You need your money," she told him. "I'll move in with your sister." Lashon's other daughter, who was still living at home, went to live with her grandmother.

Of course, Lashon knew how to access the family reserves for emergencies or must-haves. Ahead of the arrival of her first grandchild, she stocked up on cases of Pampers, formula and clothes. "That's what he needed his money for, and that was my concern," she said.

It was around this time, in the fall of 2015, with Dominique set to become a father from within a maximum-security prison, that Lashon started to notice a change in him. The goal-oriented, natural-born winner who had nonetheless found himself behind bars was going to miss the kinds of life milestones that cash couldn't cure.

"So now that you've had this experience, are you going to do the same thing, or you're going to move different?" Lashon asked him during a visit. Maybe it was time to try another career path, she offered. "Too many have given their life for the streets, and you won't be one of them."

"I'm going to move different," Dominique promised. He just didn't know how exactly. "I might want to be the president of the United States," he said.

"You have the capability," Lashon replied, both believing it and understanding full well that nobody talked a bigger game about changing their life than somebody locked up twenty-four hours a day. Still, outside of his losing battles with the police, she'd never seen her son fail. She knew Dominique, her Lil Baby, had something else in him—something positive, just like the preachers and teachers had told her, raving about his abilities for so many years. But there was one place she drew the line when it came to having full faith in her kid.

"He just called one day and he said, 'Mom, when I come out, I'mma start rapping,'" she recalled. "I put the phone on mute, and I was just cracking up laughing. I was like, *Yeaaaah, okay*. I'd heard all the stories—when they get to prison they say they going to do all this and that."

When Lashon finally regained her composure, she picked up the phone and tried to muster some enthusiasm. "That sounds good," she said.

9.

THE #BILLIONDOLLARLAWYER

NOT ALL RAPPERS RAP ABOUT CRIME. AND NOT ALL RAPPERS WHO do rap about crime are criminals, obviously. These are writers, directors and performers. Some may be Iceberg Slim or Donald Goines—grounded and gritty, with firsthand experience. Others are Quentin Tarantino, John Singleton, Melvin or Mario Van Peebles—cinematic, gory, over-the-top. Chris Rock and Mario Puzo have their hip-hop imitators, too. But few modern MCs anywhere, and especially in Atlanta, will cop to just flat-out making things up. *That's cap*, as they say.

Exaggeration is expected and accepted. Run-ins or wins witnessed, or knowledge passed down, may come out in the first person. Aspirations are expressed as possessions. But among a crowded field—where threats and brags quickly become standardized—believability, conviction and reputation are assets to be exploited, played up, underlined. Authenticity might be the biggest flex of all. Sometimes it is simply unavoidable. But in America, the truth can be dangerous.

Trap music, in particular, often represents a last resort—painful, exposed, desolate music from those whom society has tossed aside or never held on to in the first place. Almost always Black men. So it is not surprising that much of the most popular rap music ever made—and the core of hip-hop in Atlanta—is illicit, subversive and even antisocial in subject matter, even when it is celebratory and communal in sound. Lyrically, there is shooting, selling, fucking and fighting for dominance, cash and revenge—music about the guns that flood the streets, not just in Atlanta but across the nation. Glocks and AKs, Dracos and Berettas, MACs and Rugers, KelTecs, SIGs and Uzis. Nearly half of all households in Georgia, where the laws are among the loosest in the country, have a registered firearm, and that allows the black market to flourish, too, with thousands of stolen guns circulating in Atlanta every year. Because poverty and racism, plus their attendant dangers, beat a person down. Law enforcement and other impossibly big systems conspire to keep them in place, and conspicuously so in the South, where the still-lingering effects of slavery, Jim Crow, segregation and redlining are as unavoidable as 808s. Then the record labels swoop in, seeking street credibility, and sell that back to where it came from—and also to the cultural pilgrims, the teenagers seeking rebellion and bounce, the Black-curious consumers.

But whereas corporate labels are keen on scooping up and selling a gangster image, they often throw up their hands when they get what they paid for in real life. As Black men in America, rappers are vilified before *and* after they make it. While the fans flock, cops keep a closer eye on you; songs can sound like confessions. In this spin cycle of capitalism, rap, race and the justice system, total stability is rare, and money is typically the motive on all sides, though the most vulnerable at the beginning continue to bear the brunt of the risks. When you're celebrated as a modern-day rock star with an outlaw spirit—that is to say, a rap star—prison and death don't stop looming just because you're on the radio. If anything, your outsiderness—the target on your back and front—is only amplified.

But a good lawyer can save you some headaches.

Before Drew Findling became known as the criminal defense attorney for Gucci Mane, P, Offset and much of Quality Control—and therefore, before he became known as a god in the streets of Atlanta—he was a Jewish latchkey kid from Long Island, raised by a single mother who instilled in him a boundless intellectual curiosity and the confidence of an only son. In New York, Findling did not grow up particularly religious. But he was taught to be civically engaged, attending peace rallies and political events at his mother's side throughout the early 1970s. At her urging, he studied the writings of Abbie Hoffman and Jerry Rubin, their radical idealism mixing well with his family's own financial struggle. His racial and class consciousness developed early.

Thin and compact, with feathered hair past his ears and the beginner's mustache of a *Dazed and Confused* character, Findling played baseball and ran track in high school. It was sports, not politics, that led him to a strange land he'd never thought all that much about before arriving—the American South. In 1977, still splitting the difference between hippie and jock, Findling moved to the Northeast Atlanta suburb of Brookhaven on a cross-country running scholarship at Oglethorpe University, a small liberal arts school. He found the nearby metropolis to be diverse, open-minded and affordable. He never left.

Findling had never met a lawyer in the flesh before moving to Atlanta and going prelaw at Oglethorpe. He wasn't even sure what one really did until he took the classes. But by 1984, he had graduated with his JD from Emory University School of Law in Atlanta, one of the first private institutions in the South to be racially integrated.

Even then, Findling didn't love the law, per se, although as a smooth talker and assertive arguer, he did get a special kick out of his trial techniques program. Then, one Sunday morning while reading the newspaper, he came across a story about the new local public defender, Vernon Pitts. At 9 a.m. on the dot, Findling gave Pitts a cold call looking for a job. Some twelve weeks later, Findling was trying murder cases in Fulton County.

It wasn't long before the young lawyer was making headlines. In one of his first major cases, Findling backed up a more senior public defender in the trial of a woman who had choked, stabbed and decapitated her seven-year-old son because, she said, God had told her the boy was Satan. In the middle of jury selection, the older attorney pushed Findling to take the lead. The jury went on to find the woman not guilty by reason of insanity. Not long after, Findling earned another news-making acquittal when he argued that a woman who had killed her boyfriend did so as a result of battered woman syndrome, even though she had been the victim of only threats and verbal abuse, not physical violence, marking one of the first times such a defense had worked with a jury. With these big wins under his belt, he founded his own practice, the Findling Law Firm, in 1987. He wasn't yet thirty.

Throughout the 1990s and into the new millennium, as Atlanta evolved into a glitzy destination for athletes and entertainers, Findling remained on the periphery of the culture, picking up a few high-profile cases, like representing the NBA bad boy Dennis Rodman when his name came up in the racketeering trial of a strip club owner and his associates. (Rodman was never charged.) But Findling made his name steadily on less flashy cases while starting a family. By the early 2000s, he was a father as much as a star lawyer, coaching his son's travel baseball team and then his daughter's softball squad, sometimes showing up to meetings with judges while still in uniform. Once, he wrote the closing argument for a death-penalty trial in between games on napkins at a Shoney's buffet.

Findling's firm, a three-lawyer operation, had set up shop in the upscale neighborhood of Buckhead, home to Georgia's most moneyed good ol' boys, as well as the designer shops in and around the Lenox Square mall. But while Findling and those in his cohort were building up their quiet Buckhead lives, the district was also developing a parallel reputation as the center of hip-hop nightlife in Atlanta, home to a cluster of bars and clubs that didn't close until the loose local curfew of 4 a.m.

At its peak, about one hundred liquor licenses existed within about three Buckhead blocks, and the soundtrack was increasingly 808 driven. For young people from every neighborhood, the city's rap music was hard to ignore. But for family-oriented professional types in the tony suburbs, that late-night scene might as well have been a galaxy away, at least for a while. "Truth be told," Findling said later, "I'd never even listened to a rap song." But that was all about to change.

In 2000, the Buckhead culture clash intensified following Super Bowl XXXIV in Atlanta, when the Baltimore Ravens star Ray Lewis was charged, along with two friends, in the stabbing deaths of two men not far from a club called the Cobalt Lounge. Seven months later, Cobalt was closed and the cries to tame Buckhead—a not-so-discreet attempt at re-whitening the area—grew louder.

In 2003, Findling was called to the front lines of that ongoing fight, introducing him to an altogether different moneyed cohort than the one he was used to—one that operated mostly in cash and courted its share of danger. His new high-profile client, a thirty-five-year-old Black man from Detroit, was listed in court documents as Demetrius Flenory. The name meant nothing to his latest defense attorney. But in the streets of Atlanta, Flenory was Big Meech, the head of the cocaine syndicate–slash–record label Black Mafia Family, or BMF. Findling didn't know those terms either. But his work with the man atop the Atlanta drug pyramid would soon send the lawyer's career and his personal notoriety in certain circles into a new realm.

When he hired Findling, Flenory was the prime murder suspect in a nightclub parking-lot shooting that left two men dead. Up until that Monday in November, Meech had been untouchable in the city, the MVP of every night out. But a scrap outside of a club called Chaos resulted in nearly forty rounds fired from multiple weapons, and at least four men hit. A former bodyguard for Puff Daddy who'd settled in Atlanta to try to make it as a rap promoter was killed, along with a friend. One BMF associate caught a bullet in the foot. Meech, who said he ran as soon as the first blasts rang out, got hit in the butt.

In keeping with BMF's reputation for commanding street-level respect and fear, witnesses from the parking lot weren't talking. But the cops received an anonymous call from a woman who said she'd seen a man pull a pistol from his waistband and fire at least seven times. "They have a lot of money," the witness told an investigator. "They have a lot of drugs. You don't know what you're getting yourself into." She identified the shooter as "Meechie."

Flenory denied his involvement and said he saw nothing. Asked by police during his interrogation where he lived, Meech told them, "All over." He also hired Drew Findling.

As Meech's lawyer, Findling called the whole thing "just comical." His client was nothing more than another victim. "Law enforcement and politicians think they appease the public by making a prompt arrest instead of learning from their past mistakes," Findling told the media, alluding to the Ray Lewis case, in which no one was ever convicted.

At every turn, Findling punished the prosecution for their flimsy case. A search of Meech's Atlanta residence, known as the White House, would turn up a notebook filled with drug-dealing code words, an electronic money counter, sacks of rubber bands and three guns—all helpful for investigators in their eventual federal indictment against BMF. But for the time being, when it came to the double murder outside of Club Chaos, the authorities had nothing.

At a hearing, Findling aggressively cross-examined the detectives on the case in front of a packed courtroom, harping on their sole anonymous witness, who was never identified or called to testify. Meech was released on a $50,000 bond—low for an alleged double homicide—and made to wear an ankle monitor. But Findling never even needed to win at trial, where he was best. No indictment against Flenory was ever filed.

"I'll never forget at the press conference afterwards," Findling said at his office in Buckhead years later, surrounded by press clippings featuring his boldface clients. "The reporters were laughing at the case that was brought against him, it was so obvious that he was innocent. They just literally threw charges at him because he was Big Meech." As the lawyer would come to learn, Flenory might as well have been a rapper.

For Findling, this was just another courtroom victory in a string of them, and he didn't assign any particular significance to the outcome. For a while, the two men remained close. Findling was even preparing to help defend the kingpin against that federal indictment in 2005 until Meech and his brother Terry opted to plead guilty, taking thirty years each in prison. More than one hundred people with ties to the Black Mafia Family were charged in all. But it wasn't until later that Findling realized just how effectively news of his work with BMF had traveled. In the years that followed, the defense attorney started to notice a new kind of client flocking more and more to his office, and many of them remembered his big win on behalf of Big Meech.

It's possible, considering the makeup of Atlanta in those years and

Findling's reputation as a formidable trial lawyer, that he would have crossed paths anyway with many of the prominent Black celebrities in need of legal assistance. The city had them in droves. But as Findling continued to work diligently for clients with connections to the world of rap and sports—from the R&B singer Faith Evans to Shaquille O'Neal—he realized he'd found a niche. Always good for a quote on cable news or in the paper, the lawyer benefited from his prominence in local media. But it was the strong word-of-mouth chatter among Atlanta's Black elite, where the barrier between the streets and the upper echelon remained porous, that would eventually transform Findling into rap's #BillionDollarLawyer.

One of the Atlanta hustlers who heard Findling's name through the grapevine and would come to rely on his services was Pierre Thomas, then firmly in the thick of his "before music" phase and thus in need of reliable counsel at a regular clip. On paper, they couldn't have seemed more different. It would be years before P had any name recognition of his own. But Findling's work on behalf of the hustler-turned-executive would lead to a bond between the two men, as well as plenty of referral business, after P founded a rap label dedicated to turning Atlanta's wayward youth into street-rap superstars.

But first, as usual in Atlanta, there was Gucci Mane.

After Meech, it was Findling's work with the man born Radric Davis, the troubled rap star and P's good friend, that cemented the defense attorney's name as a fixture in Atlanta hip-hop circles. Findling came on board with Gucci during his turbulent nadir in 2013, playing a crucial role in the legal team that negotiated the rapper's federal plea deal and probably saved his life.

But it was in between the cracks where Findling really proved invaluable. Once, at the height of Gucci's paranoia, he stormed into the lawyer's office and caused a big enough scene to require the police. As the cops got Gucci out of there, they found a loaded Taurus 45 in the office—a huge no-no for a felon already facing an assault charge.

But Findling's levelheaded loyalty would save his client another one. "I told them it wasn't mine," Gucci wrote in his autobiography. "My lawyer didn't say anything different. I think they call that attorney-client privilege."

In helping an Atlanta folk hero, Findling became one in his own right. He also learned, a little bit at a time, the intricacies of the music business and how best to manage its mercurial personalities. Findling's designer sunglasses and taste for flashy Italian suits helped him fit in, and he could've passed easily for a label exec from New York or LA, his slicked-back hair falling below his ears into his fifties.

"Clearly, I presented to Gucci a completely different representation than he'd had before," Findling said. "Very seriously speaking, there's a business element."

Findling's substantial price tag was actually a point of respect among his rapper clients, who knew he wasn't in it for shine alone. His high hourly rate communicated a certain bar for quality, like Chanel or Louis Vuitton. "I save pro bono for poor people, for causes that are important," Findling said. "Trying to promote myself at the expense of somebody famous is not a good business idea. When people do that in my business they underestimate the intelligence of the client. They're not interested in a free lawyer, they're interested in a great lawyer." Coach K, who estimated that a murder case might run a Findling client half a million dollars—easy—called him "a miracle worker," "a witch doctor," "a magician" and "the illest."

No sooner had Gucci gone away for a while than Findling became enmeshed in another rap saga, one that would take him even deeper into the world of Atlanta music. His work with Kiari Cephus—by then known to some as Offset, the most enigmatic of the three Migos—would also change Findling's life and career in ways both personal and political. And it started with the United States parole system, a practice that Findling, dripping with righteous disdain, called "modern-day shackles."

When Offset was released from prison in October 2013, Migos' career was moving at 150 miles per hour, but Offset was stuck going the speed limit—and it was holding everyone back. For one, the terms of the rapper's probation restricted travel, with any trips requiring preapproval from a parole officer, something that could get tricky in the last-minute world of club appearances, where bookings popped up with little notice.

There was also the question of company kept. For safety reasons, Migos had moved—at P and Coach K's urging—to a country club McMansion that looked straight out of a catalog in the suburb of Stockbridge, southeast of the city, the opposite direction from Gwinnett. The house sat alongside a golf course behind a manned gate. But while Offset wanted to make up for lost time with his band of brothers, the group filled the place with more weed and heavy artillery than furniture.

In an online Vice documentary that would become infamous, Takeoff, Quavo and friends proudly showed off their equipment, including a brand-new AR-15, for the world—and law enforcement—to see, a scene made all the more jarring by the fact that it played out in front of decorative HOME and LOVE signs seemingly straight from Target. Offset was wisely left out of the garish display at its most potentially incriminating moments. But the precarity of the situation meant that instead of falling back in fully with Migos, their third member was forced to live at a separate apartment to avoid violating his probation—a distance heightened by the fact that the group had set up a studio downstairs in its barebones basement to mimic the feel of Mama's Bando as they worked on their first official album.

Throughout 2014, the group's career-making mixtape tear landed them two more hit singles. "Fight Night" starred Takeoff on his first prominent hook, while "Handsome and Wealthy," a more melodic song steered by Quavo, showed versatility. Both were strip club fixtures, as were various cuts from the *No Label II* and *Rich N—— Timeline* mixtapes that flourished on websites like DatPiff and LiveMixtapes. But Migos was also now finding success on national radio, with both "Fight Night" and "Handsome and Wealthy" charting higher on *Billboard* than "Versace," a sign that the wider industry was catching up with their sound and methods of music distribution.

Migos' increased visibility and obvious commercial promise had once again brought the major labels sniffing around Atlanta, but P, still mostly playing the background, used his deep pockets to hold out on a standard deal. As Migos' stock was rising, Quality Control turned down offers from Def Jam, Atlantic and RCA for the rights to put out the trio's proper debut. "I wanted five million dollars, but didn't none of them wanna come with five million dollars," P said. "They'd come with one, two, two point five. But we already came in the game with that." In the meantime, Migos had started clearing around $40,000 per show, the source of most of their income. All they needed was a major release to really bum-rush the mainstream.

Instead of signing with a major, Quality Control and Migos entered a partnership with a startup label, 300 Entertainment, that would take 30 percent of future royalties in exchange for marketing and distribution services, while leaving full ownership of the master recordings to QC and its group. 300 was cofounded in New York by the former Warner Music Group CEO Lyor Cohen and two of his protégés, Kevin Liles and Todd Moscowitz, who had worked closely with Coach in the Gucci Mane days. The veteran record executives were now pursuing a Moneyball model with a focus on regional rap, and they had a $5 million investment from Google to make it happen. They also claimed to have special access to Twitter data that the label said would help them break artists strategically online. In signing Migos, Cohen said he wanted "to import the essence of Atlanta to the world." The trio even got their first passports in anticipation of overseas travel.

P and Coach had also turned to Findling for help smoothing out Offset's predicament. Through a series of motions in court, the lawyer worked his magic within the system and got the rapper's travel notice changed from weekly to monthly, eventually getting him off probation completely for the first time since Offset was a teenager. "That corresponded with things' really taking off," Findling said with pride.

Quality Control was also in the process of professionalizing. After the studio on Metropolitan got too hot—with neighbors complaining about a shooting and various other disturbances nearby—Coach and P spent a year and more than $1 million building a new four-room studio, complete with office space and a shower, in a better part of town. Yet even as things seemed to be falling into place, there were missteps and growing pains—the kinds that came with being a group of young Black men in America, suddenly flush with cash and the risks associated with it.

In March 2014—the same month Migos announced that their first album would be released later that year—a Mercedes Sprinter van carrying the group was driving south on I-95 in Florida when a vehicle pulled alongside them and opened fire, starting a shootout that resulted in at least forty rounds fired back. News reports said a Migos bodyguard was shot in the leg, but the group denied that anyone had been hit. Multiple other altercations at concert venues would follow, with grainy clips surfacing online that showed Migos fighting fans who reached for their jewelry or proved otherwise disrespectful. On one hand, the mayhem—and the fact that Migos escaped all of it unscathed—backed up the group's claims of invincibility and gave them a rebellious, renegade sheen. But the cycle was also self-perpetuating, attracting the wrong kind of attention from all sides, with those news-making events—combined with the assumptions that already followed rappers as they moved through the world—leading to increased law-enforcement scrutiny wherever they went.

In early 2015, when the student body at Georgia Southern University voted overwhelmingly to have Migos headline its annual spring concert, the school administration even "advised and encouraged" the program board to reconsider its guests. GSU was located in the Southeast Georgia town of Statesboro, in Bulloch County, an area once known for its cotton plantations and later its lynchings. But the kids wanted Migos for their Spring Bling festivities in April, and Migos wanted their money. The album they had teased the year prior was now scheduled for release that summer, and performing for a bunch of college kids would be a good warm-up. They agreed to a forty-five-minute set for $33,000.

P had a bad feeling upon arrival. The group was scheduled to start its show around 9 p.m., with a hard curfew of 10:30, but Migos turned up closer to the mandated end time. Then they decided to get high backstage despite P's easily ignored protestations. By the time Migos appeared in the crowded school gym for a performance of about six songs across half an hour, the crowd was disappointed and the rappers' fates were sealed. The trio and its hype men looked up from the stage to see local police blanketing the stands. "Man, twelve up there looking crazy," Skippa Da Flippa warned Migos' manager Jerel midperformance. But it was already too late.

As Migos and its associates left the college kids wanting more, they returned to the arena locker room to find that cops had already searched their vans, using the smell of marijuana as pretense. Police discovered less than an ounce of weed, some lean and guns. Fifteen people present were arrested and thrown into a paddy wagon with little explanation, their jewelry and hard drives full of music confiscated along with the weapons and drugs. With Migos' first album due out in a matter of months, they were all sitting in a rural Georgia jail.

"Our whole label was locked up," P said, recalling his lowest moment as a young executive. "I'll never forget it. Our whole label!" Quavo, Takeoff, Offset, Rich the Kid, Skippa Da Flippa, Jerel, plus a cameraman, security and anyone else unlucky enough to still be hanging around that night. The Migos members were all charged with the same contraband, crimes made worse because the stuff was discovered in a school safety zone, adding a whole other charge. But while Quavo and Takeoff were granted $10,000 bond almost immediately—and could count on minor sentences, given how thin the charges were spread—Offset was already a convicted felon. He was in serious trouble.

In their mugshots against a white cinder-block wall, the guys appear dour and run ragged. Quavo, whose dreads fall unevenly on his shirt, wears a stunned look. Takeoff, his hair pulled back, seems ready to spit at the camera, while Offset, his baby dreads exploding in clumps, glares even more icily, nostrils flared. In court, the guys were made to appear in faded black-and-white-striped jumpsuits, like old-timey villains.

Drew Findling leapt into action. Over the next eight months of meetings and hearings, he would get much closer with the man he would continue to call by his legal name, Kiari Cephus. On top of everything else, Offset was being accused of violating the Street Gang Terrorism and Prevention Act by being the man prosecutors dubbed the "CEO" of something called Black Migos Gang. The rapper was denied bond three times, even with his mother and Todd Moscowitz from 300 testifying about his budding career and newfound maturity. Two weeks into his stay at the Bulloch County jail, Offset picked up another set of charges for battery and inciting a riot in a penal institution after he allegedly kicked a white inmate in the head on a Saturday afternoon. Once again, while his friends were trying to finish and promote their music, Offset was behind bars and away from the action at an inopportune moment.

Findling, who passed a Confederate monument on his way into the Bulloch County courtroom, saw racism, plain and simple. This was a small Southern town, marinated in centuries of bigotry, that was inclined to assume criminality and be offended by the brazenness with which Migos flaunted its hard-won successes, looking to put these young men back in their place. Findling argued that not only had the prosecutors failed to link any of the guns or drugs from the college show to Offset—or anyone—but the jail "riot," according to security footage, had lasted about twenty seconds, involved just two people, and was set off when the white inmate, who was prone to racial slurs, shouted something toward Offset. One witness—the victim's cellmate—testified that the guy had been told he could "make some money off of this rapper."

For Offset, the days in jail started at 5 a.m. with two boiled eggs, a little sausage and a milk carton. He read, watched TV and played poker or charades with his fellow inmates. But mostly he thought all over again about the money and opportunities he was missing—not to mention his children. Jordan, Offset's first, was now four, and he'd had a second son named Kody. Stressed, anxious and angry, he relied on phone calls with Quavo; Takeoff; his mother, Latabia; and his lawyer to keep him positive and engaged. Though Findling knew he wouldn't be able to spring Offset in time for Migos' album release in June—or the headlining tour planned around it, which the group was forced to postpone—the voluble lawyer would often find himself driving the four hours to Statesboro just to comfort his client with some words of encouragement.

That December, the whole group, exhausted and deflated, took plea deals, paying fines worth about a single designer shoe, with Quavo and Takeoff agreeing to misdemeanor marijuana charges. Offset, in turn, pleaded guilty to the riot charge using an Alford plea, meaning he did not exactly admit that he did it, and all the other charges—the ones that put him in the position to get into the jail fight in the first place—were dropped as a result. Less than a year after getting rid of the shackles of probation, Offset was back under the thumb of the court, this time for a maximum of five years. Barring any additional slipups, he could be off again in two. He was also banned from Bulloch and three surrounding counties, as if he ever wanted to go back.

With Offset a free man again thanks to time already served, Migos were back to being whole that winter. But it was too late for *Yung Rich Nation*, their only shot at a mainstream debut, which came and went that summer as something of an afterthought amid the real-life stressors, following an additional six-week delay. Despite a persistent, generational Rorschach test of a Twitter meme that declared Migos better than the Beatles, the group's first official album sold just 14,596 copies in its debut week—proof, depending on whom you asked, that Migos had foiled their own ascent or that their audience was, in 2015, not the music-buying demographic. It was probably both.

Yung Rich Nation received favorable enough reviews, with the veteran rock writer Robert Christgau dubbing the group "generically opportunistic and endearingly jolly." The singles "One Time" and "Pipe It Up" were pure, unfiltered Migos, but they failed to chart or generate the energy of "Versace" or "Fight Night." The album also contained some awkward attempts at diversification, including a track with Chris Brown that felt like ignorable radio bait, and a few songs that tried to pay homage to West Coast gangster rap, like an earlier generation of Atlanta artists, but came off as empty and pointless. Since "Bando" and "Versace," Migos had faced skepticism from hip-hop purists about their lack of lyrical substance or complexity, and questions lingered about the trio's authenticity, artistry and how long their relentless chanted sloganeering could hold up. The group seemed to take these criticisms to heart, turning defensive in its storytelling—"Remember the time we broke in the neighbor's house? / That was our first paper route"—where they were once aggressively celebratory.

The album topped out at number 17 on the *Billboard* albums chart, way under big releases by Drake, Meek Mill and Future, whose Atlanta wave had seemingly swallowed up Migos' moment. *DS2*, Future's album featuring some repackaged mixtape cuts, dominated 2015 thanks to his psychedelic experimentation and focused sexy-villain persona. The attention of rap fans was ever fleeting, and Migos still sounded something like 2013.

Atlanta rappers with one or even three big hits were by then as common in the city as Waffle House. But the failure to convert momentary success into a reliable establishment career could send you right back to the local circuit of mixtapes and Southern clubs, where your fee might drop every time a new hit wasn't by you. And there were always fresh acts bubbling, younger rappers willing to take a bit of your formula and add just enough innovation to move into the ascendant spot.

With Migos grasping for connection, the expressionist Atlanta warblers Young Thug and Rich Homie Quan were huffing Future's melodic chemtrails, mutating the local sound once again. Whereas Migos were angular and punchy, rapping in all caps, Thug's writing was backward and in cursive, taking more from Lil Wayne at his most experimental than Gucci Mane. Atlanta rap had always depended on the borrowing, stealing and warping of ideas from within a small circle—many of them working with the same producers—but the center of gravity was liable to shift at any moment, leaving things that once felt fresh quickly sounding stale, especially if it was too easily imitable.

Still, it was inarguable that Migos had tallied a lot of wins over the last eighteen months, changing their own circumstances and those of the people around them—not the least of which, P's—for the better. But when Offset was released from behind bars this go-around, the moment lacked the feeling of infinite potential that came with his first reemergence. He remained adamant that he would not return to prison—for real this time. "I don't belong in there," Offset said. Yet it was impossible not to see the group as having fumbled a make-or-break moment, dropping the ball at the one-yard line of pop stardom. The legal struggles hadn't helped.

For Findling, the experience in Bulloch County was eye-opening—and ultimately life-altering. "They were hunting for Migos," he said. "To all of their all-white staff, all-white prosecutors, all-white law enforcement, they were nothing but gangsters. That hardened my resolve in many ways. If they could do this to Migos—international mega-superstars—they could do this to any poor African American in any small town in America, let alone the South."

Luckily, the lawyer had managed to pull another legal rabbit out of his hat, giving Quality Control a chance to regroup. They had been here before, backs against the wall, and Migos were more comfortable being underdogs anyway. So with Offset once again free, the only thing left to do was get back in the studio.

10.

PERFECT TIMING

On the first day of July in 2016, Dominique Jones left prison for good. And while he had entered as a son, he left as a father. There couldn't have been any better motivation.

His first child, Jason, had been born the previous September, just shy of Dominique's twenty-first birthday—the same age his mother, Lashon, was when she had his oldest sister. For Dominique's final stretch in prison, he relied on Lashon to keep an eye on things, and she reported proudly on Jason's development in calls and visits. But hearing secondhand just wasn't the same, particularly for someone who had grown up without a father himself. It was ten months before Dominique could hold his son.

On the summer day he got out, Dominique was picked up by a new girlfriend—not Jason's mother, whom he had already broken up with before he went away—and she brought him straight to Lashon's house to meet the child. "That little boy cried and cried and cried," Lashon said. But the emotional homecoming would be relatively brief. Only a few hours later, Dominique surprised his mother by asking for a ride to the studio.

"Studio with who?" Lashon asked.

"I'm finna make a song with Young Thug," Dominique replied.

"For real?"

She could only shake her head, as she had done so many times before, and get in the car.

Lil Baby never really looked up to rappers. For as long as he could remember, it was the dope boys. Even when he was little Dominique, sneaking out of his mom's house on Inman Street to shoot dice and find trouble, the heroes he could reach out and touch weren't the struggling nine-to-fivers like Lashon, whom he loved and respected nonetheless, and certainly not other authority figures, like the teachers and cops who slagged off him and his friends. Even the rappers on BET and MTV, who sometimes rolled through the neighborhood, seemed a world away. "They ain't really inspiration, because I don't know them," Baby said.

He listened to rap, of course—Gucci, Jeezy, Wayne, but also under-the-radar Southern mixtape storytellers like Yo Gotti and Starlito. But as an always-skeptical observer, Baby needed a tactile and 360-degree experience, the ability to assess people with his own discerning eyes up close. A rapper, he figured, could always have fake jewelry or borrowed cars that looked gleaming enough from afar. Worse still, they could be disloyal, fake people. But the drug dealers—they were immediate, right there in his face, followed by reputations like weighty shadows and always willing to engage with him. They also tended to shine.

Ced, the mean-mugging older boy whom Baby used to beat gambling before they teamed up, put it more plainly on behalf of a generation of Atlanta kids that grew up amid the city's rap music renaissance but didn't necessarily reap the rewards right away. "Rapping used to be corny," he said. "We always been on another type of level, know what I'm saying?" Having money in the streets and *not* rapping came with a different strain of respect. It meant you'd figured something else out.

P, a guy in that mold, first met Lil Baby when he was a scrawny kid of thirteen or fourteen, already commanding respect. He admired the way the younger man carried himself, and P came to know him as an apprentice for some close mutual friends—a guy known as Dolla and another spectral figure referred to only as Big, who had taken Baby under his wing as a street entrepreneur in training. "He looked at us, trying to get in where he fit in," P said knowingly, having once been that type of eager learner. "He was a hustler—all the way dedicated and motivated to getting the bag. He really reminded me of myself."

Baby likes to tell a story about seeing P on the block one day as a teenager. This was right around the time Quality Control was conceived as a label but before the company was anything much, even locally. Baby was still trying to get his name and his money up, and he was having problems with the battery on his first-ever car, sweating under the hood. Right then, P rolled up in a vehicle that made the junior hustler embarrassed about the ride he'd finagled not from a job at Zaxby's or Chick-fil-A, like some of his peers, but from the streets, which required more risk, more ingenuity, and yet wasn't getting him anywhere close, at that point, to P's kind of money.

P's ride was the sort that could stop the block, which was what everyone aspired to—a red and white BMW M6 with Forgiato wheels like gleaming razor blades, up to a few thousand dollars apiece just for accessories that were bound to get scuffed anyway. The car, Baby knew off the top of his head, was worth six figures easy. P pulled up, and he blocked in Baby, who was stuck tending to his inferior machine. "He hopped out dead fresh," Baby said—shining right there in his face. That was motivation.

Coach K met Baby around the same time and came to know the confident teenager as something of a financial liability for his rapper clients. "Lil Baby was the little dude that you used to ride by in the hood," Coach said. "He's pulling up gambling with the OGs, pulling up at these studios with these rappers who have millions and millions of dollars and he's got a hundred thousand dollars, saying, 'Put down.' Never wrote a record, but he's known for gambling through the whole city."

Forever a talent scout—and well aware from his work with Jeezy and Gucci that in hip-hop, the music could usually come later, after charisma, authenticity and star power—Coach was insistent that Baby needed to rap. The kid owed it to himself to try. Baby's swag on its own was nearly enough to get him over the hump, Coach thought. "Dude," he told Baby whenever the young man would come by the studio to smoke and gamble, "most of these rappers out here are rapping your story."

But there was something else to Baby beyond the confidence, the dimpled smile and the pockets stuffed with bills, fuller each time he came around. There was also that gravelly, marble-mouthed voice, with something musical in its vowel-heavy lilt. It was similar to what had drawn Coach to Jeezy all those years ago—a twang, a dialect, unmistakably Southern and even more irrefutably local than that. The swag teased it, but the voice confirmed it. "To me," Coach said, "he is the epitome of Atlanta."

It would be a long road until Baby listened. "In two years, probably caught five cases—pistol charge, weed charge, another trafficking charge, all types," the hustler could reel off, recalling his pre-prison days, glossing over his rap sheet like a string of minor inconveniences. "I was out on like four bonds at one time."

And yet, before he went away, rapping was not even an afterthought. Baby was just too fluent in the streets, too savvy in the ways of his specific world, to give up what he was building—selling pounds of weed out of the West End, Oakland City and the surrounding neighborhoods. For a time, he dabbled in affiliating with a local offshoot of the Rollin' 60s Neighborhood Crips, originally from Los Angeles, wearing a lot of blue and replacing his *B*s with *6*s on social media. (Baby, Young Thug and their future collaborator Gunna shared an early mentor in the Southside Atlanta OG figure Keith Troup, a widely respected Crip and connector who was murdered in 2015, shot fourteen times outside of a Chevron in College Park.)

Baby always had designs beyond the block—they just weren't musical. For years, the ever-present reality of dead-or-in-jail hardly fazed him, and he remained confident that his business acumen would take him further eventually. That was one reason why, unlike nearly everyone he hung around with—basically everyone he knew in Atlanta, friend or foe—Lil Baby never inked an inch of his skin.

"No tattoos," he said later, as if it had been the most obvious long-term calculation in the world. "I always knew I was going to run my money up, and I was going to have to go sit in front of some people to do something with my money, and I didn't want them to look at me like a dope boy."

He would not ever be confused for a simple thug, Baby promised himself, despite the provenance of his early funds. "I knew I was going to have the money, so I had to keep my appearance straight. I literally said, 'When I sit down in front of these white folks, I don't wanna have no tattoos or nothing.'"

In a way, it was still like that, even after he finally broke down, listened to Coach and started rapping, ultimately working for corporations run by those same white folks. But unlike many young artists of his generation, for whom a face tattoo was the ultimate fuck-you—a promise to the world to never go straight, never get a real job and never need one—Baby's visage, and his neck, his arms and even his torso, stayed blank, like a choirboy's or a good Jewish son's. "When I'm sitting in these meetings, I know they'd have to think something if I've got tattoos on my face," he said. "At least you ain't thinking *that* of me."

Even after he started getting arrested, Baby slithered out of enough close calls that pursuing rap almost felt like a cop-out. He'd heard his family tell the stories about his gift for words—those preacher-man days—but a passion for making music was harder to muster. Rapping just didn't drive him like it drove some of his friends—or like his passion for money did—and throughout his teenage years, that money was coming readily enough from elsewhere. Why dream unnecessarily?

But when all of Baby's hardheaded recklessness eventually caught up to him, he knew those two years in a rural federal prison were not something he ever wanted to repeat, even though he'd taken them like a champ. Hustling, like gambling, was a known unknown—equally likely to take you up or down at any given moment. But life in prison was something else entirely, a hell so dehumanizing that Baby swore to himself—and to his mother—that he'd never go back. "No way," he said. "I'd die before I go back to jail. On God." Two years was all he needed to see. "Hell nah." *Never again.*

Inside, Baby encountered no shortage of friends and people he'd grown up around who were serving life sentences. "I ain't trying to go through that," he said. And so while he was in there temporarily, a switch had flipped. In calls and messages home, he had vowed to pursue a safer path, and he really meant it.

"We used to be talking on the phone—'Bro, when I get out, I'm gonna start rapping,'" Ced remembered, though he, like Lashon, never took it too seriously. Sometimes, from the prison phone, Baby would even reach a friend who happened to be at the Quality Control studios, and he'd fantasize about being back in the mix. "When you get out, man," P would tell him, "let's find something for you to do."

It made some logical sense. Besides Coach's urging, so many of Baby's peers, from Migos to Young Thug, an old friend and fellow Washington High dropout, had transitioned to music with great fanfare and financial success. Baby was never one to be left behind. But actually becoming a real rapper still seemed like a long shot—not far from deciding at age twenty that the NBA was still within reach.

In prison, though, Baby had developed an intensity of focus that he hoped, when paired with the natural skill he brought to most things he tried, would serve him well in his future pursuits, shutting out distractions that could stunt his growth, drawing him back into his old life and old ways. At first, this mental discipline had been a survival tactic, a way to disassociate from those cell walls, the shitty food, the days that bled one into the next. "You there, but you not there," Baby said.

He knew that dreaming about home couldn't do him any good in prison, and that was a mindset that he wanted to carry over to freedom, keeping him in the studio through the late nights required to try his hand at a new hustle. "I ain't think about what the bros doing, what the hoes doing," he said. "It keeps me going." *You're there, but you're not there.* It was almost a form of meditation.

But when Dominique did get out, starting on his path to becoming Lil Baby full-time, it wasn't a clean break from the streets—it never was. Still, there was something prodigal about his return to Quality Control, not as a weed dealer or a gambler, but as someone finally ready to start from scratch with music. After his first studio try that July, Baby began spending more time around any rappers who would have him, soaking up whatever knowledge he could from the QC roster and Young Thug's budding YSL label, which included Gunna, a round-faced, smooth-voiced neophyte from College Park.

Baby also practiced with Ced when no one was looking, recording sloppily with an at-home setup. But unlike some of his peers who were treating the possibility of a rap career like a scratch-off ticket, Baby was intent on improving—and fast. Ced recalled his friend throwing down cash so more experienced rappers like Gunna and Thug would come to the studio and teach him the basics—how to start a song, how to make a catchy hook—the same way someone might compensate a guitar instructor. "You gotta pay the teacher!" Ced said.

At the same time, Baby dabbled in his before-music ways, turning again to dealing drugs, gambling and stacking money any way he could to try to make up for lost time. But he knew that well was starting to run dry, and he also knew its consequences. Fortunately, one line of work was providing both material and investment capital for the other as he considered a permanent career change.

Everything Baby had done, seen and been through in the streets would help make him the kind of rapper he wanted to become—a memoirist with gems of wisdom that would ring true and inspire the dope boys like him. Baby wasn't yet thinking about white kids in the suburbs or international crowds as a potential audience—just the people he knew who craved a soundtrack to their struggle and their deliverance from it. As a rapper making his own myth, he needed his persona to feel tactile—*real*—not like the holograms of hip-hop that he'd dismissed as a kid. Because while rap may have mostly overcome its obsession with authenticity on a critical and commercial level, the financial and spiritual symbiosis between the music and the streets in Atlanta made everything verifiable. And the reason Baby's early music about his life—and his friends' lives—could sound so vital and so true was that both things were happening simultaneously, until they weren't.

"I didn't choose to get out the streets," Baby explained. "I wasn't getting a lot of money at the time. But I thank God that it happened like that, because I got more focused on rap." In the hierarchical business of the streets, he also knew there were factors at play beyond his control.

"It was over with not by my force, but by somebody else," he said cryptically. "So it was like, '*Shiiiit*, I ain't got nothing to do but this.'"

P, it turned out, was making moves behind the scenes. Not long after Baby was released from prison, the blooming Quality Control executive had called Baby's OG—their mutual street connection—with a bold idea. "Let Lil Baby go," P insisted. "Let me have him."

II.

WORK

DESPITE APPEARANCES, TO HANG OUT WITH A FAMOUS RAPPER OR three can be pretty fucking boring. It is the sort of enduring monotony that, God willing, might be injected with glitz or excitement at any given moment, inflating every phone call or change in plans with pregnant potential. But by the odds of the universe, things tend to stay pretty much as low-key as they seemed at first, for minutes and then hours at a time.

This is in part because rappers are almost always either in a city they know barely at all—save for a few restaurants, stores, airports, hotels and stages—or they're in a city they know all too well, a place swarming with overzealous fans and stewing enemies. Streets they've driven ten thousand times and establishments where they've bought everything they could ever want and then everything somebody they know could ever want, probably twice over. What do you even do after that?

Home, to an active musician, is a slippery concept, given that they probably spend most of their time on the road. And so even when they're at a house that they own—or one they rent for some absurd amount of money—it rarely feels lived in, because it's probably not. It has most likely been decorated by some professionals hired by some other professionals, and the furniture probably still has tags on it, if there's furniture at all. Such is the life of a wealthy drifter.

On the other hand, being at work for these rappers consists mostly of advertising themselves—either onstage or in song, or in song onstage, or often with various industry and media gatekeepers, who decide where those songs will go. Every radio station visit bleeds into every other radio station visit—interviews, song premieres, promo spots—and those don't differ much from having to flash a smile at a magazine or a newspaper or a website or a streaming service or a rolling paper startup or a classic car dealership, except at a classic car dealership you can actually buy something expensive at the end.

There are only a few things to do on a given day when you're this young, this rich and this anxious about every kind of snake that could possibly be surrounding you at any given moment. You can shop, which, at least for an observer, is less fun when you don't have to make choices between the things you really want and the things you don't really want but can buy anyway. You can try to find women to spend time with, or talk about finding women, or talk about having found women. Or you can wait around, probably in a greenroom or a hotel lobby or a Sprinter van, and do the aforementioned things—like most people under forty—on Instagram. It's about as fun to watch a rapper scroll through Instagram as it is to watch your significant other do it, except your significant other probably isn't DM-ing with as many potential partners.

The other possibility—and it's an endless one for any time of day or night—is to record. A studio, to these artists, is a windowless haven, a place where art and money can be made in relative peace, but also somewhere to eat, smoke, nap, drink and listen to music (or look at Instagram). And if a studio isn't available—though it probably can be, depending on your budget—you can just set up, bando-style, in any hotel room, bus or basement, assuming you keep a microphone and a computer on hand, which it's almost definitely someone's job to provide.

One rainy winter day in New York City, Migos' calendar was packed with the kind of promotional obligations that come with being famous rappers, until suddenly it wasn't. It was January 2017, and the group had found itself with about three hours of rare downtime in between interviews, a fashion expo for their new YRN clothing line and a trip to the Google offices in Chelsea. There, a few dozen people would listen to the new Migos album through headphones at a "silent listening party," meaning everybody would just stand around watching everybody else listen on their own, together.

Originally, the idea was that The Boys, which is what everyone affiliated with Quality Control called the three Migos now—*the boys*, like a worn-out mother might refer to her rambunctious brood—would spend those unscheduled hours tucked safely away in their Times Square hotel rooms, storing energy for the weeks of album promo to come. But when the Sprinter carrying Quavo, Takeoff and Offset—plus their manager and utility appendage Jerel and a few others, including a videographer and a DJ—pulled up on the neon-lit block where the hotel was located, one of the guys noted that the famed hip-hop recording space Quad Studios was just across the street. (Quad was where, in 1994, Tupac Shakur was shot five times and robbed in the lobby, setting off the chain of events that led to his falling-out with the Notorious BIG and, most likely, his death.)

The final seat in the van that afternoon was supposed to belong to the trio's publicist—their timekeeper and secretary at moments of so many clashing professional obligations—but since I was hoping to get a few minutes of interview time with Migos ahead of their comeback album, the PR professional agreed to take a cab and meet us at the hotel. I sat in the way back with the videographer, while Quavo occupied the front seat next to the driver, the others sandwiched in between.

"We going to the hotel?" Takeoff offered half-heartedly.

"For what?" Quavo shot back. "What's the point of going to sit at the hotel?"

The group had not reserved any studio time in advance, but Quavo seemed confident that saying *It's Migos* into the street-level Quad intercom—and actually being Migos on the other end—was enough to get them inside on a weekday afternoon. Still, the front desk person upstairs balked at Jerel's first attempt, explaining that the studio couldn't let anyone in without their boss's approval.

"We trying to pay!" Quavo protested in the van. "This the only studio in New York?" He insisted on trying again. "Pull up and pop up," he said, describing his MO. "Ain't nobody in there, anyway."

In the meantime, there was Instagram. As they each scrolled individually, sometimes showing one another what they found, the guys argued over the relative badness of various women before they learned that the founder of WorldStarHipHop, Q, had died of heart disease at the age of forty-three. They also debated the merits of various New York cuisines, namely pizza versus chicken and rice. "I'd eat some Applebee's," Takeoff suggested. "I just had some weak-ass pizza last night." He absentmindedly sparked a blunt.

"Who just fired up?" Quavo spat from the passenger seat as soon as he noticed the smell. "Who just fired up?"

His sheepish nephew, Takeoff, held the smoldering evidence.

"Put that shit out, man," Quavo said. "We right in front of the goddamn hip-hop police at this studio."

Another of the guys backed up Quavo's pragmatism. "Remember what happened last time we were here? They were just waiting on the corner for us, and we pulled off on them." No one, including Takeoff, fought back; even among those from Atlanta, the NYPD's reputation as overzealous antagonists to rappers was secure. In fact, in the early 2000s, when the department's task force dedicated to surveilling artists started giving "hip-hop training sessions," officers from Atlanta reportedly attended the seminars.

After a few more tries on the intercom and a couple of strategic phone calls by Jerel, word eventually came down that Quavo had been correct, and the studio was empty. "Wake up," Quavo told the van. "Time to work."

As everyone piled out into the drizzly midtown grime, I tripped a bit over the second row of seats and my Timberland boots, already a little soggy and speckled with the day's puddles, grazed Takeoff's fabric-heavy Pharrell Williams Adidas, earning me a vicious glare. I apologized profusely and Takeoff, assessing the limited damage of a small smudge, seemed to let it go. We all piled into the Tupac memorial lobby and then the industrial elevator, arriving as a damp mass on the tenth floor, where the studio employees, so recently dismissive, greeted Migos as they liked to be greeted—like royalty. In the studio's A-room, Quavo immediately assumed the role of genial host, having occupied so many A-rooms before, and he ordered the help—in the form of the studio "runner," whose job it is to obtain anything the musician wants, to be charged to the record label or artist later—to find some pepperoni pizza, ignoring Takeoff's earlier protestations. He also requested Backwoods cigars, cranberry juice, apple juice and Hennessy.

"Make sure they cook it well-done," Takeoff requested, resigning himself to the pizza order. Then he began counting comically large stacks of money on top of the studio microwave. In the other room, Quavo changed into a fuzzy pair of spotted socks, which he put over his existing, plainer socks. "My studio socks," he said. "They're lucky." The runner was handed $40 in cash but suggested that he might need double that for the errand. "I'll bring back the receipt and change," he promised before setting off into the rain.

While the group got situated, rolling weed and ignoring the television—MSNBC on mute, showing clips of President Donald J. Trump, inaugurated just days earlier—DJ Durel, the group's traveling sound engineer and in-house producer, plugged in one of the many hard drives he held on to for moments like this. Without prompting, Durel queued up a twinkly Zaytoven beat with thick low end and an ominous, looped piano melody, blasting it over the studio sound system, the way all 808 beats—and therefore most of Atlanta's music—sounded best.

A woman with a thick New York accent joined the party, breaking up the all-male energy. Quavo flirted innocently, teasing her about not smoking with him until she offered a convincing out. "They about to test my ass," the woman said as she settled onto the couch, where she'd remain for hours while The Boys recorded.

The session was approaching full swing when my cell phone buzzed. It was Migos' publicist, who had not been apprised of the group's change in plans and had therefore been waiting in their hotel lobby for more than an hour. I started to explain where we were and why. But before I could announce our location, Jerel grabbed my iPhone and hung up without a word. Having ditched their handler to squeeze in a little extra work, Migos wished to record in peace.

To watch the group in the studio was to witness a start-and-stop relay race that was also a magic trick. No one seemed to be exerting themselves all that much, and yet by the time they neared the finish, everyone but the rappers was exhausted and dizzied and unsure of how they'd ended up where they had, having heard the same few bars of music repeated for hours.

In practice, there is no actual *writing* going on while Migos writes a song. Their style of rapping—eons away from the old-school idea of a guy with a pen and a pad—was learned from their idols, like Gucci Mane and Lil Wayne, who freestyled at will. But instead of coming up with lengthy stanzas in their heads and then rapping them in full, à la Jay-Z, the Migos members craft songs directly into the microphone, one syllable and then one word and then one phrase and then one line at a time—starting, stopping and rewinding over and over and over again, until there is something resembling a verse. This requires a nearly psychic bond with a recording engineer—usually Durel—who is not just pressing "record" but performing surgery in real time, chopping up some words and discarding others while fitting them into place on the beat and taking instructions that are more like grunts of approval or disapproval, saying next to nothing in response.

For an Atlanta rapper, *Come on* or *One more time*—which usually means many more times—indicates that they want another micro-take, which lets Durel know that he must rewind the beat a few seconds, giving the artist another trial-and-error attempt at extending the line in progress. *Keep that* means to save what was just rapped, a Lego clicking into place with the previous block, becoming the new lyric to build off of. As the flow and rhyme pattern start to reveal themselves, these instructions pick up speed, as do Durel's mouse-clicking and keyboard punches, with *Keep that* becoming *Ki-da'* and *One more time* shortening into *Mo-ti'*. The beat plays aloud throughout, in fits and starts, and just about every word said into the microphone is recorded, then either saved or deleted.

Instead of more traditional rap storytelling, such improvisational methods lend themselves to capturing bursts of personality, surrealist description, flashes of memory and landscape and brand names rattling around in rappers' heads. It isn't easy to do, but it can sound like it is, which is to say, it sounds *cool*, effortless and, like them, of Atlanta, even when they aren't there physically. The resulting lyrics are grounded in a specific set of references and phrases that are passed around through songs by their local cohort and later slip into the mainstream until they are one-upped, refined, refreshed. Then the cycle starts again.

On this day, Quavo took the mic first with no discussion, his voice soaked in a light, echoey Auto-Tune effect, making him sound like a lovelorn, short-circuiting AI creation. At first, he multitasked, rolling a blunt in the booth while feeling out the beat with his mouth, mixing gibberish sounds with a magnet-poetry grab bag of Migos keywords: "Ride. . . *Ehh, ehhh . . . Uhhh, uh, uh, uhuh* . . . I got fifty K on me . . . Extra . . . Serving fiends, my dog . . . *Eeeeaaaaaahhhhhh. Ay! Uh!* Yep. *Yessssiiiiiirrrrr.* This is . . . Ride. Up. Vibe. Drop-top. You dig? *Dah, dahdahdah . . . Ay. Ay. Ayyy.* Riding in that . . . drop-top. *Miiiigooos.* Big dogs."

The other guys barely paid attention to Quavo working his clay as they tended to their phones, weed and food. "Come on," Quavo told Durel, who brought the beat back to the top again and again. Eventually, the sounds started to rhyme. "Chopper . . . Dirty . . . Kawasaki chopper, it's dirty. Thirty . . . Thirty . . . That's Curry . . . Big dope. Bass drop. Drop-top. Ain't opp. I can't stop. Drip wet. Drop-top . . . *Brrr brrr* . . . Drop my, *uh*, foot . . . Get in there, get in there, get in there. Diamonds, water, swimwear."

This was a word game, a crossword puzzle, a rhythmic exercise, and while the genesis may have given ammunition to those who questioned Migos' lyrical intent, it was an expressionist performance with precision, a conjuring of vibrant imagery where the delivery could invoke as much feeling as the words. Quavo's early brushstrokes went on for almost exactly five minutes—start, stop, rewind, start, stop, rewind—with no obviously discernible direction, lyrically or melodically, until all of a sudden, he hit on something that made him switch palettes. This sudden lightbulb moment, while simple, seemed to imbue his free-associative mumbling with purpose.

"Just look *wiiide* awake," he rapped, clipping the final word. "I'm gonna go count this cake / Make 'em look wide awake / Take your bae on a date." It was basic, but it had bounce.

"One more time."

"Just look wide awake / Take your bae on a date / N—— might pull up on skates."

"Keep the first part."

"Watch these n——s throw shade / Watch these n——s throw shaaade!"

"*WAKE UP!*" Quavo hollered behind his own voice, echoing the order he'd given to the van barely half an hour earlier. "*WAKE UP!*" With those trademark ad-libs added, a Migos song had started to materialize. Quavo hammered on the theme. "Look wide awake! You can't sleep on a n——! You know you can't sleep on me! Know they can't sleep on me! Know they can't sleep on me!" And that was how a Migos hook was born.

It wasn't until the catchphrase chorus was more or less finished that Quavo took off his headphones for a gut check. "I don't know, bro," he said to Durel, and also implicitly the room. "You fuck with that?" Durel nodded silently, no one else reacted and that was enough—Quavo kept right at it. About thirty minutes later, including one brief conversational detour in which the guys argued about what Maybelline was—"They clean your face, right?" "But like, what about the girls who do the commercials!"—Quavo's parts were complete. It was somebody else's turn to take the baton.

Again without discussion, Offset, matching Quavo in a Migos hoodie and dad hat, stepped into the booth, immediately attacking the beat with the same free-associative approach, but in a more rat-a-tat fashion, adding ferocity and eventually humor. "*I'mana, danana, danana, danana*," he began, evoking a typical Migos triplet flow in gibberish. "*Dunanana, nanana, nanana, danana* . . . Dive in the sea. Dive in the sea. Diamonds, Patek Philippe."

Before long, Offset had formed some punch lines, threatening to hang a rival "out the window like Suge (*Suge Knight!*)" and somehow managing to pseudo-rhyme the word *Suge* with the phrase "Watch 'em go live—Jimmy Kimmel!," a reference to the late-night show where the group had recently performed. He finished his verse on a well-earned note of victory: "They laughed, they thought it was over (*it's over!?*) /

Yeah, we took the game over / Then we kicked down the door with the polar / We came from the trap, hold the bowl up!" Nobody in the room acknowledged the lines, but everyone knew what they meant.

Five months earlier, in late August 2016, Migos had released a song that breathed new life into the group's declining stock and salvaged Quality Control's dream of becoming an Atlanta rap empire. Before they happened upon another hit record, the trio's career had seemed moribund, its musical effectiveness and visibility declining simultaneously, even as the Migos flow came to dominate rap radio—and even bleed into white pop music. Their rhythmic triplet raps were now being used often and prominently by artists from Atlanta (Future, 21 Savage, Young Thug) and those pretending to be from Atlanta (Desiigner, Travis Scott, Drake). But despite their reputation as a spigot of new music, Migos had not released an album since the commercial failure of *Yung Rich Nation* in 2015. With the exception of a few here-and-gone mixtapes that failed to reignite the trio's initial spark, its official output had ground to a halt due in part to an ongoing contract dispute with 300, the larger partner label that had expected to make Migos into international superstars.

For the last eleven months of 2016, the trio released only a brief, noncommercial EP. Such a fallow period might have been enough to write them off entirely if not for the life support provided by a string of Quavo guest verses with a resurgent Gucci Mane, 2 Chainz, Travis Scott, Meek Mill, Kanye West and Post Malone, whose hit single "Congratulations" was whetting Top 40 radio stations' appetite for the sound of Quavo's digitized smoothness. Some speculators in the industry were left to assume that Migos' best bet for a second act was a Quavo solo career.

But it was Offset—whose incarcerations had stunted the group at two key moments—who, alone one night in his basement studio, wrote "Bad and Boujee." Over a lightweight, spacious beat by the Atlanta producer Metro Boomin, Offset was trying out ideas when he uttered a simple opening phrase that would come to rival "Versace, Versace" as the defining Migos exclamation, birthing a million internet memes and the biggest song of the group's career.

"Raindrops / Drop-top" might as well have been a throat-clearing studio placeholder. But in its Seussian alliteration, the words had the effect of feeling like they'd always existed in that order, giving way to the Platonic ideal of a Migos hook, one that mixed sensational drug-and-gun talk with an overriding sense of personal uplift. When it came time for Offset to start his actual verse on the song, he could barely form words, instead making his exhilaration visceral with probably the least eloquent, most evocative opening lines he'd ever rap in his life: "Offset! *Woo! Woo! Woo! Woo! Woo!*" In that moment, he gave himself chills.

In the New York studio months later, as "Bad and Boujee" reverberated around the world, Offset's relief at being able to make up for his earlier missteps was palpable and a point he kept returning to. For the first time, he was carrying himself like a chest-out star instead of a brooding one. "Some opportunities were probably lost because of my situation, but I was fortunate to have brothers that could keep the train moving," he said. "This song is like a rebirth."

The best part about "Bad and Boujee" was that it wasn't trying to be a crossover hit. Light on melody, with no singing, heavy on verbiage, proudly explicit in content and sinister in its skeletal sound, the song represented the upside of sticking with your subject matter—trapping, shopping, fucking—and assuming the world would move toward you and toward Atlanta. Beyond the thundering beat drop that could shake any party, its icy charisma and unabashed hedonism could tickle even those furthest from its content, listeners who could sniff the fumes of abandon and opulence and feel adrenalized by proximity. It was at this exact moment that the streaming revolution was revealing what the youthful masses would choose to play, repeatedly, without the top-down hierarchy of radio programmers and corporate CEOs or bloated CD prices as determining factors. The answer, it turned out, was raw rap music that sounded like winning.

The first thing Offset did with his demo for "Bad and Boujee" was send it to P. The QC executive lit up immediately—and then he got to work, passing the song along to Coach K, who heard what P did and began devising a tactical game plan. "Tell the other boys it's outta here,"

Coach advised his partner, urging the group to finish the track as soon as possible. And while Takeoff would never actually get around to adding a verse, a lasting sore point later, a guest appearance by the effervescent Lil Uzi Vert provided a dash of freshness for a group that had now been releasing music consistently for five years—enough to no longer be the hot new thing in rap.

The song's timing could not have been better for Migos and Quality Control on multiple levels. Migos had taken to posting bitterly on social media about its label situation with 300 Entertainment as early as the fall of 2015, when its failed debut album was still a fresh bruise. But the relationship had turned worse than anyone knew after *Yung Rich Nation* tanked. QC wanted its group out of the deal, but 300 refused to loosen its grip on the trio, leading to more than a year of litigation, with all of Migos' royalty money tied up in escrow as the two sides battled largely out of the public eye, in clandestine legal maneuvers.

"For eighteen months, we couldn't sell no product," P said later. In the mind of a hustler, that was business suicide. "It was like we was shackled down." He estimated that the court battle cost nearly $500,000.

Yet for all of the agita that the label drama brought, P seemed to relish the principled ugliness of the fight, which melded the ruthlessness of the streets with the ruthlessness of the music business. "Man, Lyor Cohen?" P said one afternoon in the Quality Control studios, considering his rival executive, the 300 founder whose earliest days at Def Jam helped lead to the commercial explosion of hip-hop. "He ain't nothing to play with. You feel what I'm saying? I respect him a lot. I respect Todd. But it was a real war. It got real ugly. They know all the tricks. Lyor started this shit, bro. You trying to go against some veterans!

"That's Lyor mentality: *You think you gonna fuck with me?*" P went on, getting heated at the memory. "You know what his thing is? To smash an ant with a sledgehammer. Overkill. You ain't gotta smash no ant with no sledgehammer! But I love that, because I learned the business, even though we were warring with each other. Coach used to call me, 'P, don't let him get you out your character.'"

Coach, too, shook his head at the recollection. "He's a master manipulator. *Master. Manipulator.* He had my man off his square!" Coach imitated P, his more intimidating half, defending his Atlanta turf from Cohen, the rap carpetbagger. "'*You better not never come down here!*'"

"Let me tell you something, he never backed down," P said, slipping into his best Schwarzenegger-esque Lyor impression. "'*I'm coming! I'm coming by myself!*' Yo, no, no, no, for real. He's not backing down from *nothing*. He Israeli, man—he a fighter! Let him tell you the stories when he was a kid, really having to be out there fighting with guns and shit." P paused for a moment, reflecting, before a smile crept over his face. "I really miss talking to him."

Mixing street code with legal muzzling, P refused to detail exactly how the two sides had come to an agreement over Migos' contract, offering only cryptic mythologizing. "If anybody ever finds out how we sorted it out, folks gonna be like, *What the fuck, are you serious?* Put it all on the line. Everything. Me and Lyor. The lawyers were looking at me crazy." Still, Migos owed 300 one more album, and it was in everyone's best interest for it to be a hit. A week after they reached a detente, Offset sent "Bad and Boujee" to the team.

Quality Control put the single in the best position to succeed with a few deliberate distribution tweaks. First, they premiered "Bad and Boujee" only on SoundCloud—"where the kids live," Coach K said, comparing the rising platform for streaming rap music to the role MySpace had played earlier in his career. That helped to build hype, giving the song a subterranean feel that cast Migos once again as upstarts. QC then timed the wider release of "Bad and Boujee" to Labor Day weekend, not only to take advantage of the nonstop parties and celebratory mood—a Freaknik-type tactic, if there ever was one—but because holiday weekends were when rap radio stations relied on DJ mix shows instead of more fixed official playlists, leaving the door open for emerging sounds and songs. (The next Migos single, "T-Shirt," was released with similar precision—first with a majestic Arctic-and-fur-themed music video, with the official audio coming ahead of Martin Luther King Jr. Day.)

Coach and P also sent Migos back to basics—working the Atlanta strip club scene—to build momentum and "get the vibe of the people," as P described it. "You can't go to radio and try to force a record, you have to let it organically grow and let the people feel it." He invoked a metaphor he'd learned from none other than Lyor Cohen: "It's like having sex without having foreplay first."

"That's what really set it off," P said. "We went back to the clubs, going out every night—Magic City, Onyx, Blue Flame, Follies. When you have a song and you see them girls on that stage shaking their ass on that pole and singing the words to your song at the same time, when you see the guys singing word for word—that's when you know you got a hit on your hands."

This was a tried-and-true tactic that relied on a simple idea, one that defined the symbiotic relationship between Atlanta's gentlemen's clubs and its rap music: People tended to develop—and hold on to—positive feelings about a piece of music that they first consumed in front of, and would probably forever associate with, the memorable image of a beautiful naked woman in motion. The dancers, in turn, were liable to keep requesting the tracks that they enjoyed moving to or that made them the most money, which were often one and the same. And the artists themselves—or at least their cash-happy benefactors—had historically been glad to grease the wheels by breaking off some for the DJs and keeping the dollars flying so long as the soundtrack was theirs. (This, too, was its own economy, as DJ conglomerates compiled up-to-date playlists of hot rap songs—the specter of under-the-table payola always lingering—and sold subscriptions for, say, $10 a month to their colleagues around the city, saving them some legwork.)

From bass music to crunk to snap to trap, Strokers to the Cheetah to Follies to the Clermont Lounge, songs had broken out in these spaces at least since the onetime Magic City DJ known as DC the Brain Supreme played "Whoomp! (There It Is)" by his duo Tag Team in the club on the day the song was finished in 1992. And while the adult entertainment industry, much like the musical genre that provided its bass, was not always fully embraced by the city itself—with Atlanta's tourism chamber opting not to track the economic impact of Atlanta's strip clubs—few would deny its centrality to the place's pull, for business conventions and aspiring musicians alike.

So legendary are the strip clubs in Atlanta that they manage to be borderline-parodic theme-park versions of their reputations and also live up to the hype—more homey, more intergalactic, more diverse, more carpeted in cash than could seem possible on a nightly basis for decades. The rare mix of full nudity and liquor licenses always helped, a reality that took root in Atlanta in the early 1970s after a judge ruled, in reference to a performance of the musical *Hair*, that obscenity and nakedness were not the same, allowing the dancers to ditch their bottoms and pasties. The strip club food—wings, lobster tails, steak and potatoes—was also well-known for being way better than it had any right to be.

By the start of the 2020s, thanks to labor disputes, law-enforcement pressure and zoning requirements, barely more than a dozen such clubs remained in Atlanta, and the good old days were missed. "What you see today is not making it rain," explained Lil Magic, the private-school-educated, second-generation proprietor of Magic City, Atlanta's Disneyland of ass, one evening behind his desk downstairs.

"You don't throw a hundred dollars to make it rain," he said, in between using the corporate chat app Slack to check in with dancers and order a tequila from the bar above. "If you've only got a hundred dollars, don't throw that shit—put it on the floor or tip it a dollar at a time. If you want to throw money to make a point, it can't be less than a thousand dollars."

Still, the current generation was doing its best to keep the BMF legacy alive. The very night of the club heir's complaints, after 21 Savage's crew was rejected from a nearby establishment due to a lack of IDs, the local fixer and neighborhood fairy godmother Baby Jade ambled downstairs to ask Lil Magic for a cool $17,000 in ones for the rapper and his friends to spend. That amount—and then some—happened to be sitting at the ready in a safe within arm's reach.

Big Magic, the club's founder and Lil's father, was a former Duke University running back who opened the place in 1985 and later did most of a ten-year sentence on drug conspiracy charges. He tended to be more insouciant about the ebbs and flows of the business and its royalty of the moment. "They hot as pussy grease right now!" he said one afternoon about Quality Control, as Migos videos and ad-libs blanketed the surprisingly small space. "Everything I'm hearing is they got it! They on fire!" He compared the label's run to Motown's success with the Temptations and the Four Tops. "That's how this thing goes," Big Magic said. "It's their turn."

Because at the same time as QC was working its proven ground game, the methods of distribution for the industry were finally catching up to Migos' mixtape-loving ways. Digital streaming was now allowing tracks to build from the bottom up, all but forcing more traditional power brokers to eventually acknowledge the viral velocity. After a summer of grassroots growth for "Bad and Boujee," Migos' zealous army of online supporters—the same ones who had earlier proclaimed the group "better than the Beatles"—did its part, drawing attention to the song on social media with a series of "Raindrops / Drop-top" Mad Libs jokes that allowed users to fill in a rhyming third line about anything from *The Office* to the "Bad and Boujee" meme itself ("rain drop . . . drop top . . . these tweets really need to stop stop").

In December 2016, when the group took a trip to Lagos, Nigeria, to perform, the crowd was practically levitating, flinging water and rapping every word as the beat for "Bad and Boujee" hit, cementing the song as an international phenomenon. Strategic dissemination of video from the Lagos performance, shot at stage level to emphasize the absolute mayhem, also went viral, creating a positive feedback loop for the track that made anyone who didn't know the words feel irrelevant. By then, "Bad and Boujee" and its accompanying music video, released on Halloween, had tens of millions of plays and was running up the *Billboard* Hot 100.

"The game has changed," Coach declared.

But it wasn't until "Bad and Boujee" was mentioned onstage at the Golden Globe Awards in early January 2017—just weeks before the release of the second official Migos album, boldly dubbed *Culture*—that the final hurdles to mainstream pop stardom started to fall. Donald Glover—the multihyphenate who once joke-rapped as Childish Gambino, wrote for *30 Rock* and starred in *Community*—had come into serious auteur status as the creator and star of the FX show *Atlanta*, a deadpan, experimental satire of Southern rap life. Glover played Earn, a Princeton dropout who starts to manage his tougher cousin's music career. In its first season, the show mixed rap in-jokes, arcane Atlanta-specific references and enough canny social commentary and absurdist humor to make specific Black concerns feel cosmically relevant and relatable to multiple audiences, elevating the city's surging cultural brand to high pop art. *Atlanta*'s pilot even began with the song "No Hook" by OJ da Juiceman, one of Gucci Mane's most underrated associates.

Glover knew this world inside and out. Before thriving in comedy and rap, he was raised in Stone Mountain, Georgia, the DeKalb County suburb known for being the site of the cross-burning that restarted the Ku Klux Klan in 1915, and also for its gigantic bas-relief monument, carved into Stone Mountain itself, that depicts the Confederate heroes Robert E. Lee, Jefferson Davis and Stonewall Jackson. *Atlanta* was a tribute to—and send-up of—the violent local juxtapositions that made him.

In the first season of the show, Glover had cast the three Migos as caricatured versions of themselves, showing them dealing drugs and keeping a kidnapping victim in a camper secluded in the Georgia woods. The fictional rapper Paper Boi, who doubles as a small-time hustler, comes to re-up his supply with Migos, and he tells Quavo that he's been "busy, busy." Quavo, with pitch-perfect comedic timing, replies, "What the hell you mean, n——? Trapping boring as fuck."

When *Atlanta* won the Golden Globe for best comedy series, Glover closed his speech by giving a special shout-out to the city. "I really want to thank Atlanta and all the Black folks in Atlanta, just for being alive," he said, clad in a brown velvet tux and bow tie. He also singled out the local group of the moment, thanking "the Migos, not for being in the show, but for making 'Bad and Boujee.' Like, that's the best song . . . ever." Backstage later, Glover doubled down in response to a reporter's question about "*My*-gos," correcting the pronunciation and calling them "the Beatles of this generation." Glover also noted that "they don't get a lot of respect outside of Atlanta." But that was about to change.

Behind the scenes, Coach and P had been trying for weeks to get Migos booked to perform "Bad and Boujee" on national television, to no avail. The day before Glover's prime-time remarks, a publicist had forwarded the Quality Control execs an email thread filled with all kinds of excuses from the cadre of late-night bookers who picked the musical guests that would be allowed to perform for millions. *It's not the right time*, they all said—even as "Bad and Boujee" was climbing the charts.

But the day after the Golden Globes, *Billboard* announced that "Bad and Boujee" had completed its rise and hit number one on the Hot 100 (replacing another Atlanta-made, internet-driven hit, "Black Beatles" by the Mike Will Made-It–produced duo Rae Sremmurd, featuring Gucci Mane). It wasn't Glover's namecheck that did it—the song had secured its top spot days prior to the Globes—but his mainstream shout-out would still prove invaluable. "Soon as Donald Glover did that, the following morning, our publicist hit us back," P said. "All the people that just denied us wanted them on the show." A week later, Migos performed "Bad and Boujee" on *Jimmy Kimmel Live!*

"Hip-hop is the number one streaming music," P said, vindicated. "We're the leaders of the culture." And so it was. "Bad and Boujee" went on to go four times platinum and spend four weeks at number one, becoming one of the biggest songs of the year and earning a Grammy nomination for best rap performance.

Culture, the new Migos album released in the song's wake, matched its success. At just thirteen tracks, it was the group's most focused and potent release since the *YRN* mixtape, relying on more airy, ornate trap beats that allowed the three rappers to tame their staccato verbal onslaught, making better use of empty space for melodic hooks and adlibs. The album, which also included the hits "T-Shirt" and "Slippery," catapulted Migos to A-list status for good, selling 131,000 album units in its debut (including the newly counted streaming metrics)—dwarfing the 15,000 copies *Yung Rich Nation* sold in its first week—and becoming their first release to top the overall *Billboard* album chart. Just one year after it looked as if the group might be another casualty of rap's on-to-the-next-one mentality, Migos was hotter than ever. Coach called it "a minor setback for a major comeback."

AT THE STUDIO in New York, the group knew it had pulled off a magical reversal of fortunes, though they insisted their approach had never wavered. "We're doing the same thing we've been doing," Quavo said. "I feel like the world just caught up." Takeoff compared releasing *Culture* to Christmas Eve. "You just know that everything you asked for is going to be there up under that Christmas tree," he said. "It's our time right now."

But they still had a song to finish. Takeoff, who split the difference between Offset's jabs and Quavo's vocal curlicues, was the last of the three to take the booth, and that evening his verse was coming the least easily. With work on the track approaching the four-hour mark, he sipped lean from a Styrofoam cup as he struggled to come up with lines. Giving him cover, the group continued to dodge increasingly agitated calls from members of their team, who worried that Migos would be late for its own album listening party. But Quavo, Offset and Takeoff, unbothered by the outside commitments, would not even consider leaving the studio until all three had finished their parts.

Sensing his nephew's vocal-booth frustrations, Quavo offered a few suggestions, but it was past 7 p.m. when Takeoff wrapped his section. By then, the trio should have already been some twenty blocks south promoting the album. Instead, they were adding more ad-libs to their new song, like students scribbling the last few answers on a test after the bell has already rung. Even still, when the track was finally finished, the three Migos took a celebratory moment together to play it over the studio speakers, dancing in a triangle formation and rapping along to the words they'd just blurted out.

Despite their elation in the moment, that particular track, like hundreds of others Migos had made the same way over the years, was never released. It was just a moment in time, and there would be plenty more.

12.

"I'M TRANSFORMING"

When Lil Baby was ready to let Atlanta know he had turned to music, he let his cash do most of the talking.

J Rich, a reliable studio engineer in the Quality Control rotation, would never forget their first session together. Right away, he was impressed by the budding artist's natural facility on the mic. But it was the rapper's nonmusical attributes that really convinced him that Baby had what it took. Namely, it was the stacks. "You know you're supposed to bring money and stuff for in-studio video," J Rich said. "But he brought like a half a million dollars, bro. I'm like, *What!?*"

According to Ced, it was really more like $300,000. But the effect was the same nonetheless once it hit Instagram. "We had to let folks know he was rapping," Ced smirked.

The announcement did its job and immediately, the local scene was chirping. "I think I should sign this young n——," Gucci Mane wrote in the comments underneath the video. He was followed swiftly by his own former protégé, Young Thug, who got competitive. "Fuck that uma sign this lil n——," Thug replied. The established local rappers actually picked up the phone, too, offering Baby up to $500,000 for an artist-to-artist deal before he'd even put out a real song. But given his roots and the label's foundation, Quality Control was always going to be Baby's rightful home. Now all they needed was some actual music.

Like most artists in Atlanta at the time, Baby was not writing down his lyrics or even thinking much at all about his songs before getting in the booth to lay them down. Instead, Baby's engineer would play a beat that felt motivating enough on loop as Baby mumbled and hummed vocal patterns to himself in a stop-and-start fashion similar to what he'd seen from others. "He'd freestyle all the way through, four or five times, and then I would put the song together word by word," J Rich explained.

By early 2017, Baby was finally ready to show Coach and P his progress—a batch of seven or eight songs. P had seen no shortage of people decide one day that they were musicians, but he was blown away by what was happening right under his nose. "It happened so fast," he said. "I knew he wasn't no rapper. For him to just go in and make those songs like that . . ."

Off the bat, Baby's sound was familiar without being rote. Like Young Thug without the whimsy, he relied on drawled sing-rapping to soften his street tales, using plentiful Auto-Tune as both a sweetening accent and a vocal crutch. Preferring hazy, minor-key piano beats that put him in confessional mode to celebratory stomps that might start a party, Baby sounded worn down and ragged from the beginning, even as he blustered.

On "Option," the track that would become one of Lil Baby's first official releases, he began with a statement of fact that explained the song's simplicity, functioning as equal parts brag and sheepish apology: He had been home from prison for only 120 days. The rest of the song leaned on Migos-like repetition and directness—"I want money, I want money, for real," Baby intoned in various permutations—but you can hear him working through the process of putting words and phrases together, with dashes of personal insight and specificity starting to set it apart from more generic trap fare.

"Option" also hinted at a melodic sophistication beyond Baby's experience level, a promising starting point for the downbeat, melancholic music that would become his bluesy signature. Baby's friends thought the song was a smash. P considered it decent, something to work with. But Baby was wholly dissatisfied, cutting himself no slack. "I don't like that song," he told them flat-out. "That song really ain't me."

So he pressed the gas harder, cutting his common kingpin talk ("Shout-out to the plug, he keep bringing all these drugs," he rapped on "Plug") with detailed disclosures about his current circumstance—the liminal state between a life of dope-boy excess and the scabs that that life left behind.

"I got out of prison at the perfect time," Baby warbled on "Days Off," sounding spent yet determined. "Got out, I was fucked up, Big gave me a dime." He was also direct about his self-medicating, which had picked up after prison, outright calling himself a "junkie" and copping to needing rehab because of his intensifying addiction to lean. The drug tests required by his probation had sent Baby deeper toward opiates, which, unlike weed, didn't violate the piss tests he was required to take, a fact he rapped about economically and without pretense. That pain was, in many ways, his new product.

At the same time, P was still working behind the scenes to fully sever Baby from his other hustle. After Baby played him his second batch of recordings, P doubled down on his earlier executive decision. "We're going to freeze on whatever you're doing in the street," he told his new protégé. "Let's focus on this. I got a vision."

Just as a younger P, dubious and stubborn, had been advised by Coach K and others that there was money in the music business if he applied himself, he was now turning those lessons toward Baby. "If I can just get Baby to listen to me and follow whatever guidelines, we gon' make this work," the executive told his old friends who'd long backed Baby in the streets. And there would be something in it for everyone. "I promise you, bro, if we make this work, it's going to benefit everybody," P stressed to the crew. "This gon' be y'all way to get out the street, this gon' be y'all way to make some legit money, take care of y'all family."

Quality Control knew they officially had their latest prospect. "Whatever you was doing in the streets, just apply it to the music business," P told Baby. He also assigned him a more specific task: "Go to the projects, to your neighborhood, and take a picture." They needed an album cover.

Lil Baby's debut mixtape, *Perfect Timing*—featuring a sullen, amateurish shot of him in all black amid the wreckage of an abandoned house—was released by the label in April 2017, much to the surprise of Baby's own mother. "Mixtape of what?" Lashon scoffed. Her son handed her a CD.

At home, Lashon started at the beginning, playing each of his songs over and over again, sometimes for days, until she'd learned and digested every line, breath and beat, before moving on to the next track. "By the time I'm on the fifth song, he said, 'Mom, you got my new mixtape?'

"I'm still on the first one!" she replied.

P was equally floored by Baby's work ethic and improvement. "Did somebody write these for you?" he asked the rapper not long after *Perfect Timing*, when Baby played him another pile of songs. Baby assured P they were all his. And so the executive got back to work.

This marked the beginning of a Pheidippidean run by Lil Baby and Quality Control, who followed the early Migos plan of attack—release, release, release. After *Perfect Timing* in April, Baby would drop a mixtape in July, October, December and the following May—a total of five album-strength releases in his first thirteen months as a rapper, with each mixtape demonstrating a legitimate artistic leap and noticeable refinement. And while Baby's affiliations with artists like Thug, Migos and Gucci did help draw early ears, his tapes were not overly bloated with features from his more famous friends and labelmates. Establishing his own voice took precedence, and everybody involved knew that Baby had too much potential to be introduced to the world as a Migos hanger-on.

P and Coach had better ideas for presenting Lil Baby as a fully formed artist from a distinct genealogy. For Baby's second mixtape, *Harder Than Hard*, they secured a stamp of approval from DJ Drama, who hosted the release as a *Gangsta Grillz* special edition, harkening back to the buzz-building days of TI, Young Jeezy and Lil Wayne. For the cover, P instructed Baby to take a picture with his shirt off. The executive then fired up Google and searched, simply, "Atlanta." He sent the most relevant results to a graphic designer.

What came back, woven collagelike onto Baby's torso as he gripped two phone books' worth of cash, was exactly what P had in mind: bricks of cocaine, piles of guns, dice, crime-scene tape, a man smoking crack, the chalk outline of a dead body, and local signage and signifiers representing the MARTA train, the historic West End, Blue Flame and Magic City. "Everything that define a street cat coming from Atlanta," P said.

The songs on *Harder Than Hard* accomplished the same thing as its cover, beginning with the first track, "A-Town"—"A-T-L-A-N-T-A-G-A, that's where I'm from," Baby declared, in case there was any doubt. The song featured another homegrown, from-the-dirt native and emerging QC prospect, Marlo, and the pair traded hood history about bygone hustlers, establishing themselves convincingly as the city's next-generation trap griots.

But beyond the arcane and provincial, there was also the universal. It was on *Harder Than Hard* that Baby hit upon his first *Billboard*-charting single—and first Atlanta club classic—"My Dawg," which established him as more than just another local aspirant or neighborhood hero. He had national potential, and the song's music video would make that clear.

Situating Baby along the continuum of rap history—at least in subject matter and swagger, if not sound—the video for "My Dawg" began with a clip of Ice Cube rapping, "It was once said by a man who couldn't quit / 'Dope man, please, can I have another hit?'" Through this single indelible line from an early N.W.A song, Baby amplified his personal mythology for a new audience that didn't already know his reputation. The rest of the video underlined that essence, showing Baby rapping shirtless among dozens of young Atlanta dudes in front of a trap house and alongside a bright red, doors-up Lamborghini parked ostentatiously in front of a weathered corner store. But even beyond the evocative visuals, it was Baby's little pockets of nursery-rhyme rapping on the song that really stuck—especially in his yearning slurred post-chorus hook: "I'm on my way / I'm goin' fast / I'm comin' home to get you." In a song full of X-rated relations and violence, this romantically horny moment of plainspoken guard-dropping hinted at additional musical depth from a still-unproven artist. The video for "My Dawg" would go on to be viewed more than 130 million times.

Just as important as its reach, the song also became a bona fide street hit in the strip clubs and nightlife spots of Atlanta and their parking lots, where it represented a textbook stepping stone for an emerging rapper, creeping onto mainstream radio playlists, first locally and then beyond. It was the success of "My Dawg" that increased the demand for Lil Baby club appearances, the first way most Southern rappers get a direct payday. But while the clubs were now offering Baby a few thousand dollars to come and rap a few songs from a small stage or a VIP section, he spent far more than that paying to get all of his friends into the venue—usually in matching outfits that he also paid for. Then, like a mini-Meech, Baby would buy them all bottles, eating up any hope of a profit for the night. But whatever he sacrificed in immediate cash, Baby more than made up for in the priceless word-of-mouth accounts that told of some new rapper from the West End and Oakland City who rolled deep and had money on him. Lil Baby, much of Atlanta soon learned, had a movement building behind him.

At this point in any rap career, consistency was key. Although Baby's star had risen significantly in his hometown and was starting to glow online, too, the spoils of real rap stardom still remained distant and hard to fathom when compared with the fast street money he was accustomed to. A few thousand dollars here and there for shows was nothing to Baby, and although he'd piqued the wider industry's interest, those checks took time to clear. One medium-sized hit song, even if it made it beyond the South, was far from enough to sustain a career. And while the craft of rapping had captured Baby's attention—and his songwriting progress reflected real dedication to the form—he remained ambivalent about the 360-degree commitment that would be required to make the next leap.

When Baby arrived at the Quality Control studios one day in November 2017 to begin the process of assembling the track list for his latest mixtape, he was restless, withdrawn and even a little awkward, as Coach K and P talked up his development.

"I'm so happy for this kid, it's so crazy just to see this," Coach said like a proud uncle, even as he ribbed Baby for taking so long to get started. The three men reminisced about the days when Baby would say the label was too busy with Migos to give him the attention he needed as a new artist. Now, with Migos ascended, there was no question that it was his turn as a priority.

IT WAS AT this moment that Quality Control was beginning to flower as a record label, its ethos now spread among multiple artists of different levels. Outside of Studio A, in the company's pristine and oddly quiet studio and office space, a worn piece of printer paper was taped to the wall, broadcasting the tenets of QC's DIY professionalism. The rules may not have been enforced at all times, but they were displayed for everyone to see, just in case they needed to be invoked.

QUALITY SOUND STUDIO GUIDELINES

1. Book ALL APPOINTMENTS with Corey. (NO POP UP VISITORS WILL BE ALLOWED IN!)
2. We are ALL ADULTS, PLEASE CLEAN UP after yourself.
3. NO propping/jamming doors open.
4. NO Smoking in unauthorized areas.
5. DO NOT come to the studio UNLESS you are working. Engineer must be here and ready to work for your scheduled studio session.
6. NO sexual activity in the studios or lounge areas and PLEASE PROPERLY dispose of ALL condoms and condom wrappers!
7. BE RESPONSIBLE for the company you bring. LIMIT your Guest per studio session, UNLESS it is a producer, engineer, or artist working in your schedule studio session. Homeboy/Homegirl hanging is UNACCEPTABLE!
8. ONLY ARTIST & STAFF are allowed in the kitchen area. NO EXCEPTIONS!
9. Please use the parking spaces properly. DO NOT make up your own parking.

10. DO NOT have anyone dropping off or picking up drugs at the studio.
11. EVERYONE must enter through the SIDE DOOR and SIGN IN.
12. During your studio session DO NOT allow your guest to ram around the building or go into someone else's studio session Your guest must remain in your assigned studio AT ALL TIMES!
13. This is not your home, this is not a hangout, this is a place of business. PLEASE conduct yourself accordingly and in a professional manner.
14. ANY gambling, all parties involved must pay the house 30%!

FAILURE TO COMPLY WITH THESE RULES CAN & WILL RESULT TO FINES AND/OR SUSPENSION FROM QUALITY SOUND STUDIOS!!

Just beyond the printed rules, Lil Baby diligently wiped his Chick-fil-A sauce and crumbs from a marbled studio countertop. His new go-to producer and engineer, Quay, whom he'd met through Thug's former studio hand, pulled up tracks of varying degrees of completeness to play for Coach and P. But before they could get to the music, there was business to attend to: the QC team needed to update its major-label partner in New York on the rollout plan for Baby's next release.

On a video conference with their new New York colleagues, Coach and P were informed that Baby would need to turn in his finished mixtape four weeks before its planned mid-December release, in part because the corporate office would be largely empty over Thanksgiving. In Atlanta, Coach and P bristled at the strict due date, arguing that in the post-CD era, when albums and mixtapes were all but interchangeable and fans were more and more using only digital streaming platforms, top-tier artists like Migos and Travis Scott were turning in their completed projects only hours before they were released. But their pushback was met with the words "global supply chain" from the New York side.

"We're just always trying to take you next-level," a label guy offered meekly. There were streaming companies and radio programmers who needed preparing, not to mention a digital advertising plan to whip up.

"We don't need no marketing plan," P countered. "That ain't how we operate over here. We just want to drop it."

"What's the drop-dead deadline?" Coach interjected, ending the conversation with his obvious impatience. The label promised to get him a real due date on paper soon. Like a kid at a parent-teacher conference, Baby—in all-black Balenciaga sneakers, a Versace belt, four chains of various thicknesses, three pendants, two bracelets and two watches—futzed with one of his two iPhones, barely paying any attention at all.

About four years into its existence, QC was still functioning with the ragtag spirit of an independent label—and it had the single-digit staff in Atlanta to prove it. But now there was corporate parentage to answer to, as well. In 2015, with Migos still stuck in an unhappy marriage with 300 Entertainment, Coach and P had entered Quality Control into a joint-venture agreement—typically a fifty-fifty partnership in which the companies split profits and co-own the master recordings—with the largest music company in the world, Universal Music Group. They joined its Capitol Music Group division, which included the renowned labels Capitol Records and Motown.

The deal was not their first choice. Earlier, they had flirted with the onetime Atlanta godfather LA Reid at Sony—Universal's corporate rival. But a dream deal offered by Reid had fallen through after his C-suite overseers balked at the numbers, and QC remained on its own for a little while longer.

But it was another child of Atlanta—and of Reid's—that finally brought QC into the corporate fold. Tall, striking and glamorous, usually in gold hoop earrings, the young executive Ethiopia Habtemariam had moved to Atlanta from Tuskegee, Alabama, in the early 1990s as a sixth grader, quickly making friends with a pre-fame Kris Kross and dedicating her life to local music. Habtemariam got her start in the business interning at Reid's LaFace Records, and she was eventually tapped by

Universal to rebuild the dormant Motown brand as the highest-ranking Black woman at the company.

Habtemariam knew at the outset that Capitol and Motown lacked an authentic presence in modern Black music. In Coach K, whom she had known for more than a decade, she saw a scout on the ground with a keen eye and eclectic taste. Combined with P's love for the streets, QC represented the duality of Atlanta music, Habtemariam knew—"We love trap music, but we also love alternative soul"—and she signed the label to a three-year deal, with the possibility for more. The assumption was that Migos, still signed to 300 for the time being, would join the rest of the QC family when it was contractually possible.

"They saw an open lane here," Habtemariam said. "There was nothing in the hip-hop or urban space at all—that didn't exist here at the company. We were betting on each other."

That bet turned out to be a lucrative one for all involved, one made at an opportune moment, just as the music industry was reversing its fifteen-year slide, thanks largely to the way rap songs were clicking online. By the end of 2015, streaming music had arrived in full force, with Apple Music and the Jay-Z–owned Tidal joining Spotify and Google in offering unlimited access to seemingly infinite catalogs of music for the monthly price of a café breakfast. The result was a rapid turnaround for the music business, and Black artists, as they'd been so many times before, were its most viable stars. Two years later, in 2017, the industry grew its revenue to $8.7 billion, the highest level in a decade, with 65 percent of that coming from streaming, where rap dominated.

For years, rap fans had been taught through the high-volume, instant-gratification culture of mixtapes and blogs to anticipate something like streaming's water hose of content. An insatiable young audience, combined with the artists' ability to rapid-fire write and record songs from anywhere and post them online, made for a perfect union. Soon, hip-hop and R&B—which were combined in the corporate imagination as Black music—became the most consumed genre overall, dethroning rock in 2017 for the first time since such stats were monitored. The market share for rap/R&B would keep increasing for the next three years, accounting for more than 30 percent of all streaming in the US in 2020. And with the rise of official playlists, which Apple and Spotify needed to replenish constantly with new music, Quality Control was determined to be a reliable supplier—a twenty-first-century hit factory, the Motown for the beginning of the streaming era. That they would be able to do it under the old Motown banner was just a cosmic bonus.

But things hadn't clicked right away. While Migos was still finding its footing, the constellation of would-be rappers around them had suffered some stunted artistic development, and a few promising QC contenders from outside of the group's orbit faltered, too. OG Maco, the punk-rapper whom Coach had plucked from the hipster underground, never topped his debut single "U Guessed It" despite some buy-in from Capitol Records. A second attempt to break an artist through the major-label system fizzled as well when Young Greatness, a New Orleans transplant with a triumphant hit record called "Moolah," failed to generate excitement with his follow-up songs. (In 2018, Greatness was shot and killed at a Waffle House in New Orleans. He was thirty-four.) Quality Control's deal with Capitol and Motown might have gone down as a failed regional experiment if not for an unlikely interim success that had little to do with the company's repeated attempts to rescue guys from the streets.

Miles McCollum, a Technicolor teenager who had recently dropped out of Alabama State University, was raised in the small suburb of Austell, west of the city. His mother, Venita, was an elegant pharmaceutical rep. His father, Shannon, was a renowned Atlanta hip-hop photographer who had worked with OutKast, Goodie Mob, Pastor Troy and Lil Jon. As a child, Miles accompanied his father as he documented the lives of rappers. But at first, the kid found himself more drawn to the business and fashion on display than the music itself.

"I would let him help direct photo shoots, and I would always show him my invoices so he could see what I made," Shannon said. He also turned the lens often on his son, who from a young age vowed to become famous. "I used to photograph Miles every week. By three or four, he was so comfortable in front of a camera."

Born in 1997, and therefore raised online in the time of André 3000,

Miles was early to develop a taste for dressing flamboyantly. "Once, when he was about seven, we were picking up his friend, and Miles had on a pink polo shirt," Shannon recalled. "The little boy got in the backseat and started laughing uncontrollably at Miles, calling him a girl. Miles just said, 'You don't know nothing about this, man.'" In high school, influenced by the bright colors favored by Pharrell Williams and Tyler, the Creator, Miles would spend the money he earned working at McDonald's or as a photography assistant for his father at local thrift stores. "Ninety-nine cents, fifty cents, I just knew how to put it together," Miles said. His mother even taught him how to sew.

But when thrifting lost its charm, Miles developed a taste for the designer clothes favored by his mother and, increasingly, his friends and the rappers they looked up to. He decided that he needed to make his own money, fantasizing about the day he wouldn't be able to walk around the mall anonymously. "I always knew I was going to be something," Miles said. "I didn't know what."

For a time, he dabbled in ill-gotten gains, but they were not his specialty. In the fall of 2015, when Miles was eighteen, he and a friend were shopping at the hat store Lids in a Florida mall when an employee called security on the two shoppers. Police found thirty-nine fraudulent credit cards on them. In his mugshot, Miles resembled Sideshow Bob from *The Simpsons*, his loosely braided fluorescent red hair sprouting out in all directions.

By then, Miles had been accepted to Alabama State University, but he found himself unhappy and isolated during his first months away from home. In hopes of developing a different hustle, he began recording lo-fi rap songs in his dorm room. Free from judgment, Miles experimented with simple melodies; bright, bubbly production; and an affecting falsetto that he smoothed with Auto-Tune. He loved Kanye West and Kid Cudi—elder statesmen to someone his age—but his most direct influences were cult-favorite, unorthodox internet rappers like Soulja Boy and Lil B. He also had a taste for the pop and rock acts that he'd learned about from his father, like Coldplay, Daft Punk, Fall Out Boy and Radiohead.

Above all, though, was his knack for social media, including an innate sense of brand building. Soon, Miles started calling himself Lil Yachty, and he conceived of a clique of collaborators known goofily as the Sailing Team. A marketer above all else, Yachty started uploading his music for free on SoundCloud, the streaming site favored at the time by anyone with a hipster edge. He proclaimed himself the King of the Teens.

As Lil Yachty, Miles also traveled repeatedly to New York and Los Angeles—Shannon's day job at Delta gave him access to free flights—and he slept on couches while working to ingratiate himself with rap-adjacent tastemakers. When Instagram exploded, Yachty already had a signature look that made him instantly recognizable: dyed cherry braids that dangled over his eyes like a cool-kid bowl cut, each strand accented with six translucent beads.

Lil Yachty was sober and in college, so his subject matter, like his rapping skills, remained limited. But that left him to preach an all-purpose positivity that was fueled by timeless adolescent ambitions: chasing girls, looking cool and hanging out with friends. Even Yachty's attempts at aggressive raps could feel impish, his beginner's boasts and disarmingly juvenile sexuality betraying his age. "Parents mad at my ass 'cause their kids sing my song in class," Yachty warbled. He may have looked like Sideshow Bob, but he played the role of Bart Simpson. His fellow teens ate it up.

In late 2015, when Yachty's warped bubblegum-trap ditties like "One Night" and "Minnesota"—in which he brags about spending $8,000 on a lawyer to get him off on the credit card charges—were starting to snowball online, Yachty's father, Shannon, reached out to an old rap industry contact for some help.

"I hadn't talked to Shannon in a minute," Coach K said later. But when he saw a message from the photographer—"Dude, my son is blowing up and it's getting out of hand"—Coach was immediately curious. "I was like, 'I love high school sports—what high school does he play for? I want to go watch him play.'"

"Nah," Shannon clarified, "he don't play sports. Have you ever heard of Lil Yachty?"

Coach, of course, had heard of Lil Yachty. In fact he'd been looking for him for weeks. As part of the executive's constant drive to stay current, Coach often hosted dinner parties at his house with younger DJs and street A&Rs, where he provided the food and wine and they brought the music. When someone played him Yachty's SoundCloud experiments with some nervous caveats, Coach was immediately intrigued. "I like weird," he said. But once Coach saw the kid, he knew he had to have him.

Unbeknownst to his father, Yachty had also been trying his luck in Coach K's inbox. "I'm Yachty man I'm 18 and i rap. But I got the image and the sound boss! What 80% of the 'game' is missing. All I need is that correct 'push' ya know?" he wrote in a cold pitch. "I know your the guy to help me prosper."

When Coach finally went to meet Yachty in person, it was like all of his Atlanta connections were folding in on each other, leaving small-town coincidences to feel like fate. In addition to going way back with Shannon, Yachty's mother, Venita, like Coach, was from Indiana, and the two had actually been college classmates at Saint Augustine's in North Carolina.

Coach vowed to take Yachty on as a management client. But it was more than that for the executive—Yachty represented a special project outside of the trap mold, a vehicle for the exact Atlanta eccentricities that Coach had long fostered but never successfully launched on a mass scale. "You've got this freakish look," he said, "but he's not scared of who he is."

P was skeptical at first. But with enough plays of "Minnesota" in his car, he would eventually dub Lil Yachty's decidedly not-hard songs to be hard enough, if only because they were so different. In its ability to polarize rap purists, Yachty's music was not unlike "Bando" and "Versace" had been a few years earlier. "He's not a street cat," Coach admitted of his oddball client. "But, in the streaming world and online, his credibility was real—he was authentic."

He was also endlessly marketable. "Rappers don't have endorsements because of their images," Yachty said early in his rise. "Endorsement money is huge. And I care about my character." Coach had a plan.

Over the next two years, Lil Yachty, who subsisted almost entirely on Domino's pepperoni pizza, candy and cookies, would release popular mixtapes like *Lil Boat* and *Summer Songs 2*. He even reached the *Billboard* top 10 with his taffy-like digital wails and cartoon melodies. But more important, he became a cultural phenomenon and generational lightning rod, pissing off critics and fellow artists with his stated indifference toward the catalogs of Tupac and the Notorious BIG. Yet even as Yachty became the poster child for a style-over-substance new school dismissively dubbed "mumble rap"—a catchall pejorative also leveled at Migos and other Southern artists who favored the outré over old-school lyricism—he collected more endorsements than hit songs. He modeled for Kanye West's Yeezy line at Madison Square Garden, starred in a Sprite commercial with LeBron James and teamed up with Nautica and Urban Outfitters, Target and Chef Boyardee, while also actively seeking out movie and TV deals. With Coach and P in his corner, Yachty vowed to become the next Will Smith.

Along with bringing a younger audience to Quality Control, Yachty's development allowed Coach K to hit the pavement all over again like he'd done in his early days. The executive even rode with Yachty in a van on a twenty-five-city, mosh-pit-heavy tour that served for Coach as a nightly marketing focus group for hip-hop youth culture. "It was a pivotal time to do that, right after everything was switching" in the industry, Coach said. "As soon as I got off that tour, we put out 'Bad and Boujee,' which was the first Migos record we put on SoundCloud."

The specifics of QC's deal with Capitol and Motown, meanwhile, allowed Coach and P to function independently as they always had back in Atlanta. They could develop a pool of embryonic artists at will, for little cost and at their own speed. But they also had the ability to "upstream" an act into the major-label system when they felt like they had one who was ready to blow up and deserved a big-league promotional budget. Lil Yachty signed officially with Quality Control and Capitol Records in June 2016, receiving a hefty personal advance that, per industry contract norms, he'd have to earn back for the companies before he would see any profits from his recordings. But by January of the next year—before releasing an official album—Yachty had recouped the entire cost of his deal. "That's unheard of," Coach said.

Teenage Emotions, Yachty's proper debut for Capitol, would ultimately be met with a broad critical "meh," selling just 46,000 copies in its first week in the spring of 2017. But critical acclaim—and even album sales—was not the point. Lil Yachty had made, according to his backers, $13 million in sixteen months. "Brands last longer than songs," Coach said. "I tell every artist when we sign 'em—I'm real with 'em—'You have an expiration date on you as an artist. Let's turn you into a brand.'"

Yachty's success in that realm also cemented QC's worth to Capitol, proving that the Atlanta label could mint another superstar—and an atypical one, at that—from scratch. Now, in a notoriously "What have you done for me lately?" business, all QC had to do was do it all over again with Lil Baby.

Back in the studio at the label headquarters, with the deadline for Baby's upcoming mixtape punted for the moment, Quay queued the rapper's new songs from various unorganized Gmail attachments. P took notes on his phone, jotting down track titles, as well as the producers who'd need to be compensated, while Coach vibed on a nearby couch with his eyes closed. "You got fifteen songs that's stuck in my head," P told Baby. "They're hard as hell."

The tape, not coincidentally, would be called *Too Hard*, following Baby's earlier releases *Harder Than Hard* and *2 the Hard Way*. In Atlanta, everything good was *hard*, and often just that—*hard*—with no additional descriptors necessary. But even with the encouragement, Baby seemed uncomfortable with what he was hearing and soon turned petulant, decrying his new songs as old.

"It ain't old if nobody's heard it!" P laughed.

Coach, with a grown man's serenity, added: "Every artist, their newest song is their best song—'*I'm on this new wave!*'"

In fact, the unreleased music represented Baby's best and most introspective songs yet, his complexity as a lyricist and songwriter sharpening into a distinct point of view. Prison, he explained on one track, had made him a better version of himself even as it haunted him: "I can't get no job, I got too many felonies / I been on probation since I was like seventeen," he rapped, delivering rough stories in little flutters of melody, balancing his newfound confidence with world-weariness, and vice versa. "Last year I was sittin' in a cage, this year I'm going all the way," Baby promised on another song before jerking back toward reality: "Taking drugs, trying to ease the pain." P, visibly energized by the somber number, announced that it would work perfectly as the intro to the mixtape.

But Baby wasn't having it. "That's an outro, if anything," he said.

"Listen," P shot back, making the case that every Atlanta street rapper had emotional opening tracks. "Go back to Jeezy—I'mma send you some intros. Then you just go hard on the next one."

Baby still seemed unconvinced.

"You're getting overruled on this one," P said, ending the discussion. "Have I told you anything wrong yet?"

LATER, IN THE driver's seat of his dark-maroon Maybach, P gestured to Baby's swollen pockets in the passenger seat, as if to explain his charge's hard head. "This is why it's so hard for us to stay on track," he said, palming the stacks of twenties and hundreds that had been crawling out of Baby's pockets as if seeking a breeze. "This is real—this is his life," P said, making meaningful eye contact with me through the rearview mirror. "I'm trying to get him to transition from this. He walks around like this every day."

The three of us were sitting in the parking lot of Magic City, anticipating some wings and seafood from a menu that was as legendary as the women inside. It was not yet 6 p.m. on a Wednesday. "I'm telling him like, yeah, you can go get that fast money right now, but you got to get older and put yourself in the safe zone," P said, gesticulating with the loose cash. "Sometimes he gets frustrated because he doesn't understand."

Finally, Baby was starting to see some real money from rap. But he still referred to the ever-increasing sums as if they were equal to a minimum-wage fast-food check. "I'm going to pick up ten thousand dollars for a show," Baby said, "or seventy-five hundred dollars, eight thousand dollars, but I can sit here and don't gotta go nowhere and make twenty, thirty, forty, fifty thousand dollars." He didn't mention the drugs that would have to change hands to make that so, but he didn't have to.

"You got to trust the process," P said in rebuttal. "It's fast money, but there's a lot that comes with it. Stay in the safe zone. Just trust the process. You really gotta have patience. Man, I been sacrificing for five years. I'm really used to a certain lifestyle. But I got dreams and goals.

"I learned this from my pastor—your breakthrough comes from the sacrifices you make. You got to be willing to give up something to get your blessings in life. I know you're getting a lot of money. But if you put your full time and effort into this—I know it's not what you're used to—the reward will be greater at the end."

I asked Baby, who was tucked deep into a bright yellow hoodie, as if it protected him from lectures he'd heard before, if he found P's logic at all convincing. "You don't hear nothing, you know what I'm saying?" Baby said, letting loose a waterfall of brutal honesty even as his musical benefactor sat inches away. "You have to see it and go through it. I've been in it now, like, a good six months. I ain't going to lie—I be like fifteen percent knowing.

"Some days I get frustrated—*P, I don't want to hear that shit. Fuck that. I ain't going.* But I think about it and I look around—I'm living in the best of both worlds right now. I'm still seeing what goes on in the hood every day, and I'm still involved every day. And I'm still in the process of becoming a superstar. Both roads. *Which way do you want to go?*"

By this point, Baby was basically arguing with himself. "I done been through all the bad parts of the streets," he said. "I've been to prison, seventeen years old—level-five prison, the worst kind you can go to. Shootouts, I done watched my bros die. I've been through all that. You know what I'm saying? I ain't never had nothing good in life.

"But now I'm seeing there's actually something good. On the road, people know who I am, people chanting my song, girls willing to do whatever for you."

He knew prison loomed heavy over the other path. "Even though it sounds like, *Okay, duh*. But it's hard to transition. I've been rapping for six months, but I've been in the streets heavy for like twelve years straight. So it's like, I'm already stuck on this path, versus I'm trying to get on this other path. But I be telling P, I'm a money-over-everything type of n——. So, like, once I start getting the money for real out of rap, I don't care. Game's over with. It's more about the money with me."

And it wasn't only P on his back. "Artists like Thug sometimes try to give me ten thousand dollars to leave the hood and go to the studio for a week," Baby said. "I don't take it."

Yet even just hearing himself talk through it, something seemed to click, like Baby was convincing himself by talking about being unconvinced. "I ain't going to lie, I'm transforming," he said. "Like right now, P talking about a meeting at two o'clock with you—I don't really care about that. I'd rather be in the hood. But I made myself. My phone's been ringing uncontrollably." Baby pulled out his cell phone and scrolled through the missed calls—old friends luring him back.

"I ain't did it," he said. "I'm with P.

"Prison helped me. Right now, I would've called me a ride, go to the hood. But now I'm starting to build this patience. God got something else for me. I need to be with P. Ain't no telling what's going on in the hood right now, what I could be going into. I look at P as a savior. Everything he tries to do to get me away from the hood, that shit saved me. I don't know what's going on. Twelve could be about to hit my little spot right now—and if I'm at Magic with P? I'm gonna be so happy.

"I'm getting through it," Baby said. "Slowly, but surely, I'm getting through it. I'm getting through it. I'm getting through it. I'm definitely getting through it, though. Definitely.

"But I ain't going to lie and tell you, *Yeah, I'm there*. I ain't going to lie." He exhaled, and then he followed P into the empty strip club.

PART II

13.

RAP DREAMS

ALL ACROSS ATLANTA IN THE 2010S, EVERYDAY KIDS WERE CATCHing rap dreams. Like the songs coming out of the city, these dreams could be contagious—viral, even—and there was a practical component to their spread: once one was achieved, the ability to put other people on, to give friends and collaborators a chance, was a built-in perk. Everyone knew someone who was bubbling—or else they knew someone who knew someone. They'd seen it with their own eyes.

As unlikely as the odds might be on paper to really make it in music, the Atlanta essence hung so heavy in the air during these days—and had wafted so far beyond the city's boundaries—that it could only feel like it made some practical sense to try to bottle that product for oneself. The chief export, after all, had its foundation in their own naturalness, the lives they were already living. To retain that authentic sense of self and place, to dress it up, drench it in melody and in bass, and then to monetize it—even the ugly parts—was to make the best of a bad hand. It was also fun, freeing and competitive, with local encouragement and rivalries each acting as an accelerant.

There was another business reality at play in the ubiquity of fledgling rap careers at this time, too: When something from somewhere specific was proving valuable in the music industry, there were always more prospectors inclined to show up and start digging. Luckily, Atlanta had no shortage of gems.

A FEW MONTHS before Tyrek Curry signed his first major record deal, he graduated from high school in size-five Prada sneakers with a Velcro strap. The ceremony, which preceded *The Graduation*, his first independent mixtape, by a couple of weeks, was held on a late May day with cartoon clouds in a sweltering Clayton County church south of the airport, at the bottom of Atlanta. Though fewer than fifty kids from Life Christian Academy School of Performing Arts were walking across the stage that day representing the class of 2018—girls in yellow gowns, boys in green—both levels of the stuffy building were packed with friends and family amped on the occasion. Their excitement sent the imposing digits on the upstairs thermostat from eighty-one to eighty-five in a matter of minutes. Certain men came prepared, draping washcloths over shaved heads in a futile attempt to keep their shirts crisp. Most accepted the moisture as inevitable.

Tyrek, whom everyone knew as Lil Reek, or just Reek, stood out for his size, or lack thereof. Even among the adults-in-progress, he appeared Doogie Howser–like—tinier but more magnetic than any person onstage, student or otherwise. Including the bubbled white soles of his designer sneakers, Reek would've needed his toes to top five feet, and a three-digit weight seemed like a stretch. At eighteen, he looked closer to ten years old than twenty.

Yet around those who knew him best, Reek's physicality, while striking, went all but unremarked upon. He would cop to being short every so often—"It taught me to really be humble and how to carry myself," he once said—but little was mentioned about his stature outside of his occasional reminders that he was not to be fucked with in spite of it. The exact science behind his body—possibly a hormone disorder—did not seem important to his friends or his girlfriends. It was no one's business, really, and beyond his vitamin regimen, Reek was a typical teenager. Besides, in the line of work he aspired to, any shortcut to standing out could be considered an asset.

By the time of Reek's high school graduation, those paying close attention to Atlanta's overflowing talent pool—or the corners of the rap internet dedicated to magnifying it—might have recognized him, novel as he was, as a prospect. In the universe of aspiring rappers, where every artist who makes it big transmits that what-if bug to a handful of those around them, Reek had a special vantage: he had been on the periphery of fame enough times to make it feel not only possible but likely. And it wasn't just proximity; Reek had the unsnuffable star gene, too.

In his first taste of notoriety beyond his neighborhood, Reek became a character with recurring cameos in the Snapchat videos of the once-popping New Jersey rapper Fetty Wap. On trips down south years prior, Fetty leaned into the visual absurdity of allowing Reek to drive his BMW i8, the childlike teenager's neck craned in order to see over the steering wheel. Some online incorrectly assumed that when Fetty referred to Reek as his "little bro," that meant biologically. Nonetheless, the famously one-eyed rapper bragged about his pocket-sized companion as the "smartest n—— in the goddamn school, man—and he got money." For Reek, it wasn't a bad place to start.

Though still anonymous as an artist in his own right, Reek received more visibility a few years later with an equally jarring cameo in Lil Baby's breakthrough music video. "My Dawg," which would be seen by millions, including many record executives, may have been packed with undiscovered Atlanta talent, but Reek again stood out. Immediately arresting among the dozens of other young men gathered, a baby-faced Reek first appears flashing four fingers—for Baby's Zone 4–residing 4 Pockets Full crew—in a slow-motion establishing shot. Later, he's shown again, furtively passing off a handgun while making ever-skeptical eye contact with the camera—and by extension the viewer—daring anyone to wonder about the details of his life. The subject of an almost excessive number of close-ups framing his cherubic visage, Reek pops up once more in a final upward pan. He is shirtless, with a leather holstered weapon tucked against his Hanes behind the zipper of his tiny pants. A lollipop peeks out from his pocket and Reek grips an ice-cream sandwich with a bite missing. In a few brief frames, he can't help but steal the show.

Reek never claimed to be part of Baby's 4PF, and he never played up his other associations with anyone who had their own thing going. But he and Baby both heavily overlapped with the extended Southwest Atlanta network of Young Thug, the influential rap eccentric who birthed a hundred local imitators. Before Thug's YSL—for Young Slime Life, as a clique, or Young Stoner Life, as a company—was a rap brand or a proper record label, it was a loose but loyal neighborhood crew (plus imitator offshoots) of young men who called one another "slime," guys who might get one over on you while wearing the coolest sneakers and skinniest jeans imaginable. Reek was raised at first around Zone 3's Dill Avenue, not far from Baby's Oakland City and West End stomping grounds in Zone 4. But after moving a few I-85 exits south with his mother while in middle school, he came up as a rookie rapper in the Young Thug–stamped strip of a neighborhood known as Cleveland Avenue, for its main corridor, in the southwest suburb of East Point.

Far from the most basic understanding of a tough urban neighborhood, Cleveland Ave. is leafy and dotted with little hills. The opposite of crowded, it maintains the tired vibe of a small town, its activity centered around a loose constellation of gas stations, strip malls and a standalone Checkers, with modest family homes tucked away in cul-de-sacs and ungated subdivisions off the main road. A well-known little brother figure around the neighborhood, Reek could often be found outside the Chevron or the wing spot in the company of older men, an obvious diamond in their midst. Even in a small circle, his unique beauty and spark plug energy made his potential feel boundless.

In 2018, Reek employed the same outrage-baiting collision of apparent innocence and vérité street life that he embodied in the "My Dawg" video for his own proper debut as a rapper. The music video for "Rock Out," Reek's sneering first single, pushed that dynamic to an artistic extreme, offering authenticity and creativity in equal measure, and its originality would set a nearly insurmountable standard for his future work. It also got him noticed.

In the video, which is edited more like a short film, Reek is seen in grimy handheld footage once again behind the too-large steering wheel of somebody else's car, rapping in a raspy squeal about gunplay over a horror-movie beat. He appears shirtless on a boxing gym stationary bike, ribs protruding; in night vision with a grimace alongside a jaws-open boa constrictor named Cupcake; dancing maniacally on empty train tracks;

and intermittently donning a satanic goat mask with a broad grin—an Atlanta teenager as a Harmony Korine wet dream, bugging his eyes to deliver sucker-punch lines like, "You a little bitch when I pull this Glock out / Let's see how fast you gon' run your fucking mouth."

When "Rock Out" dropped, without context and thanks to a few pulled strings on the all-purpose, cross-platform rap clearinghouse WorldStarHipHop, no one knew how exactly to receive what was being served to them. The video could have just as easily resulted in a call to child services as in a major-label deal. Peeling back the layers only led to more intrigue. Behind the video was Kim Chapiron, a French filmmaker who in 2010 made a movie about a juvenile detention center in Montana. The link between the disparate worlds of Reek's Cleveland Ave. and France's art house exports was another unlikely Atlanta interloper—Louis Rogé, a Paris-based DJ and producer known as Brodinski.

"I needed to vouch for Kim on Reek's side and vouch for Reek on Kim's side," Brodinski said in the back row of the second-floor balcony at Reek's high school graduation, recalling how he'd brokered the guerrilla-style video shoot. "I was taking a risk on both sides."

Slim, tattooed and stylish, usually in tight all-black ensembles, Brodinski—Brodi for short and Louie to friends on either side of the Atlantic—could have passed for a French actor. In fact, he represented a benevolent version of another common hip-hop archetype: the white ambassador—usually a writer, DJ, producer, designer or executive, who at various points in the genre's jagged commercial development had helped take rap to different places in the popular consciousness out of some combination of self-interest, artistic commitment and opportunism. At the graduation, as in many of his Atlanta exploits, Brodinski—like me—was one of the only non-Black people in the room. He'd promised Reek he would be there, and he came through, flying in from Europe for the occasion.

The cofounder of the electronic label Bromance, which rode the early 2010s dance-music boom to international notoriety, Brodinski, a native of Reims, in northeastern France, had entered the hip-hop hierarchy at its highest level: alongside Daft Punk, he lent abrasive, bespoke industrial sounds to Kanye West's stripped-raw 2013 masterpiece *Yeezus*. It was only from there that Brodinski worked backward, sliding happily down the rap totem pole into the Georgia mud, choosing to cash in his musical credibility after *Yeezus* in the streets of Atlanta, where star power was thought to be as common as Chick-fil-A.

Once on the ground, the producer found himself further inspired by rap's instinctual songwriting and creative risk-tasking, and he recruited artists like iLoveMakonnen, Bloody Jay and Peewee Longway for his first solo album, *Brava*, in 2015. The next year, Brodinski doubled down on his new locale, setting up shop in more Atlanta studios and scoring early songs with local talent like the cousins Young Nudy and 21 Savage, a morose, deadpan rapper from Glenwood Road in DeKalb County, who would soon become an unlikely crossover superstar (and be revealed, in an even less likely twist, as an "unlawfully present United Kingdom national" when he was arrested by ICE for overstaying a childhood visa just ahead of the 2019 Super Bowl in Atlanta).

Brodinski wasn't just pilfering from the Atlanta coffers as a tourist. "I'm here to try to build something," he said in 2017. To him, that meant spending more of his EDM money to record and release little-heard mixtapes with fledgling rappers from forsaken neighborhoods. He successfully plugged himself into Atlanta's always-overlapping social and musical networks by putting in endless hours of good vibes and strong beats—trap with a French accent, adding an analog, idiosyncratic techno feel to the established sound. "It's the most creative and open-minded place I've been to," Brodinski said at Reek's graduation. "Rap is the most important music in the world—and it's still weird."

Yet even as he tapped in early with Atlanta artists, the French producer yearned for fresher material to help mold. It was Brodinski—not Young Thug or Lil Baby—who first encouraged Lil Reek to really try rapping. Despite being born with a performer's twinkle, Reek had only rhymed playfully at school and with his older cousins, and he barely thought of music as a creative pursuit, let alone a career. "I didn't know who the hell Brodinski was," Reek said. "At that time, I didn't even know what the hell a producer was."

But a DJ, photographer and blogger known as Drug Money, another white guy with an outsider's ear to the Cleveland Ave. pavement, "used to come through the hood with his camera," Reek recalled, and soon he was recruiting neighborhood kids to go record. "I'm like, 'Shit, boy, I ain't got no money, no weed, no nothing,'" Reek said. "I ain't finna go down there with no producer from Paris."

But as more of his friends took the fish-out-of-water Frenchman up on his offer of free recording time (plus the obligatory snacks and weed) at studios like Stankonia, the storied home of OutKast, Reek found himself drawn into their orbit. "I ended up doing my research on him, seeing who he was, ended up fucking with him," he said. "I followed the trail, which definitely paid off." Reek had even taken some French in school, and upon meeting Brodinski, he greeted him in the producer's native tongue: "*Bonjour, comment ça va?*"

Using this parade of eager teenagers with stories to tell, Brodinski and Drug Money put together a free mixtape, *Young Slime Season*, featuring a crew whose ages hovered somewhere around fifteen. In a statement announcing the project, Drug Money described the music as "a look into the unrest, the urgency of survival, and the bonds of friendship that are forged when young people from the proverbial jungle grow up with nothing to rely on but themselves and each other." Most had never made music before, and some of the boys were forced to come up with rap names on the spot. Reek appeared on just one song, but his nimble, melodic verse on an otherwise unremarkable track called "Money" showed serious potential as he stretched his syllables and bounced from bar to bar, declaring, "I pull up, I dip and I dab / I got *moooooney*." Even on a first attempt, his dynamism was undeniable.

Reek and Brodinski came out of the experience with a true bond. The producer, in his role as a label owner, had a scout's eye for the intangibles that could make a young artist really pop. And Reek realized quickly that it was a once-in-a-lifetime chance to have someone in his corner who was so engaged and intent on giving back in exchange for whatever he was taking culturally. "He developed my sound and the whole rap melody and all that," Reek said. "Other producers, to them, it's just a beat. To him, that shit is a piece of art—like Picasso. He know every beep, bop, beep to that motherfucker."

In addition to producing Reek's "Rock Out"—one of Brodinski's finest and most chaotic compositions—the producer would also work his connections for the ambitious teenager as he neared the end of high school. Through a mutual associate who worked at WorldStar, Brodinski set Reek up with a makeshift manager—another producer known as Roger Beat who lived in Washington, DC, but had worked with Gucci Mane and was well connected in Atlanta—insisting that the young rapper at least needed someone in the same time zone. Brodinski also gave Reek a crash course on the business, breaking down how to make a budget for a release and explaining concepts like distribution (the middleman companies that used to get CDs into stores but now mostly just make songs available across streaming services online) and publishing (the process by which songwriters are paid for their compositions, separate from the actual recorded music).

"It's my turn to help," Brodinski said. "I'm not here for me."

Like a good big brother, the producer encouraged Reek's studies, as well, and he often bragged about his young charge's grades. Reek had ended up at Life Christian Academy after being expelled from public school for what he brushed off as "some bullshit." A small, Black-run private school, the academy billed itself as a place that could handle students with behavioral issues or "academic obstacles" from Atlanta's "under-resourced neighborhoods." But Reek still supplemented whatever financial assistance he received from the school with some small-time hustling, spending most of his extracurricular hours around an illicit subterranean enterprise known as the Donut Shop, a trap where Reek fell under the tutelage of a mentor known as Big Jack Racks. Reek credited Racks with making sure he didn't drop out of school and commit to street life full-time. "If it wasn't for him, there wouldn't be no me right now," he said. "He really made sure I did what I had to do."

At the same time, through his proximity to both poverty and the drug dealing that could be its cause and its cure, Reek dedicated himself at an early age to an American tradition, the one he rapped about on his first track: getting money. Legitimate employment hardly felt like an option for Reek and his friends. By twelve, Reek had bought his first handgun from a kid he knew for $200, and he started smoking weed soon after, falling in with the neighborhood hustlers. "I was out here going with the flow—doing whatever the people around me were doing, trying to get some money," he said. "That's all my mind was set on: a bag!" As a preteen, Reek tried working under the table at the corner store, stocking drinks. But even then, he knew a service role wasn't for him. "I wasn't fucking with that working-no-job shit," Reek explained. "I need everyday money. Can't wait." He vowed to never take orders from anybody else: "I'm the boss."

Still, it was obvious to the adults around him that Reek had real potential in many arenas not limited to entertainment. He was a good student, taking to language, history and science, and he had a giddy curiosity about the world. Reek liked to read, and he was liable to spelunk down a YouTube rabbit hole on his iPhone, coming up with trivia about volcanos, deadly pink algae, Pangaea or the origins of wasabi. In college, he planned to study business and marketing.

Reek's early songs were at their best when he weaved in the full breadth of his life as a high schooler, letting violence, gloating and academic requirements coexist. On "Rock Out," he rapped about having to pay his "motherfuckin' senior *duuuuues*," while mentioning his pistol ("my motherfuckin' tool") and rhyming that with a non sequitur that also functioned as a novel crow: "Yes, bitch, I love going to school."

When it came time to release the music video, Brodinski arranged for "Rock Out" to premiere on WorldStar that March. (Hosting a video on the site could run a rapper about $3,000, give or take, depending on the strength of their connections.) But while WorldStar guaranteed a built-in audience for an entirely unknown artist, it was not a cerebral one. "He looks like a damn alien," one commenter wrote of Reek. "Hes gonna get kicked out of preschool if his teachers see this," said another. "Only in America lol."

Brodinski compared it to the Roman Colosseum. "His mom was like, 'Oh, I read *ze* comments and they're crazy,'" the producer recalled in his exchange-student English at Reek's graduation. "But it's like putting you in *ze* biggest arena in the world. It's like ancient times, when people would fight in front of 20,000 people—that's WorldStar. And all of the ones that are commenting are dumb as *sheeet.*

"It's a *sheet*-ton of people not liking it," Brodinski added, "but at least they saw it."

For Reek, that reach was enough, and those in the digital peanut gallery questioning his age, his gender or why a small child was driving and smoking weed were easy enough to ignore. The video would go on to top a million views. "I just felt like I was worth a million after that video, for real," he said.

The industry's curiosity was piqued as well. Reek's emergence online coincided perfectly with the boom moment in the business, as rap became a growing focus for the major labels. And for those chasing viral moments, Reek occupied the heart of a Venn diagram between novelty, talent and realness, a crucial nexus in the nascent rap streaming economy. In May, the month he was set to graduate high school—and only two months after the release of "Rock Out"—Reek flew to New York City for his first round of business meetings. Even that close to the academic finish line, and with labels eager for access to him, he didn't want to miss any classes, so Reek limited his big-city schmoozing to a weekend. Roger, his reserved and unpolished manager, had enough industry knowledge to maneuver the ladder's lower rungs, and he served as Reek's chaperone and representative. They had known each other about a month.

For any budding regional artist, an early-career trip to New York or LA is typically an awkward handshake tour with low-level executives and members of the media who have been closely watching WorldStar or its competitors. An office visit—a *We'll keep an eye on you* nod of affirmation—could be the extent of it, or maybe there's content to be made. If you're lucky, a YouTube channel with a focus on emerging artists might ask you a few questions on camera. If you have a song or music video gaining some traction online—or if a member of your inner circle is already a known quantity—maybe label A&Rs (those responsible for finding new signings) might want to hear a few unreleased tracks. And if a prominent artist from your hometown has already appeared on your songs, shown up in your music videos or even just followed you on Instagram, that counts as an advantage. By the time you get to the contract stage, which could happen in a matter of hours or days, even those small advantages turn into leverage. Leverage means more money.

Lil Reek, though intriguing, especially in a seller's market, still needed more material to prove that "Rock Out" was not just a one-off. So after a few introductory meetings around town, Roger set up an impromptu showcase at a midtown Manhattan recording studio that could prove the rapper's legitimacy beyond YouTube while also building up his catalog of music. Scouts from Def Jam and Republic Records, two of the largest major labels, promised to stop by.

Along with a photographer and a videographer to capture social media content, Roger brought along a friend and potential co-manager for Reek. A portly white guy with a Caesar haircut and an outer-borough accent, he introduced himself as C. Another aspiring executive, a New Yorker known as Birdman Zoe, in a tribute to his Haitian heritage, posted up on the couch nearby. Eventually, the label reps showed up, too, taking it all in from opposite corners of the room. No one wanted to seem too eager.

As Reek started to record, C ran through the business possibilities that were already springing up around the teenager. "It's happening super fast, but it's an organic process," he said, warning that all sorts of people were starting to sniff around the emerging Lil Reek market. "People want to attach themselves to it if they feel there's money to be made." C's own vision for Reek's career included building an independent operation with a small team, running up the numbers on social media and then seeking investment from a label when the time was right—and the price tag appropriately high. "We'll do the independent thing—I have enough money to cover it—because I believe it'll make me tenfold down the line," he said.

"Any deal we do, they've gotta pay for his full education," C added. "Reek said that—'They gotta pay for my college!' Smart kid."

Even based on a single meeting, Republic seemed like the most promising corporate partner, according to C. "I almost feel like this kid's on his own, that's why I want to expedite things," he explained, all of a sudden less interested in playing the long game. He noted that Reek's paying his way through private school by doing a little trapping on the side was "a sick backstory."

"Roger, what you think?" Reek shouted from the booth after making some headway on a song.

"That's the hook right there," Roger said.

Even the engineer was vibing as Reek picked up steam. "Now she's in the moment," the engineer said from behind the computer in the control room. "Now she's got it."

Roger shook his head, laughing. "That's a boy," he said. "He's eighteen."

Reek, encased in the recording booth, didn't seem to notice as he sipped tea and fielded a call from his mom back home.

"GOOD AFTERNOON—LET ME say praise the lord, everybody. Praise. The. Lord. Every. Body."

The Life Christian Academy graduation speaker, a faculty member from a Southern Baptist college, roused the crowd before the diplomas were awarded. "You are not at a jail, you are not at court, you are not at a funeral," she boomed. "You are at a graduation. So we have reason to celebrate."

She led those gathered in a call-and-response affirmation. "I am. (*I am!*) Good. (*Good!*) I am. (*I am!*) Better. (*Better!*) I am. (*I am!*) Best. (*Best!*) I am. (*I am!*) Above the rest. (*Above the rest!*)"

When Reek crossed the stage to accept his diploma, he dabbed, nestling his tiny, delicately featured face into his elbow crease to loud cheers. Up in the crowd, Brodinski beamed, and he greeted Reek's family and friends, who thanked the producer for everything he'd done.

Out in the sweltering parking lot, which was still less humid than the church, Lil Baby songs blared from the cars of kids and their parents alike. Reek pinballed from group to group, exchanging hugs and hand slaps, posing for photos and grinning ear to ear, his bow tie hanging loose. Brodinski hung back, waiting politely for his turn to hug the graduate. But when the producer finally caught his eye, Reek rushed over for an embrace before quickly being pulled in another direction by still more joyful friends.

"I love you, bro!" Reek yelled to the Frenchman on his way back through the parking-lot crowd.

"I love you, too!" Brodinski volleyed back.

"Studio session tonight!" Reek shouted over his shoulder, his shiny green gown flapping in the breeze.

14.

PARTNERS

AROUND THE CITY, IF NOT THE COUNTRY, IT DIDN'T TAKE LONG before both P and Coach K had earned themselves the title of OG—the now fully co-opted term, once only short for *original gangster*, that bestows a lifetime's worth of respect on a person for his past victories and also his foibles. As such, upon Quality Control's arrival as an established label, the pair was treated with recognizable reverence by most everyone they encountered in their daily lives, from preteens to major-label presidents, although they leaned into their elevated status as local celebrities and rap kingmakers with different energies.

Coach, with his full, snowy beard grown out a few inches from his chin and a now-bald head gleaming above it, had the debonair essence of a gallery owner or architect in good sneakers, glad-handing when he needed to but more often receiving the ring-kisses. He presented the open posture of a modern Zen master from the school of Phil Jackson, hands back or by his sides, confident and seen-it-all in his standing. P was about a decade Coach's junior but more youthful still, even as he towered over him. He preferred the crossed arms, jutted chin and tense shoulders of someone playing both offense and defense simultaneously, his weary eyes never still, always in room-scanning mode.

Both men carried some version of the bountiful middle-age belly, though Coach, who often ate vegan, was known to be up by 8 a.m. to swim laps. Each dressed flashily in his own way, with Coach favoring the couture and internationally chic streetwear boutiques of a self-proclaimed urban aesthete; P, with his wider frame, opted for greater glamour when not in refined dope-boy mode, like neck-open, four-figure designer dress shirts by Versace or Louis Vuitton. P was more likely to wear a chain or two—CEO, read one of his smaller pieces in bubble letters—and Coach a plain T-shirt that was obviously still expensive. Both, however, would gladly rock a run-of-the-mill hoodie if it plugged a brand they owned, like QC, or one they might as well have, like Magic City.

A smile from P was not easy to earn—as rare among strangers as a sun shower. When he did break, it might still not include teeth, but Coach, whose caterpillar eyebrows usually betrayed his mood, was quicker to offer a full set of pearly whites when thrilled by music or money talk. Both men had the sense to only speak when they really had something to say. Both carried two cell phones at once, minimum. Neither liked to be run up on, surprised, caught off guard. Both had bullet scars on their legs.

"They're like *Bad Boys*—P is Martin Lawrence and Coach is Will Smith," said Simone Mitchell, one of the two women who kept the Quality Control trains running on time from the office attached to their studios—booking flights and hotels and appearances, keeping track of everything on a color-coded whiteboard, with one marker for each main act on the roster. Tamika Howard, Quality Control's sunny but stern general manager and Simone's boss, agreed. "P is the street one, Coach is the suave one," she said. "Yin and yang, but it's the perfect match." More of a known quantity than his partner in the boardrooms of New York and Los Angeles, Coach tended to politick upward on behalf of QC and its artists, while P kept his ear to the concrete, working his donlike connections at the intersection where the subterranean street-level business of rap edged up against its burgeoning corporate concerns.

One afternoon in the fall of 2017, in Coach's slate gray Range Rover, I had watched the executive field a series of overlapping phone calls, each of which sounded profitable. In barely twenty minutes, with the beep of another intruding call interrupting every conversation, Coach agreed to approve a Quavo feature on another artist's song ("We clear our own records"); negotiated the filming of a potential QC documentary ("Here comes the question: are they going to own it? We can shoot our shit ourself, but let's set that call up"); discussed producing a movie with Queen Latifah; asked for more money to expand Lil Yachty's endorsement deal with Nautica; and, in the exchange that got him most visibly charged up, brainstormed ideas for a televised wedding special starring Offset, who was in the midst of becoming a gossip-page leading man. "Fox is where we need to be!" Coach told the guy on the other line. "*Shiiiit*—fuck BET!"

As Migos settled into superstardom, the trio's once-combustible wild card had entered into a much-speculated-about relationship with a matching supernova—a surefire way to shore up rap celebrity. The object of Offset's affection was Cardi B, a former New York stripper and foul-mouthed social media sensation turned reality star and rapper, whose charisma could be said—without exaggeration—to match and contain elements of such disparate personality bombs as Lucille Ball and Spike Lee. That October, at a radio station concert in Philadelphia, Cardi, who had found her own "Bad and Boujee" in the number one song "Bodak Yellow," was performing with Migos when Offset snuck up behind her and got down on one knee. Arguably romantic, their public engagement was definitely pure savvy. A month earlier, the couple had gotten legally married in Fulton County as a spontaneous show of eternal commitment between numerous breakups and makeups. But private acts of devotion can be hard to sell against.

On the phone, Coach dreamed about airing Offset and Cardi's wedding extravaganza in between episodes of the music soap operas *Empire* and *Star*. "Everybody's calling me about this," he said. "*Ev-er-y-body*."

P, meanwhile, remained more comfortable with the ground troops. After years in the shadows as the deep-pocketed mystery Migos investor, he had only recently started to put himself out there as the Master P, Birdman or Suge Knight figure of his late-blooming hip-hop daydreams. He knew that 2018 would be boom times for Quality Control, street music and Atlanta in general, and he finally felt far enough from his imperfect past that missing out on celebrating the spoils in public would be unnecessary. P knew that he might never be able to outrun the streets entirely—nor would he want to. But his distance from them had started to feel safer.

P also knew that hip-hop was a streaky business—one in which it was easier to win if you've been winning. This was not some abstract idea of momentum but a quirk of the overlapping online-attention economy and rap patronage system of artist cosigns, which gave any hot rapper the ability and power to transfer some of that momentary heat to another affiliated artist of their choosing. LaFace spun the success of TLC into OutKast into Goodie Mob into solo careers. Jermaine Dupri turned Kris Kross into Lil Jon into Lil Bow Wow. Gucci Mane went from OJ da Juiceman to Waka Flocka Flame to Young Thug, Migos and so on. Rocko gave the world Future, who gave the world Young Scooter and his Freebandz affiliates, or at least tried to. One man came from the next, and for everyone who made it, dozens got closer, through blood and friendship, than they maybe had any right to. In other words, QC had the chance—with the trust of fans and also the ear of the corporate powers-that-be—to multiply its recent successes with Migos, Lil Yachty and Lil Baby and grow the label exponentially. Or as Coach and P would put it, to keep their proverbial foot on the necks of the competition.

"Other labels have these A&Rs and CEOs and chairmen, sitting in an office looking on the internet at numbers on SoundCloud and Spotify—they're just into the analytics," P said as his confidence grew. "That's part of it. But if I'm being honest—and it might sound ignorant—I don't own a computer. I'm really out here in it."

While hoping to expand the QC brand into television, film and fashion, the executives knew they needed to personally tend to their growing "farm team" of Atlanta talent, as well. Instead of chasing viral moments already in progress, like the majors, Coach and P passed out beginner's contracts and small cash advances (or just free studio time) to small handfuls of developing local artists who could then be activated when the market called for it—or when the label's elders finally found the time to really invest, hands-on, in new blood. With Baby now an auspicious rookie in the big leagues, the QC studios were hosting a revolving door of aspiring weirdos and gangsters like Mak Sauce, a hyper, willowy teenager who claimed to be from Saturn (but was really from SoundCloud) and clearly worshipped Young Thug, and Kollision, a thoughtful and polite young father with braces and kind eyes who rapped and sang interchangeably while taking Adderall pills to last all night in the studio.

While P and Coach loved all their artists in different ways, each according to need, there were clear passion projects among the bunch, which had swelled beyond the single digits, including those in preliminary development. Lil Yachty—that started as Coach's thing. Lil Baby and Migos split the difference. But Marlo, probably the label's thorniest prospect yet, was pure Pierre Thomas.

Even at twenty-seven, Marlo—born Rudolph Simmons Johnson IV and known to everyone before rap as Rudy, or Rude—was weathered in a way unique to those who grew up fast out of necessity and didn't blame anyone else for it. Instead, like P, he had internalized the unfairness of the world, pushing it down and to the side until it just looked like all-around hardness.

Marlo first met P when he showed up to support his friend Lil Baby at an early music video shoot. The executive had heard tell of the kid—"Atlanta really small, you hear about a lot of these guys"—and vice versa, but the two kindred spirits had never crossed paths. Baby, though, had come as something of a package deal for Quality Control, having decided to make music at the same time as Marlo, a child of the Bowen Homes projects off Bankhead on the West Side. Though they could have been rivals, hailing from different neighborhoods on the same side of town, Baby and Marlo were instead peers and partners—young leaders and street colleagues favored by the local OGs, pockets fat and toughness confirmed, a cavalcade of others falling in place around them. "He the man where he from, and I'm the man where I'm from," Marlo explained. "His name ring, my name ring."

Marlo, like Baby, was familiar to P, someone who made him feel comfortable and nostalgic. "That's Lil Baby right-hand man, he automatically my right-hand man," P said. "I ain't gotta do nothin' but see some potential. All of us come from the same background. I know the lifestyle. Ain't nobody growed up rich or nothin'. Everybody came from low income. I know what it's like trying to get out the hood, trying not to make the same mistakes and putting yourself in the position to go back to prison."

Immediately upon seeing Baby and Marlo together, P had flashed back to the early days of Migos and their always-present collaborators. "My vision was so big," he said. "I don't know them from a can of paint. But I just know they were with them and they rapped together. I had a studio—*Come on, I'mma sign y'all, too. Just get in there and work.*"

It wasn't long before P was giving Marlo the same spiels he gave to Baby. "Hey, the streets gon' always be there, you know what I'm saying? But it's got consequences," the executive said. "You don't gotta be the best rapper, you just have to have the work ethic. You might just fuck around and make a hit by mistake."

On any given day, in one of his many spaceshiplike sedans, P fielded his own versions of Coach K's phone calls. Somebody always needed something, and it was the responsibility of a manager and label CEO to provide, to negotiate and to show up. One afternoon that fall, Marlo was filming a music video and P wished to convey his enduring support. He whipped his Mercedes through Midtown congestion toward downtown, pulling off on Ted Turner Drive, near the CNN Center and Centennial Olympic Park, in the area of overgrown railway beds, abandoned buildings and parking lots known as the Gulch. Billions of dollars had recently been pledged to redevelop the postindustrial ghost town of a neighborhood, with a wave of gentrification occurring in the shadow of Mercedes-Benz Stadium, the new home of the Atlanta Falcons and Atlanta United soccer club, and the planned site of Super Bowl LIII in 2019. At the same time, the city's generous entertainment tax breaks and spacious, anonymous-enough landscape had turned it into "the Hollywood of the South," with productions from the Marvel Cinematic Universe to *The Walking Dead* calling Atlanta home.

Under a weathered awning reading SOUTHERN RAILWAY, ten young Black men in skinny jeans and designer sneakers or Timberland boots gathered near an expensive-looking camera. The eight-story former Norfolk Southern railroad office complex, a once-vibrant symbol of Atlanta's transportation past, had been gutted for more than a decade, but plans to turn it into luxury apartments and complementary commercial spaces were now under way. In the meantime, it was the perfect stretch of Atlanta-specific concrete on which to shoot a video.

In a Gucci T-shirt and constricted, cargo-pocketed blue jeans, with a faint, line-drawn cross and a friend serving life's initials tattooed between his eyes, Marlo did not immediately stand out as the star of the proceedings. At first, he wore just a single diamond chain reading PFK—the *K* in the form of a bejeweled AK-47. But when Lil Baby hopped out of his ride and placed three additional chains from his own neck over Marlo's head, P beamed at his protégés.

"Two words," P said of the pair. "Real Atlanta."

In between takes, Marlo said he was shocked by how easy it had been to be welcomed into the mix as a musician. He just hadn't expected the demands that came after. "I love they studio, I go there every day—eight o'clock, and I might not leave until eight in the morning," he said. "Then P is calling me soon as I'm closing my eyes: 'Marlo!' Like, bro, he be on you!

"I be like, 'All right, P, whatchu want me to do? I just left the studio, I'm laying down, can't I get some type of . . .' He's like, '*Shoot the video! Do this, do that!*' He a big inspiration, a real battery pack into me—he's gon' give you that push," Marlo said. "I love P like I been knowing him all my life. I be really just trying to show him—both of 'em," he said, gesturing to Coach, who had also pulled up to check in. "Whatever they say to do, I'mma do."

Behind them, the director called for a location switch before sunset, and P urged Marlo on. "Go catch as much light as you can," he said, soaking in the camaraderie as his charges dispersed and Marlo peeled off in the passenger seat of a doorless Jeep. "I'm just trying to give these dudes an opportunity," P added.

Even more than Baby, the executive knew that Marlo represented a special, specific archetype in the annals of Atlanta rap. He was not the blessed prince who seemed to float as he walked, not a natural for whom most things just clicked and who collected regard and admiration as if they were God-given. Instead, Marlo was a determined bruiser who, while cunning, could not help but make everything he had seem hard-earned. These were the types of Atlanta guys—Peewee Longway, OJ da Juiceman, Young Scooter, Fatman Key—who were not likely to scan immediately as superstars to a wider (or whiter) listening public. They might even end up forgotten. But their status in the city where they were raised was firm and indisputable, because they were soldiers, loyal comrades and proven enforcers—rappers not because of any innate ability or interest, per se, but because of neighborhood stature, sheer will and circumstance.

Marlo had attitude. His stories were vivid and his voice, like Baby's, was distinct—a wheezed squeal that worked as a vehicle for tragedy, for history, for warnings, vaunts and regrets in equal measure. But early on, his rapping was not impressively poetic, melodic or rhythmic, and his spoken nuggets of street wisdom and cleverness were often buried deep beneath a local dialect of slang and tics ("Like, *gatdamn* . . ."). He could be withdrawn, even shy. But it was Marlo who, while dipping his first toe into the rap game, insisted that his street counterpart Lil Baby do the same. Unlike Coach and P, who were easier for Baby to ignore at first, Marlo spoke to his friend not from the distant vantage of an elder, but as a peer with a similar knack for stacking fast cash through less legal means.

Marlo, too, had long resisted the call of the studio in favor of hustling, even as he heard the same refrain over and over again: *You have the swag, the money and the lifestyle—go claim what's yours*. He, too, had no shortage of rapper friends, having also grown up around budding stars like 21 Savage and Young Thug, not to mention the earlier Bankhead ambassadors who had cast a long shadow over the neighborhood, like Kilo Ali and Shawty Lo. Marlo loved Kevin Gates and Future, his go-to soundtrack for trapping, and he even had music in his blood. His father, who hailed from up north, once rapped as Philly Blunt; they had cousins, Roland and Karl Chambers, who were instrumental in forging Philadelphia's soul sound.

But it had taken a bit of misdirection for Marlo to finally record a song. Big Bank Black, a hefty street CEO with a mouth full of gold, was one of the many OGs from across Atlanta who had taken a shine to Marlo when he was just Young Rude with a reputation. Big Bank had made his name in the Zone 6 neighborhood of Edgewood, on the East Side, and had dabbled in music since nearly a decade earlier, founding the label Duct Tape Entertainment. But Bank's reputation in rap circles far outpaced his team's recorded output, and there wasn't a star from the city who hadn't crossed his desk, metaphorically speaking, at one point or another. A talent scout, a settler of disputes and a godfather to many young men who needed a distinct flavor of been-there guidance, Bank spent about a week straight pestering Marlo over the phone to try rapping. But failing to get through to him, Bank eventually just picked Marlo up and brought him to a studio without warning.

"If he would've said, *Bro, we finna go to the studio*, I would've stood his ass up," Marlo admitted. Even once they arrived and started listening to beats, Marlo assumed they were for someone else. "You got me fucked up," he told Bank. "I don't have to do that. I really am doing what they talking about. I got my spot *bucking*. I don't gotta rap."

Marlo didn't really know how to make music anyway, and he had no plans to embarrass himself. But a Percocet pill and some weed later, a relentless Big Bank managed to break him down. Marlo recalled finally getting in the booth, his inhibitions muted, and making his debut rap song using the same choppy, improvisational recording process he'd seen so many others pull off. The result was simple but not half-bad, as Marlo stuck to what he knew in a halting delivery: "Bitch wait, fuck a mixtape, I got plenty cake / Yeah, I'm rich and I'm pushing weight, that's why n——s hate."

"I told you, man," Big Bank said. "You a superstar."

That may have been an overstatement, but Marlo, appropriately gassed up, passed along the enthusiasm he was receiving to his ally. "I called Baby and I hit him with the same line," Marlo said. "'Bro, you need to get to the studio, I'm telling you! We got that swag, we got the cars, the jewelry, the money . . .'" The pair started collaborating soon after.

In October 2017, with Baby riding the high of his first two mixtapes, he and Marlo released a joint project via Quality Control called *2 the Hard Way*, a nod to rolling dice, which featured Marlo's first-ever track, "Set Up Shop," now with additional verses by Baby and Young Thug. The next month came Marlo's solo debut, *The Wire*, a reference to the HBO show from which most assumed he got his name. (In the crime drama about the Baltimore drug trade, Marlo Stanfield represented the most ruthless and homicidal of all the big-time dealers.)

Those early mixtapes were far from technical feats, with Marlo defaulting to boiled-down street tales with little use for metaphor or storytelling beyond standard mob talk. But rappers had built careers out of far less. If nothing else, he was believable. Most importantly, Marlo had P, a resolute champion who plugged his music at every turn as if the rapper had given voice to his own inner monologue. From the day they met, P would keep the younger man close at hand, showing him through physical proximity to his flourishing business everything he couldn't convey with an onslaught of platitudes about persistence and dedication.

The day after Marlo's video shoot, a troop of Quality Control compatriots gathered at the studio before a night out, adjusting their chains, catching up and rolling blunts in preparation for a public show of force at a local club. Marlo would be riding with P.

At about 1 a.m., the label boss signaled to the mostly male group and the two women on the couch sipping liquor that it was time to go. He took the ringleader of the female duo, a woman from Miami, into the passenger side of his Maybach; Marlo and I piled into the spacious back, where each seat had its own throw pillow. All the way to Amora Lounge, P blasted Marlo's music. When we arrived, they were expecting us, with spots reserved right in front of the club's door for the procession of QC vehicles. We all skipped the line.

Inside, the small, chandelier-dotted space was bordered by low booths, offering hookahs and bottle service. Like any crew worth its cred, QC knew to move in formation as a synchronized mass in public places: anonymous, imposing position players took the outside to control traffic and prevent unnecessary proximity to any other patron, while those with more recognizable names, faces and expensive jewelry occupied the well-surrounded center. P, Marlo and their friends were ushered quickly through the thick crowd to a raised spot in the corner near the DJ booth, giving them a full panoramic view of the place if you stood on the vinyl seating, which everybody did. Almost no one danced to the music, but nearly everyone filmed the scene with camera phones.

P wore a red Givenchy hoodie, tattered with intentional holes, and a QC medallion on a fat gold chain. Marlo, dressed down in a plain gray hoodie over a plain gray T-shirt and green sweatpants, let his cluster of rocky necklaces left over from the video shoot do all of the talking. He also fisted a personal bottle of pink Moët rosé champagne.

All through the night, half a dozen barely dressed waitresses tended to the section. Even though blunts were being blown through at a much higher rate, the women raised bottles of champagne, Patrón and Ciroc overhead and delivered them with gusto as clusters of light-spitting sparklers let everyone know they were coming. Every half hour or so, the club's staff also dropped off more banded stacks of dollar bills, which then sat somewhat pathetically at everyone's feet until someone with authority decided to let them flutter atop the heads of the bottle-service squad in an approximation of a strip club celebration.

"Where them ones at, P?" the DJ shouted, catering directly to his celebrity clientele. The goading worked, and in response, the QC section casually flicked hundreds of dollars at a time into the air.

For hours, Marlo stood stoically next to an equally unmoved Kollision, with each man breaking character only to shout along to songs from their record label. Offset, fresh off a flight, joined the group around 2 a.m., with a string of Migos songs soundtracking his entrance.

Later, some grumbled when the playlist veered too far from Atlanta artists as the DJ attempted to stoke some friendly competition between the various VIP factions by sampling a few hits from the Memphis rappers Yo Gotti and Blac Youngsta, who occupied a section across the club. "This is our city!" one QC hanger-on screamed. But a third run-through of Lil Baby's "My Dawg" diffused any lingering concerns, earning the night's biggest reaction, with everyone from wall to wall sing-rapping in unison.

"QC is in the building!" the DJ bellowed. "What you say, P?" Even TI wandered over to pay his respects.

Around 3 a.m., the party moved to the parking lot, where the luxury vehicles were rearranged like Tetris pieces to allow P and his fleet the ability to pull off at will. Instead, the group lingered, their impromptu, up-close car show greeting all exiting attendees as the guys joked and waited for stragglers still inside, posing for photos together and calling after women on their way out, successfully bringing a few into the fold.

An old friend of P's, his white T-shirt damp from the party, had helped himself to plenty of the bottle service and constant rotation of blunts. Noticing me, an outsider in the inner circle, he began vouching unprompted for the credibility and loyalty of his clique. He had recently been released after a decade in prison, and he'd tracked P's rise through incessant daily phone calls to his friend, hoping to catch snippets of rap life happening in the background.

"P a real street n——," the man said, citing the money he could always count on for his commissary books, as well as the care package of cash that the executive had waiting for him upon his release. "Picked me up from prison in a Maybach."

P, in the eye of the swirling parking-lot circus, waved off his friend's effusive, drunken ramblings, preferring not to stew on stories of his past exploits and his old friend's glory days. "I'd die for this n——," the guy said, sentimental and undeterred.

When P finally accelerated away from the club, hitting ninety miles per hour on the darkened, twisting back streets on the way to the QC compound, the executive once again queued up unreleased songs by Marlo, who had resumed his post behind the label boss. "That's how you drive leaving the club," Marlo chuckled after one brisk turn.

In the darkness, a drunk and extra slurry Marlo rapped along with himself, reacting to his lyrics and teasing out their meanings in real time. "'*If I pull it, bet I pop it*'—that's, like, a rule coming up that old heads always taught you," Marlo said, zeroing in on one line. "You better not pull the gun if you ain't going to use it.

"I'm just giving you the game, same as it was given to me," he said. "It's a street tradition—somebody give you the game, you give it someone else.

"Live by the gun, die by the gun," he added, as if it were simple.

But there was less and less explication needed as the song went on, and everyone sat silent, Marlo's words echoing through the empty streets. "I'm just thinking out loud, got my hand to the cloud," he rapped. "I wish C could see me now, I know he'd be proud."

15.

THE GOLD RUSH

THE SUMMER AFTER HIGH SCHOOL GRADUATION, AS FOR MANY teenagers, was the most carefree time in Lil Reek's young life. Unlike most of his peers, however, Reek was traveling the country in high demand.

"Eighteen years old," one record label A&R scout in New York marveled. "This is a lot of attention from adults. How does that feel right now? You can vote now, and you're in these meetings, talking to these business folks."

"This is what it's all about," Reek said, eyes barely rising from his Nintendo Switch. "Making it happen."

The get-to-know-you consultation with the young Atlanta rapper had been scheduled on a few hours' notice, at a semi-independent label closely affiliated with Sony Music. Reek, in Umbros over tights, a fanny pack and a tiny hoodie, was already in town with his manager Roger for another round of these check-in chats, and also a meetup with Brodinski, his Parisian mentor. But a record deal was what they were really after. They just had to play it cool. The nibbles of interest from outsiders had been steady enough that summer, following the release of Reek's eight-song mixtape *The Graduation* and a few more music videos. But none of the tracks had exploded organically online, so no one had come to sweep the rapper and his rookie representation off their feet.

"We got the momentum," Roger said in the meeting, promising a second Reek mixtape within a month.

"You not fucking around," the label rep, another young Black man, replied.

"I ain't going back and forth," Reek said in agreement.

"You gotta go hard, man. Keep warming the streets up and weigh the options."

But Roger, not wanting to shut the door on the possibility of Reek's signing a contract sooner rather than later, interjected. "If something comes before we drop another project, then we're all ears," he clarified. "Until then we got our own game plan."

Like uncertain suitors, the two sides continued to feel each other out, with no one wanting to appear like they wanted it more. The conversation was halting at best. Reek, content with his video game, stayed silent unless asked a direct question. After some prompting, he fiddled with a faulty aux cable, attempting to cut the small talk by playing some of his new songs for the scout. "Still doing my homework while the crack on the stove," Reek rapped quietly along with his recorded self.

When the music finished, Roger wanted to talk money, but without appearing too eager. He settled on general questions. "What type of situations would be in hand for an artist like Reek?" he asked. "My goal, and I know his goal, is to get him out the door as quickly as possible—like, skyrocket, of course. That's why we going back in July to drop another tape and be consistent with visuals and stuff like that. But what type of situation—what machine would be put around him to help with the process?"

A second label employee, who specialized in marketing, had joined the conversation, and he took this opportunity to launch into his pitch. Steadier than his counterpart in A&R, the marketer stressed the advantage of a small label with a dedicated team and only a few artists, as opposed to a corporate behemoth concerned only with "inventory control."

"Because Spotify effectively saved the music business—and saved hip-hop—all these labels are kind of doubling down and just signing everything," he said. "I've been on both sides of it: I know what it's like to have one of a hundred artists and whoever's moving gets put to the front. But there's very little in the way of artist development, still, when it comes to major labels because it's a very frontline type of thing. You're trying to make that profit, get your numbers for the year and get your bonus." Their label, on the other hand, was diverse and focused, split between a few aspiring pop stars, rock bands and street rappers—but definitely "hip-hop-minded," the marketer said.

"We get the culture. I would say that our passion is hip-hop, all the way, hands down. It's not one of those things that can be taught." Roger nodded along.

As an example of their services, the label guys offered the case of a drill rapper they'd recently signed on the strength of one song that was hot on YouTube and in the artist's hometown of Chicago. The first thing the label did was put the Atlanta star 21 Savage on a remix, the marketer said. "That brought him from the core blogs—Say Cheese TV, Kollege Kidd, Chicago stuff—and elevated him to *Billboard*, *Fader*, *Complex*. It got us more playlists on Spotify, all that kind of stuff. He's in a different light now."

"How soon, you know, would the ball get rolling if a decision was made . . . ," Roger tried to ask again. "Some artists do sign and get left behind."

The marketing guy assured him that this company didn't work that way. "We got a chip on our shoulder," he said. "We got something to prove." The meeting ended with hand slaps and a promise to keep in touch. Nobody mentioned a number.

"The young G himself—thank you for your time today," one of the label guys said to Reek. "Keep doing what you're doing out there."

Only on the sidewalk out front did Roger let on what he'd been looking to hear and would continue searching for across Atlanta, New York and Los Angeles: a million dollars up front in Reek's pocket. Factoring in lawyer fees, taxes and his own cut as manager, that meant a deal between $2.5 million and $4 million, Roger estimated.

"I need the bag, bruh!" Reek said, more animated than he'd been inside.

THIS WAS NOT an entirely unreasonable request. The demand for fresh rappers—and for those with some semblance of connections in a hot city like Atlanta—had reached such a fever pitch by 2018 that these kinds of conversations were now happening everywhere, all the time, for talented young people like Reek.

With most "sales" now coming in streams, Swedish hitmakers paired with bubbly pop vessels were no longer the surest or most economical way to a hit in an anxious, overmedicated and underpaid America. The appetite for something grittier appeared bottomless, and rappers had taught themselves in the fallow times to be self-sufficient, reliably pioneering how to reach their expanding audiences early in unlikely places online. For labels, these once-regional or pigeonholed acts were now an easy, hands-off investment that allowed them to tap into the excitement and the malaise of the underground, where cathartic rage reigned and was obviously resonating.

For the artists, large record labels had long been a necessary evil whose necessity was now in question. After decades of taking advantage of musicians—Black ones, in particular—through unfavorable contracts that traded money up front (an "advance") for perpetual rights to the recorded music and low royalty rates, artists had recently started to take some power back. Whereas the labels once justified these deals based on the risks and expenses they were taking on, from studio time to CD packaging to radio promotion, the internet had reoriented the business, making it technically possible for an artist to record, distribute, promote and blow themselves up from a bedroom with little capital.

But in reality, those who could make it on a mass scale while remaining wholly independent remained rare, as streaming services, award shows, venues and other significant channels of attention continued to operate hand in hand with the major-label system. (A company like Quality Control, a local independent business with corporate partners, could ideally function as a middle ground.) There were also the questions of patience and need, an issue often starker in rap, where young kids from little or nothing were unlikely to be able to turn down the life-changing sum of a fat advance, leaving the labels an opening to take advantage of, not unlike they always had.

In 2017, the three major record companies signed 658 acts—about two artists a day—up 12 percent from a few years prior; around the same time, Spotify was seeing 20,000 tracks uploaded every 24 hours, a number that would soon double. Most would never be heard on a wide scale. By 2020, only about 870 artists—from all genres across all of time—were generating more than $1 million annually via the top streaming service. But 97 percent of artists on the platform weren't even making $1,000.

Still, when the labels did come sniffing around, the results for the right individual could be nothing short of transformative. "It could be two hundred fifty thousand dollars, it could be three million dollars—depends on how hot it is," said Barry Weiss, a veteran record executive who had helped to bring once-regional rap acts like DJ Jazzy Jeff & the Fresh Prince, Too Short, A Tribe Called Quest and UGK to Jive Records—and international acclaim—in the late 1980s and early 1990s. "What's also happening now is artists are coming out, and if they get one significant cosign from a Cardi B or a Drake, it's a million-dollar deal—plus recording costs. Just on cosigns."

Back in the day, when Weiss first started finding rappers from outside of New York or Los Angeles, he would routinely call radio stations, record stores and wholesalers to ask, "What's the hot local rap thing?" Then he would assess the records that were moving well in certain cities and decide who had the broadest national appeal—"merging ears and instincts, research and energy," he said.

Today, "everybody sees all the same data, so the minute someone sees something popping, everybody is seeing the same shit, so then it becomes who's going to write the biggest check," Weiss explained in his New York office. "It's much more competitive." He added, "It's financial exercises more than A&R exercises."

But Atlanta, on the ground at least, was a different beast. Given how deep its talent river ran, and how insular the city could be, the major record companies, in search of any edge, wanted more and more to rely on locals—and notably, Black executives—for their instincts and relationships. Coach and P had helped set the tone for this shift when they signed with Capitol Music Group, the company all but outsourcing its rap division to them down south. Discovering an artist *before* their numbers popped could save a label some money and headaches.

"That's what makes Atlanta so cool, that everyone is in a circle," Amina Diop, a well-known connector in the city, told me one day in her quiet office, just outside the city's perimeter. "It's a small group of people that make a big impact in the industry. Everyone kind of knows each other, been around each other, come up with each other, in one aspect or the other. If they're from Atlanta, then they've gone to school together or they've grown up in the same neighborhoods and they have a deep connection, street connection, family connection, stuff like that. It makes the music real."

A New Yorker by birth, Diop had attended Georgia State University and stumbled into the music industry through a side door—as the manager for early 2000s video girls like Buffie the Body, crucial figures in the rap economy. "We monetized it and made it a business," Diop said. "We were selling calendars and CDs, ringtones and wallpapers for cell phones. Remember, this is like a decade ago—this wasn't two hundred years ago."

After social media took over, burying her specific niche—Instagram was "the Napster for pinup girls," she said—Diop turned to rap more directly through her connections with Gucci Mane and his manager at the time, Deb Antney. "Men at that young age are super-unorganized," she said. "I was just like, 'I could help him out, just his day-to-day, you need a little bit of structure.'" She noted that every successful male rapper had at least one strong woman in his corner—platonically—even if they were out of sight, behind the scenes.

Gucci's life and career were at their most turbulent then, so he proved challenging to wrangle and protect. But Diop would remain a constant throughout his rehabilitation and rebirth. Gucci also introduced her to his many protégés, and Diop eventually took on an unpolished Young Thug as a management client. "I did everything," she said. "It was just him and I. Paperwork—from creating YSL as an entity, all of that—setting up bank accounts, houses. Everything. Cars. Just everything."

Thug, the tenth of eleven children and not one to take direction, trusted her guidance from the jump. "He needed someone to wholeheartedly believe in unicorns," Diop said. "That was beautiful. He needed someone to be on his team for real, and be like, 'This shit is dope, this shit is normal.' Or even if it's not normal, to be like, 'I'm with you, too. I'm riding with this. I love it.' Reassurance." She added of Thug: "He's good. He's bad. He's male. He's female. He's dark. He's light. He's everything. Whatever kind of person you are, you can find solace in him. That's what the culture needed at the time."

In 2018, Republic Records, a major among majors, named Diop senior vice president of A&R. She would remain based in Atlanta. "They'll sign any-fucking-body at this point," she said of the record companies like the one that now employed her. What she hoped to add was a better ear and "connectivity," she said. "If there's a conversation to be had in Atlanta or you need a feature for somebody or whatever, it's a phone call. Not red tape and paperwork. You can only have that with a true person who is here in this culture."

About ten miles toward downtown, in a windowless office attached to a recording studio, Ray Daniels was doing something similar for Republic's rival, Warner Records. Like Diop, Daniels was a quick-talking New York transplant, having moved to Atlanta as a child, and also like her, he maintained his own management roster on top of his label A&R job during the rap boom.

"It's a fucking gold mine," Daniels said. "It's football money. It's scary, but it's incredible. I come from the era where if you were a rapper and getting half a million, you're like, *What!?* Now everybody's getting millions." He was fresh from finalizing a seven-figure deal in LA. The rapper was sixteen. "It's just a gold rush, bruh," Daniels said. "It was at an all-time high yesterday, and then today it became higher."

His concern was what came next for most of these artists. "Say if you had fifty Rolls-Royces to give to people—are you going to give one to a sixteen-year-old? Are you going to give it to somebody who just got their license? That's what you're doing when you're giving two million dollars to somebody who's never had that kind of money. That's what's happening right now. That's what's scary."

It's also where someone like him came in. "We need a lot of motherfuckers out there saying, 'Hey, let me start teaching y'all motherfuckers how to drive.' And we don't have enough of that."

Daniels was nearing forty, with two kids, and he had been in the industry nearly fifteen years, working under Black music legends like LA Reid and Sylvia Rhone at Epic, Interscope, Motown—everywhere that mattered. But some labels, he said, were chasers ("It's hot, go get it") and some were builders.

"This new game we're in, these kids are waking up and numbers are saying they're worth something that they haven't proven to be worth," Daniels said. "What happens if you wake up today, upload a song to SoundCloud, and now you've got millions of dollars? In your mind, you think everything you're doing is right. Which is good, I like that.

"But eventually the money starts drying up," he said. To become a *superstar* required another level of guidance. He recalled sitting in a meeting with Reid and Travis Scott at Epic. Scott, an Auto-Tuned mishmash of mimicked influences and self-marketing magic, had found success live with small shows that became fabled (and then infamous) for their high-energy mosh pits and stage diving. "You know what's better than fifteen hundred people singing your name and your songs?" Reid asked the rapper, according to Daniels. "*Twenty thousand.* How are we going to get to twenty thousand? We need *hits*, Travis. We need hits."

"You got all these kids who are from the hood—from low backgrounds, who are really pretty much fucking fighting this gauntlet to get out—finally getting money, selling out shows," Daniels said. "Somebody is not in a room telling him, 'Where you at is good. *But there's more.*'

"How do you tell a young Black kid that's working that it's not enough? But still make him feel like he trusts you? Somebody that he looked up to had to tell LeBron, 'You can be better than Jordan.'

"I remember the first time somebody told me I had potential. That was like, *Holy shit*," Daniels went on. "That's important." He praised Coach and P for their work with Lil Baby. "Someone who had Jeezy told him, 'You're going to be as big as Jeezy.' So now it's like, 'Okay, what I gotta do?'"

That's where Black executives had an advantage with Black artists, Daniels said. "We're more like coaches. But it's not like coaching a basketball player—Xs and Os. This is like, these kids have daddy issues.

Mother issues. Brother issues. These young Black guys need a father figure. And I hate to say it like that. They need to know that somebody's going to be in their life that's not going to leave them or desert them."

At the same time, that dynamic could introduce some latent class anxiety, Daniels pointed out. He mentioned a white guy who had the same job he did—signing rappers. "He drives a Volvo—I could never drive a Volvo. Because a little Black kid sees me and I gotta be in something else—I got a Sprinter and a Maybach and a big-ass house. I have to have that. These little kids will never respect me if I don't have what they want.

"You, on the other hand," he said, pointing to me, "could come in here with some fucking Asics and Kia and no one's going to judge you because you're white. I don't have to brag, I just need to make sure these kids know I'm not the n—— in the room trying to get in your pockets. That is important to a young Black kid. 'Oh, you don't need me for money—I can listen to you.'"

He'd had a telling experience with his own family. "I remember when my little brother was making money when he was in the streets real heavy," Daniels said. "One day I asked him how much his chain costs. This is my real brother, who I raised, mind you—I bought him his first car, his first chain, his first everything. And he told me, 'Mind your motherfucking business, n——! Don't be trying to count my money.'"

But the guy with the Volvo could only take a rapper so far, he said. "The minute he tells them how to make money, they're like, 'I'mma listen to you.' But the minute he tells them how to survive, they're like, 'How the fuck do you know what I gotta deal with?'

"That's where I come in."

Atlanta's greatest advantage, in addition to people like him—like P and Coach and Amina Diop—was its affordability for artists, Daniels said in closing, well aware of having floored me with the certainty and vigor of his monologue. "In New York, LA, y'all gotta have the Rolls-Royces," he said, speaking metaphorically and literally. "In Atlanta, we can drive the Chrysler 300. The Chrysler 300 doesn't cost as much." He underlined the point of Atlanta's affordability: "Any kid with five hundred dollars and a fucking dream—whether that dream is to produce, write, rap, sing, engineer, anything—can come to Atlanta and fucking make it. And that's why Atlanta is never going to lose.

"You wanna build?" Daniels said. "Come to the A."

In late August, Lil Reek took a deal from Republic Records for $350,000. It was the only number on the table. Who could say no?

Roger Beat and Birdman Zoe, the Queens guy everyone called Bird, who attended Reek's first New York recording session, accompanied him as co-managers. (C, the once-eager would-be investor, was nowhere to be found.) The two grown-ups provided a rap-fluent entertainment attorney to go over the contract and a videographer to document the big day. Reek also brought along a friend from home. Alongside the six Black men, posing against a wall decorated with the Republic logo for a celebratory group photo, was a white A&R rookie named Bryan who had gotten the deal done. He pointed proudly to Reek, who barely cleared his shoulder.

"Six figures same year as graduation," Reek wrote online. "I'm a blessed lil bastard."

It wasn't the millions they had been after, but Roger was proud of the deal, his first major score for an artist. Despite Reek's proximity to Atlanta stardom, he could not have hoped for much more in terms of immediate funds without a true viral smash or a specific rapper in his corner. The contract was also short-term, covering one release and leaving the label an option to extend it based on performance. Reek's team had spent eight hours in the Republic office, renegotiating terms and filing the paperwork.

Bryan had the advantage of being one of the first industry people to reach out about Reek months prior. "I had every label hitting me up, but no one ever followed up," Roger said. "Bryan always called me, every week, to check in. I trust him." Now they were all eager to get to work. "We're trying to tell the label there's no letting up—we need to drop music ASAP," Roger said.

Early the next week, Reek was back in New York City to record and meet the rest of the Republic staff who would be tasked with getting his career rolling. It was the night after the MTV Video Music Awards at Radio City Music Hall, so Quad Studios in Times Square was active, as artists and their labels seized the opportunity to put in some face time. Juice WRLD, a nineteen-year-old SoundCloud rapper from Chicago who had signed a deal worth more than $3 million, was set up in a room two floors down. While Reek and Roger got comfortable, Bryan went to pay his respects to Juice's team, which now shared a corporate umbrella with his.

Reek wore a G-Star camouflage jacket and carried an orange soda along with his Nintendo Switch, which was now outfitted with a special controller to better play Fortnite. His dreads, which usually hung past his shoulders, were in a ponytail, revealing shaved undersides. The engineer for the night fiddled with the computer, connecting the hard drive that contained Reek's recent work. But before everyone could settle in for a long night, a ruckus erupted in the elevator bank, where a small hallway split the floor into two separate studios.

Reek immediately ran to look for the source of the commotion, arriving right as Roger lunged at another man and began tussling, shouting and shoving, limbs flying wildly in the tight space. Launching his orange soda into the melee, Reek turned around and rushed back into the studio to grab a stool, wielding it and screaming behind Roger like a WWE star. But as quickly as it started, the men separated into their respective corners, with Reek and Roger pulling the heavy studio door closed behind them, sealing us in with a slam and a flip of the lock. A bleeding man banged loudly on the other side.

"Man, I ain't gonna lie, this shit about to get crazy out here," said Roger, who began working his phone to call in backup. He wasn't from New York, but he knew plenty of people who were.

"I don't be on that shit, bro!" Reek said, vibrating with adrenaline. "Beef shit. This shit *weird*. This shit be business gone bad."

Roger, it turned out, had busted into the neighboring session when he heard a name and voice that rang a bell. A promoter who'd stiffed

Reek recently at a small rap festival in Los Angeles, leaving him with no performance slot and no flight home, happened to be next door. The guy had put their lives in danger, Reek explained, by telling him and Roger to go collect their money from a third party; when they arrived, it was clearly a setup.

"When someone fucks you over, you ain't gon' never forget," Roger said, pacing the room.

"He didn't think he'd ever run into us again!" Reek added giddily.

Bryan, who'd missed the action and was now locked out of the session, called Roger's cell. "What's up, Bryan?" the manager said, putting on a cheery voice. "Yeah, we good!"

Reek was seething and exhilarated but no longer in the mood to record. The man outside the door was still screaming as he walloped the thick glass. To drown him out and give everybody something to do, the engineer cranked up the Lil Reek music, and within minutes, the tension had dissipated. Reek began dancing almost involuntarily to his unreleased songs. "Yeah, that's hard right there—I gotta finish that," he said when one track ended.

As Roger worked his contacts, Reek mused on his new record deal and what came next. "I'm in the game for longevity," he said. "The whole thing is a blessing." He was also considering starting online college classes, but first he wanted to get his next mixtape ready and move with his mother to a new place in Atlanta. She was proud but overwhelmed, he said. "Me too, though."

Downstairs, Roger's friends had arrived, but the studio security was refusing to let them up, citing the earlier disturbance. The cops who were already gathered close by, due to the studio's location and the talent on hand, were also getting curious. "We 'bout to roll out, man," Roger said.

But passing by his rival on the way to the elevator did not seem like a wise option, so the studio engineer, knowing the building, devised a plan to sneak everyone down via a secret stairwell in the back. Without much discussion, Reek and his crew slipped one by one onto an outside roof deck and through an adjacent door, down six flights of steps and back into the safety of an elevator. When the doors slid open in the lobby, three NYPD officers were waiting to head up. They asked no questions, accepting the group's polite nods as they slipped by, out the front door and into Times Square, quickly disappearing around the corner onto 48th Street.

Standing with Bryan in front of the building was his superior in A&R at Republic, Amina Diop, shaking her head and laughing at the scene. Nobody had a chance to say hello, let alone goodbye. Diop took in the details of the incident like she'd heard it all before.

"That is definitely Atlanta shit," she said.

16.

BANKHEAD

When Marlo called Ken, the Asian American proprietor and namesake of Ken's, his go-to wing spot, one afternoon in the summer of 2018 to say that he was coming by, the two men shouted at each other in a clipped shorthand that might have functioned as an official takeout order but was more likely just a heads-up that a regular was on his way. We reordered once we got inside.

Quick, delicious and affordable—about $5 for a ten-piece—Ken's wings were presented in white Styrofoam with crinkle-cut fries and "grilled toasted bread"—a single, perfect slice of white soaked and crisped in butter. For Marlo, the combo might as well have been a home-cooked meal, a time capsule to childhood in the form of a takeout container.

Compared to the genetic monstrosities served by national chicken chains, the wings at Ken's on Bankhead are anemic in size, short and only a little plump, like the fingers of a healthy baby, but vibrant in flavor, served fried, plain or doused in hot sauce, teriyaki or barbecue, dusted most likely with lemon pepper sprinkles resembling tiny crystals of gold dust. Each nub could be housed easily in a bite and a half. Dry or wet, drums or flats, sweet tea or peach drink, fried rice or fries, ranch or blue cheese, ketchup or hot sauce, six-piece or ten-, J. R. Crickets or American Deli—wing culture in Atlanta is serious and detailed, a staple of most neighborhoods and cultures, but extra personal in places like Bankhead, where Ken's deli has been around and feeding people for as long as most remember.

The corner store–slash–takeout spot sits somewhat apocalyptically in an unkempt island of a strip mall on a stretch of the six-mile-long Donald Lee Hollowell Parkway, a street rebranded in the late nineties for an

Atlanta civil rights attorney but still better known as Bankhead Highway (though no one says the "Highway"). A textbook "food desert," where underserved populations have little immediate access to nutritious options, Bankhead can be either barren or bustling, depending on the day and your vantage, with trees and unruly vegetation flourishing more than most businesses, which include gas stations, tire shops, barbers and beauty supply stores, some open and some abandoned, the answer not always obvious at first glance.

Ken's, for example, and the Wash House laundromat next door, appeared at first fossilized, with faded yellow signage—K&H FOOD STORE ICE COLD DRINK, it had read at one point—and bars on the windows. Inside, the place looked equally bombed out, the dirty shelves almost all empty, save for a few bags of twenty-five-cent chips and a fridge stocked full of soft drinks. Most of the action happened behind the counter and a sign reading "We no longer accept EBT," where candy boxes mingled with phone cards, hair accessories and picked-over medicine packets, adjacent to the fryers and a grill where the food was prepared. If you didn't know where Ken's was already, you probably weren't stopping by, but directions, from local to local, might have gone something like this, per one internet commenter: "On Bankhead before u get to Bowen homes if u coming from blue flame"—that is, the strip club where the casket of the Bowen Homes legend Shawty Lo was taken, via hearse, for one final goodbye after he was killed in a car accident in 2016.

A few hundred feet down the road, past the shell of one gas station across from an active Texaco, at the corner of Bankhead and Yates Drive, is a dead end with a chain-link fence that was once an entrance to another world, the one where Marlo grew up. Built in and around a circular street called Wilkes, intersected twice in its center by the roads Chivers and Walden, the Bowen Homes projects were constructed in 1964 and demolished in the summer of 2009, becoming in the intervening forty-five years one of the most dangerous, crime-ridden and notorious areas in Atlanta.

Immortalized in umpteen rap songs and OutKast's trippy music video for "B.O.B."—André 3000 once lived in the apartments across the street—Bowen Homes was made up of 650 units spread across about one hundred cookie-cutter Monopoly buildings on some fifty-four acres. Its labyrinth of two-story, pale orange brick structures were home to multigenerational families on government assistance, and also a vibrant crack trade that swept in during the 1980s and lingered until it was sent scattering elsewhere by the city's police and fed-up housing authorities.

Outside the grounds, now empty and overgrown, Marlo reminisced about the OK Super Market—long vacant, but still standing—where his family had shopped, and also the burger place next door, a go-to option after school bus drop-off. Once home to a daycare, a library and an elementary school, the Bowen Homes projects—named for John W. E. Bowen Sr., a former slave who became a Methodist clergyman, as well as the first Black person to receive a PhD from Boston University—were also, at least according to legend, stalked by an indiscriminate serial killer known as the Assassin, though he was never confirmed to exist.

With or without an actual bogeyman, living in Bowen Homes could be risky, with those advocating its razing pointing to a stretch of time not long before its demise when the area was host to 168 violent crimes in seven months, including five murders—the last straw in the place's turbulent life. In the midnineties, Atlanta had the highest number of public housing residents per capita in the country—about 12 percent of the city's population—96 percent of whom were Black and half of whom were children in families earning less than $5,500 per year. Some 93 percent of the families living in the projects were headed by single women.

When Bowen Homes was finally leveled in June of 2009, Marlo was newly nineteen. The demolition represented a symbolic endpoint for a failed experiment in Atlanta housing, as the city—which had constructed the nation's first prominent projects, Techwood Homes, in 1936—became the first metropolis to demolish them in an attempt to decentralize the overlapping cancers of poverty, crime, community disinvestment and poor schooling. Spurred in the midnineties by the federal HOPE VI Program—and by Atlanta politicians and real estate developers anticipating the arrival of the 1996 Olympics and the gentrification that would follow—the long process of destroying Atlanta's housing projects was supposed to result in more mixed-income areas and apartments. Like those from the other projects that were knocked down around the same time, residents of Bowen Homes, who paid at most 30 percent of their adjusted gross income in rent, were promised vouchers to discount rent on new places, along with counseling and other government assistance.

But while the housing authority's director at the time promised that the destruction of Bowen Homes would be the end of "warehousing families in concentrated poverty," the results were much less unequivocal. Subsequent studies found that most people who lived in Atlanta's decimated project housing didn't move far, typically relocating within three miles of their old apartments, still in poor neighborhoods. By 2017, Atlanta had one of the highest eviction rates in the country, with 22 percent of tenants living in Fulton County having received eviction notices, and that rate shooting above 40 percent in some majority-Black neighborhoods. Due in part to rampant gentrification, the city's stock of low-income housing declined by 5 percent every year between 2012 and 2016, leaving about twenty-five affordable rentals for every one hundred families who needed one. In 2019, with Atlanta's income inequality among the worst in the nation, the Federal Reserve ranked the city number 360 out of 381 in economic mobility. Eighty-five percent of the local unhoused population was Black.

When his family was forced to leave Bowen Homes, Marlo, still reserved but newly self-assured in his entrepreneurial abilities, relocated to a series of equally rough, low-income apartment complexes—the ones kids refer to, generically, as "the bricks"—a few miles away, in a dilapidated unofficial neighborhood they called the 9th Ward, in a nod to New Orleans. But Marlo had already soaked up his project's culture of sly lawlessness.

"I know how to survive in the jungle," Marlo said, recalling fondly the years he was known as Rudy, with his mischievous eyes-first smile and the gap in his front teeth giving away the kid he once was. But he also peppered his childhood memories with sharp reveals of tragedies past, like the death of his older-brother figure, his protector and idol, C. J., who was hit by a flatbed truck while riding his bike on Bankhead when he was barely a teenager.

That day in 2004, Rudy—C. J.'s more sensitive and less athletic shadow—was supposed to be riding with him. Just fourteen at the time, he was never the same. Once a raw child prone to crying fits, Rudy hardened almost instantly, and he was forced to step up in the hierarchy of the surrogate Bowen Homes family that looked after him, telling C. J.'s mother, Denice, "I'm his twin, and I got you."

Rudy's biological mother and father were around but not always part of the picture. His dad, Rudolph Simmons III—Big Rudy—was from North Philadelphia's notorious housing projects the Richard Allen Homes but had been sent to the South as a teenager after his mother saw the police stick a gun in his face while he was dealing drugs. In Atlanta, the elder Rudy kept hustling, though he met his son's mother during the week he tried to go straight, working as an orderly at an old folks' home. The job didn't stick, but Rudy IV was born on May 1, 1990, in Fulton County on the West Side, off Hightower Road. A little sister followed soon after.

But the young parents split, and life was unstable. Big Rudy was in and out of prison as a user and a seller, and by nine or ten, little Rudy had serious enough issues with his mother's boyfriend that he moved out, leading him to be raised in a collective effort by a nucleus of women—grandmothers, aunts, friends, sisters, not all of them blood—some of whom encouraged the child to get out and hustle to help however he could. Denice, a cousin of Rudy's mother, welcomed him into her brood of five, and he came to call her Mom as she called him son.

A onetime star dancer at Magic City, Denice was "street," Rudy said. "She gave me all the game, knew how to move." Denice stressed what she called the four major Cs in life: "credit, career, car and crib"—the necessities. "We never used the word *broke*—we don't claim that," she said. "We used the words *low in funds*."

For a time, from the late eighties to the midnineties, Bowen Homes had a reputation in spite of its omnipresent poverty as the Million-Dollar

Trap, a free-for-all of illegal entrepreneurship. Guys with names like Big D, Fat Steve, White Boy Keith and Milo controlled the bustling trade, which centered around crack but also included powdered cocaine, marijuana, heroin, hash and, later, ecstasy. At a young age, Rudy would get his first taste of the business when he received nickel and dime handouts from the older men, like the original Milo—his actual rap namesake, which he combined with the allusion to *The Wire*—flipping them for the things any kid might need, like school clothes and shoes.

Milo was killed in 2009, the same year Bowen came down. *Marlo*, pronounced with a classic West Side Atlanta drawl, sounds just like *Milo*. But *The Wire*'s Marlo Stanfield wasn't a bad proxy, either. "Let them know Marlo step to any motherfucker," the fictional dealer said in his defining monologue. "My name is my name!"

Like P, the head of his record label, Marlo, or Rudy from 1015 Chivers Street, #350—Shitty Chivers, as it was known—was about ten when he "hit the block," he said, selling weed and crack in growing doses, having learned to cook it from Denice's husband at the time, who charged him for the knowledge. Rudy also robbed when he needed to, and he earned the grudging respect of the big-time drug dealers who operated fiefdoms within the rowdy Wild West of the project borders. Historically, police cars that did enter Bowen Homes without backup were liable to get "rocked out," or showered with projectiles, until they drove away. One time, legend had it, some Bowen Homes kids taunted an officer enough to get him out of his vehicle, allowing one of them to jump in the driver's seat and ride off.

On the harsh stage of the projects, Rudy "turned into a bully," his father said. "You know how you play-fight? Rudy don't play-fight. If you hit him, he's gonna bust your head open. If you hit him with a brick, he gon' cut you with a knife. If you got a knife, he gon' shoot you. That's just how he is."

Once, Rudy told his father that he would steal from anyone except family—even the man who sold him his first quarter pound of weed, a close family friend. "Dad, I'll fucking rob Big Boy, I don't care," the impetuous up-and-comer said. "If he's slipping, I'll get his ass." And he followed through, at one point taking two pounds from his mother's boyfriend.

"He got that from being around me, he got that from being in that jungle, in Bowen Homes," Big Rudy said, recalling his own experiences seeing dead bodies in the Philly projects before he turned double digits. "There's so much violence every single day, every single night, it's bound to trickle on you. It hardens you. It makes you kind of numb to a lot of different things. That's what got Rudy."

Yet even as he developed a reputation as a serious troublemaker, the young man who would become Marlo was low-key about it and he never got caught—a "quiet little badass little boy," as one neighbor put it. "He sneaky bad—he gon' give you that little look." Still, as Marlo slipped past consequences, his drug-game dreams turned BMF-sized, and he kept a notebook filled with goals, like big houses for everyone who depended on him.

HISTORICALLY IN ATLANTA, even with the prevalence of high-volume drug dealing, traditional gang culture did not dominate, with local crews and cliques lacking the hierarchies, history, sophistication and order of national organizations, like the Bloods, Crips and Gangster Disciples of New York, Los Angeles or Chicago. Instead, Atlanta outfits were scattered and localized up to the turn of the century, separated by the city's big gaps of forest and highway nothingness but naturally arranged via blocks, project gates and school zoning. Burglaries, drug dealing and shootouts were still seen largely as random crimes of opportunity, not widespread conspiracies, and were therefore mostly left by federal authorities to the Atlanta Police Department and its paltry gang unit, which at one point in the early 2000s consisted of only six officers.

But many Atlantans would draw the dividing line regarding gangs around 2005—the year of Hurricane Katrina—when an influx of refugees from Louisiana, allegedly including some more established Bloods, came to the city and started wreaking havoc. One New Orleans group, the International Robbing Crew, whose MO was plain in its name, was single-handedly blamed for a spike in the murder rate, with some local drug dealers reportedly begging law enforcement to "get them off the street." A dispute between the IRC and 30 Deep, a less structured local upstart from the Mechanicsville area south of downtown, led the warm months of 2007 to be dubbed the Bloody Summer. Meanwhile, LA transplants burnished the Southern presence of West Coast collectives like the Rollin' 60s Crips, and elements of the Gangster Disciples also gained a foothold in the city and its suburbs.

Within Bowen Homes and its counterparts, groups of friends who lived on top of one another naturally got in trouble together. They sought financial opportunity by any means and defended themselves en masse against encroachment or jumpings by neighborhood rivals, like the kids from Bankhead Courts, another rough housing project nearby, where even the mailmen were scared to enter. Their sectarian divides were more often niche, geographic and social, with law enforcement eventually calling these more parochial groups "hybrid" gangs. The men involved just called one another brothers.

As the projects were flattened and elders killed or imprisoned, dispersing young people haphazardly as social media was taking off—increasing their desire to belong to something and flex in public—these band-of-brothers subsets multiplied in nearly every poor and even middle-class neighborhood, porous as they were in Atlanta. They blurred the lines between hierarchical street gangs, makeshift families, teenage social clubs, aspiring entertainment companies, labels, fashion brands and hustling conglomerates, combining seemingly every letter of the alphabet with finger-contorting symbols and secret handshakes, resulting in an overlapping excess of mini-crews and their more official gang offshoots: PDE, ATM, 2BF, YSL, SMM, ABG, CRDC, SGDB, YR and so on.

One Bowen Homes group, which morphed and grew over the years, was MDC—the Most Dangerous Click, Crew or Committee, depending on whom you asked. It was under MDC that Rudy really cut his teeth as part of the rowdier second generation in matters of solidarity and crime. But later, when he was forced to move as a teenager to the two-story brick apartment buildings on Delmar Lane off Martin Luther King Jr. Drive, where Zone 1 met Zone 4—the 9th Ward, or the Nine—Rudy and his friends joined forces with some guys from the nearby Allen Temple Apartments under a more powerful organization.

GoodFellas, also known as GF or the Mobb, had its roots in the Fulton County Jail, but the 9th Ward became its external stronghold, according to gang investigators. Aiming for a more old-fashioned structure, it took inspiration from the Italian Mafia, with a pope and godfather—both incarcerated—overseeing a system of dons and capos with their own subsets of earners and enforcers. The names of these crews were fungible, the loyalty less so. The concept of omertà—a code of silence, represented these days by the zipper-mouth emoji—was invoked, and sometimes it was imposed. Known to one another as *partner* or *twin*—*shooters*, *steppers* and *soldiers*—they fought for each other for life, or at least until they didn't.

It was a rap video that first drew serious law-enforcement scrutiny to the group. In 2017, a Chicago native and 9th Ward denizen with braces who rapped as SahBabii released "Pull Up Wit Ah Stick" on WorldStar. The sound was sickly sweet, but the song was about firearms, and the video featured an array of automatic weapons that authorities would compare to a dispatch from the Taliban. "This isn't Iraq. This isn't Afghanistan. This is Southwest Atlanta," said Tyrone Dennis, a gang detective, in court testimony later. Multiple times in the video, when SahBabii mentioned the capos and dons he hung around with, the camera cut to a grinning Rudy, clutching stacks of cash.

In the immediate wake of Migos' chart-storming with "Bad and Boujee," the track became an internet sensation, resulting in a major deal for SahBabii with Warner Bros. Records. But combined with two murders in the area, the shocking music video also led to an Atlanta Police Department investigation, with cops kicking in doors and seizing more than twenty guns. The city decided soon after to raze the twenty-eight-building Sierra Ridge residential complex on Delmar Lane.

Amid that investigation, authorities learned of the recombining 9th Ward fraternity that was growing Rudy into Marlo, an Atlanta underboss and potential rap star: Play For Keeps, or PFK, which came to double as a budding record label under his partner Tweet. In time, their splintered but far-reaching team would be forced by law-enforcement scrutiny to sublimate the PFK handle and call themselves 3L, or 3 Letter Entertainment, with a rotation of other monikers representing subbranches, shifting allegiances and other attempted rebrands. The PFK motto was simpler: "Bomb first. Never get bombed."

By then, Atlanta had doubled back down on its gang unit, which had seen some success in stemming the crack trade at its earlier peak. Quadrupling its staff to twenty-six officers, the department expanded the list of eighteen identified local gangs to somewhere between fifty and one hundred, which they said were comprised of thousands of individuals who were monitored and carefully logged into a government database, largely thanks to social media and rap music.

"From a law-enforcement standpoint, they kind of do our job for us because really all I have to do is put in a hashtag that says PFK and all of them will pop up," said Dennis, the detective, comparing decoding the nicknames, hand signals and other gang accoutrements to a children's Choose Your Own Adventure book.

Periodic pushes in law enforcement, which were likely to follow upticks in violence and tough-on-crime elections, were like games of whack-a-mole in neglected neighborhoods, with federal RICO charges still rare but increasing into the 2020s. But that didn't mean every wave of aggressive prosecution wasn't felt on a human level by those being targeted, with gang conspiracy charges and their harsher sentences wielded as supposed deterrents.

Rap, then, provided a paradox. Because even as it was bringing legal heat, autobiographical art was also seen as one of the few ways to escape the cycle. Most of the earlier project legends had been killed, like Milo, or were serving serious time. Some who outlived their empires invested old money in new hustles, like small businesses and real estate. But as with the earlier offensive waves by the Atlanta Police Department and its Red Dog unit—Red Dog, taken from an aggressive blitz play in football, stood for Running Every Drug Dealer Out of Georgia, a task force that began in the late eighties—it was often the escalating threat of arrest and prosecution for gang-related activities that drove many project babies, eventually, toward the relative haven of music.

It was in this sense that little Rudy from Shitty Chivers—the kid who turned into Marlo—was a direct spiritual descendant of the most notorious and most celebrated trapper-turned-rapper that Bowen Homes had ever seen.

"I don't know who the fuck came up with him being a rapper," said Jacoby Hudson, a onetime projects resident who went on to become Shawty Lo's defense attorney. "He wasn't no rapper."

Carlos Walker—Bowen Homes Carlos before he was the chart-topping Shawty Lo of D4L—"was a *motherfucker*," Hudson recalled. "He was tough. He was fat. He would hurt you, he would hurt your family, he would do all of that. But when he got older, people started to love Carlos." Because Carlos—who was also known as the Colonel and the CEO within Bowen Homes—took care of his hood after he took it over. Then, like so many others, he turned to rap, because he was tired of getting locked up.

Carlos was raised by his grandmother, Miss Usher, on Wilkes Circle. She died when he was seventeen, leaving him to fend for himself. Carlos was a diabetic, squat like those Bowen Homes buildings he grew up in, but he could fight, and that was what gave him entree to the world of dealing, first as muscle and then as a cutthroat Bankhead kingpin himself.

Across his action-movie life, before his sudden death at the age of forty, Shawty Lo bridged the generations, from the old-school hustlers in their nylon shirts, Kangol hats, bomber jackets, rings and gold rope chains—their box Chevy Caprices, Impalas and Oldsmobile Cutlasses—to the new-school trappers and rappers, who favored cotton Ts, fitteds and diamonds, Jordans and white Air Force Ones, Lexuses and BMWs and Benzes. From 1996—when the imprisonment of some local big-timers allowed Carlos to graduate from being "a robber and a taker" to a proper dope-peddling hustler—until the 2006 peak of D4L, his irreverently bouncy snap-rap collective, with its *Billboard* number one ringtone smash "Laffy Taffy," Shawty Lo evolved with the times, helping to mold the young people on the West Side who would guide his city's subsequent waves.

"Everybody neighborhood had those guys—those guys made sure your neighborhood was good," explained another Bowen Homes staple, whom Lo christened Braski. Others knew Braski as Jimmy, the light-skinned kid. Marlo, like Lo, would come to know him as a reliable right hand.

"I'm the only one that look like me in my neighborhood—I'm damn near looking like a little white kid," Jimmy said one day on the steps of some West Side apartments, where he was still hanging like he had in Bowen Homes. "Big curly Afro, looking like a Puerto Rican or something—little bitty scrawny," he said, invoking his salad days in the late eighties and early nineties. "Whoever my mama gave that pussy to, I can't say."

To a young Jimmy, Bowen Homes was like a McDonald's PlayPlace covered in land mines—"your favorite worst project to be in." There were card games, marbles, cookouts and jump shot competitions, all broken up by shootouts on the regular—a world of experiences for Jimmy to soak up, all right outside his front door. "It was fucked up," he said. "But it was *a'ight*. At the same time! You could get into some trouble or you could get into some fun at any given moment."

Jimmy recalled seeing someone smoke crack for the first time when he was six, peering through a neighbor's patio wall and noticing a strange, burnt "test tube." Not long after, Jimmy found a similar instrument in his own apartment, and his mother and aunt fought after he secretly threw it away.

Much of the possibility—and the suffering—within Bowen Homes was due to guys like Lo, who contributed to both. "Lo didn't have to tell you shit—you saw it," Jimmy said. "Lo was a dog. He gon' piss and shit in the middle of the floor, he don't give a fuck who watching. Lo was a gentleman, but he was a monster. You see them veins pop up in his forehead and you know to leave homes alone—he finna to get crazy."

Jimmy was twelve when Lo, then a seasoned teenager, passed him his first "bomb of dope." Always an observant child, Jimmy had seen a lot already, often using the "three quarters and a dime" it took to catch the MARTA and exploring other Atlanta neighborhoods. One afternoon in Bowen Homes, he recognized a drug-buying regular, who he knew spent a few thousand at a time on rocks to break down and sell elsewhere. Jimmy was also savvy enough to notice that the guy's go-to corner boy was nowhere to be found.

He promptly ran to Lo—"I never did business with 'em, but I know to know"—and convinced the older boy to hand over a substantial package, promising he would be back with the cash in a few minutes tops. Lo, afraid the kid might get robbed in the process, sent his own watchdog to observe Jimmy's deal. But it went down without a hitch.

When Jimmy brought back the money, a glowing Lo shot him a finder's fee—"the first three hundred dollars I ever had to myself," Jimmy said. But it was only once Jimmy left that he realized why his patron had been so tickled by the transaction.

"You gave Lo all that *gatdamn* money and he couldn't believe that shit, Jimmy!" a friend ribbed him on their way home. It turned out Jimmy had sold a sack of "nicks," or $5 servings, as if they were "dimes." Only Lo—not Jimmy or his customer—realized the double payment. "That was a lesson I learned," Jimmy said. It also endeared him to Lo for life.

The exchange would put Jimmy on a path to becoming the sort of silent soldier—the dutiful background figure who always did his part and never complained—that made both the rap game and the dope game click, often in concert. "Now that I look at it, the guys who I looked up to, they were the workers," Jimmy said. "Not the kingpins. The guys who didn't ever look like they were doing something, they had more money than everybody."

Jimmy, though, was a born worker, and he was always doing something. "All the ill shit that you would never think of," like finding the right remote creek in the woods where he could bury the crew's weaponry after a battle, and then returning to find the guns again when necessary. "I was that dude—'*Jimmy, go hide these!*,' and I'm going to bumblefuck to hide these bitches," he said. "I done buried 'em, and I done dug 'em up."

Alongside Lo, Jimmy chose a life of crime over a trade, but he did have a choice. Right around the time he made his first crack sale, Jimmy was also assisting a guy who hooked up car sound systems on Bankhead, quietly learning the craft. But after tricking out Lo's brand-new Denali truck with seven TVs and a six-disc DVD changer and receiving only a small fraction of the $15,000 job, Jimmy said fuck it.

"Man, I'm finna ride with y'all," he told Lo that day. They headed directly to the mall, Jimmy said, and he "ain't never looked back since."

Jimmy was already experiencing the downsides of the streets anyway, even as he only dabbled. By fifteen, Jimmy said, he was being targeted by the cops in the area, who viewed him as a burgeoning gang leader. Jimmy and his friends, who all wore matching red baseball caps, had taken to calling themselves the Red Hat Clique, and they got into little neighborhood rumbles with other groups from school. It wasn't long before there was a knock at his mother's door and the police took Jimmy in for questioning. "They couldn't really prove shit—they were just profiling you, putting you in their book," he said.

But the next day, when Jimmy told his friends on the school bus what happened, they couldn't help but be a little flattered. "Man, we the most dangerous crew," one kid said, and the name stuck. "Basically they made MDC into a gang," Jimmy shrugged. "We weren't no gang. We were just little badass children from Bowen Homes."

Years later, Jimmy could only laugh when the next generation of kids from the same projects ran up to inform him that they had taken over the name. *We know how to use it and y'all don't*, they told him. "Y'all didn't take nothing—y'all inherited some Bowen Homes shit," Jimmy laughed. But he also realized that things had changed. "We was just fighting!" Jimmy said of when his crew was their age. "Those n——s weren't fighting. They were doing every-*fucking*-thing you can think of."

Not that Jimmy was naive. At eighteen, while riding with Lo and his friends in the same car he had souped up, Jimmy took the charge when the police discovered a pistol in the vehicle. But taking his losses like a man was how he proved his worth.

A month later, when he got out of jail, Jimmy returned to find his mother's place boarded up. He turned to Lo, moving into the seven-room, $275,000 house his boss kept out in Decatur. "You knew he had some money, but you wouldn't know he was loaded like a baked potato, extra chives," Jimmy said. "Lo was rich as a bitch by nineteen years old. You wouldn't even believe that a little nineteen-year-old kid had a million dollars—cash money, liquid."

Yet even after he made it to the safety of the suburbs, Lo was most at home—and also at work—in Bowen Homes. "Nine, ten in the morning, we on that concrete," Jimmy said. "We might not leave until four in the morning."

For his troubles, Jimmy was paid $1,000 a week, plus whatever he could make on the side—usually about $700 a day—by stretching out the extra product he had left over. As long as Lo got his share, that was kosher. But for a worker like Jimmy, the money never lasted. "I fucked it up just partying," he said.

The cops, more than anyone, knew where the cash was coming from. "They were busting our spot every two weeks," Jimmy said. "You know how many trafficking cocaine charges I done beat? Criminal trespassing, trying to catch a n—— with money and take it off you, kicking in them doors. We were like, 'Oh, fuck.'" Once, during a high-speed chase, he watched Lo throw $175,000 out of a car window, never to be seen again.

In 2004, the FBI's High Intensity Drug Trafficking Areas task force finally made its presence felt around Bankhead, convicting more than thirty people—including the Baltimore Ravens running back and Atlanta native Jamal Lewis— in a sweeping investigation focused in and around Bowen Homes. Around the same time, Lo was facing twenty to forty years on three different cases, but he worked out a deal that sentenced him to about a year for each, running concurrently. Still, the writing was on the wall, and they were tired of it. Lo had never been shy about the twenty-eight times he had been arrested, or about his four convictions, but it was Jimmy who saw that notorious rap sheet as freeing.

"Everybody know you sold dope," he told Lo. "You went to jail for it, so you can talk about it! The whole fucking state can vouch for you—FBI, police. Who don't know you from being what you was? I was there, I know, I was right beside you! You gotta give them folks these stories."

In addition to having his boss's ear, Jimmy knew how to rap. One afternoon while cooking crack together in a female friend's kitchen, Jimmy started spitting lines about what they were doing, tailoring his flow to fit Lo's well-known taste for Jay-Z.

"I've been around him, I know what he do, I know his lifestyle," Jimmy said. "I wrote it on a brown paper bag in fifteen minutes, just thinking about shit in the hood." *All you have to do is make it rhyme!* he thought. Jimmy called the song "Pusher," and right away, Lo was ready to record it, hitting Toe Jam Studios on Bankhead, where everybody bought their mixtapes not long after they were finished.

In the years that followed, with Jimmy Braski by his side, Shawty Lo honed a voice that sounded like he was whispering and screaming at the same time, a charismatic rasp that imbued his plodding raps with significance. In oversized sunglasses, with a chin-strap goatee that looked painted on and a tattoo of the Bowen Homes entrance sign ever present on his forearm, Lo used his funds, his renown and his connections to build up a credible and influential—though brief—career for his collective, which helped to popularize the subgenre of snap music. (In 2007, Soulja Boy would expand upon snap and take it global with the early viral smash "Crank That [Soulja Boy].")

Lo's D4L crew, or Down For Life, included the rappers Fabo, Mook-B and Stuntman, among others. He also invested in another group out of Bowen Homes called Dem Franchize Boyz, who had hits with "White Tee," the song Gucci Mane flipped for his first local hit, and "I Think They Like Me." Though the two groups would become rivals, fighting over ownership of the sound, Lo was a main engine behind the West Side micro-scene, building a studio and greasing palms at radio stations and Bankhead clubs like the Poole Palace, where "Laffy Taffy" earned its stripes. Along the way, Jimmy burnished his reputation as a diligent sidekick and a secret rap weapon—the hardest person in the studio to please, a nearly invisible executive producer who could also come up with a hook or refine a bar in real time.

Shawty Lo released his solo debut, *Units in the City*, on Asylum Records, a subsidiary of Warner Bros., in 2008. It was a modest hit, featuring the singles "Dey Know" and "Dunn Dunn," which inflamed Lo's beef with TI, who was also claiming to be the King of Bankhead. But Lo's defining songs developed a special resonance locally and would eventually become to wide swaths of Atlanta what "Sweet Caroline" is to Boston. Yet even as he attempted to go fully legit in hip-hop, Lo's solo career failed to recapture the national interest that his early D4L songs had generated, and he never got the chance to build out the full-scale rap empire that he and Jimmy dreamed of.

One night, in the fall of 2016, Jimmy was at Blue Flame by 8, smoking, having a bite to eat, shooting pool and watching ESPN. By eleven, he was wiped, and he left for a friend's house nearby—the same guy who had overseen his first drug deal on Lo's behalf. Jimmy knew that Lo and the other guys were heading to the club, but he was resigned to sitting the night out, plopping down on the couch and falling asleep a few blunts later. When he woke up, it was to a screaming phone call. The only words he could understand were "Lo dead."

"It was just like my mama passing all over again," said Jimmy, who went to the morgue to help identify the body. "Father figure, brother, cousin, best friend—he was all that in one."

Lo had left the strip club around 2 a.m., losing control of his coke-white Audi A7 on the I-285 Southbound ramp for Cascade Road. According to the medical examiner, the car flew off the road over a guardrail and hit a tree, tossing Lo from the vehicle as it flipped over and caught fire. Two women riding with him lived. Initially described as a hit-and-run, the accident was ultimately ruled a one-car crash.

The next night, police blocked off Bankhead as cars blared "Dunn Dunn," "Dey Know" and the rest of Shawty Lo's catalog. The locals threw their fingers in the air in the shape of an L, and they cried. Lo left behind eleven children and a whole neighborhood.

"I would've been in that car," Jimmy said, still hurting years later. The official account of the accident never sat right with him. "Did somebody bump him? Was somebody following him?" Lo was the best driver he had ever seen.

"Like a stunt car driver, a n—— that can make the car do what he wants it to do," Jimmy said. "That was Shawty Lo. I don't give a fuck if it's a truck, it could've been an ambulance—homes gon' make that motherfucker do what it's supposed to do." Jimmy didn't even wear a seat belt when they rode together. "He'd always say, 'Jimmy, I know you ain't scared—you been in the car with me since you were fifteen years old!' "

Not long before his mentor died, Jimmy had been arrested for what he hoped was the final time, serving ten and a half months on a drug-trafficking charge. Upon release, he was sneaking by on some small-time street shit, but he also continued dabbling in the neighborhood music scene, driving most days to the West Side even though he lived out in the sticks. Guys knew they could still come to Jimmy when they needed an opinion on a potential single or wanted to arrange a feature with one of the many rappers he knew through Lo. Even though Jimmy was nearing forty, his ear hadn't aged.

So when one of the next-generation MDC guys started taking rap seriously enough to need a day-to-day manager, he knew Jimmy was an obvious choice. Jimmy had toured with D4L, and he knew the players, the radio stations, the clubs, the sound and the subject matter. After Lo's death, he was also struggling.

Marlo had kept in touch intermittently with Jimmy since the days when he had watched Lo and the other older guys hustling outside of his Bowen Homes apartment door. And Jimmy recognized the blueprint Marlo was following, as the kid he knew as Rudy began to forge his own way. "When they tore the hood down, Marlo went to another hood and turned that bitch into Bowen Homes!" Jimmy said proudly. "That's why they call him the 9th Ward God. Same thing how Lo did when Bowen Homes was up for grabs—he took that bitch over."

As Jimmy observed Marlo's money stacks getting bigger on Instagram—and the uncomfortable attention that followed—he also recognized the inevitable pivot. "They name hot in the streets," Jimmy said, "and now they rapping. I'm like, *Okay, they get it!* Marlo got a story. If anybody got a story and came up hustling in the streets, you already kinda popular."

He knew that Marlo needed a little work as a rapper. But in the Quality Control infrastructure, Jimmy saw everything he had fantasized about building with Lo. "Man, that's like Cash Money and Death Row put together," Jimmy said, "*and* it's in Atlanta." He was content to watch it thrive.

But Marlo knew they could help each other. "Hell nah," he told Jimmy as he set off on the road to rap. "I'mma take you with me."

17.

800 MILES FROM HOME

MUCH LIKE WITH MIGOS, IT WAS A LIGHT FAVOR FROM DRAKE that helped make Lil Baby really happen. But as with his label-mates, it was what Baby did after the Canadian rapper's assist that would allow his life to keep changing with the same whiplash intensity the last year had brought.

By 2018, the young man once known as Dominique Jones was, against all of his own expectations, a professional musician with four mixtapes under his belt and two fistfuls of regional hits—enough to come up from about $5,000 per show toward a healthy five figures for any given concert, with demand highest in his own city. Yet even that level of success placed Baby in the company of dozens, if not hundreds—a ravenous pool of Southern rappers who were multiplying by the minute. In a mainstream sense, only Baby's breakout single "My Dawg" had really crept out far beyond I-285. And if Atlanta had a graveyard for the careers of artists who had lucked upon a song the size of "My Dawg," or even bigger, never to be heard from again, it might take up the entire West Side, with an eye toward sprawl into Douglasville.

"We got more one-hit wonders than anywhere in the world! And they songs be *super* big," a guy known as Gouch, a fixer in the scene, told me, seeming almost insecure about anointing Atlanta anything more than a fast-food-style rap song factory. "Trinidad James, Ca$h Out, Joe Gifted, Shop Boyz—who else?" he rattled off. "Man, I'm telling you—we the home of the one-hit wonder!"

In the eyes of a lot of people who'd seen what Gouch had over the years—guys like Coach K and P—rap could always be counted on for a quick come-up. But sticking around beyond a cycle or two on what is still known, in a nod to the Jim Crow days, as the modern Chitlin Circuit of Southern rap club appearances felt about as likely as winning the lottery twice, even to those who'd actually watched it happen.

So even after a nine-month period in which Baby had gone from, by his estimate, 15 percent invested in rap to an all-in major-label artist—with Capitol and Motown welcoming him to the next level with a multimillion-dollar deal—Baby decided to approach the next phase of his music career with the same intensity he'd shown the block. Baby's sister Deja had once told of the time when a teenage Dominique asked to borrow $20, only to disappear for seven full days, returning home with a few layers of grime on him, bags under his eyes and some $100,000 in cash. Baby expected his second year as a real rapper to go something like that, with probably as little sleep.

But a text message from Drake—probably the single most influential figure in hip-hop, if not popular music, at the moment he pressed "send"—made everything a little bit smoother for Lil Baby.

In the five years since Drake had strapped "Versace" to a bottle rocket with a ninety-second verse, he had lost none of his fan's ear for emerging artists, and as a savvy observer of regional scenes, from Memphis to London to Lagos, he maintained a pen-pal relationship with the Atlanta underground. Even before Baby's career had truly started to boil, Drake let the young rapper know he was keeping an eye on him, and the two exchanged phone numbers on the strength of the Quality Control connection, the possibility of a future collaboration ever dangling.

Baby, however, was not the thirsty type, and he maintained a stubborn, old-fashioned desire to never ask for a handout in music or beyond. Cordial iPhone rapport or not, Baby vowed to his friends that he would not be caught dead begging Drake for a verse.

The politics of collaboration in rap could be fraught, and never more so than when Drake was involved. Most rappers started off their careers by doing features left and right on songs by slightly larger local artists or label allies, with a strong cameo potentially earning them some early fans, like a young Busta Rhymes on A Tribe Called Quest's "Scenario" or Future on YC's "Racks." At the same time, those rappers were likely paying for more popular artists to do something similar on their songs, again in hopes of conducting heat by association. If that two-pronged attack worked, and the smaller rapper became a draw themselves, they could begin selling their own services more widely—to R&B singers, say, and then would-be pop artists in need of injectable rap credibility, and then to the next tier of more established stars, who still want that same cred.

But if a typical guest appearance on somebody else's song could be seen as a personal favor, a full-throated cosign, a strategic alliance, a cynical maneuver, an easy paycheck or a one-for-one swap, a string of bars or a hook from Drake was something else entirely—a surefire ticket to Google searches, radio play, label attention and the *Billboard* Hot 100. Drake's mere presence could throw the entire economy of rap features out of whack, functioning as a cheat code to international attention, and just as often casting a shadow that blacked out the smaller artist entirely. In no small part because of what happened with "Versace," the very act of Drake's collaborating on music with lesser-known artists had become controversial in its own right among rap fans, who referred to it alternatively as the "Drake stimulus package" or as a vampiric blood-suck of virgin creative juices. The Atlanta graveyard of once-promising careers had more than a couple of artists who'd succeeded with Drake by their side, as he absorbed their refracted glow, only to fall off a cliff once the Canadian moved on.

So when Drake did pop up out of the blue, sending Baby barely forty seconds of himself flowing over a minimal, triumphant beat by the Atlanta producer Wheezy, it was both a gift-wrapped display of generosity and also an implicit dare—a challenge for Baby to make something that would not primarily benefit the guy who needed it least.

In the studio with Drake's start, Baby added a choppy four-line chorus that was catchy but not his finest, and also a verse of his own, sending the completed volley promptly back to Drake in a show of punctuality and respect. It was only then that Drake told Baby he could keep it for himself, giving the younger rapper his next big single and a track to anchor his new project—the first Lil Baby release beyond QC, under the larger Capitol and Motown banner.

What Drake likely knew at the time, and what Baby would be forever too humble to say straight out, was that the greener artist had stolen the song, assuring that his verse would not be cut off by DJs after Drake's was finished. And Baby did it with a single memorable line—brainstormed on the spot with Offset, who happened to be in the studio—exercising a muscle that hadn't previously come naturally to him: humor.

What led up to the song's defining lyric was typically tough money talk from Baby, though he did manage to compare the color of his yellow Ferrari to Pikachu, rhyming the name of the chubby Pokémon with what he refused to do from behind his Cartier glasses ("peek at you"). But as Baby neared the end of his verse with velocity and flair, he broke his usual hustler's poker face when he said probably the first outright meme-able thing of his career thus far. "Wah, wah, wah," he squealed out of nowhere, "bitch, I'm the baby."

Snappy and silly, assured in its absurdity, the line worked as rap, and also as in-your-face marketing, firm in the hip-hop tradition, from "Snoop Doggy . . . Dooogg" to "chka-chka Slim Shady," leaving previously ignorant listeners certain who they were hearing. *Bitch*, Baby spelled out, *I'm the baby*. In classic Atlanta fashion, Quality Control quickly put the line on a big yellow billboard overlooking the city.

The song, titled "Yes Indeed," premiered that May on Drake's internet radio show, but only after P built anticipation by posting a clip of the track to Instagram Live from an Atlanta club, only to delete the snippet, further stoking fan and industry interest with his own DIY marketing. That, these days, was sometimes all it took.

Less than a week after the song's official release, Baby delivered his fifth career project, *Harder Than Ever*, which continued to erase the music business distinction between a mixtape and a digital-first album. Barely a year after putting out his first-ever songs, *Harder Than Ever* debuted at number three on the *Billboard* album chart. By the end of June, "Yes Indeed" would be his first platinum song—an achievement it compounded seven times over in the years that followed.

Now an auspicious major-label priority, Baby spent the weeks around the release of *Harder Than Ever* in a whirlwind of obligations to others, filling entire days with interviews and appearances in Atlanta, New York and Los Angeles, including promotional stops at radio stations and streaming services, where the goal was to make a good enough impression, musically or personally, to be put on the influential playlists from which casual fans took their cues.

At the sleek and snack-stuffed Spotify offices in Manhattan, Baby was visibly exhausted and equally bored, muttering with Ced about girls on Instagram and barely looking up from his two phones while his new music played for the playlist "curators." But when he was asked by Coach and P what he wanted to do that evening, after twelve hours of press and handshakes, Baby was direct and unequivocal. "Studio," he said. "All night." He had a flight out in the morning.

YET EVEN AS his music climbed the charts, Lil Baby was still being overlooked by certain hip-hop gatekeepers, the kind who might've considered "Yes Indeed" a Drake-flavored fluke. Just as the song was peaking on the Hot 100, hitting number six beneath Post Malone, Childish Gambino, a pop DJ and two other Drake singles, the legacy rap magazine *XXL* released its annual Freshman Class issue. The list of rappers anointed the genre's rising stars based on the kind of opaque criteria—like label and manager lobbying—that allowed those left out to angrily deem it irrelevant while simultaneously reinforcing its primacy by caring.

P had pushed the importance of making the magazine cover, forcing Baby to visit the *XXL* offices with his best face on and to make the kind of self-promotional pitch video that made the rapper squirm. Nonetheless, Baby was left off in favor of less successful acts. When one prominent hip-hop talking head remarked online ahead of the Freshman Class's reveal that Baby better be on it, P preempted the official announcement by admitting that his artist had not been chosen. "But he getting money like a sophomore so we ain't tripping," P commented. What freshman, after all, had already released his fifth mixtape? (Besides, two other Coach and P management clients, Stefflon Don and Trippie Redd, did make the cut.)

Baby brushed off the slight, but he was as unlikely to dwell on his recent successes. Before the year was out, he would release two more albums—*Drip Harder*, with his Atlanta brethren and fellow Young Thug protégé Gunna, and *Street Gossip*, which reached number two on *Billboard*, his highest chart placement yet. But even as his recording addiction continued apace, in line with his desire to not be defined by "Yes Indeed," Baby was honing another element of his professional arsenal, one that could be overlooked in the viral rap age.

Live shows had always been the most reliable source of steady income for musicians, and with streaming slicing up small royalty payments even further, concerts remained important and lucrative. But whereas pre-internet musicians might've spent years developing as live performers, getting comfortable on small stages and learning the right angle to hold a microphone, younger acts—and especially rappers—were now blowing up before collecting much real-world experience. Pre-fame touring was no longer how one paid dues, and it showed. Most emerging rappers could be expected to pace back and forth onstage while their tracks played in full, recorded vocals included, shouting a few words at a time over a better version of themselves, usually out of time and out of key. Muffled microphones were the norm and stage presence an obvious afterthought.

For a while, Baby didn't do much better, relying on his DJ and the crowd to set the tone, eyeing his designer shoes and failing to keep up with the verbose tongue twisters in his recorded music. Self-confidence aside, he had trouble being the sort of ham it took to command a room. Even after her initial skepticism about his new career had subsided, Baby's mother, Lashon, ribbed him about the performance aspect of his unforeseen profession. "How you gonna get out on the stage with all them people?" she asked. "You *bashful*!" At first, Baby requested that she stay on tour with him to help stave off the loneliness and isolation of the road. "He likes to know he got family somewhere," Lashon said. "He's very sensitive like that."

But by the time Baby returned to New York City for his first show there as a solo headliner a few months after the release of *Harder Than*

Ever, he had tapped into a new gear, greeting the sold-out crowd of 1,200 at Irving Plaza with his head high and voice steady.

As if to prove a point, Baby bounded onstage as Drake's "Yes Indeed" verse blared, opening the show by dispensing with his biggest song as a constellation of iPhone flashes shot upward from the mass of fans below, their bodies surging toward the front barricades. The crowd was young and diverse, with the first four ad hoc rows of standing room packed overwhelmingly with women, revealing another burgeoning side of Baby—the heartthrob. The women shrieked as he got closer and riled his congregants with a symphony of circular arm waves and the glare of glistening jewelry, with everybody anticipating the same moment.

When the song's climax arrived, Baby dropped his mic as his DJ killed the beat, allowing the crowd to shout the signature line in unison—*Wah, wah, wah, bitch, I'm the baby*—right as the rapper's son Jason, days from his third birthday, waddled up from behind, his own tiny arms swinging wildly. Baby mussed the boy's hair as he finished the song, and Jason stuck around, shadowing his dad's stage-stalking from side to side. For the next hour, the audience matched Baby word for word through singles and deep cuts. Toward the back of the stage, his Atlanta entourage swelled but kept its distance as they all admired the reception Baby—and Baby alone—was getting more than eight hundred miles from home.

Magnanimous as usual, however, Baby closed the show with a surprise throwback gesture of regional respect, one local-first artist to another. Without warning the New York crowd, the Southern visitor wordlessly welcomed a special guest, the rainbow-haired rap supervillain known as 6ix9ine—a Brooklyn native who couldn't even book a concert in town, for fear of the chaos and violence that followed his every move—for a raucous, surprise performance of his hit song "Gummo."

Instantly, the place exploded at the sight of the genre's most controversial outlaw of the moment. But as 6ix9ine dove headfirst off the stage into Baby's fans, it soon became clear that his cameo was pure spectacle; the people stopped rapping along and they buckled under his sudden weight. It was hard to hold up a man while trying to film him like a circus animal at the same time.

Moments earlier, during Baby's own final song, the venue had been more unified and more reverent as the out-of-towner led the audience in a full-throated a cappella chant of a song that received an even livelier reception than "Yes Indeed." A tumble of tangled verses with no hook and no celebrity feature, "Freestyle" had become Baby's surprise fan favorite and sleeper hit, introducing wider audiences to his world and a cast of recurring Atlanta characters, including the Zone 4–residing 4PF clique ("Me and Ced get them loads / We let 'em go for the low") and Marlo's 9th Ward compatriots alike ("We won't fall out about shit").

Bathed in blue light, Baby spit his neighborhood tales and catalogued the wins that signified he was outgrowing them, with the reaction to his intimate anthem leaving little doubt. When he finished the song, Baby was so energized by the response that he started it over again. The second time through "Freestyle," the crowd only screamed louder.

18.

"CAN'T DO BOTH"

ONE AFTERNOON IN THE SUMMER OF 2018, MARLO INSTRUCTED me to meet him at one of the many isolated apartment complexes scattered across Southwest Atlanta—just not the one where he was staying. As I sat in the nearly empty parking lot, watching a group of kids play on a creaky hoop and waiting awhile for him to show up, three young women tittered for a moment before shouting toward my idling rental car to ask who, or what, I—an unfamiliar white face—was looking for.

When I said I was there for Marlo, they cracked up laughing, like it made perfect sense but was still amusing, which it did and was. "Just making sure you're in the right hood, boo," one of the women said with a loaded shrug.

When Marlo finally picked me up in a steel-colored Genesis sedan more than an hour later, he was fresh out of bed and still groggy, apologetic for his lateness but laid-back in a white T-shirt, Philadelphia 76ers basketball shorts and Louis Vuitton slides with socks. Beyond fashion, the slides were practical: Marlo's foot was still healing from an injury that had kept him homebound while Lil Baby went on his first national headlining tour. Originally, Marlo had been scheduled to open for his friend at legitimate concert venues—not nightclubs—for the first time. Instead, he totaled his brand-new $100,000 Trackhawk Jeep—an Atlanta hood favorite for the supercharged engine that could bring it from zero to sixty in 3.5 seconds—slashing through the tendons in his foot, leaving him hobbled at home and lucky to be alive.

Marlo's second solo mixtape, *9th Ward God*, had come out that spring to some mild acknowledgment in Atlanta. But despite the Quality Control imprimatur, he received almost none of the national notice that had followed Baby almost from the beginning, a fact that made the often unpredictable business of rap feel decidedly meritocratic, given the pair's obvious difference in natural ability—but also, at that point, in dedication. Marlo had been busy beyond music, and even at its hottest, QC couldn't will a hit that wasn't there.

Driving around familiar streets, Marlo seemed sanguine about his relative lack of career development. He knew full well that not being able to tour alongside his more famous counterpart was a missed opportunity to reach a receptive new audience; he'd been hearing about it nonstop everywhere he went, as if he were the lazy high schooler who failed to get a summer job and was bumming around while everyone else was out making things happen. But the truth was that in the eighteen months or so since he'd started to call himself a rapper, Marlo had not taken music all that seriously, and he alluded repeatedly to what he still had going on in the streets, which he always pronounced with a hard K, as in *skreets*, just like Baby.

"I ain't tripping," Marlo said of his wobbly takeoff in the music industry. "I had to be new to the block before. So it just is what it is."

In this chicken-and-egg scenario—was Marlo not blowing up because he was still in the hood, or was Marlo still in the hood because he was not blowing up?—the answer was obviously both. His studio diligence had suffered as he kept one foot or more on the block, leaving his development as a rapper to stall. At the same time, Marlo was bursting with pride for the strides Baby had made professionally, encouraging his friend repeatedly to stay on that new path.

"No matter what I'm doing," Marlo had told his partner, "you keep going."

In the car, Marlo played some of the new music he'd been working on, revealing melodic growth and more experimentation with Auto-Tune, though he still had a habit of stuffing too many syllables into a line and ignoring rhyme schemes in favor of packing in names and information—rookie moves that could also double as a distinct style if honed correctly. But more than his choices as a songwriter, Marlo was adamant that consistency in output would be the key to making it in rap.

He assumed that his product and entrenched connections were good enough to attract notice as long as he kept the mixtapes coming, with their quality somewhat beside the point, especially if he could continue to enlist his more famous friends to appear as guests. "You might not like the whole tape, but you might like one song on this tape, two songs off this tape, three songs off that tape, and by the time you look up, you really just like a whole tape," Marlo explained. "It's just about: *Keep dropping, keep dropping, keep dropping.* I ain't finna never stop. That's the only way you're going to win."

He turned to parallels in drug dealing. "It's just like, say, me and you on the corner and we selling weed. If I keep my weed more than you, you might be bunking harder than me at first, but if I have my weed when you ain't got no weed, eventually, I'm going to be taking your clientele." Marlo vowed, not for the first time and not for the last, to spend more hours in the studio.

But if he had picked up anything else from Baby, who was dropping mixtapes constantly, it was a budding knack for the kind of lyrical specificity that elevated certain trap music beyond its component parts and stamped a rapper as a bona fide student of—and participant in—the streets. Hood legends had reputations like high school athletes, their glory days ever distant in the rearview, hard to monetize and eventually lost to history. It was up to a local oral tradition to keep the names alive and enlarge their myths in the process. On his least generic songs, Marlo did just that, memorializing and offering cautionary tales in equal measure.

Marlo and Baby had traded these stories with a friendly competitive edge on their earlier collaboration "A-Town," breaking down the fates of their forebears, like Shawty Lo and another local legend, Noonie (who "got hit with a whole clip"), each in enough detail to register with those who knew, and with little care for the great potential majority for whom the lines might as well have been made up. Lyrics like these went beyond establishing authenticity among those who could pick up the reference to Noonie. (The twenty-year-old born Christopher Copeland was killed during the Bloody Summer, when he was shot forty times while leaving an illegal gambling spot on Metropolitan, in a dispute involving the International Robbing Crew and 30 Deep.) The details also bred an Atlanta-first loyalty among listeners who saw themselves, their neighborhoods and the travails that affected their families directly reflected back to them in music.

Such on-the-ground reportage chronicling overlooked communities had always been a value proposition of hip-hop—"the CNN of the ghetto," as the genre has famously been called—but as regional distinctions were being decimated by the great leveler of the internet, and artists could explode on social media without ever gaining favor in their own city, certain street rap remained a quaint refuge for the close-at-hand, the esoteric, the hyperlocal and loaded. As P explained it, pointing to the underestimated marketability of this musical niche, "There's more poor people and people in the street than anything. So the young folks coming up in poverty, they can relate to this."

On *9th Ward God*, Marlo returned to this well of street stories in bursts, exalting and mourning Bowen Homes ("Home of the murderers and them drug dealers"), the MDC boys ("we more dangerous") and Milo ("a motherfuckin' real one"), as well as Lo, Chivers Street and a seemingly endless list of nicknamed compatriots who had fallen to prison or gun violence along the way. His verses could sound like stream-of-consciousness diary entries or therapy sessions, their poignancy ratcheted up by the Auto-Tune drenching his pleas to all those he wished were still around—Fresh, C. J., Die, Joe Bad, Milo and more.

As both a rapper and a hustler, Marlo had always seen himself as a carrier of the Bowen Homes torch, an ambassador and a historian who, through his proximity to giants past, took on some of their authority, his pedigree strengthening his own well-established "face card." To guys like Marlo, Baby and P, the concept of a face card was the ultimate claim to neighborhood renown—a reputation that followed, preceded and protected a respected figure in the streets, allowing them to walk through certain areas and do business with certain people, confident all the way in the strength and thoroughness of their past dealings.

As if to underline the sway he held in certain Atlanta neighborhoods, Marlo described how he'd really won over P in the first place, beyond being a friend of Baby's and whatever embryonic musical talent he showed. In fact, he had worked his street connections to right a wrong on behalf of the executive.

"It was just some serious shit happened, and he seen how I really get down," Marlo explained, tiptoeing around the particulars but describing a situation in which somebody close to P was relieved of something valuable, only for Marlo to see to its safe return. "Somebody had gon' done took somebody shit, and I pressed it and got the shit right back"—he snapped his fingers, *like that.* "It ain't even about no money, we going to do this on the strength of love," Marlo recalled P's telling him afterward. "As long as you loyal to me, I'm loyal to you."

"And he knows I'm straight loyal to him," Marlo said. "That's all it takes."

Baby had once flexed a similar muscle on behalf of Quality Control after hard drives containing unreleased music by Lil Yachty were stolen along with the unattended car of a QC employee. "Attention: Atlanta," P wrote on Instagram in a panic. "Whoever just jumped in the Dodge Journey and stole the car at the Chevron on Northside dr. That was my engineer car with an important hard drive in it. I know you just doing what you do and I'm not knocking your hustle cause I use to steal cars in the 90's. I have 20k cash money for the hard drive back."

Hours later, Baby FaceTimed P grinning and holding up the devices. The message was clear: while P had gone wide with his plea, it proved to be unnecessary—QC's own young guys were connected and certified.

The trick, for Marlo, was cashing in one kind of credibility for another, with authenticity only going so far in music without the songs to back it up. He knew the city's network of clubs and studios afforded the possibility for a rapper to campaign on a grassroots level, getting their friends on board, then their neighborhood and then the whole metropolis before going national. But that was an old-fashioned way to build a fan base in the twenty-first century.

At the same time, the small-town feel of Atlanta street dealings and gossip could lead to plenty of backbiting, pissing matches and attempts to undermine a rapping hustler's influence, be it through crude means (chain-snatching, girlfriend-stealing, Instagram exposés) or more artful ones (like diss songs). But driving around the West Side with Marlo, the risk of someone testing him to prove their own toughness or avenge some perceived slight couldn't have seemed further from his mind.

"Ain't nobody never gon' say nothing to you if they see you with me," he said. "Period." Still, Marlo backed into every parking spot, from Ken's to the barbershop to the mall, like a mafioso demanding a restaurant's corner table with a view of every entrance and exit.

On this particular afternoon, Marlo was feeling especially nostalgic about his neighborhood and those he'd learned from. It was, after all, Bowen Homes Day, the almost-always-annual block party on Bankhead for those who lived in the projects or wished they did. One of many "hood day" celebrations around the city, Bowen Homes Day was like a family reunion if your family was a thousand people strong and also interested in drinking, smoking and screaming Shawty Lo songs on the street while staring down the police.

In preparation for the party, where he expected to be one of the more prominent guests, Marlo planned to get a shape-up and some new clothes. But he needed to grab some money first, so we stopped by another apartment complex, this one pristine and quiet, with a security gate. "This ain't no projects," he said, "but it's still the West Side—I can take some back streets and be right in the hood."

Marlo liked to keep about four or five apartments around the city at any given time, a constellation of crash pads and stash spots for clothes, cash, a good night's sleep or whatever else might need safekeeping. Inside, mountains of shoeboxes, black trash bags stuffed with who knows what and loose garments were piled high on a white faux-leather sofa and the floor around it—Gucci, Nike, Prada, Jordan—alongside zipped-up suitcases and two unplugged, tipped-over flat-screen TVs, like a ransacked Christmas morning at Daddy Warbucks's bachelor pad. The blinds were drawn, and the only thing on the walls was a painting of Clint Eastwood as Dirty Harry, gun drawn.

Only one corner near the bedroom made the place feel lived-in. Neatly arranged on a card table, and also scattered around the couch, were various statues in carved wood—thin, sleek and covered in what looked like melted wax and dried blood. Propped alongside the figures on the white tablecloth were yellowing family portraits in frames, dusty and worn, adorned with beads and candles.

"That's my religion," Marlo said. "Ifa." He beamed at the altar. "My family's from here, but we study an African religion. This my oldest brother, C. J.—he passed. This my great-grandmother, my great-grandfather. We just praise God."

An ancient spiritual system that survived the transatlantic slave trade, Ifa, the religion of the Yoruba people, has its roots in West Africa, in what is now Ghana, Benin, Togo and Nigeria. Over the centuries, it morphed and combined in some places with Christianity, but the religion remained, in its ritualistic incantations and divination, a bedrock of what is known variously around the world as Santeria, vodou and Sango Baptism. Practitioners of Ifa are taught that deceased ancestors and loved ones become spirit guides to be venerated and consulted in moments of uncertainty as one seeks to fulfill one's destiny.

In Atlanta, Ifa had recently gained a word-of-mouth popularity among the Black youth as they sought to reconnect with their African roots. It even took on a certain trendiness in the streets after a group of Marlo's 9th Ward compatriots, including 21 Savage and No Plug, began advertising their faith, carrying stones and wearing beads for protection. On Marlo's left wrist, next to two diamond bracelets, a rubber band and an iced-out Rolex, sat two strands of green and brown known as *ide*, beaded bracelets tied off by an Ifa priest for personal preservation. Coach K, he noted, had also dabbled.

For a couple summers, Marlo traveled to Nigeria to learn more about Ifa. But while the trips had expanded his spirituality, the grueling eleven-hour flights there also helped introduce him to using Percocet, the opioid pills that, along with Oxycontin, had become a raging American health plague. In a less-seen slice of the crisis, opioids had also grabbed hold among young Black people, for whom weed, lean and pills seemed to supersede most other recreational drug combos, a reality reflected and possibly encouraged by rap lyrics about the most effective ways to numb one's pain.

At this point, Marlo considered himself addicted to Percs, as they were known around town. "I have to have those motherfuckers every day," he said. "I'm trying to get off them motherfuckers, but I'm telling you, that shit hard as hell to kick."

What started as a way to chill during international travel had quickly spiraled—"just started taking 'em and taking 'em and taking 'em"—and Marlo had even gone to the hospital with stomach problems brought on by the pills. But for him, the connections between chronic self-medication and the traumas of racism and poverty that touched nearly everyone he knew were almost too obvious to remark upon at length. "N——s be having so much on they mind," Marlo said. "N——s just be wanting to cool it. Either they on Percs or they on lean."

He had recently stopped smoking weed cold turkey, an achievement that was somewhat comforting as he struggled with the pills. "That's how I know I can stop taking Percs," Marlo said. "Whenever I put my mind to something, I can just stop doing that shit." But his car accident and injured foot didn't help.

AT THE BARBERSHOP around the corner, a song by Lil Baby and Offset was blasting as two kids rapped and danced along in between PlayStation trash talk. But it wasn't long after Marlo entered that the current of the ribbing changed directions, as the large customer already in the chair, midcut, revealed his level of intimacy by leaning into the rapper's birth name.

"Rudy be hot just like Lil Baby, but he don't be serious," Gouch said, revving up his shit-talk engine.

Marlo rolled his eyes and settled in for the roasting he knew was coming. "I hear this shit every day," he muttered, failing to break eye contact with the video game he'd gotten in on.

As Gouch carried on, Marlo reluctantly introduced his friend as "the West Side A&R," an old neighbor from Bowen Homes and fellow MDC ally who had grown into an Atlanta bon vivant, the kind of guy who knew everyone and hustled constantly but didn't actually sell any drugs. Gouch had instead made himself a respected celebrity on his side of town with relentless good vibes, a generous spirit and a feisty, community-oriented Instagram page, where he was as likely to be seen shooting dice as he was to be leading a ten-mile bike ride, organizing a school supply giveaway, starting a weight-loss competition, buying up junk cars or selling tires. When Baby got out of prison in 2016, it was Gouch who took him to the strip club. A nightlife promoter, small-business marketer, hood philanthropist and all-around social facilitator, Gouch could also play the role of pastor, politician, gossip columnist and middleman depending on the day, an Atlanta character and chameleon through and through.

"If you got something, it's best to take it to a n—— like Gouch," Jimmy, another old friend from the projects, said. "He knows somebody who wanna buy the shit—he's like a broker."

One product whose movement Gouch facilitated with ease was music. Though not a rapper or producer himself, he, too, had an ear for hits, an eye for star power and an endless contact list, which had put him on the fringes of breakout rap success more than once. Another lifelong student of Shawty Lo's, Gouch was in the midst of rebranding the aging rapper's career as his fresh-minded manager when Lo died in 2016.

"Music always was the center of our projects," Gouch said of Bowen Homes, where he was raised by his grandmother and helped to take care of his three sisters. "Music and drugs.

"I never saw myself being a drug dealer," he said. "But I saw the things that they had that I wanted."

Gouch's entrepreneurial streak had led to a wide variety of semilegal "juuging," he explained, using the all-purpose term for finessing a payday by any means—hustling with a dash more creativity and no sense of consistency. "In Atlanta, sometimes you just come around and make some money," he said. "That how Atlanta go: up, down, up, down, up, down."

Once, around Christmastime, Gouch was tipped off about a Target semitruck pulled off on the side of the road and open for business, its driver distracted but accounted for and the merchandise ripe for the taking—after an entrance fee. "They keeping the driver high and be charging people fifty dollars to get on and off the trailer with whatever you want while the dude do his drugs," Gouch explained. "So me and my brother might have got over forty thousand dollars' worth of stuff—we made forty thousand dollars off a hundred dollars."

Jimmy had gotten by on similar juugs. When OutKast shot the "B.O.B." music video in Bowen Homes, they used his mother's apartment to hook up the electrical power, and Jimmy saw an opportunity. "They gave me five hundred dollars for that shit," he said. "I ain't playing with they ass! I said, shit, it's already three hundred dollars for the bill, so give me two hundred dollars on top of the three. I gave my mama a hundred dollars—'Here, Mama'—put the four hundred dollars in my pocket. We don't even pay light bills! It's the *hood*." That, to guys like Gouch and Jimmy, was the essence of Atlanta.

So was putting those profits into music. Gouch estimated that he had spent some $250,000 over the years trying to help break various rappers. Along with a few rotten business arrangements and artists who cracked under the pressure or were arrested midclimb, Gouch was an early proponent of Young Thug, whom he called his cousin—"He not really my family, but my cousin is his cousin"—helping him sign his first local mixtape deal at a pizza joint called Slice. But being a behind-the-scenes link didn't come with a percentage in most contracts.

Recently, Gouch had settled on calling his own fledgling record label Group Home, running it as an all-purpose studio and marketing apparatus out of a wood-paneled building on the West Side. But even as Group Home failed to launch, Gouch's reputation as a good hang and strategic thinker—as well as a loyal compatriot of Baby's and Marlo's—allowed him to fall into the Quality Control nest, with P taking him under his already-crowded wing. As part of the entourage on trips to Miami, Las Vegas, New York and LA, Gouch got to see a previously walled-off echelon of the music industry up close, gaining favor as P's trusted confidante and gut-check counsel. "I don't even talk when I be around," Gouch said. "I just watch and listen. Because I know if I talk more, I'm going to miss something."

It was all of his reverent soaking up of P's knowledge, pet peeves and preferences that allowed Gouch to absolutely fillet Marlo at the barbershop. "'What you gon' do—you gon' hustle or rap!? Because you can't do both,'" Gouch bellowed in his best P impression, recalling a conversation on a recent stop of the Lil Baby tour. "P was just going in," he said. "He told his driver and security to go ahead so he could walk with me down Hollywood Boulevard—boy, he going crazy!

"'Rap, not rap, think he missing something in the street—fuck that shit! They don't be understanding me. Stick to my plan! Marlo wanna go over here and gatdamn do what he do, come rap when he wanna rap, but man, he could be getting fifteen, twenty thousand dollars! You don't wanna do nothing but hustle. You don't wanna do nothing but sell shit, stupid bitch. All these *gatdamn* millions! We gon' get these millions—fuck wrong with you?'"

Marlo had heard it all before. "They be on my ass!" he said. "Don't even trip. I'm going on tour!"

Back in the car, Gouch's pep talk–as–roast seemed to have sunk in. As Marlo maneuvered along I-285 North toward the Cumberland Mall, he made and fielded a constant stream of FaceTime calls to friends and associates—including "OG P," as the executive was listed in Marlo's phone—each of them soundtracked by the soft ding of his no-seat-belt alert. Sometimes, like when he put on his chains while going eighty miles per hour, Marlo steered the car with his knees, his iPhone rattling around the cup holder as his array of check-ins continued, always on FaceTime.

"I might go fuck around with some of them dates," an invigorated Marlo told one caller who also inquired about the Baby tour. "I'm just trying to get my lil tape together, to really build up my archive. Songs everywhere."

"You in there! Especially if one of them really catch, it's gone!" said the voice on the line, echoing up from the compartment next to the gearshift. "Ten K, fifteen K a show ASAP—that shit gon' be so easy. You ain't gotta do shit, boy, except keep doing what you're doing. Shit gon' come right in your lap. I know you the next one. Whatever P gatdamn doing—probably joined the Illuminati. P like, *Fuck that, I don't give a damn who I gotta sacrifice.* I'm telling you."

The two invoked other rappers like sports radio jocks did professional athletes, assessing their up-or-down stock based on recent streaks or slumps. "I know what these folks wanna hear, and they wanna hear that trapping shit," Marlo's friend said.

Satisfied and gassed up, Marlo pulled off the highway and into the mall parking lot, ending the call without a goodbye. It was time to go shopping. But we were barely onto our first escalator when it became clear that Marlo was being followed.

He glanced over his shoulder but ignored our tail—three young boys who looked between ten and thirteen years old. In the women's department at H&M, they mustered the nerve to make up the distance between us and approached the rapper in their midst, asking if he was, in fact, Marlo.

"See! I know my rappers, boy," one of the kids hissed at his friend. "I rap, too," he said, turning his attention back to the local celebrity. Marlo, trying to suppress his obvious pride, handed over $40 and told them to split it.

But the group had ballooned from three to five as some stragglers caught up to their braver friends, and no one wanted the interaction to end. The shortest of the bunch asked if he could rap right there, and Marlo, sufficiently tickled, pulled out his phone to record the impromptu cypher as each kid took turns freestyling, whether they knew it or not, in Future- and Migos-style triplets.

As we parted, Marlo shook his head. "I didn't start rapping till I got grown!" he said. "When I was a kid I would've never walked up to nobody. I was busy living."

* * *

Bowen Homes Day was just starting to coalesce when we finally made it to Bankhead. At the mall, Marlo had opted for an all-H&M outfit, pairing gray sweatpants with a Velvet Underground & Nico T-shirt under his QC and PFK chains. On Bankhead, he wrapped a red flannel around his head like a turban and marched down the main drag alone to nonstop calls of "Rudy!," "Rude!" and "Rudy Marlo!" from those with the familiarity to chide him for having a stage name.

"That ain't gatdamn Marlo—I don't know no Marlo," teased Jacoby Hudson, the Bowen Homes–born defense attorney, who rocked a blanket-size red Polo T-shirt, a Braves hat and a Jesus chain. "I know *Rudy*."

Cars crawled down the thoroughfare, which some lifers referred to playfully as Ocean Drive, though it had neither the glitz nor the waterfront view. They blasted Atlanta-only music and shouted out to friends as the clusters of people along the road swelled into the street. A half dozen cop cars rolled back and forth, too, mostly ignoring the light revelry as blunts were sparked and drinks poured, including one into a Versace teacup. The police sometimes flashed their lights to keep traffic moving, receiving occasional jeers, but the air was thick with humidity and cross-generational jubilance, and not even the APD was itching for a confrontation before nightfall. Grills the size of coffins sizzled with barbecued chicken. A man draped in a thick yellow python prowled the area, placing the snake around the neck of any willing woman or child for a photo op.

As the sun started to go down and the crowd swelled, Marlo greeted his sister, their mother figure Denice and her teenage son, who asked first for a pair of sneakers and then, more quietly under his breath, about when he might be able to come live with his more established sibling. Marlo said soon, but he sounded noncommittal and handed the kid some cash. The boy tapped at Marlo's diamond-encrusted QC pendant as if to confirm it wasn't a figment of his imagination.

"This is how the projects used to be," Marlo said as he moved slowly down the street, surveying the celebration, soaking up the adoration, issuing hugs and handshakes.

In front of Continental Seafood—the neighborhood spot for fried shrimp and crab legs—the greetings got more complex as a cluster of young men in PFK chains interlocked fingers with one another in graceful swoops, their hands dancing together as choreographed mirror images. Percocets, Backwoods and crumpled cash changed hands with equal fluency. Each overlapping group of people revealed a distinct layer of communal bond, be it from blood, business or friendship. But Marlo's air of authority was impossible to mistake, with children, peers and elders alike approaching to whisper something in his ear or take a photo.

Across the street, Gouch held court in a stretched-out ribbed tank top, pouring sweat and leading the charged-up cavalcade in Shawty Lo sing-alongs like a pep rally director. All the while, the cops' ineffective blue light show and symphony of horns added to the cacophony and made Bankhead look like a nightclub. An urban cowboy trotted by on horseback.

When it was time for me to leave, Marlo gestured wordlessly to a friend who, without my knowledge, had become my ride. The man introduced himself as Thumb, "the only one who's actually legit with a gun," and he told me to stay close as we slipped through the block party to a beat-up sedan. The air-conditioning wasn't working, so we rolled down the windows, letting the summer air whip through the car as we rumbled through the back streets of Bankhead and beyond, past boarded-up houses invaded by vines, yards dotted with browned and cracked plastic lawn chairs, piles of worn tires and twists of trees.

Thumb said he hadn't even grown up in Bowen Homes, but down the street in Bankhead Courts, which meant that he and his friends had feuded with Marlo and his. "I couldn't go hang in their hood, they couldn't go hang in my hood. When you saw us, we were fighting or you were getting jumped on," he explained. "Now we grown, and I'm proud to see you doing what you're doing, if you ain't locked up or dead."

They'd all done what they had to do to survive as men, Thumb said. But at a certain point, whether it was a court case or a killing, most everyone got tired of the grind, of being seen as a "hoodlum or a menace to society," of getting harassed by police, of having cash confiscated. "You just get so tired of this shit," he said.

"We tend to stay on the path we know because that's where we come from. Some folks be looking like it's a gang—it's not a gang, it's a family. You might not be my blood but, shit, the struggle made us blood."

Thumb mentioned that he did security and that he hoped to one day become a personal bodyguard for Marlo or Baby. "I know the ins and outs of them, I know their daily routines," he said. "They shouldn't hire outsiders to be with them, should be somebody that know 'em.

"Staying alive is harder than staying out of prison—that's the real risk," he said. "N——s envy n——s if they feel like you getting too much money. N——s'll kill you.

"But if we can all stick together and come as one," he said, "it's an unstoppable city."

19.

THE STARTING LINE

THROUGHOUT 2018, IN THE HONEYMOON PERIOD THAT SURrounded Lil Reek's record deal, the teenager made the traditional promising-artist rounds, learning that his new job would be grueling, repetitive and also full of wonder. With his managers Roger and Bird by his side, Reek visited the corporate offices of YouTube; he made his live debut at a taste-making concert series hosted in the courtyard of a modern art museum; and he was the subject of his first extensive profile, telling Pitchfork, "I'm just trying to handle my business while I'm young, so when I get older, I'll be set for life."

To celebrate what he'd accomplished already, Reek bought himself a small gold Rolex that fit his slim wrist perfectly, with a custom diamond bezel and ten more petite diamonds in its face, along with a matching ankh chain. He increased the percentage of luxury brands in his wardrobe and shoe collection, helped along by burgeoning long-distance friendships with the designers and tastemakers Virgil Abloh and ASAP Bari, who sent Reek clothes and played his music in DJ sets or on internet radio shows. And he left the country for the first time, visiting Paris, London, Berlin and Milan, captioning one Instagram post, "Thousands of miles away I'm sorry but fuck the USA."

Back stateside, Reek was booked for a few other small performances that fall, including his first college show—and first time as a headliner—at Lawrence University, a private liberal arts school and music conservatory with fewer than 1,500 undergraduates, located in Appleton, Wisconsin. The student in charge on the booking committee, a smiley blond kid named Elijah, who scoured rap blogs and didn't look much older than Reek, initially offered $3,000 for the concert. But Bird, more in the driver's seat as a manager lately given his experience advantage and assertiveness compared to Roger, talked Elijah up to $5,000 from the school—plus airfare for Reek and his two managers (comfort-plus seats), a three-star hotel or better (the Marriott) and a suitable rental car (a hulking Mercedes).

Upon arrival, Reek hit up the sleepy Midwestern mall near the school and was confused to find a lack of designer on offer. He opted instead for a fresh pair of Timberland boots and a kid-size Green Bay Packers jersey, knowing that repping Aaron Rodgers would endear him to the local crowd. "Who would have thought I'll be in Appleton, Wisconsin," Reek marveled online, taking in the hotel's lakeside view. "The power of music."

At the show, about a hundred excitable students showed up to watch him rap, posing for photos with Reek before and after in their Vans and Hood By Air. Reek, still curious about the college experience, took it all in. But classes and a campus would have to wait.

Because after having attracted the attention of the music industry, and even putting their stated interest in writing, the key now was to do it again. For the hundreds of artists signed to major labels every year—and the innumerable aspiring amateurs right below them—a contract could feel like a culmination. It was really more like a starting line. Commencing the slow build of collecting a fan base through steady releases and shoestring appearances technically came next. But what the labels were really waiting on, often passively, though few would say it outright, was a self-generated spark.

Usually, this came in the form of a hit, or at least a viral moment that could lead to one. But whereas some select few of priority artists—typically those who fit snugly into a preconceived idea of a Typical Pop Star—would be assigned a team whose job it was to extract that hit song out of them, or else create it themselves, the purpose of spreading around small bets on eager self-starters with auspicious beginnings was to be in position in case they happened upon it on their own.

Giving artists like Reek room and some budget to develop as musicians while they collected their small club, college and festival show checks along the way could be fruitful. But in all likelihood, it wouldn't be. That was the gamble. In the meantime, there was the motivating hope—on both sides, though more so on one—that the next big break was ever imminent. After all, they had made it this far. Still, the cloud of inertia always loomed.

At home in Atlanta, Reek was building mostly by himself. No tier of his small team was from the city, and so in between trips out of town, he was left to his own devices, living basically the same life as before, but with more spending money. His finances, too, lacked much oversight. Reek remained proximate to a few Atlanta crews and fledgling labels, like Young Thug's YSL and Lil Baby's 4PF, but not fully in the fold with any of them. And while he partnered with Republic—home to blockbuster artists like Ariana Grande, the Weeknd and Drake—some of the rappers he had grown up with around Cleveland Ave., like Lil Keed and Slimelife Shawty, both of whom had also started with Brodinski and featured on some of Reek's earliest songs, opted for more domestic operations. In addition to a built-in local hype squad, such arrangements meant the freedom to release music at will, without corporate approval, and to more pointedly work the strategic alliances of the Atlanta pipeline, including clubs and DJs. Reek's most immediate circle in town—the guys of the Donut Shop trap referenced in most of his songs—did not have a major footprint in music. There was no sign of his second mixtape.

For his first real hometown concert that October, Reek was treated more like an independent artist than a major-label one. Booked alongside a slate of his still-green peers, including Lil Keed, another disciple of Thug's with a movie-star smile, Reek was scheduled to do a brief set at a rap showcase during A3C, Atlanta's annual music conference and festival à la Austin's South by Southwest. He would not be paid outside of travel expenses, so Roger and Bird flew in, along with Roger's brother, who would serve as Reek's onstage DJ. Expected early for sound check, Reek pulled up in a dark and shiny Corvette, blasting Baby and Gunna's days-old *Drip Harder* mixtape and using a pillow for a boost in the driver's seat. He had paid a friend $1,000 to hold on to the car for a couple months.

"He wouldn't be doing anything else tonight," Roger said about Reek's low-key appearance, which was being held at a small, barlike venue on Euclid Avenue in Little Five Points, the hipster neighborhood filled with coffee shops, new age boutiques and thrift stores.

After making themselves known at the venue, Reek's managers were on their way to meet him for a preshow meal, musing together about the rapper's potential in the viral marketplace, given his look and magnetism. "He should be on *Ellen*," said Bird, a barrel-chested operator with a New York slickness that stood out down south, about his kid-sized client. He predicted that Reek, the individual, would "get bigger than his music."

At the restaurant, Reek bounced with anticipation, shimmying to a muffled soundtrack and snapping pictures of his twinkling watch. Unfailingly polite to the waitstaff, he drank a Shirley Temple and munched on a plate of lemon slices as if to prove he could. A screenshot of a to-do list saved as his iPhone background reminded him to take his vitamins, keep up with his nutritionist and "stop smoking, stay drug free." One by one, a small parade of friends joined the party for moral support.

Back at the venue, the entourage grew to include Reek's on-again, off-again girlfriend, whose long braids rivaled his body in length, and his mother, who was her son's compact doppelgänger plus a few facial piercings. Huddled on dirty couches crammed backstage, the group matched Reek's nervous energy and stayed mostly silent. When he finally took the stage, illuminated in red, Reek gave the spotty but curious crowd a performance befitting a beginner, with admirable pluck but a lack of breath control. It was a start.

After the show, there was little to dwell on but plenty to plan. Where Reek did have an advantage, thanks to his record deal, was in access to funds, and the concert crew included a young music video director who was scheduled to shoot Reek's first single as a signed artist. They had $65,000 of Republic-fronted money to spend.

But, three months later, when the video for "Door Swing"—an eerie number produced by Roger that included Reek's unforgettable line about studying while cooking crack—was finally released in January 2019, it received little if any promotion from the label. With its science-lab drug motif, including two women handling test tubes, cash and literal donuts on a scale, the video collected barely 50,000 views out of the gate on YouTube, a fraction of what "Rock Out" had done independently a year earlier.

Another half-handful of one-off tracks dropped by Reek into the streaming rapids also failed to find any traction. "Door Swing" would turn out to be the only music video he ever released under contract at Republic Records. Bryan, the A&R who signed him, was not long for the company either, leaving Reek no real advocate in the building. A still-embryonic rapper now frozen on a high corporate shelf, Reek knew he wanted out. To the label, which had offered him nothing in the way of artistic development, he would only ever be a rounding error anyway.

By the summer of 2019, just one year into his first record deal, Lil Reek was once again without one.

20.

MORE AND MORE

WHILE LIL BABY WAS HITTING HIS MARKS AND MARLO WAS DEciding how much he really cared to, the rest of Quality Control was churning at an unprecedented pace.

Migos had long set the tone for the label's everything-all-the-time ethos, recording and releasing mixtapes as if every idea had an expiration date, and the industry's new reliance on streaming playlists was helping to do away with the traditional album as the default vehicle by which an artist was judged. The ease of uploading music online—with physical packaging an expensive afterthought, if required at all—and the bottomless appetite for new content from distractible audiences with scroll-happy tendencies gave an advantage in visibility to musicians willing to create fast and frequently. So QC, name aside, was willing to serve, serve, serve most of what its rappers delivered.

At the end of 2017, to set the tone for the year to come, the label had executed a hard-drive dump in the form of a compilation album, not unlike the *So So Def Bass All Stars* collections of the midnineties—except this one existed only online, as a one-hour-and-forty-five-minute pseudo-playlist. *Quality Control: Control the Streets, Volume 1* was thirty tracks long and featured the full spread of the label roster, like an appetizer sampler platter with Migos as the hot wings, Baby as the potato skins and Lil Yachty as the mozzarella sticks, plus plenty of lesser-known crudités.

In addition to songs sprinkled throughout by Marlo and Kollision, the compilation introduced the idea of getting all three Migos à la carte, since Quavo, Offset and Takeoff had increasingly taken to recording song ideas alone. Sandwiching the release of *Control the Streets* was further evidence of this divide-and-conquer strategy: Offset dropped *Without Warning*, a collaborative mixtape with 21 Savage and the producer Metro Boomin, while Quavo put out *Huncho Jack, Jack Huncho*, an album-length collaboration with Travis Scott.

But all of that was just a warm-up. In January 2018, right around the one-year anniversary of the Migos album *Culture*, the group released its sequel, *Culture II*, abandoning the focused economizing of its thirteen-track predecessor. Billed as a twenty-four-track double album, *Culture II* was another 106 minutes of maximalist rap music featuring input by Pharrell Williams, 21 Savage, Drake, Gucci Mane, Nicki Minaj, Cardi B, Kanye West, Post Malone, 2 Chainz and the trio's usual stable of producers (Murda Beatz, DJ Durel, Zaytoven). But whereas *Culture* had been credited for filtering the Migos sound into its purest form and tightest hooks, *Culture II* was received skeptically as opportunist bloat, the beginnings of inevitable oversaturation.

"If *Culture* marked the very peak of the Migos' triumphal arc, buoyed by a swell of goodwill, *Culture II* is simply . . . here," the Pitchfork critic Meaghan Garvey wrote. "Where *Culture* was an event, its sequel feels more like an occurrence, the quality of its songs handicapped by the artlessness of its presentation."

DJ Durel bragged that the tracks on the new Migos album had taken about twenty minutes each to write and record. "If they really want to take their time on it, they'll take forty or forty-five minutes," he said. "No more." But while the group said in the past that its music came easy, the bluster had a different ring coming from multimillionaires considered to be at the peak of their profession than it did from the punkish upstarts they once had been. New songs like "Stir Fry," "Narcos" and "Walk It Talk It" (another QC hit featuring Drake) displayed Migos' trademark pep over novel-enough sounds. But its effectiveness waned across the two dozen tracks, which felt more like attempts to find another "Bad and Boujee"–style breakout than a diverse whole—an exercise in brand extension rather than an artistic statement. The album was rolled out along with a merchandise collection at Bloomingdale's.

Yet the trio and its label were also shrewd, the perfect musical avatars for a bacchanalian moment in the music business. In streaming terms, a runaway smash hit was worth more than a pile of solid songs, so Migos' swinging for home runs and accepting strikeouts made sense—the more tracks they put out, the more chances they had to happen upon a huge single. And because of the way streams were counted on the *Billboard* charts, long albums could also benefit at first, with any combination of 1,500 streams across songs counting as the equivalent of one album sold. The more tracks for fans to sample, the thinking went, the higher the total streams.

Such number grubbing was hardly hidden. Around the release of *Culture II*, if a listener searched for "Migos" on Spotify, the first result was not just the new album but an official playlist that repeated the album three times in a row, perhaps in the hopes that someone would press play, get distracted and just let it run for the three and a half hours it took to play the seventy-two-song loop. This was music optimized to keep playing, as immersive an experience as one could handle while also going about their daily life.

Atlanta, in this sense, was once again ahead of the curve, meeting the consumer where they stood, much like the city's rap artists did in the mixtape days. The traditional album format, after all, only existed because of technological limitations—about four to six songs, or twenty-two minutes of music, fit on each side of a vinyl LP, with its invention kicking off the "album era" that lasted through cassettes and CDs. But that was no longer a concern. And Migos, in line with its young listeners, whose attention spans might have waned as technology made finite delivery systems obsolete, was helping to dismantle the hegemony of the capital-A album—a standard upheld for decades by mostly white rock critics who often valued the cerebral preciousness and audible labor of art over its visceral immediacy, the essence of innate style, the creativity of abundance and the impact of instinct. Whereas George Harrison once recorded 102 takes of a song that did not even make the Beatles' *White Album*, Quavo was improvising slogans that could nonetheless move millions, even if only for a time. Then he would put out another song.

In the short term, the gambit was working: *Culture II* gave Migos a repeat victory, debuting at number one on the *Billboard* album chart and selling 199,000 "album-equivalent units"—which included streams—more than the 131,000 *Culture* did in its first week the year before. Based on the middling reviews, the modest uptick in activity might have been chalked up to the larger portion of the listening public now streaming its music regularly. But that was hardly enough to convince anyone at QC to change course. The label forged ahead with its plan to release another volume of its *Control the Streets* compilation by year's end, and it followed up *Culture II* with three more albums from the Migos universe—the first full-length solo releases from Quavo, Takeoff and Offset.

"It's all about market share," Coach K told *Complex* that fall, spelling out the plan to continue the flood of content. "We love domination."

At the same time, Quality Control was diversifying beyond its Atlanta bread-and-butter. *Control the Streets* allowed the label to introduce a new perspective—the female one—in the form of a raw, unproven duo called City Girls, from Miami, Florida. Made up of JT and Yung Miami, two twentysomething rappers with brash style and defiantly dirty mouths, the group combined the sass of Salt-N-Pepa with the knowing lewdness of Trina, and nodded toward the booty-shake bass music that once linked Atlanta and South Florida. In one unforgettable lyric, JT described her female anatomy as "so tight it could smoke a Newport."

The overwhelming domination of the straight male perspective in Atlanta rap was in line with the genre's—and the country's—broader limitations and failures regarding gender. Even after the political (and racially motivated) freak-outs of the nineties, misogyny in rap, from the industry back rooms to the lyrics, continued largely unabated, with listeners and collaborators of all sorts compartmentalizing certain standards of morality or decency for access to celebrities, danceable beats, sticky flows, fun and a commitment to uncensored freedom of expression.

Beyond the musical content, Atlanta trailblazers like TI and LA Reid would even face accusations of using their power in the industry to commit systematic abuse. In 2021, at least four women accused TI of having drugged and raped them over the span of more than a decade beginning in 2005. Reid had been pushed out as chairman of Epic Records following a sexual harassment complaint in 2017, one that tracked with a similar account from earlier in his career. (TI denied the allegations and a criminal inquiry in Los Angeles was dropped due to the statute of limitations. Reid apologized for anything that could have been "misinterpreted.")

Still, this reality couldn't help but be reflected in the pool of successful artists, which, despite early Atlanta-based innovators, like TLC's Left Eye and Crime Mob's Diamond and Princess, remained basically all men. There were, eventually, glimmers of progress: after decades of an unwritten, one-at-a-time rule when it came to female rappers, the success of Nicki Minaj, Cardi B, Megan Thee Stallion and more seemed to be shifting the gender dynamic for good as women across the South started coming up with the same ferocity (and support) as men, as seen in talented Atlanta newcomers like Latto, LightSkinKeisha and Baby Tate.

Though less heralded, women had always been crucial to the city's music ecosystem. From the early influence of Bunnie Jackson, the mayor's wife turned funk manager, to the work of Deb Antney and Amina Diop with Gucci Mane and Young Thug, their centrality to the business was never in question on the ground. Future and 21 Savage had women as managers in Ebonie Ward and Kei Henderson, respectively, and QC would not have functioned without the day-to-day oversight of the unsung Tamika Howard and Simone Mitchell, to say nothing of the invisible labor of rap mothers like Lashon Jones (and surrogate mothers like the indomitable and omnipresent Baby Jade of the Duct Tape family). Ethiopia Habtemariam was working her way up at Capitol/Motown, and as these executives accumulated influence, they vowed to keep widening the path for female artists and employees of all varieties.

At QC, City Girls fit right in. P said he first heard about the group from a Miami club waitress who showed him the SoundCloud diss track "Fuck Dat N——," the first song the City Girls ever recorded, which was then catching on among the local stripper population. Coach probably had flashbacks to Freaknik. And even when the duo sheepishly admitted that JT was about to be sentenced to jail time for identity theft—a fact Coach already knew before meeting her, having done his research—the label signed them anyway and got to work.

Though the package was new, the blueprint was familiar. QC enlisted their go-to criminal lawyer, Drew Findling, to argue on JT's behalf at her sentencing, pleading to the judge about how a record deal with one of the hottest labels in music had given her a new lease on life. Findling succeeded as usual, getting JT's surrender date pushed back six months to allow her to work.

As Coach had done previously with Gucci Mane—and QC had mastered with Migos sans Offset—the executives used that extra time to begin banking two albums' worth of songs (and six music videos) to keep up a steady patter of releases during JT's incarceration. City Girls released two albums, *Period* and *Girl Code*, in 2018, eventually landing two songs in the Top 40.

And then, once again, there was Drake. On the day before JT turned herself in to serve a two-year sentence for credit card fraud, Drake released "In My Feelings," an earworm borrowing from New Orleans bounce (a cousin of bass music) in which Drake referenced both City Girls by name and gave them a scene-stealing bridge: "Fuck that Netflix and chill—what's your net-net-net worth?" the women demanded. The song would spend ten weeks atop the *Billboard* Hot 100, and QC, thanks to its Canadian patron saint, could say it had broken another artist that came out of nowhere.

These were, in many ways, the money-counter days for Quality Control—the montage scene in every hustlers' tale when the cash is rolling in, the cigars are being lit, the women are falling over themselves, the songs are shooting up the charts, the mansions are being moved into and the cash registers, from Rodeo Drive to Lenox Square, are *cha-ching*-ing. The stacks of bills on display had gone from brick size to cinder blocks, and everybody on the team seemed to be locked in an arms race of foreign cars, Swiss watches and diamonds, with Lil Baby setting the bar for creativity in the form of a jewel-encrusted baby head, complete with a swirl of hair and a pacifier. His diamond baby pendant was even wearing a tiny diamond chain of its own.

The family was also growing. In the fall of 2018, Baby was expecting his second child, this time with an Instagram influencer known as Jayda Wayda, who had more than a million followers and ran an online boutique selling wigs, clothing and accessories. Offset and Cardi B had welcomed their first child—a daughter aptly named Kulture—that summer. And in December, the gossip pages that were now tracking QC's every move reported that P, already a father of three, was expecting two more, almost simultaneously, by two different women.

For someone who so steadfastly avoided attention and publicity for most of his life, and even the beginning of his career in the music business, P's becoming a hip-hop tabloid fixture was an uncomfortable new reality. But it came with his dreams of moguldom on par with Diddy, Master P and Birdman. When one of P's paramours, the model and video girl Lira Galore, started airing his dirty laundry on Instagram—"We both knew she's been pregnant," Galore wrote, accusing P of "cheating, gas lighting, taking my stuff away when u get mad" and having thrown a "temper tantrum"—the executive remained largely silent but allegedly texted an associate ominously, "She gone see."

There were hurdles on the business side, as well. With Cardi B and Offset's personal and professional lives becoming more intertwined, the executives behind his career were also invested in hers, which had flowered beyond anyone's wildest hopes. Even though the televised wedding special that Coach K had been plotting never came to fruition, the couple established itself as a tumultuous Jay-Z and Beyoncé for a new generation, and as their reality show unfolded over social media, Coach and P's management wing of QC, known as Solid Foundation, helped guide Cardi through the industry. This was an unwelcome intrusion for the man known as Shaft, Cardi's manager from her *Love & Hip Hop* days, who claimed in a $10 million lawsuit against Cardi, Coach and P that he had "conceived, arranged and orchestrated Cardi B's rise to become the biggest music sensation on the planet," only to be frozen out.

In legal filings, Shaft blamed Offset for steering Cardi toward the rapper's own team, resulting in a breach of contract and defamation, as the couple claimed that Shaft had been stealing from her. "U a snake," Offset texted the ex-manager. "U can't hide from me n—— and u not bout to play my WIFE."

Cardi B countersued Shaft for $30 million, claiming that he made her sign record deals without a lawyer, giving himself a 20 percent cut and failing to properly account for the money she made as he pocketed more than his fair share. But even as the lawsuit inched its way through the legal system, the couple was on the upswing, at least in the business and celebrity sense.

"Man, my girl sold ten point eight million dollars in three hours," Offset said, beaming, one afternoon that November, while scrolling through Instagram in the basement of the pair's sparsely decorated mansion in the leafiest part of northern Atlanta. Not satisfied with the social media headline about his wife's sold-out fast-fashion collection, he FaceTimed Cardi to get the specifics.

"Hey, baby, how much royalties you got on your Fashion Nova shit?" Offset asked, preening for his audience of employees, family and hangers-on. "You might as well start adding that money up. You know you sold ten point eight million dollars in three hours? Ten point eight million dollars in three hours! Bruh, I'm doing my own math . . . What was the cheapest piece?

"Sold out!" he reiterated with more excitement than she could muster on the other end. "You going to re-up or do another collection?"

With insane schedules and an infant daughter—Offset's fourth child with a fourth woman—quality time had been hard to come by for the couple in 2018. But business was obviously their love language. Multiple times, against the glare of their public on Twitter and Instagram, the pair had broken up, only to get back together, with Offset, like any good rock star, trailed eternally by cheating rumors. Once, internet sleuths even attempted to authenticate a video of him allegedly in bed with another woman by matching his designer pants—the kind rarely worn twice—to photos of him wearing the same yellow pair in public.

But Offset remained visibly and vocally in the thrall of Cardi's successes, bragging often about her dominance across music and merchandise. He blamed jealous, shit-stirring internet commentators for their marital struggles—"Y'all won," he wrote online during one of their splits—and vowed repeatedly to cut out all of the distractions in his life to devote himself to being a family man. Settling down, Offset said in his basement, was "the best thing that's happened to me personally, which helps me make the music, which helps my career.

"I'm building a dynasty," he said. "I have no distractions. I have a wife and a child—that changed my whole everything. I was a young hothead, but now I understand the value of life."

When his phone vibrated again minutes after he and Cardi's first FaceTime, Offset fished a second cell phone from his sweatpants pocket and sought some privacy. "That's the wife," he announced with diligence.

Offset was still glowing when he returned. "At first n——s was talking shit," he said. "'Oh, you're with a stripper, you're this, you're that.' But I'd seen her potential, her vision, her grind. Whatever she does, she's going to master it. She's like me."

In fact, Cardi was even savvier, using her ease of intimacy on social media—where, for instance, she cataloged Offset's obsession with limited-edition sugary cereals—to round out his image, too, making him more relatable by proxy while flexing her business sense to motivate him. "I ain't never had nobody I could do that with," Offset said. "We're talking real business—big scale. She brings excitement and pressure to me, but I like that. I like the pressure of my bitch doing her thing. She's number one, so every time I'm hitting the charts, I've got to be top ten."

Still, Cardi made no secret of preferring her native New York to Atlanta, and her presence felt negligible in their rented mansion. A Mercedes SUV, a Jeep, a baby-blue Lamborghini and a McLaren 720 sat in the driveway, next to a statue of a Rottweiler by the front door that screamed bachelor pad. More luxury cars hid in a garage the size of some family homes. Inside, much of the furniture still had its tags on, even in the movie theater. The platinum plaques had yet to be hung and the only thing on the kitchen counter was Michelle Obama's memoir.

Offset's mother, Latabia, sat a table nearby in a QC sweatshirt, overseeing a spread of breakfast food, while his friends and former stepfather, Kevin, milled with other insiders about the home, tending to the rapper's space, his schedule, his plentiful suitcases and pairs of shoes. Just two of Offset's nearly a dozen dogs—the pit bulls known as Bentley and Fat Mama—were in the backyard, dining on Waffle House straight from the takeout container. Offset, smoking a Newport in Palm Angels flip-flops, showed off a doorframe that one of them had chewed through. "All this stuff I have to pay for," he sighed.

The hub of activity, and the most finished room in the house, was the basement. It was down there that Offset's home studio was coming together as he tried to put the last touches on his solo album, the third and final installment in the individual Migos trilogy, while also finishing a sold-out, fifty-plus-date arena trek with Drake dubbed the Aubrey & the Three Migos Tour. Fittingly, the final three concerts were scheduled for back-to-back-to-back nights that weekend in Atlanta.

"This is what it is right here," Offset's engineer J Rich said, recounting their busy schedules and motioning to the bando-style setup of hard drives, laptops, speakers and monitors scattered about. "Studio, studio, studio, studio, studio, studio, studio, studio, studio, studio, studio, studio, studio, studio, studio, show, show, show, show, show, show, show, show," he said.

Already, Offset had spent the year spreading his wings, earning three top 15 hits without his groupmates, but he wanted his first album alone to be something different altogether. While the preceding Migos solo releases—Quavo's *Quavo Huncho* and Takeoff's *The Last Rocket*—further demonstrated the ephemerality of the modern music deluge, largely fading from the public consciousness after streaming and charting just fine in their opening weeks, Offset was betting on a more substantial breakout moment because he was adding an element seen only in flashes throughout the expansive Migos oeuvre: introspection.

The album, which he hoped to put out on his twenty-seventh birthday in December, would be titled *Father of 4*, and as Offset played his new music for those gathered downstairs, his hushed, intimate tone was the first sign of a fresh approach. Though Migos had never presented or been received as particularly reverent of Atlanta history beyond Gucci Mane, Big Rube of the Dungeon Family opened the album with a weighty spoken-word verse. The songs that followed included Offset's detailing of his own youthful rebellions, his experiences with the criminal justice system and its effects on his mother, friends and children, all four of whom he addressed by name with personalized apologies for everything from missing birthdays to his dependence on lean and Percocet.

Carlos Desrosiers, a friend and A&R executive who was helping with the solo albums while the group was on tour, said he made it a point to push Offset to uncomfortable places. "A lot of people know the Migos, but they still don't *know the Migos*—they just know the sound and the vibe," he said. "What's the core? People need to know the story. Nothing's better than your fans knowing who you are."

Offset had plenty of material, but he needed the space, mentally and physically, to let it out. "When I'm making those records, I'm not making them type records in front of n——s," he said. "It's me breaking the barrier of myself, opening myself, opening my head and playing with my thoughts."

He definitely didn't need the usual parade of yes-men that surrounded a typical Migos recording session. "I don't like a lot of n——s in the studio anyway, because everyone wants to say something is hard. I like critique n——s that are like, 'Nah, we can leave this off,'" he said.

As Migos had helped to make trap culture into popular culture—landing a number one song about cooking up dope with an Uzi and bringing its *Scarface* tales to James Corden's family-fuzzy "Carpool Karaoke"—Offset came to realize that he felt a different level of satisfaction from reaching those outside of what he assumed was his target audience. He liked surprising people. When I told him that my mother had sent me the James Corden segment approvingly, he seemed genuinely touched. "Hell yeah," Offset said. "Them the most important people. You just said your mom—that shit's big to me, my n——. For real."

A near-fatal car accident had marked a turning point for his sense of perspective. About six months earlier, with Cardi B seven months pregnant, Offset, never much of a sleeper, made a middle-of-the-night store run alone in his two-door, lime-green Dodge Challenger SRT Hellcat. When he staggered back through his bedroom door at 5 a.m., he was bleeding from his mouth and hands. He could hardly stand or speak, and he gripped a thick Cuban link chain that had fallen from his neck.

Cardi was already awake, getting her makeup done ahead of a long day of appearances, and as Offset collapsed on the floor soaked in his own blood, she went ballistic, certain he had been shot. Even in the ambulance later, as Offset insisted that he had only been in a car accident, the paramedics said that he might be delusional, and they cut off his designer clothes in search of a bullet wound.

"I had so much blood on me I didn't even notice," Offset said, showing off scars on the backs of his hands that marred his tattoos of Jesus and the Quality Control logo. His voice caught as he recalled the carnage.

It was raining that night, and somebody was walking in the street just around the corner from Offset and Cardi's home. Offset swerved to avoid the pedestrian, he said, and crashed into a tree, leaving his Hellcat looking like it had run over an IED, its front end crunched like a torn-up tin can. The point of impact was directly in line with the driver's seat. Offset was not wearing a seat belt.

"I had enough reflexes to put my arms up in front of me," he recalled. But when two airbags deployed, the force sent his arms back into his face, breaking his bottom teeth. When he tried to escape the flaming vehicle, he found his door was stuck. His chest felt like it was caving in. "I just kept screaming, '*I'm not finna die! I'm not finna die like this!*'"

Offset squeezed out of the passenger side, but he passed out when he tried to stand up. It was then that someone approached him, and the rapper, in a cloud of smoke, his vision blurred, was certain even in that state that he was about to be robbed. Instead, "it was like a guardian angel."

A man heading home from his graveyard shift had seen the accident, recognized Offset and walked him the few blocks back. The next day, bandaged like a mummy, his eye socket broken, Offset was released from the hospital and headed right back into the recording booth.

When I asked how the accident affected him, Offset didn't even have to think. "Slow down," he said. "That's the biggest lesson: Slow down. Take your time. Think through your moves." He caught his breath again. "That was my life."

Typically impulsive, Offset knew that patience was never his strong suit, no matter how many signs from the universe he had received. One summer afternoon two months after his crash—ten days after the birth of his daughter Kulture—he posted a brief video to Instagram that showed him visiting an out-of-the-way pawnshop. In no time, Offset and a friend were pulled over in the rapper's Porsche 911 Carrera for what the police called an improper lane change and potentially illegal window tinting.

They were in Clayton County, south of Atlanta, an area not unlike Bulloch, where Offset had been locked up after that ill-fated college show. This time didn't go much better. Once again citing the stench of marijuana, the cops searched the vehicle and turned up three handguns and ammunition, some weed and $97,290 in cash. Offset and his passenger were both arrested and charged with possession of the drugs and guns. But it was worse for the rapper, who remained a convicted felon and thus unable to legally own a firearm. Offset also got hit with the traffic violation, and both men were taken straight to the local jail.

Right away, Drew Findling was on the case, arguing that all Offset was guilty of was "driving while Black." The lawyer pointed out that the rapper's companion was a licensed gun holder who was working as his bodyguard, but the authorities were not convinced. In fact, they pushed harder, insisting that the car and cash were subject to civil forfeiture because they were "derived from, or realized through a pattern of Street Gang Terrorism." Offset, who was on the cover of *Rolling Stone* alongside a pregnant Cardi B at the time, wouldn't get his money or car back for another six months.

"There's a tremendous amount of money in this industry and law enforcement is clueless," Findling said. "So what will happen is, they'll see a young African American man driving a shiny, beautiful, three-hundred-fifty-thousand-dollar car, he is laden with diamonds, and there's automatically an assumption that he's a gang member or he must be a drug dealer."

Though Offset was never indicted in the incident, chalking the dropped charges up to another magic trick from Findling, the rapper was forced to perform the entire Drake tour while out on bond. And the threat of a more serious case still loomed: in deciding not to prosecute Offset, the Clayton County district attorney's office invoked a "much larger" "ongoing federal investigation."

Findling, who by then had been dubbed the #BillionDollarLawyer by his rapper clients, still had more work to do on behalf of Kiari Cephus. "There's such a target on these young guys," Findling said one afternoon in his office. "It is increasingly disturbing to me, the X that is on the forehead of people in this industry. Every once in a while someone is going to make a mistake. But no one looks at all the good that comes out of what they do."

Findling seemed both enraptured by his celebrity clientele and yet still partially—and purposefully—oblivious to the intricacies of the rap world. ("I'm always going to hit that seventies channel on Sirius, man," he said about his own musical tastes.) But he was adamant that "people go to Wharton to try to achieve the business acumen that just naturally flows through the veins of these guys." And he wasn't shy about assigning motivation to the government forces that kept him busy on the fringes of the music business.

"There's a failure to understand that this is an art form and that this is just a new generation, just like all past musical generations," Findling said. "Blues was the devil's music, everybody thought jazz was this horrible thing that was going to change mankind, and rock 'n' roll was going to destroy the earth. The earth was going to implode because of rock 'n' roll! So now we have this new industry that has cross-appeal to all socioeconomic groups, people of all races, all ethnicities. But those on the outside want to associate some negative connotation to it."

It felt as if Findling might be testing courtroom material, or at least recycling it. Either way, he was on a roll. "The guy that started the posse was Henry VII," the lawyer said. "Read the history! Mickey Mantle talks about his posse—everywhere he went, he had his boys with him.

"To me," Findling concluded, "it's all just motivated by racism."

DESPITE A HANDFUL of mysterious cancellations by Migos, the North American arena shows with Drake that summer and fall were a whopping success, selling more than half a million tickets and grossing $79 million, enough to put the tour in the top ten highest earning for the year behind acts like Ed Sheeran and Taylor Swift. But even with seven straight dates in New York and Los Angeles, respectively, the whole run was leading up to Migos' three hometown shows just ahead of Thanksgiving, at the State Farm Arena downtown.

On a Saturday night in November, the second-to-last date of the tour was the only event that mattered to the city's rap fans. Clusters of vibrating young people dressed in their finest flocked to the venue as the Quality Control team prepared for a friends-and-family extravaganza, arranging piles of complimentary tickets for everyone from Migos' jewelers and their mothers to the R&B singer Monica and her two sons. Offset even requested that Drew Findling meet him at home and travel to the concert with his entourage—a conquering hero returning home from battle to greet his faithful, flanked by loved ones.

Migos were technically opening for Drake, performing for forty-five minutes before the bigger artist took the stage. But every night, the group returned for an additional half-hour segment during Drake's set—a typically benevolent gesture from QC's big brother. "That n—— a real n——, man," Offset said. "I fuck with him. People can say what they wanna say. He solid."

The night before, Drake had brought out Lil Baby as a special guest, allowing him to soak up the adoration of the Atlanta crowd. On Saturday, in an attempt to return the years' worth of collaborative favors, P took Drake aside and presented him with an honorary QC chain, which the rapper immediately put on over his white crocodile-skin vest, a celebration of their tactical alliance.

Backstage, the mood was convivial and the hallways were crowded as the rappers' dressing room overflowed with their VIP guests. Takeoff and Durel were running late, but Quavo and Offset played host, shaking hands and posing for photos as their crew rolled blunts and dealt with the stress of the guest list. Even Findling, in a gingham blazer and sunglasses, was sought-after, recognized by two women in the crowd, who cornered the lawyer for a conversation.

Given the commotion, it was not surprising that Migos took the stage thirty minutes behind schedule. By then, the crowd was seething with anticipation. "It's every fucking day with these guys," Migos' tour manager said, rolling his eyes, as he corralled the trio. "Every day."

But when the lights went down and DJ Durel bellowed "*Atlaaaaaaaaanta*," by way of introduction, thousands of people started pogoing along to the beat as the trio took the stage chanting one of its earliest mantras about trapping all night: "Hannah Montana! Hannah Montana! Hannah Montana!"

Each Migos member was outfitted in an absurd matching getup—jumpsuits in three colors that were part NASCAR, part skydiving, complete with reflective tape accents (and available for purchase on the Migos website as a $125 Halloween costume). But the wreaths of chains around each of their necks were the sartorial centerpieces, and Offset's jeweler estimated that he was wearing $600,000 worth of regalia, including diamond rings on eight of his ten fingers. Digital screens cycled through abstract graphics, and pyrotechnics flared in harmony with the trio's Auto-Tuned chirps as they bounced through five years of exuberant hits.

But when it came time for Migos' grand finale—an inevitable yet eagerly expected rendition of "Bad and Boujee"—the atmosphere of swelling hometown pride between the group and its audience turned to one of sputtering anticlimax. Not even halfway through the song, the arena crew appeared on the catwalk that led to the main stage, beginning the work of turning over the setup for Drake's more elaborate production.

At first, Offset, Takeoff and Quavo failed to notice the commotion on the fringes, continuing their performance as the house lights turned on and audience members exchanged puzzled glances. Even a few seconds later, when the arena speakers went silent, the group kept at its animated performance of "Bad and Boujee," unaware of the fact that no one in the stands could pick up what they were saying. The onstage monitors were still blasting the sound from their microphones back at them, but Migos were the only ones who could hear it. From outside the trio's bubble, there were only disappointed groans.

As the rappers gradually realized something was wrong, a few fans, assuming technical difficulties, tried to keep up the sing-along—"My bitch is bad and boujee / Cooking up dope with an Uzi"—but the chant stood no chance against the audience's chattering as heads swiveled left and right for any source of clarity. Looking equal parts confused and humiliated, the three Migos were forced to jog awkwardly down the catwalk and into the bowels of the arena, waving halfheartedly to feeble applause. "They cut the mic on the Migos, y'all!" one spectator observed. "What the *fuuuck*?"

By the time the group reached its dressing room, followed by a tense trail of caretakers and companions, it was clear that the unceremonious end to their homecoming had been deliberate, a decision made over their heads for the sake of the concert's schedule. Jerel, Migos' manager, met the fuming trio, trying to say something about the venue's curfew. But no stagehand union contract bullshit was going to explain away the blatant affront. Quavo, asserting his role as the group's leader, demanded answers about who made the call.

Just then, Drake's manager, a diminutive Somalian Canadian known as Future the Prince, came rushing down the hall, giving Quavo a target for his ire. Future the Prince was being trailed by two hefty security guards.

"You don't disrespect me in my city!" Quavo shouted as Drake's manager stammered over his reasoning and claimed that he had informed the Migos team ahead of time what needed to happen.

"In my own city?" Quavo repeated. "With our kids out there?"

A half circle formed behind Migos in the narrow hallway, but no one else said a word as Quavo and Future the Prince stood face-to-face. A police officer assigned to the arena joined the security guards tentatively in the back, but all three kept their distance. Drew Findling pinned himself to the wall, staring straight ahead, like a child avoiding eye contact with his arguing parents. Behind Quavo, Offset's teeth were clenched.

"I come from *nothing*," Quavo said, establishing the source of his outrage—the fact that what should have been a triumphant moment, the endpoint of a lifelong arc, had been snatched out from under him. Not to be outdone, Future the Prince countered that he, too, came from "zero-zero." But that only inflamed Quavo further.

Not taking full responsibility and not really apologizing, but clearly hoping to defuse the situation, Future the Prince said he would get to the bottom of it, and he rushed back to where he came from, closing the doors behind him that separated Drake's portion of the backstage area. But just as quickly as Migos and its entourage stormed into their dressing room, still audibly incensed, a group of more than a dozen, still led by Quavo, burst back out, stomping with purpose down the hallway toward Drake's side. Each man tucked his chains under his shirt in the process. Those VIPs lingering near the dressing room exchanged nervous glances, but no one moved. Drake was due onstage at any moment.

"They were very late, though," Offset's mother offered, having missed the showdown. Migos would be expected to join the show again in less than an hour.

Offset said later that the whole thing had been a big miscommunication, telling *Billboard*, "It wasn't anyone's team or anything. It was arena issues . . . Sometimes you could uppercut somebody, but you got to make the best of it."

In the moment, the guys seemed less understanding. But the dispute didn't detonate—they had come too far from the bottom Quavo had invoked and there was too much at stake to risk this particular alliance.

Still, when Drake welcomed Migos back to the stage for their second performance slot, their hand-slap greetings lacked some of the enthusiasm from previous nights on the tour. It was hard not to think back to 2013, when Drake had big-footed the trio, however inadvertently, on "Versace," getting most of the credit for a wave they started and leaving Migos to find their own way to stick around.

But stick around they did, and Drake's subsequent QC collaborations—which could be seen as either penance, passion or trend chasing, depending on one's generosity of spirit—no doubt made up for a lot. That night in Atlanta, Drake once again ceded the spotlight to smooth things over, giving Migos an extra few minutes in front of their hometown crowd.

"We gotta do this shit the right way," Quavo said onstage, only a hint of a grudge in his voice. "If you're representing Atlanta, light this motherfucker up." Then they played "Bad and Boujee" one more time.

PART III

21.

A NEW BEGINNING

THE INEXTRICABLE LINK BETWEEN ATLANTA RAP MUSIC, THE streets and the law would not be broken by a mixtape, a hit single, a record deal, a mansion, a private jet or a Grammy. Marlo knew that reality, and he accepted it, having never blinked in the face of his circumstance, defined as it was by his race, where he grew up, the choices he made and the choices made for him. Fame could never erase what he had endured or done, nor would it ever fully alleviate the pressures that came with his life up to this point or the lives of all those around him. But by the end of 2018, with three solo projects in the world and dozens of unreleased tracks on his hard drive, Marlo could safely write "rapper" on his taxes, even if most of his income wasn't yet from songs, concerts or endorsement deals. He had largely settled into the irregular grind of studio life, recording in marathon late-night sessions like his collaborators, and although nothing he made caught anything close to fire, he was a good soldier and teammate, hewing closely to his label's oft-repeated credos: *Wait your turn*, *stay down until you come up*, and so on. Marlo wasn't much of a complainer in general, and jealousy, he knew, was the quickest way to spoil any successful squad.

"You one hit away," P would tell Marlo—along with the other bench-warming Quality Control compatriots—again and again, by way of encouragement. A single song couldn't change everything, but it could change a lot.

"The Real 1," the title track from Marlo's latest mixtape, may not have been his breakout, but its sound and accompanying music video showed a new sheen of professionalism—the kind of subtly perceptible upgrades that differentiated a rickety regional airline from a slicker, well-marketed international carrier. The triumphant, horn-heavy beat by Twysted Genius was pure vintage Jeezy—in case the mixtape's opening song, "Trapping Ain't Dead," wasn't tribute enough—and the dope-man subject matter was meant to again underline Marlo's trap music heritage. In the video—which featured a background role for Jimmy, along with other Bowen Homes and PFK loyalists—a Shawty Lo deep cut played over a scripted intro that showed Marlo working a flip phone and a money counter like an old pro, while his associates warn him that life as a hustler can't last.

"I made a million dollars on Bankhead," Marlo shoots back, even as the video's existence belies his stance. "Fuck wrong with you, man?"

Behind the scenes at the video shoot, Marlo promised anew that he was taking rap "serious like a motherfucker now," calling himself "Bowen Homes' last hope" and crediting P for staying on his ass. "Me and Lil Baby call him Pop," Marlo said. "He wanted more for us than we wanted for ourselves."

But as usual, Marlo still oscillated about the odds of his life transition's sticking, forever managing expectations. "Streets like crack to me, you feel me?" he explained to a videographer following him on set. "Like, just imagine a crackhead trying to get off of crack instantly. He ain't going to never do that, you feel me? 'Cause that ain't something that he can just instantly stop when he been smoking crack all his life. It's like me—the streets are all I know. I've been in the streets all my life. I ain't never thought to myself that I'm gon' give the streets up."

The video for "The Real 1" premiered on WorldStar in September and racked up more than a million views. But that initial bump of curiosity seemed to be its ceiling, and Marlo would remain one hit away a while longer, his chief authority still coming from another realm—the one he had known the longest.

"Rudy wasn't no big-ass drug dealer in Bowen Homes," Jacoby Hudson, his lawyer, said one weekend afternoon in his windowless law office, not long after the annual block party for the old projects. "But he met his connect, he met his plug, and his plug put him on and he started up his crew. Rudy was running the 9th Ward at twenty-four."

As for many from the neighborhood, Marlo would always be Rudy to Jacoby, who had seen it all. A onetime gang prosecutor turned criminal defense attorney also raised in Bowen Homes, Jacoby knew the game from every side. "I never sold drugs, but I hustled," he explained, a preemptive clarification that was not defensive in nature but telling nonetheless.

Coming up when he did in those Bankhead projects, a child of Yates Drive in the crack-smoke eighties, Jacoby knew the distinction was both nuanced and necessary. "It took over my neighborhood," he said of the drug, which loomed over the lawyer's whole history and upbringing in what he called "one of the roughest neighborhoods ever," even if it never landed on him directly. Rap was always on the periphery, too, but even more so as he aged, falling in with Marlo and others as a guardian angel for hire.

In his thirty-five years, Jacoby had occupied an eye-of-the-storm role often. Once a gambling bookworm with a jump shot, he was a favorite of the local hustlers even as he abstained from drinking and smoking with them in the shared space of the projects because he was a teenager with school the next day. He was always known as the smart kid, and his neighborhood wanted to help him stay that way, supporting his potential however they could, even if it was just by leaving him alone.

"I be lying a lot and shit when I be at the functions and everything—'Man, I was all out in the hood!'" Jacoby said with some embarrassment yet more evident pride, rubbing his creased bald head. "But I was in my books, I was all in school."

Still, even a student as diligent as him had to dabble in some moneymaking mischief. "Small-time—playing cards, shooting dice, playing basketball, just using what talent would get me through," Jacoby said. "When Puff Daddy had a concert here back in '98—when they came to the Georgia Dome—the day of the concert, me and Carlos was down shooting jumpers. I beat him out of like four thousand dollars. We was shooting like three, four hundred dollars a shot." That was hustling, too.

Now sweaty and substantial, with a white towel close at hand to keep the summer off him, it wasn't hard to imagine Jacoby as a sneakily athletic kid and a semisecret nerd, winning over Carlos—a pre-rap Shawty Lo—with his full-cheeked smile even as he emptied the older guy's pockets. Jacoby was always relentlessly, contagiously cheerful, a few years younger than Lo and a few years older than Marlo, straddling the Bowen Homes generations. But he came to know both men like brothers, going from neighbor and familiar face to lawyer and sensible confidant after he was done working briefly for the government, putting people like Lo and Marlo away.

Jacoby said he knew by the sixth grade that he wanted to be a criminal defense attorney. He had seen them operate on TV and also witnessed firsthand the ramping up of mass incarceration in real time, as the Red Dog unit and the drug war became the 1994 crime bill and the pre-Olympics crackdowns, and more and more of his friends and neighbors fell into a system stacked against them. But his path to starting his own defense shop—Hudson Legal Firm, "Tipping the Scales in Your Favor"—was roundabout, coming only after his dreams of playing basketball or football at the University of Georgia, like his running-back hero Garrison Hearst, had faded. Jacoby's father was a truck driver and his mother worked the grounds at Bowen Homes when it still stood. They never stressed college, but a high school diploma was mandatory. The rest was up to him.

Jacoby attended West Fulton Middle School, right on Bankhead, as did Marlo, and then did well at Frederick Douglass High. After he graduated from UGA (sans his coveted Bulldogs jersey), he took a bill-paying job as a Delta ramp agent at Hartsfield-Jackson airport, saving money for whatever came next. After two years handling baggage, Jacoby enrolled at Atlanta's John Marshall Law School, finishing in 2009 and falling right into the end of the recession. Fortunately, his interest in helping out his old neighborhood went both ways, and one of the older Bowen Homes hustlers contributed to his law school tuition. "Our whole neighborhood gave Jacoby money when he was going to school," Jimmy recalled, mimicking the refrain he heard repeatedly: *That's Coby—give gatdamn Coby what he need.*

By then, Paul L. Howard Jr., the first Black person in history to be elected district attorney in the state of Georgia, had become DA in Fulton County. Howard's constant presence in the media made Jacoby "switch sides": "Instead of being a defense attorney, I wanted to become a prosecutor and send people away."

Ideology aside, working for the government was a steady and prestigious job, and too much life was happening for his Bankhead friends to really hold the pivot against him. "At the time, it didn't resonate with them," Jacoby said, and he remained a sympathetic, if pragmatic, presence when he encountered his people in court, working with them on fairer plea bargains and lighter sentences.

But he didn't last as one with The Man, even if this particular authority was an elected Black man. "In 2013, through deep prayer and life circumstances, I changed and went to the defense side," Jacoby said, recalling the move that would bring him ever closer to the rap business. And it was Marlo—Rudy—who helped make the switch stick.

Even with the projects gone, Bankhead was a small world, and Jacoby's cousin ran with some of Rudy's Play For Keeps guys, the fearsome clique from the 9th Ward. When the crew inevitably needed legal assistance, they knew where to turn. "Man, your cousin Coby, he's a lawyer, ain't he?" Rudy asked one day.

Jacoby, fresh out of the DA's office, had handled a few possession and trafficking cases for his friends and acquaintances already, but he was still unsteady in his new role on the defense side when he took the meeting with Rudy on the strength of their shared Bowen Homes connections. "Shit, bruh, I want you to do this murder case for me," Rudy told him. He handed the lawyer $12,000—"straight cash."

Jacoby almost balked, knowing full well that he wasn't prepared to be the lead attorney on a murder trial just yet. But he agreed to help out on the case, and in the interest of fairness, he handed Rudy $4,000 back. ("I did file taxes on it!" the lawyer insisted.) The case involved one of Rudy's closest PFK partners, known as Tweet, a former rival with whom he had joined forces in music and more, but who had now been charged in a murder. "His friend really was innocent," Jacoby said. "Police know who did it, and the prosecutors know. But they come from a powerful organization, so it was alleged that they put a hit out on somebody, which they did not."

At trial, with Jacoby assisting a more established colleague, the verdict came back not guilty, and after fifteen months in jail, Marlo's friend Tweet returned home victorious. But Jacoby might have been the biggest winner of all. "My name became legendary after that," he said. "Everyone was like, 'Who that lawyer from Bowen Homes?' '*Coby!*' 'Rudy, ain't that your lawyer?' "

All of a sudden, after a single resounding "not guilty," Jacoby's counsel took on a new air of authority, his reputation as a seer and a truth teller booming along with his business. There was something about freeing a man from behind bars—saving his life, essentially—and especially "beating a body," the evocative brag attached to any murder acquittal, that imbued a lawyer with an otherworldly wisdom, like being the coach of a team and the star player at the same time, a man with all the right answers and the right moves.

"Rudy put me on," Jacoby said, as if he, too, were an aspiring rapper.

For Rudy, Jacoby quickly became a mentor and an older brother figure, though he was also unmistakably an employee who provided an important service for a budding boss. The irony was that Rudy, out of all of his friends, probably needed Jacoby the least, despite the reach of his reputation.

"Rudy doesn't have a record," Jacoby said, like he couldn't believe it himself. Rudy had been caught with a pistol when he was a teenager, and there were various smaller arrests for driving with a suspended license and possession of less than an ounce of marijuana in the years since, "but he's not a convicted felon," Jacoby said—an important distinction in both men's lines of work. In the long run, as Rudy began the process of blooming into Marlo, the rapper and local street legend, his lack of convictions would be a point of pride, not a ding against his credibility. Prison, he liked to say—usually referring to it as the "chain gang"—was "for suckers."

"Hell nah, I ain't going," Marlo bragged, deploying his most incisive smirk. "I'm smart as hell, n——. I ain't with that. I like being comfortable."

Instead of using Jacoby for his own cases, Marlo was known to generously secure his lawyer's services for those in need, even if he was not affiliated firsthand with their particular crimes. Once, a friend from outside of Marlo's immediate circle received a jail visit out of the blue from Jacoby, who assured the man that he'd already been paid for the work he was about to embark on.

"Why you spent that bread, bro? I already got two lawyers on the case," the friend asked Marlo in a call home from jail.

"Well, now you got three," Marlo said.

At the same time, he kept Jacoby close as a strategic adviser, sleeping sounder all the while knowing that, if and when it came down to it, he had someone trustworthy on standby for his own protection, too. The law, of course, was always lurking. "Just because he doesn't have a record doesn't mean he ain't about what he says he is," Jacoby cautioned. "He got street credibility—he just don't get caught. Rudy gonna get out and get in there now."

Because of his relative luck with law enforcement and lack of firsthand experience in the penal system, rap never represented the same refuge from real life for Marlo as it did for guys like Shawty Lo or Lil Baby, who had served actual time and knew they never wanted to again. As a result, Marlo's own turn toward music was taking a bit longer, if it was to ever really take at all. But the personal impetus that really pushed him onto another path was even more tragic than a long sentence. To hear Jacoby tell it, the thing that made Marlo try to change his life for good might well have been a sign from God.

On January 20, 2014, Marlo—who didn't even have an Instagram account at the time, let alone a rap name—welcomed his first child with his girlfriend Tammy, a little girl they christened Rihanna and called RiRi, like the chart-topping pop and R&B singer. Tammy, who met Rudy as a teenager at the Delmar Lane apartments in the Nine, had an older daughter, but RiRi was everything for Rudy, who was twenty-three and immediately smitten. Although his shifts hustling in the 9th Ward were long and treacherous, and he might not see RiRi for days at a time, a daughter was a new kind of eternal motivation for a man, and Rudy was exploding everywhere with pride for his wide-eyed angel, whose little mushroom puff of curls would rest so serenely on his bare chest when he had the time.

But the bliss of fatherhood would be all too brief. By her first fall, RiRi was seriously ill, and her parents rushed her to a top-of-the-line children's hospital in the city's tony northeastern quadrant, where Atlanta faded into its suburbs. There, sick and wailing, the child was initially misdiagnosed and sent home, with doctors failing to recognize the extent of the pneumonia that was ravaging her tiny body. When it became clear later that RiRi would not make it, Marlo, bereft and racked by guilt, called Jacoby to his side. The lawyer headed straight to the hospital, where Marlo asked him outright, "Coby, you think this is my fault?"

He could have been there more, Marlo told his lawyer in the child's final hours. Jacoby, at a loss for a suitable answer, told him that this could only be God's plan.

At Rihanna's funeral, almost everyone wore white. The church ladies' hats were white and the dope boys' jeans were white, as well. The casket was white, carried into the cemetery by a white carriage drawn by two white horses, with white roses placed on top. Rudy wore a white Nike sweater and an all-white fitted hat turned 105 degrees over his right ear, though his Timbs and Louis Vuitton belt were black, a look matched down to the details by his most reliable partners, who stuck close to his side. Rudy and Tammy held white doves, releasing them into the sky as their daughter was buried two miles from Bowen Homes, her small children's coffin covered in kisses.

At the service, Jacoby sobbed as the hymns played—*I learned to let go and let God have his way*. Rihanna, the preacher said, was now heaven's special child. *Let the end of her life be a new beginning for your life*, he told Rihanna's parents.

Marlo had always been drawn to numerology, divination and omens, the parts of his West African Ifa faith that were only whispered about in mixed company. But Christianity had its superstitious aspects, too, its messages from on high. Seven was the number for completion. But eight—Rihanna's age in months—was for a fresh start.

"Let the number eight be a new beginning," the pastor said.

These shifts couldn't happen overnight, Jacoby knew, having seen people age out of hustling his whole life. But in the months and years that followed Rihanna's death, the lawyer started to notice a change in his favorite client—some slowing down, some manning up, a shift in focus from the monomaniacal need to take over every block, every apartment complex. It's not like the business of drug dealing was all that steady anyway, and Marlo, like everyone else in his world, could be down financially as easily as he could be up, especially with so many people counting on him.

Sometime after the funeral, when Jacoby pulled up on Marlo one day in the trap, looking for $5,000 he was owed, he could tell times were tough. "I think he had maybe twenty thousand dollars to his name," Jacoby said.

But as Marlo gave his lawyer the cash, Jacoby could also sense that something else was on the horizon. Set up in the corner of the house was a makeshift studio, and Marlo was recording a song.

A FEW YEARS later, Lil Baby represented motivation, or a maddening point of comparison, depending on one's self-confidence as a musician. Upon the release of his album *Street Gossip* just after Thanksgiving in 2018, Baby landed ten individual songs on the *Billboard* singles chart—"I'm ten percent of the *Billboard* Hot 100," he boasted—giving him twenty-one entries on the Hot 100 for the year, a monster total that fell behind only indisputable fixtures of the hip-hop A-list: Drake, Travis Scott, Lil Wayne, Cardi B, Nicki Minaj and Post Malone.

"No radio single, no videos, no big marketing, just our normal grind," P noted. And while the album could have easily been a collection of workmanlike songs to capitalize on Baby's buzz, *Street Gossip* managed to raise the bar again with still more autobiographical insight, experimental vocal cadences and increasingly grandiose beats. At a tight thirteen tracks, and with the usual inner-circle cameos (Gunna, Young Thug, Gucci Mane), the release represented Baby's first postcard from the stratosphere—the moment where his street stories began to feel as if they were more firmly in the past tense and the boasts, paradoxically, more down-to-earth, because now they were literal instead of pure aspiration.

"We turned a Section 8 'partment to a condo," Baby rapped on one hook, detailing matter-of-factly the incrementalism of his rise via real estate. These particulars were scattered throughout every song but packed together most effectively on the opening number, "Global," which captured the extent to which Baby had already succeeded and also how he had not yet been afforded the time to really soak that in. The first words on the song and the album—"We global now"—were technically the producer tag of Baby's go-to beat maker, Quay Global, but they doubled as a factual marker of real-world progress. Still, every victory remained couched in a cloud of ambient anxiety, and Baby would cut the celebration short even when memorializing that it had only taken a year to make himself a millionaire. "Thinkin' 'bout what I been through, I can make a tear fall," he rapped immediately after.

That seesaw between the sweet and the bitter had become Baby's trademark, but it was not a rhetorical contrivance as much as a stream-of-consciousness representation of his everyday psyche. "The adjustment from coming where I come from to where I'm at now is like—I'm still adjusting. I haven't even made the full adjustment 'cause it happened so quick," Baby explained, breaking down his lyrics. "I grinded up on a million dollars. That shit felt great 'cause I'm like, four hundred, five hundred, six hundred, seven hundred, seven fifty, go back down, go back up, then you become a millionaire."

In the song's chorus, Baby hinted at the coming birth of his second child, another son due in early 2019, by cataloging his recent purchase of a Gucci stroller—a splurge he'd made the very day the song was recorded. Then, almost out of nowhere, Baby added a line that may have been meant specifically for Marlo but could have applied to any of the ever-expanding list of friends who considered taking music more seriously since Baby's own liftoff: "My dog rappin', hope he blow up."

"I got a couple of homies rapping and I be having so much going on, I feel sometimes they might feel like I ain't really with 'em," Baby said, expanding upon the sentiment with ample self-consciousness. "I really be having a lot going on, but God knows my heart. I really want everybody to blow up."

The plights of his non-rapping friends remained front of mind, as well. In the second verse of "Global," Baby mentioned two younger boys by name, Jock and Dee, lamenting their two life sentences and adding that he hoped the lawyers he got for them would lift their spirits. Just as he had done before music, diligently putting money on everyone's commissary books and trying to help with legal arrangements when he could, Baby's new tax bracket allowed him even more options when it came to spreading around the work of top-shelf attorneys, whom he hired for others in hopes of reduced sentences, better plea deals and a fighting chance at looming trials.

In addition to funds, Baby now had something else to offer those who were locked up—hope, or at least vicarious thrills. When his incarcerated friends called—and they called every day—"I let them know what we doing," Baby said. "I don't tell them I'm going to call them back when they want to talk." Jock and Dee, in particular: "I leave them on the phone with me on three-way, just let 'em stay on the phone with me for three, four hours." He did so whether he was in the studio or with a woman—"Whatever I'm doing, I just let them hear."

Earlier in the year, inside the drab conference space of an Atlanta-area Marriott Marquis, Baby had appeared as one of four formerly incarcerated men—two of them now involved in truck driving—on a panel discussion titled "I Am My Brother's Keeper: Guiding Principles of Re-Entry," about successfully reentering society after prison and "shattering the shackles of collateral consequences."

Looking slightly bored and more than a bit nervous behind a paper placard displaying his government name, the rapper was there as a favor to Quality Control's go-to attorney, Drew Findling, who had recently become the president of the event's host organization, the National Association of Criminal Defense Lawyers. To celebrate Findling's new role as president, QC even footed the bill for the NACDL's annual party.

Despite the rapper's success so far at not reoffending, Findling had taken an ascendant Baby under his wing much as he had Offset a few years earlier. At the panel, Baby spoke only when prodded by the moderator, but he did so with rising emotion when discussing just how consuming it could be to try to keep his people—and himself—out of prison.

"That's an everyday challenge, honestly," Baby said. "There's so much you can get into."

Looking like he had been woken up too early, Baby, in a Fred Perry collared shirt and two fat diamond earrings, rubbed at his face often. But he commanded the room whenever he piped up. "Coming out, it's hard to even just make a change completely," he said. "I been doing whatever I've been doing for my whole life."

He traced his imperfect path back to his lack of a father figure, as well as the racism he experienced from all sides, even within his own community. "I do feel like the Black youth is getting profiled, but not just by white people—just by people period," he said. "I got a nappy Afro, dirty little clothes, I go in some places and it be a Black person—they judge you, too."

When asked about his childhood dreams, Baby demurred. "As far as aspirations growing up, like, 'What you wanna be?'—I never wanted to be nothing," he said—not a race car driver, not a marine biologist, not even a rapper. "I only wanted to get me some money. How I got me some money didn't even matter.

"It's a lot on what you see, too," he continued. "If you grow up around doctors in the household, more than likely you can become a doctor. Not saying you can't, but it's more likely not to happen if you don't see it. If you see drug dealers every day, you kinda turn out to be a drug dealer. You don't have to be. But it's your environment.

"I definitely never had a mentor, really, as far as like, to do the right thing," he said. "All my mentors is, like . . . drug dealers, you know what I'm saying?"

Even after prison, Baby wasn't sure he had any real options to go straight, he explained, emboldened by the applause that grew each time he unloaded some real talk. "If I wasn't rapping or nothing, I wouldn't know where to go to get back into society if I was stuck," he said. "I wouldn't know where to go."

It was important that his music reflected that dead-end reality, Baby said—the most likely outcome of all he had seen and all he had experienced. In one of his heaviest verses, Baby had described the silence that filled the car carrying him and his friends home after a shootout in which they thought they had hit a child bystander, the dread at watching the local news for confirmation—and then the eventual relief of realizing they were wrong. "I'm just glad the kid didn't die," he rapped.

"I actually let young brothers know that when you do do violence or you do criminal acts, there's a consequence," Baby said in the conference room. "Because I know—I've been through the consequences. In my music, I ain't just shooting 'em up, kill kill. I ain't on that. I do say stuff about shoot and kill, but I say if you shoot and kill, you go to jail and don't come home." The professional crowd applauded again.

It was easier, however, for Baby to identify the cycle than to break it, even within his ranks. On November 30, 2018, the day *Street Gossip* was released, real life was interfering again. According to police, one of Baby's closest friends, known as G-Five or Lil Steve, spent a fateful part of that afternoon at a luxury apartment complex in the Atlanta suburb of Brookhaven, where he and an accomplice attempted to rob a man during a drug deal. Two people were shot. The bleeding victims drove themselves to a Waffle House, where they called 911. One man eventually died.

G-Five had been one of Baby's most loyal 4 Pockets Full associates, alongside Ced, since they were teenagers. Born Stephen McCallister, he spent much of his young adult life in and out of jail but became a recurring character in the Lil Baby musical universe when he was mentioned frequently in song while behind bars ("Do this for Lil Steve, they gave my lil homie a dime"). When free, G-Five was pictured as Baby's right-hand man, on private jets or in luxury vehicles with gargantuan Jenga towers of money.

Boxy in stature, with a pencil-thin mustache and a tattoo across his trachea, G-Five's rap sheet included aggravated assault and gun possession. When he was twenty-one, he had been wanted on twenty-four simultaneous warrants for what authorities estimated as no fewer than 118 car break-ins, where he allegedly targeted guns, cell phones, laptops and GPS devices—crimes all carried out while he was already serving decades' worth of probation on earlier charges. Yet somehow, with Baby's rap money and lawyerly connections in his corner, G-Five was freed on appeal in the spring of 2018—Baby's breakout year—an occasion the rapper celebrated by gifting his friend $100,000 cash and another couplet to match ("G-Five out the can / Give him 100 bands").

"Baby made a way for everybody," his friend told a reporter two months later. "Everybody he around, he changed everybody's life."

But that December, about two weeks after the Brookhaven shooting, G-Five was taken back into custody by local police, with the assistance of the DeKalb County Sheriff's Office and the United States Marshals Service. Charged with felony murder, aggravated assault, armed robbery and possession of a firearm by a convicted felon, he was ordered to be held without bond at the DeKalb County Jail.

Arrested the same day, and alleged to be G-Five's accomplice in the shooting, was his mirror image in Marlo's PFK circle—an enforcer known as Head, who had more recently billed himself as Marlo's road manager. What happened next was as promised by the respective crews' biggest breadwinners and de facto leaders: Baby brought on Drew Findling. Marlo brought on Jacoby Hudson. G-Five and Head would get the best legal defense on offer, and the money was of no real concern.

* * *

A FEW MONTHS later, Baby and Marlo were heading back on the road, each down one ally. Baby needed to run with the heat he had been generating, regardless of what was going on in his personal life. This time, Marlo would not be stuck at home in Atlanta missing out.

With rap having already taken him global, to Freeport, Manchester, Lagos, Paris and more, Baby's New Generation tour was set to begin in the spring of 2019, with Marlo and City Girls opening concert dates across the United States. Also joining the caravan would be two rappers new to the intimate fold: Rylo Rodriguez and 42 Dugg, who were not Quality Control artists but Baby's own personal protégés, signed to his burgeoning label. Named for his 4 Pockets Full crew, the 4PF imprint would give Baby a chance to play talent scout and CEO, à la his own mentors. It would also help provide employment for his friends, like Ced and, eventually, G-Five.

This was how quickly the generations could turn over in twenty-first-century, internet-fueled hip-hop. Although he had been rapping for barely two years, Baby was already flipping his audience and influence in service of others, going from hanger-on and understudy to star to executive in about the same amount of time that it took to get an associate's degree.

But having a label of his own wasn't an exercise in pure autonomy for Baby either. It also demonstrated the Russian-doll-like nature of the modern music business, where an artist could be signed to any number of other artists through their boutique labels or production companies, which then lent their services up the chain to larger and larger organizations.

Baby, for instance, released music on behalf of a small parade of businesses that each had a role—and a financial stake—in his career. There was 4PF, his personal pet project, which grew out of Wolf Pack Global Music, the investment vehicle for his original street patrons, which fed him into Quality Control Music, Coach K and P's funnel into Motown Records, which was itself part of the Capitol Music Group, an umbrella organization under the Universal Music Group (UMG) corporate structure. UMG, meanwhile, was owned by the French media conglomerate Vivendi, though the Chinese tech company Tencent was sniffing around obtaining a minority stake as the company also considered an IPO.

The contracts, it would be safe to say, were complicated. But as long as things were going well, everybody would be winning, and few would complain. Still, in almost all cases, the artist was likely to be both the most crucial cog in the machine and the last one paid. But recorded music was just one revenue stream of many available to the top-line talent, with concerts representing a more rapper-friendly flow of cash. So back on tour they would go.

First, however, there was family life to attend to. With his headlining concerts scheduled to begin in Houston in mid-March, Baby would get just a few weeks at home with his next newborn son, his first child with his girlfriend Jayda, who was set to give birth at any moment.

It was while rushing to Jayda's pregnant side one evening that February that Baby would have his most serious run-in with police since leaving prison and making a name for himself. Driving an orange Corvette through Oakland City and the West End, Baby was pulled over by a Georgia State Patrol officer on Lee Street for failing to signal as he weaved and sped through the Atlanta traffic. When the officer, a Black man, caught up to Baby, he removed him from the vehicle and placed him facedown on the pavement in handcuffs, much to the surprise of passersby who recognized the rapper around his old stomping grounds, in his sports car and matching tracksuit.

"Fuck the police who be on that bullshit," Baby said when he bonded out with just a signature a few hours later. "Shout-out to ones who get you through the process ASAP."

It was not an auspicious start to the year, but for Baby, these days, it was surmountable. Ten days later, he named his second son Loyal. Three weeks after that, he was crisscrossing the country once again.

This time, Marlo was on board and committed, delivering passable performances to somebody else's crowds. As he rapped every evening about trying to stay above the odds on "2 the Hard Way," Marlo concluded his opening slot with one of the sharpest lines he had written thus far—one that directly addressed the possibility that his career might never explode.

"I won't fold," he promised, via one of the first songs he had ever written. "And if I never sell a record or a song, in the trap, I went gold." Then, night after night, Marlo would watch from the curtain's edge as his superstar partner commanded the room.

22.

NO SLEEP

BASED ON THE RELENTLESSNESS OF THE LABEL'S HOT STREAK, Memorial Day 2019 seemed like as good a time as any for Quality Control to shoot from deep three-point range. The heat check, in this case—and in basketball terms—was "Soakin Wet," a club song by Marlo, who didn't exactly scream light and fun. It was the sort of shot just outside of a comfort zone that you take when you know you're on fire but aren't sure whether it's a once-in-a-lifetime, *Anything I put up is going in* kind of heat or the sort that burns bright briefly before sizzling out.

QC's current run, continuing well into the new year, might have been most evident in Lil Baby's nonstop string of successes, but the label's ability to break a third major artist after Migos and Lil Yachty seemed to make the winning contagious, and more so when the acts worked together. City Girls, the female rap duo from Miami, had successfully become a fan favorite, even with one-half of the group still incarcerated, and their track "Act Up" was a slow-burning smash starting that spring, taking off in strip clubs and nightclubs, on social media and eventually on rhythmic and rap radio, which pushed it into the pop Top 40.

Love for the song only grew when Yachty, who hadn't found a hit for himself lately, revealed that he had semicovertly written some of City Girls' kiss-off raps, earning his keep as a playful, transgressive feminist lyricist and keeping it all in the family with a single that would soon go platinum. Migos, too, was hanging around the radio with collaborations that felt fresh enough and kept their voices feeling inescapable. And hits, in the streaming era, could beget more hits on the basis of name recognition alone.

This was a moment when rap—and culture—felt like an all-you-can-eat buffet, with an overabundance of options in every direction, the street music both more popular, poppier or harder than ever, depending on where you looked and what you wanted to see. Melody was everywhere, with Drake, Future and Young Thug having carried on the Auto-Tuned influence of T-Pain, Kanye West and Lil Wayne, and the generations coming after knowing no other way. But other than the prevalence of 808s and some singsong touches, the only rule in pop at the moment was that there were no real rules about what could catch on and when. There was no reason Marlo couldn't get in on the fun before summertime.

"Soakin Wet," while cynical as a commercial play, had the right ingredients for a warm-weather breakout. The beat was airy and unassuming, with a pleasing intermittent whistle and skittering drums that begged for twerking, and Marlo, awash in vocal effects, was a casual presence. His trap-god persona may have been established locally, but it hadn't really traveled, so QC sought to re-create the tactical magic it had used with "Bad and Boujee," releasing Marlo's frothy, stripper-friendly track near a holiday weekend that required a surplus of bangers. Still, it remained to be seen whether the label, through sheer audaciousness and reverse engineering, could will a single into existence for one of its lesser-known artists using the local clubs and radio stations as a sort of home-court advantage.

The single had actually been sitting around for some time already. Marlo only put one verse on the song the night it was created, but even then, he was bullish about its chances. Still, he kept it from P for a while, knowing it wasn't what the executive expected from his most undeviating trap rapper, and he opted to show Coach K first, receiving a thumbs-up about its potential as a hit.

When Marlo did get around to playing it for P, he got dinged for procrastination. "Boy, you been had this?" the executive chided. "We coulda been outta here! What's wrong with you, boy?"

"You ain't my daddy," Marlo responded, only half-kidding. "You need to stop yelling at me!"

But the plan was put into motion, with Marlo asking his labelmate and fellow Lil Baby opener Yung Miami of City Girls to add a verse to the track, thus throwing her growing clout into the mix. Then, as P and Marlo listened back to what she'd recorded, Offset just happened to walk into the studio.

"Whose song is this? This hard," the Migos rapper told Marlo. "You gotta let me get on that. I won't let you tell me no."

This was rap synergy at work, and the QC circle had a phrase for when everything was lining up just right with a new record that imbued everyone with high hopes: *This one of them ones*, they told each other. *This one of them ones*.

In the weeks that followed, Marlo's song did its thing without blowing anyone away. First, in May, "Soakin Wet" swept the local strip clubs as expected. In July, its yacht-and-ass-heavy music video hit YouTube to decent views. By August, the Atlanta radio stations were at least curious.

Hoping to grease the wheels, and maybe make the song into a meme the way a new rap track seemed to spread every week, Marlo, Baby, Ced and P also started pushing what they called the "Soakin Wet" Challenge, a not-exactly-original concept to encourage virality. The rules were simple: the person—woman—who could post the best video dancing to the song would receive $10,000 as a cash prize.

After a healthy number of submissions, the winner was unanimous and no one else really stood a chance. In the victorious clip, a young woman in white hot pants twerked outside against a backdrop of Astroturf and a wooden fence, holding a big glass bowl beneath her bottom with her left hand and a half-gallon of milk in her right. With the whole thing set in slow motion to "Soakin Wet," she poured the milk down her ass crack, some of it sloshing into the bowl, and followed the liquid with a waterfall of Fruity Pebbles, wasting most of the cereal on the way down. The edible props eventually paid for themselves. The contest's effect on the song was more difficult to ascertain. There was still work to be done.

On a Monday that summer, Marlo received a call from P around 8:20 p.m., informing the rapper that he needed to be at a radio station downtown by 9:00. At this point in his song's young life span, saying no was not an option for Marlo, and so he and Jimmy, his old Bowen Homes elder turned day-to-day manager—the one charged with getting him up and at 'em for opportunities like this—rushed to the car, knowing that traffic would be a nightmare. They also knew that Greg Street, the influential prime-time DJ at V-103, was expecting them. Neither man seemed excited, exactly, understanding that there would be little glamour in the workaday promotional stop, which was more like being called into a service job to fill a coworker's shift than any sort of VIP celebration. But such was the grind of a handshake tour, the sort expected by program directors and DJs citywide.

When the pair arrived, Street had been on the air since rush hour, just like he had been every day for years. Marlo carried a double stack of Styrofoam cups, personalized with a PFK logo in purple, and Jimmy handled the two-liter bottle of Minute Maid fruit punch, a combination of accessories that indicated Marlo was once again sipping lean. Perhaps due to the opiate, his drawl was extra pronounced, so his words were less so. But Marlo's gap-toothed smile was winning as ever as he greeted Street and begged for more opportunities from the Atlanta radio authority.

After some brotherly banter, Street transitioned to hyping up "Soakin Wet" on air without breaking the casual stride of their rapport. Marlo, on the other hand, clammed up once he was live on the mic.

"Lil Marlo! Marlo's world! Tell me about this single, man."

"I already had this song like a whole year ago," the rapper said in a near-whispered slur. "We gon' make this motherfucker go viral."

But before the sentence was finished, Street shot Marlo a look, reacting to the on air curse like a strict parent. "We gon' make *it* go viral," Marlo said, correcting himself. "Most definitely gon' make it go viral." Street cued up the track.

IT WAS AFTER 10 p.m. when Marlo left the station, but his shift as a rapper was just beginning for the night. With about the same amount of notice as he received for his radio appearance, Marlo had been asked to cut an original song for a cable series that no one seemed to know much about.

"P done got me an agent," Marlo said, and the agent had arranged for a Marlo song to be used by a fictional rapper in an unnamed show that was set to air eventually, at some point, probably.

"It's a dude . . . some producer . . . some new show," Jimmy said. All he knew was that it was for the network Starz and that the song needed to be completed that night. Also, the money would be right. They set off together for the Quality Control studios.

Out front, a single car idled with its lights off, doing security. Behind the password-protected gate, the parking lot was crowded with expensive rides, but only Kollision was inside working. Marlo had changed into a Nike tracksuit and red Supreme slides with Gucci socks, the better to pull an all-nighter in, and he gathered sustenance as well. On top of his dwindling bottle of fruit punch potion, he brought along a pack of Newports and an aluminum plate of fettuccine Alfredo with shrimp and scallops, a hunk of corn bread on the side. A friend joined to serve as his recording engineer for the night, and that guy brought a friend, too. They brought the sour candy and the blunt wraps.

Despite the growing group, Marlo opted to set up in Studio D, which was about as wide as one man's wingspan, and he plopped down at the computer desk, forgoing the vocal booth altogether by bringing the microphone to him. While he got settled, Marlo FaceTimed Tammy, the woman he called his wife, and he cooed at their son, Rudy Jr., or R. J., who was three years old and actually the fifth in the line of Rudolph Johnsons. (The same month R. J. was born, in 2016, Marlo had welcomed another son, whom he named Marlo Jr., with a different woman. "Don't ask me how I did it," he said of the arrangement. "I just did.")

"Dada! Daddy, music!" R. J. said on FaceTime, babbling happily in the background. Marlo set the phone to the side, making it clear that the call was not a pointed one, but rather atmospheric, allowing him to spend time with his family while he worked. They chatted intermittently when Marlo wasn't blasting his in-progress music over the room's speakers, and neither side seemed concerned about staying in frame for the iPhone camera; mere presence was enough.

In the background, a hook Marlo had recorded for another artist played on a loop. "In the trenches sipping on some codeine," he crooned. "Hope my past don't ever catch up with me."

He cycled through other drafts on the computer, each more promising and soulful than the last, revealing that he might've found his voice as a lyricist not by tallying his wins, but by leaning further into his losses. Rapping was clearly coming easier to him, too, in concert with the idea of baring his soul.

"My crazy lifestyle, I hope I make it," Marlo began on another track that was oozing with pathos, even before it got to the lines about his late daughter, Rihanna. "The first girl I really loved, she had to leave my life / Why you do your dad like that? / Girl, you did me wrong / And on this song my heart cry, my baby girl gone."

"That song hard as hell," Marlo said under his breath when the track finished.

"I ain't never heard you rap like this," one of the other guys in the room remarked.

But it wasn't right for Starz. "You have a good trap beat?" Marlo asked the engineer, an aspiring producer, who fished around his files for a track the rapper might find inspiring.

For the next few hours, Marlo nibbled at a spread of sounds—some with ominous synths, some with soothing acoustic guitar loops and some in between—never getting beyond one stilted, generic verse. At his side, the engineer clicked around the screen, moving multicolored bits of vocal takes like Tetris blocks. But Marlo was antsy, and he kept commandeering the mouse to scroll through disorganized Gmail attachments in search of the perfect beat. Sometimes, for motivation, he played a song that he had already written, leaning back and zoning out with his eyes closed, the end of a Newport burning dangerously close to his fingers. He never left the desk chair.

At some point past midnight, Marlo's FaceTime call disconnected, and he spread a few fat white pills onto his pants, popping one. A few hours later, he took another, along with a quarter of a pink pill from his friend. "I might have to go all the way left field to get right field," Marlo said, frustrated yet realistic about his quest for the right idea. "*Gatdamn*, when I catch my groove, this shit be easy. But I really start getting blocked."

From the hallway, where there was more room, Jimmy nodded along with each attempt at a song, occasionally offering a word when Marlo seemed stuck. But mostly Jimmy just rolled blunt after blunt, dutifully getting up every now and then to refill the ice in Marlo's cup.

"Don't nobody sleep," Jimmy said, apparently bullish about the possibility of finishing a song good enough for television before the sun came up. "At nighttime, this city don't be sleeping. Folks who normally get up, nine to five, go to work, they sleep at nine, ten o'clock. That's when all the entertainers—that's their hours. Go out, get paid—after that, studio.

"Your bitch might be going to work, she mad, but she knows where you are, you know what I'm saying? That's just how this shit go. All night. Studios be dead in the daytime, on God. You gotta feel that vibe."

But by 3 a.m., with Marlo still at the computer and showing no signs of stopping, Jimmy was horizontal in the hallway, and he was snoring.

23.

ESCAPE THE TRAP

"SEAT BELTS!" LIL REEK CALLED INTO THE BACK OF THE SUV he was captaining for the afternoon. The Cleveland Ave. carpool that day included his nine-year-old brother and his twelve-year-old sister, whom Reek had scooped up early from school to make sure she had a way home. Young Thug's son, who lived nearby, didn't have a ride either, so he hopped in at one point, too, wearing Balenciaga shoes and a translucent plastic backpack. In the passenger seat was Reek's new music industry associate-in-training.

"Y'all hungry?" Reek asked the group.

It was November again, a year on from Reek's brief career high point as a major-label rapper, and his concerns for now were mostly familial and financial: scrounging up $8 for his brother's upcoming field trip; dropping off a salad and wings for his mother during her shift at the beauty supply store; making sure the front door of the house was locked. Regular shit. "My brother and sisters are my kids," Reek said. "Gotta give them what I didn't have."

He didn't much like talking about the aborted record deal that had momentarily changed his life. "They wasn't doing shit," Reek murmured, settling in for an after-school meal with his siblings at the original Chick-fil-A location, known as Dwarf House, in Hapeville. "They wasn't seeing it through my eyes, like, from my perspective of how I wanted to be portrayed as an artist."

Republic had agreed to let him walk after a few failed singles, but the money from his advance was already long gone. "I spent that shit," Reek said tersely—helping to pay bills, treating himself occasionally, plus the chunks for managers, lawyers, taxes. "It goes faster than it came." There was no way around it. "I'm broke," he said.

"And for you, ma'am?" the diner waitress, an older white woman, asked.

"I'm a man, ma'am," Reek replied.

"I'm sorry," she said, not missing a beat, "but you sure are pretty."

Reek smiled convincingly and ordered a spicy chicken sandwich and a chicken noodle soup to save for later. He planned to be at the studio all night—"whichever one the cheapest"—and hoped to fully reprioritize music soon, despite his daily obligations and lack of capital. But the false start of his career wasn't the only thing that had proved destabilizing for Reek in recent months. "Lost my granddad, lost my fucking partner," he said.

The toll of mourning two of his towering male role models had snuck up on—and then pummeled—Reek. He recalled the stories of his late grandfather's gambling houses around town, where men played Georgia Skin, an old favorite of workers down south. Big Jack Racks, the patriarch of the Donut Shop collective, who had always looked out for Reek, died not long after, compounding his grief. As the oldest child in his own immediate family and with his father in and out of contact, Reek had looked to Jack for guidance and support. "I still see my dad," Reek said. "But I don't fuck with him like that, though. I don't know what the hell he doing, I ain't going to lie."

All he could do now was regroup. Reek's managers Roger and Bird remained supportive, but usually from afar. Roger was still producing music, and he had taken on a French rapper client from Martinique who was blowing up, with hundreds of millions of plays online. Bird, too, had found platinum-level success managing some white teenage beat makers who started on YouTube and became go-to hit machines for rappers not unlike Reek. But it was hard for a client to stay top of mind when he wasn't all the way up.

In their stead, Roger and Bird had recently sent Reek an emissary charged with turning his career around. Elijah, the goofy Wisconsinite who'd booked Reek for his concert at Lawrence University, began interning for Bird when he moved to New York City after graduating college, getting by on the money he'd made selling weed at school. "I was really good at it," Elijah said, "because I'm really reliable and on my phone all the time." He hoped the same would be true of his new job.

A classically trained piano player, Elijah grew up in the nowhere town of Appleton and initially attended the Lawrence Conservatory of Music. But like many his age, he became obsessed with rap during college and got curious about the business side, helped along by a job at the campus radio station and a friendship with the son of a prominent Midwestern indie-rock musician who lived across the hall in the dorms.

For his first real assignment under Bird, Elijah was named Reek's new in-house A&R, tasked with putting together a mixtape from the unreleased songs that were still lying around. After weeks of Elijah's trying to get in touch, Reek finally started replying, and eventually he welcomed Elijah to Atlanta for work trips that began administrative but blossomed into friendship. The car Reek was using to transport his siblings was Elijah's rental—a white Dodge Durango SUV with a digital dash and Hemi engine that Reek loved to rev. Elijah, who had a nervous laugh and blemished, nearly translucent skin, always rode shotgun.

"I can't let him down," Reek said earnestly of his new partner, though he would also occasionally bully Elijah for not rolling blunts properly or asking too many questions, treating him like a star might treat an assistant. Still, Reek remained grateful for the good-faith investment. "I feel like God sent him to me," he said.

Together, the two young men compiled Lil Reek's *Slime Bizness* EP, his second independent mixtape, which was released on the rapper's twentieth birthday in 2019. The songs were clever and melodically sophisticated, covering much of what had occurred in Reek's life lately, although his voice—which one critic called "odd, pre-pubescent but also slightly raspy"—remained an acquired taste dependent on investing in Reek as an individual. In what would remain an eternal challenge for his career prospects, Reek's most distinctive selling point—his childlike tone and appearance, as contrasted with his subject matter—was also his biggest limitation for casual listeners.

"Man, you got me fucked up, I ain't signing shit," Reek rapped on one track called "Vette," coproduced by Brodinski, that hinted at his recent label woes. "Rather stay motherfucking independent." But the mixtape's opening song, "Maintain," with a beat coproduced by Roger, painted the richest portrait of Reek's journey, invoking how the struggles of his mother and father had landed at his feet, down to the mundanity of day-to-day bills: "We had some problems and I made 'em right / Stayed in that trap all night—water, rent, gas, lights."

Another recurring specter in Reek's music that was popping up more, given his somewhat brittle state, was the shooting death years earlier of his friend Rudy, another of Brodinski's Cleveland Ave. finds, who rapped as Babysnake. Rudy was just fifteen when he was killed in a pointless tussle, and his murder had shaken the neighborhood, even making an episode of *The First 48*. One of Reek's new songs was titled "LLR"—for *long live Rudy* and *long live Racks* both—and when their names or stories came up in his music, Reek's voice tended to flutter with unvarnished fragility but also resolve. "I'm tryna just make a lil change," he rapped to close one verse. "And make a lil change."

Riding around Cleveland Ave. and its neighboring South and Southwest Atlanta neighborhoods could turn Reek wistful beyond his years. Across Zones 3 and 4, Capitol View and Perkerson Park, he pointed out the house where he'd lived for a few years with his father, his grandmother, his uncle, his aunt and his sister, then the apartments he moved to with his mother, the hoop where he learned to shoot a basketball and the woods where he learned to shoot a pistol.

"My youngest siblings, they don't have the manners we grew up with because of my grandma," Reek said, recalling the daily breakfast of pancakes and sausage she would prepare for him when he was a child. A social worker at a school, his father's mother liked to make Reek complete her own supplemental lesson plans on top of his assigned homework, teaching him cursive, integers, electronics and art. "She was strict, but she was nice as fuck," he said. "My grandma a real one—no cap!" He vowed to go visit her the next day.

Yet even amid the warm glow of nostalgia on every corner, Reek could also turn frustrated by the monotony of his surroundings, bored of the same invisible borders he had been penned in by his whole life. "We need an itinerary for these days," he told Elijah curtly, though he seemed as mad at himself as anyone. "We don't need no more days like this. We need to start planning shit, for real."

Ideally, Reek would release the sequel to *Slime Bizness* within a few weeks. Roger and Bird, according to Instagram, were together in Beverly Hills, but Elijah's job was to help prep the track list while holding on to the files and getting the sign-off from producers to use their beats. For promotion, the pair arranged to film a new music video the following afternoon with a hungry director who had driven down from North Carolina in a weathered Honda Civic and promised to do it for free. But Reek didn't yet have a song picked out, and whichever it was going to be, he probably still needed to finish it that night. First, however, he dropped off the jacket he wanted to wear for the video shoot at the dry cleaner. Then came the search for a studio.

"How much is it going to be for four hours?" Reek asked a friend, working his phone to lock in a schedule for the evening. "How much you got on you? You can do sixty dollars? All right, I'mma make the rest work then." He stopped by the Donut Shop to get some weed for the occasion and fielded a call from his annoyed girlfriend.

"You think you're all that because you're riding around in that Durango?" she asked.

Lately, Reek had been splitting his time between his mother's three-bedroom brick home and his girl's place, where he was expected to pay rent and help with her two children. He told her to meet him at the studio.

When Reek and Elijah arrived, five guys were already inside the cramped, humid room, trying to make the most of the hours they'd pooled funds to pay for. Two of Reek's good friends, Reo and Luquae, were most of the way into a song already, and Reek took about fifteen minutes adding a perfunctory verse. He spent another fifteen tacking on a second verse to the half-finished track he'd decided to make the video for, and eventually he asked his in-room adviser how it was sounding.

"I think it's good?" Elijah said tentatively.

Even with every minute of the essence, an unspoken peer pressure to not write down any lyrics in advance of recording permeated the room, with each rapper taking turns punching in using the typical Atlanta mode of freestyling one line at a time, even though not everyone was good at it. Nothing anybody came up with garnered much of a response, and an hour into Reek's time in the booth, three of the guys were fighting sleep, stirring only to cough or sip an orange juice. At some point, Reek's girlfriend showed up with a sidekick, sitting quietly on the couch, save for some friendly banter with Elijah and less friendly banter with her boyfriend.

Rather than work to win her over, Reek opted to use the rest of his allotted time to cram in an attempt at one more track, playing with permutations of the line "I'd sacrifice it all just to have you here today / I'd do life in the pen just to see my brother's face." All told, the crew finished most of four songs in four hours. But before calling it a night, Reek asked me for $75 to pay for his portion of the session.

The traps scattered around the neighborhood were not exactly subtle. A near-constant procession of vehicles, from junkers to foreigns, crowded the driveways and front lawns of single-family homes on active residential blocks made busier by the illicit business. Different from the dilapidated, boarded-up abandoned houses of the popular imagination—places that did still exist, say, off Bankhead or the Bluff, near the football stadium—a trap house near Cleveland Ave. or another in-between area might be set up in a well-appointed, six-figure split-level with cut grass and a barbecue grill on the porch, a steady flow of all-ages patrons knocking on screen doors and being let through dead bolts after a careful peek by an armed doorman.

Inside, the spots—which tended to specialize in weed or lean or Percocet or some combination thereof—could be clean and well stocked with amenities for staff and customers, done up not unlike the legal drug depots that were popping up in states like California and Massachusetts, with a selection of storage worthy of the Container Store (mason jars, plastic crates, airtight dry-food canisters), comfortable couches, video game systems, card tables and big screens. The lack of transparent windows and the excess of security-camera feeds tended to match the recording studios around the city, and many traps were known to have music setups of their own. Like a coffee shop or juice bar menu, whiteboards in the main area were updated with multicolored markers, listing strains, weights, prices—up to $400 for an ounce and as little as $10 for a gram—with graffiti-style decals on the walls to bring the room together.

Typically, no one lived in these man caves—they were places of business. And due to the obvious rotation of short-term guests and the experience of the neighborhood cops, the drug houses never stayed at the same address for long, moving around within a contained radius like a marble in a shell game. But even if they were ephemeral, these traps were Atlanta cultural landmarks, enduring and evolving to the point that their reputations could be sanded down enough to anchor tourist attractions and legitimate businesses, from wing spots (Trap Wingz, the Bando) to the TI-backed Trap Music Museum near Bankhead. There, beginning in 2018, any rap fan could pay $30 to experience a replica–trap house–as–escape room, plus a reproduction of Gucci Mane's drug-cooking kitchen and a mock jail cell. ("Only three ways out of THE TRAP: death, jail or you a lucky muthafucka," read the wall text.)

Reek stopped by the Donut Shop, the go-to clubhouse for his surrogate family, many times a day, to borrow or buy or just to pee. Having a car while Elijah was in town made his daily errands and family responsibilities much simpler. But it was also invigorating to have a mobile home base, and the Durango provided a rare place to himself, good for sitting around listening to music, smoking, snacking, speeding, napping and changing clothes. All day, Reek whipped the car around the neighborhood in circles, always with one more stop to make—buying blunt wraps to roll with or chips and candy to eat after smoking, but picking up a friend first and then switching locations based on the movements of the East Point police or some other imperceptible whim. Sometimes

Reek jumped on the highway just to turn up the music and go extra fast while getting high in peace.

Cam, the music video director, who had a scraggly beard and a chipped front tooth, was ready to get to work. But Reek enjoyed hazing him, pulling off unexpectedly and challenging the out-of-towner to keep up on the Cleveland Ave. rounds. "You got him whipping that Honda like a Porsche," Reek's friend Luquae laughed.

Filming in quick bursts whenever Reek felt like it that weekend, the director ultimately gathered enough footage for two short videos. He captured Reek in front of the Cleveland Ave. Exxon, rapping into the camera while the regulars stayed posted in front of the store, and in a more inspired, fictionalized attempt at visualizing the music, recorded Reek and his buddies running up on an unsuspecting target, played by Elijah. In black-framed glasses and a respectable sweater, Elijah was a central-casting college nebbish perfect for fake-robbing with a real handgun.

On Saturday night, Reek and Elijah packed the Durango with three of their video costars and two pistols. Luquae, a girl-crazy class clown with braces, had graduated from Life Christian Academy with Reek the year prior and recently started rapping while on five years' probation for possession of weed and a gun. Reo, another guy from the recording session, could be alternately woozy and cutting, and he carried himself as the slickest of the bunch. A chubby dude with a loaded backpack was wordless in the way back.

After a few days in Atlanta and a marathon of blunts, Elijah was a seamless addition to the clique, a perceptive and respectful presence who knew his place in the unspoken hierarchy. He played aux-cord DJ during every ride, taking Reek's demands or otherwise cycling through a playlist heavy on the guys' own music, plus their go-tos—Lil Baby, Young Thug, Future, Gunna and NBA YoungBoy, who was from Baton Rouge but functioned as an honorary Atlantan.

Elijah also code-switched some among his Black peers in age, if not circumstance. Around his Atlanta pals, but even when they were not listening, he began dropping his *G*s or the second half of contracted verbs, among other tics ("We on the way," "It be the same . . ."), while sometimes faltering over his "fa sho"s. Reek and his friends didn't seem to mind, but at times they acknowledged the skepticism or confusion of others around the neighborhood when they spotted white people—myself included—in the car.

A token white guy or two with a group of young Black men in certain Atlanta neighborhoods was usually assumed to be rap-related. "You somebody famous's manager?" a teenager asked me when we stopped by Greenbriar Mall to eat, show off and let Luquae holler at women. "People think every white person is a millionaire," Reek offered matter-of-factly.

Around the mall he stood out as well, recognized by strangers, acquaintances and old classmates who nodded, waved or dapped him up. As we were leaving, a toddler with a big smile and a small jean jacket approached for a hug. "I saw you in the video," the kid told Reek. "You was singing!"

"Man, we was like some superstars in the mall," Luquae said on the way back to the car.

"I knew everyone in that bitch, for real," Reek agreed.

But the main event for the night was a nineteenth-birthday party for a friend of Reek's known as Meatt, another aspiring rapper and next-generation associate of Marlo's who repped PFK. Digital flyers posted to Instagram advertised a dice game, good vibes and a planned music video shoot. The hosts had rented a two-story Airbnb for the gathering, about twenty minutes north of Cleveland Ave., not far from Bankhead. "Bring your own weed," they warned.

When Reek and his friends arrived on the early side in a different part of town, they announced their presence and allegiance by blasting an obscure YouTube video from within the Play For Keeps family—"No Evidence" by Check PFK, another student of the 9th Ward—circling the block twice, hanging out the windows of the SUV and screaming the lyrics: "*I was going to school, the only reason 'cause I was selling shit!*"

When they entered the house, about two dozen young men were already inside, gathered in the fluorescent-lit kitchen. Resting on the

L-shaped counter were about a dozen guns of all sizes—Glocks and FN pistols, Draco assault rifles and a janky-looking shotgun that somebody joked was from the Revolutionary War. The birthday boy wore a nonfunctional $220 bulletproof-vest-as-accessory that read RESISTANCE across the belly strap. Everyone was jovial and fluent in secret handshakes, lifting a weapon only to pose for a photo or hot-potato it to whoever was answering the door, just in case. A rotation of music videos from friends, associates and local heroes played on the living room television.

Outside of the general lack of alcohol and the kitchen firearm stash—or those otherwise stuffed into skinny-pant waistbands—it was a teenage party like any other. Blunts and Percs, along with the conversations around procuring them and their subsequent quality, stood in for beers and shots. No one looked much older than twenty-one and some much younger. One baby-faced boy, glued to a love seat, claimed he was fourteen—"But I'm telling them I'm seventeen," he said, pointing to a group of giggling girls. Most everyone wore streetwear or athleisure, Uggs, Jordans, Converse or Air Force Ones. As the house filled up, it remained divided by gender like a school dance, with most of the young women huddled on couches in the front room, showing each other their phones. When the two sides did mingle, it was under the pretense of flirty teasing, like playing keep-away with a bag of candy. Lil Baby's latest single, "Woah," came on at least five times, exciting the girls as much as the guys, but no one danced together. A few people snuck upstairs to the bedrooms.

Elijah and I were the only white people present. On top of that, I had at least a decade on most of them, so I remained more or less invisible, approached only by two separate teenage girls who asked, sheepishly, if I owned the house. I told them that thankfully I did not, nodding to Reek as my ticket in. They understood.

Towheaded, with a cowlick and a weed stash, Elijah proved even more of a novelty. Egged on by Luquae and Reek, he danced unnaturally with his arms and rapped along to the soundtrack, eventually drawing a small crowd that couldn't decide if they were laughing with or at him. A superb sport, he took instruction on various moves, making funny faces and breaking the ice for everyone as a semicircle of guys filmed his awkward jerks and hip thrusts on their iPhones to the sound of Young Thug's "Surf." Reek cheered. "*Aye! Aye! Aye!*"

Later, on the ride back down I-85 toward Cleveland Ave., Reek tried to hit a hundred miles per hour in the Durango, swerving around anyone in his way. The night, like most Saturday nights in one's teens or early twenties, had proven somewhat anticlimactic, and everyone was exhausted. Reek, though, was locked on the road and to the music, screaming along to a YoungBoy song blasting from the sound system, harmonizing an octave higher and adding his own ad-libs over wailed lines about being a "lonely child," head running wild with pain and longing.

"*I need some help because my life been real hard*," the speakers said.

"NO CAP!" Reek yelled back.

"*The way I approach the game, it seems that I'm hard / But I got feelings, too, just like a lil boy, oh, lord.*"

· 24 ·

ALL GOD'S SIGNS

It wasn't long after P started leaning into his life as a suburban dad, just shy of his fortieth birthday, that the ducks moved in.

While many of the Quality Control CEO's musical progeny were flourishing, his fourth and fifth biological children—a boy and a girl, the latter to be named for a *Games of Thrones* queen—were due within weeks of each other in the spring of 2019. Their mothers, two models and Instagram fixtures, were also public figures, ratcheting up the prurient interest of TMZ and the Black gossip pages. But P, for his part, generally continued his attempts not to spar in public with either woman, or anyone else for that matter. He preferred to float above any pointed shots at his alleged misdeeds as a man or a boss.

Instead, on Valentine's Day, P publicized his lavish gifts to both pregnant women, telling one (and everyone watching) on Instagram, "I look forward to us both doing the right things as two grown adults co parenting. Enjoy your new Bentley Truck and your New Home. You never have to pay rent another day in your life." He signed the message, "A Responsible Father."

At the same time, like Tony Soprano before him, P was learning to live with waterfowl. In frequent dispatches from his palatial home—the sort of distinctly Atlanta McMansion that the local paper called the real estate equivalent of a Big Gulp, and which, in this city, could belong to a dentist, a lawyer, a club promoter or a music mogul—P showed off his shimmering backyard pool, always perfectly manicured up to its edges, the water dancing like diamonds. It wasn't surprising then that a local duck may have confused the man-made expanse for a proper lake, and the bird became a recurring character on P's otherwise flashy online feed, a droll domestic headache that at first annoyed, and then tickled, the executive.

"*Gatdamn* duck," he said one afternoon, Gucci flip-flops visible in the frame. "Still in my gatdamn pool." But his tone was playful, and P seemed resigned to the wildlife that came with a yard of such square footage. So, he scattered some white bread outside, ensuring that the freeloading animal would stick around. But the saga intensified when it became clear that the duck had laid her eggs in a planter overlooking the water.

P, appropriately softened by the opening stages of the circle of life, kicked into patriarch mode, taking ownership of the would-be flock. "We gonna make sure these babies come out healthy. We gonna take care of them, we gonna feed em," he told his million-plus followers.

"Bruh, you don't want nobody to be talking about no animal cruelty," P put out there preemptively. "We love ducks. They can have the pool, man."

In his new role as duck dad-to-be, he crowdsourced some dietary options for the mother-in-waiting, who sat warming the nest in her new upscale neighborhood. Not long after, P displayed a lush Tupperware cornucopia overflowing with grain, shredded lettuce, loose corn and meticulously halved green grapes. Quavo had sent him a "spiritual and really deep" message about the significance of the bird's presence, P noted, and he'd received it with an open heart.

"I take heed to all God's signs," he said. "That was really big for Quavo to send me that message and let me know what ducks represent.

"She know I'm feeding her. She know daddy gon' take care of her," P continued, emphasizing the responsibility that had been foisted upon him. "She comfortable. She know she at home now." But like any working father, P also feared not being around enough. "I hope I don't be gone when these babies born," he said.

Unfortunately, the harmony across species would prove short-lived. A few days after P's show of devotion, his pool cleaners came by for their regular appointment and informed the homeowner that there was duck shit everywhere. P's pristine water, the cherry on top of any luxury property in the area, was being contaminated, the experts said, and the bottom of the pool coated with slimy feces. P would have to call animal control; they would make sure the duck knew she would not be returning.

"My kids have to swim in that pool," P announced, newly stern at having to relearn a lesson he had already absorbed elsewhere, as the caretaker of so many surrogate charges: *If you give handouts, they'll shit all over you.*

Outside of his personal palace, P tended to approach his growing music empire in the benevolent spirit of munificence, tamping down any internal competition among artists and always insisting that there was plenty to go around. Wizening in real time as an executive, and increasingly looked to as an elder statesman in the wider hip-hop sphere—an honor, or else an inevitable side effect of great monetary success—P in turn embraced his motivational self-help side, reading daily from a modern prayer book, *Praying Through It: 365 Days of Prayers That Make Praying Easy*, and broadcasting his favorite passages under headings like "Fix Me" and "I Pray for Discipline." He stressed the importance of Black property ownership ("INVEST IN YOURSELF") and reminisced often about his down-bad days as they faded further and further into the rearview.

In line with the enduring rap ethos, which had for decades embraced the most competitive and consumptive aspects of American capitalism with a semiconservative bootstraps mentality, P framed even his flexing of outrageous material possessions as motivation for others—and as a rejection of a system designed to hold people like him back. For the executive and his artists, diamond chains and six-figure watches were armor, trophies and talismans—a celebratory middle finger to a world that looked down on, and even disdained, them. But P also subtly differentiated the drug-dealer flashiness of his old life from the more IRS-and-FBI-proof grandeur he had earned with his new one.

Once, in a throwback lesson for his followers, P recalled the in-between days of 2010, when he was preparing to buy his first Rolls-

Royce Ghost—easily a $300,000 car—to the chagrin of the man they all called Big, the one who'd linked P and Lil Baby in the first place. "He told me if I buy the car, don't come around him no mo bringing the wrong kind of attention," P wrote. "He told me just keep stacking and hustling. The man even told me to find a new church to go to." Big did so in front of Baby and Ced, younger men who were soaking up competing knowledge from both sides.

At the time, P thought of Big as nothing more than a hater. But he had come to understand the warnings he once scoffed at after he was able to purchase cars of equal or greater value "without the stress of what I was dealing with" all those years back, before music. "Moral of the story, if you stay down and focus on the positive and trust God, he will bless you with a overflow of things that you never imagined could happen," P concluded. "Get people around you that want to see you win and motivate you to do better."

He also vowed often to continue paying forward the blessings he had received. "Gon' help a couple mo' n——s become millionaires this year," P wrote in a public affirmation of his intentions that doubled as a New Year's resolution. "On God."

Yet the executive's attempts to present as a smoothed-out version of his former self, a man calmed by faith and a financial windfall, were belied by the knottier reality of his personal life. By mid-2019, P was engaged in a brutal custody battle that would drag on for the next two years, as Lira Galore, the mother of P's youngest daughter, accused him in detail—and with what she said was photographic evidence—of abuse. In court papers, Galore said that P had "consistently demonstrated physically violent, emotionally abusive, irrational and erratic behavior," including choking and beating her several times while she was pregnant. Estimating P's net worth at $50 million, Galore sought at least $15 million in damages.

P denied the allegations, countering on social media that Galore was a drug addict and a liar engaging in a shakedown. "One thing I don't play about is my father hood. I have 16 artists on my label, I still make time to see my children 4 times out of the week," P wrote. "No I'm not perfect but if anyone knows me they know I go hard every day so my children will never have to go through what I've been through."

But his post, which included text messages from Galore meant to bolster his side, violated the judge's gag order in the dispute, resulting in an $11,000 sanction. The case was eventually settled, with both sides agreeing in court to seal the specifics. The music industry, including P's corporate partners, stayed mum on the issue.

Compared to the few years prior, 2019 would be a relatively fallow one for the broader Quality Control family, at least when it came to music. The same could not be said for Atlanta rap in general, as its influence and impact continued to proliferate across culture, both in its purest forms and in Xeroxes of Xeroxes of Xeroxes. *Billboard* number one albums for the year included inescapable, evolved trap music from 21 Savage (*I Am > I Was*), Future (*The WIZRD*) and Young Thug (*So Much Fun*), plus the compilation *Revenge of the Dreamers III* from J. Cole's Dreamville label, an album recorded over ten days in the famed Atlanta-area studio Tree Sound. *Dreamers* centered some outré, trap-adjacent up-and-comers from the city, like EarthGang (a spacey, OutKast-esque duo from the SWATS) and Young Nudy (the giddily nihilistic 21 Savage affiliate who also repped Marlo's 9th Ward), and the project would go on to be nominated for Best Rap Album at the Grammy Awards alongside Savage's *I Am > I Was*. Also reaching the top of the charts: Trippie Redd, the SoundCloud warbler, Atlanta transplant and onetime QC affiliate; Roddy Ricch, who was from Los Angeles but sounded more like Atlanta; and Post Malone, a white, Southern-raised, beer-guzzling Auto-Tuned interloper who made a habit of collaborating with Migos.

Even the Nickelodeon-spawned pop star Ariana Grande tried trap accoutrements on for size, dropping the album *Thank U, Next* with the quick casualness of a mixtape—and with the 808 drums and sing-rap cadences to match. "7 Rings," Grande's dominant number one single, even found itself the subject of controversy regarding appropriation and outright creative theft, with listeners accusing the singer of lifting her flow wholesale from Soulja Boy and 2 Chainz, with Chainz eventually added to an official remix as an emissary. In a show of hip-hop transactionalism, Grande returned the diplomatic favor by appearing on the veteran Atlanta rapper's next album, *Rap or Go to the League.*

But the biggest musical moment of 2019—and probably the biggest pop culture phenomenon period, on its way to becoming the defining song of the streaming era so far—was also an Atlanta story, albeit in less obvious ways. "Old Town Road," by Lil Nas X, was considered a novelty song by most, dubbed "country-trap" by its creator and may be remembered as more of a meme than a piece of music. But the song's combination of Southern caricature and hip-hop irreverence could only have come from one city.

Lil Nas X, who was nineteen and entirely independent when he released the track on SoundCloud, was born in Atlanta in 1999. He moved as a child from Bankhead Courts, where his mother and grandmother lived, to his father's place in the Cobb County suburb of Austell, where Lil Yachty was raised. "If I would have stayed there, I would have fallen in with the wrong crowd," Lil Nas X said of his time on the West Side.

Instead, the kid born Montero Hill became a savvy internet prankster and meme hustler. He had just started dabbling in music when he sourced a Nine Inch Nails–sampling pseudo-trap beat from YouTube, leasing it from a rap-loving Dutch stranger for $30. That banjo-plucked, internationally born instrumental would become the backbone of "Old Town Road." Lil Nas X then recorded the track in under an hour at the studio CinCoYo, a couple miles from Bankhead, because it offered a special rate known as $20 Tuesdays.

After releasing "Old Town Road" online and boosting it with homemade cowboy memes on Twitter, YouTube and TikTok, Lil Nas X did not make much use of his city's rap infrastructure or boosterism, bypassing the local power structures like clubs and radio stations with his mastery of social media. But he nonetheless carried the mantle and credibility of being "from Atlanta" as his song went viral—and then beyond viral—with a nineteen-week streak at number one on the Hot 100 that set the all-time record.

Though "Old Town Road" was not necessarily of the same on-the-ground, overlapping and borderline incestuous scene that had made Atlanta rap an international touchstone, the song and its cultural domination encapsulated how Atlanta's music had morphed and spread, influencing everything it touched and becoming a lingua franca across ages, races and beyond. Eventually, even Young Thug—not one to pander—blessed the song with a hyperlocal verse, shouting out "South Berry Road" in his native East Point.

But even as the planet was becoming more Atlanta-fied, learning its minor roads subconsciously, Quality Control was pulling back and plotting. What had become clear after the tepid reaction to the Migos solo albums was that for QC's already established artists, there were now diminishing returns to rushing out even more new music. The problem with a game plan that called for oversaturating the market, it turned out, was that eventually the market gets oversaturated.

With four nationally certified, prolific in-house acts—Migos, Lil Yachty, Lil Baby and City Girls—the label had a proven track record that put it in conversation with the rap empires of yore, the ones that had served as its blueprint. QC was no longer considered merely lucky and no longer banging at the industry's gates to be taken seriously. But rather than continuing to claw for attention share from a fragmented and overserved audience, the label, for the first time since the pre-*Culture* Migos drought of 2016, considered creating some scarcity while expanding in other ways.

Which isn't to say that the organization took any time off. As Migos and Yachty tended to their packed appearance schedules and corporate endorsements—like the Mountain Dew commercial, set to a custom soundtrack, in which the rap trio rode man-sized, gold-plated tricycles across a mansion, or Yachty's starring role in the stoner sequel *How High 2*—Coach and P were tending to their JV squad of hopefuls. They were also making rap's inevitable sports metaphors more literal, launching the Quality Control Sports agency quietly but effectively, finding the perfect early client in Alvin Kamara, an NFL running back for the New Orleans Saints who won Offensive Rookie of the Year honors in 2017. Kamara, of course, was from Atlanta.

That summer, in lieu of proper albums from its biggest names, there was also the second volume of the label's *Control the Streets* compilation, another thirty-six tracks from its dependable stars and auditioning postulants. New to the party were the R&B singer Layton Greene, an inevitable expansion lane for QC; 24Heavy, an Auto-Tuned ex-convict who trickled up from an affiliated fledgling Atlanta label; and Duke Deuce, a high-energy crunk revanchist and Offset affiliate from Memphis with improbable dance moves; plus a fourteen-year-old local Quavo signee called Street Bud. The QC compilation reached number three on *Billboard*, almost as an afterthought, but the critical reaction continued to emphasize the label's overexposure. (The critic Sheldon Pearce called it "an attempt at crowd control, like trying to wrangle a disinterested mob" of rap fans, adding that the collection had "the reek of desperation.") But the tossed-off digital album did have the benefit of shoring up industry alliances for the label, with guest features from the next microgeneration of rap stars, including Megan Thee Stallion, Playboi Carti and DaBaby, who rapped on the album's best track, a diplomatic offering with Lil Baby over their shared moniker called, naturally, "Baby."

His label having exhausted some listeners, Baby was still zooming on pure momentum. For the first time in his short career, he would release no new albums or mixtapes for a full calendar year, itching to all the while, but not even needing fresh product to keep achieving exponential growth in radio spins, name recognition and streams. Baby continued to record new music nonstop, including amid a lucrative run of international music festival appearances—England, Germany, Switzerland, Ireland, the Netherlands, Sweden and so on—but he was sowing with one hand and reaping with the other, all while building anticipation for whatever he did next by trying something new: staying quiet.

"The year that I didn't drop was the year that I blew up," Baby said later, with incredulity, never acknowledging that he had already packed a decade's worth of output into the first two years of his career.

But with expanding fame and family came the sort of life changes that don't get listed in a Celebrity 101 manual. Baby knew these were the things that could sound like ingrate griping to most, the stuff not taken seriously by anyone but other successful artists and their intimates. But they could wear a person down.

Among the stresses were constant travel, with private jets and helicopters deployed to sometimes make two separate paying obligations in one night; the nonstop surveillance of anyone associated with you by the iPhone-wielding amateur paparazzi known as modern fans; the expectation of financial assistance from everyone you've ever known; and the kind of limitless access to material possessions, women and drugs that could turn anyone into a selfish, hedonistic glutton.

From his earliest songs, Baby had always been preoccupied with his dependence on chemical substances to even out—declaring, for instance, that he was done with drugs on "My Dawg," right after admitting to having a bladder full of codeine—but his consumption habits were now part of the broader public record and thus subject to wide speculation. Baby's natural twitchiness on camera led some to declare that he was going too hard on the Percocet pills, with the fan diagnosis even becoming a recurring topic of conversation online. But Baby's biggest personal struggles had always been with lean and cigarettes, since weed failed to register as a concern. At his peak usage, he was drinking up to five or six ounces of prescription opioid syrup a day, going through a pint—with an everyman street value up near $1,000—fast enough to result in a $20,000-a-month habit.

Baby had taken up sipping lean while on parole after prison, when he was regularly drug tested and thus barred from smoking marijuana, and he'd nursed an on-and-off dependency ever since. "That shit started fucking with me," he said once upon quitting temporarily. "Breathe different, talk different, feel different, everything." After two months off from the drug, he lost twenty pounds.

But backsliding could happen just as easily. And as Baby's station rose, so did the expectation of leadership on such issues. Baby had always preferred to refrain from passing judgment on those around him, particularly in public, ever wary of being considered a scold. "I ain't telling 'em—that shit lame. I ain't really on that," he said. "To each his own."

But he had also seen enough fellow rappers and regular people around him die from opioid abuse that he knew it was something to be taken seriously. Even beyond concerns over health or morality, addiction represented the greatest affliction of all in the eyes of a dedicated hustler—laziness, an overall lack of grind.

One summer afternoon, in the parking lot of the Quality Control studios, a label affiliate tended to an RC car, a favorite grown-up toy for the guys when not playing with their life-size versions. With single-minded focus, the man twisted the little vehicle's wheels back and forth in place, not far from three stacks of cash totaling some $150,000 that were strewn on the dirty pavement.

Baby had dropped the money there as a lesson, right at the feet of another friend who sat curled in on himself on an overturned yellow bucket. The target of Baby's lecture was dressed in a tight, all-black ensemble with matching Nike Air Force One mids, and he put his head in his hands as the rapper stood over him, incensed.

Hands on his own knees, Baby bent down into his friend's face like a coach laying into a moping player on the sideline bench. "So you don't wanna be no rapper?" Baby asked him, voice raised high and piercing. "You said you don't wanna be no rapper 'cause what?"

His friend refused eye contact, looking down into his clasped hands, not far from the money. "I wanted to, but . . ."

"'Cause you love them pills, bruh?" Baby yelled over the weak protestations. A small crowd had gathered behind them, and someone else chimed in. "Check him in somewhere," they said.

"I'm telling you to go to a doctor!" Baby shouted. "I'm dead-ass serious." The man with the remote-control car continued his maintenance work, tossing his cigarette butt and not even glancing over.

"I worry about myself, and my close loved ones," Baby said later of his begrudging role as guidance counselor. "I ain't going to let nobody with me do something I'm not going to do." He was back to sipping lean himself, but less intensely. "I drink a little bit here and there, and this and that, so I can't be too hard on you," he said. "But if you are just like, obsessive, I'm going to be on you. I ain't for that. I really ain't for that. To the point now where I stopped putting it in my music."

"You're rapping less about doing drugs?" I asked.

"I'm trying," Baby said. "Because I done rapped about drugs that I don't even take. People think I take 'em and then people take 'em thinking I take 'em. Like popping Percs. I don't pop Percs, period! Hell nah. Every now and then I used to take a half of one, but I say it in my raps, because I *might* pop one and that's what's going on. Now I done seen people actually tell me I inspired them. N——s done actually told me, *I'm fuckin' with you and these Percs!* But I don't even take Percs!

"Shit's real," he said.

Cigarettes were a more mundane, personal issue. He had publicly vowed to quit—and later, letting on that he'd failed, would rap, "I'm too rich to be smoking these cigs," continuing to pepper his verses with millionaire problems that overlapped with everyday anxieties. But Baby's main concern was his new teeth.

Along with jewelry, foreign cars, sneakers and designer clothes, "aesthetic dentistry" had become a bragging right in rap, another expensive flex that could appear superficial at first but actually revealed the depth of the race and class divides in America. Living in "dental professional shortage areas" was something that affected nearly fifty-eight million people across the country, and while one-third of white children did not get proper care, about half of all Black and Latino kids lacked access—never mind the thousands of dollars for braces and other orthodontics. So, like movie stars before them, when some rappers made it big, fixing their smile was often near the top of the to-do list.

Taking the throne as the poet laureate of perfect smiles, Cardi B, on her first smash hit, rapped that she "got a bag and fixed my teeth." (She later responded to fans who said they missed her old, crooked grin by stating definitively, "Bitch, you and my old teeth was not friends.") Young Thug, who was said to be so self-conscious about his mangled and rotted pre-fame smile that he often spoke with his hand in front of his face, had spent hundreds of thousands of dollars to retool his mouth. And though Baby's situation was less dire, cosmetically and health-wise, he would follow suit. "Just 'cause you bought 'em don't mean you ain't gotta brush 'em," he declared, though his fresh set made sure to maintain his trademark gap front and center.

As with other luxury items, the quality of one's pearly whites even became a competitive battleground, with bad, budget versions of veneers a cause for ridicule. "Hundred thousand in my mouth like, 'What's happenin'?'" Baby rapped on "Woah," his comeback single in late 2019. "Not the big cheap teeth, that's embarrassing." Smoking cigarettes, he knew, was akin to putting a bumper sticker on a brand-new Lamborghini.

ONE HUMID ATLANTA morning that June, Lil Baby's mother, Lashon, pulled up looking like royalty. She arrived at a crowded soul food brunch spot, located in an otherwise desolate strip mall outside of the city, way west of the West End, in a shimmering gold Mercedes-Benz E-Class convertible Cabriolet, her short hair dyed a complementary blond. Lashon wore a Rolex that matched the vehicle and a Tommy Hilfiger dress shirt, with a Louis Vuitton pocketbook in hand, and she greeted me with warmth and obvious pride at the unlikely arrangement, sitting gamely on a plastic chair out front to wait for a table.

The Benz was a Mother's Day gift from her youngest child and only son, Lashon said, and it followed the earlier, less flashy Dodge Durango SUV he'd bought for her. The combo of cars—one better for carting around grandkids—suited the large suburban home he'd also paid for. Soon Dominique, as she still called him, would buy her an even bigger place, along with homes for his sisters, at once confessing and bragging on a record that he didn't even have the time to go admire them. "That's a great feelin'," Baby rapped. "I'mma go there when I get a chance."

Lashon appreciated the tokens of gratitude that her son's new life provided her, of course. "He spoils all of us," she said over breakfast. "Because of him, I have experienced stuff that I never, ever thought I would experience." But her chief concerns remained maternal above all else. "Do it for your kids," she told Baby, trying and failing to brush off his constant offers of more cash. "Make sure they have a future." Her grandson Loyal was still an infant and Jason only three. But thinking ahead was a luxury they could now afford.

"So if they decide that school ain't for me, working for somebody ain't for me, give them options," Lashon said. "Give them some businesses in their names, give them a dividend every now and then, so when they're eighteen, they can go in there and take it over." Generational wealth was the end goal.

Lashon knew she could get her recompense elsewhere. Recently, she had been sitting in her new home, in her favorite chair, and she was able to rely on her smart speaker to underline how far her family had come. "Alexa, play some Lil Baby," she commanded.

Lashon beamed. "I texted him, 'You did that shit. I was just getting teary-eyed.'" Baby replied to his mother that he, too, got emotional all the time at the thought of their journey.

But Lashon continued to stress to her son the importance of fatherhood, not to be measured monetarily but in physical presence—something she knew Dominique had missed out on from his father. "Time is what they remember," she said. "They ain't going to remember the stuff, because people buy them stuff all the time. They gon' look back and say, 'My dad was at my game.'"

At the restaurant, Lashon wiped away a tear. She noted that Dominique still called his own father by his first name, Thom. But she was heartened of late that the two men had been talking more since her ex-husband was diagnosed with cancer. Baby had even let his father borrow one of his cars, earning a text from his mother about how proud she was of him for growing into such a forgiving person.

"Time," she repeated. "You can't get it back. Your dad wish he could—I hear it in his voice every day when I talk to him. He texts me like, 'Congratulations on the BET nominations.' I said, 'I didn't make him by myself.' I raised him by myself, yeah. But I didn't make him by myself."

Yet Lashon's life, too, had also shifted in less storybook ways that she never expected—all from the runoff of fame. "You hear stories about celebrities, and they talk about their family, and you're like, *Oh, Lord . . .*," Lashon said. "I thought I had the best family ever—*No, my family ain't like that.* Oh, I lied!" She cried out with laughter. "I lied! It's crazy."

It wasn't that she didn't want to chip in where she could. "I'm always helping people," she said. There were local charities, like a friend's nonprofit for drug-addicted mothers, and she took to keeping a stash of bills in her car, to give away to friends, family or strangers—anyone who approached her with a hand outstretched.

"You don't think if I could help everybody I would? I can't say yes to everybody. It's never enough. At some point you have to say no. I can't save the world. If that was the case, it'd be saved already," Lashon said. "I still have a life! Bills don't stop. I have two daughters—they don't work, so when he helps me, I help them. And they have babies."

The outside pressure had gotten to be so great that Lashon deleted her Facebook page and changed her number. Dominique, she knew, would brush these things off, honored that he could be of service to those around him. But in the lyrics to a new song, he confessed: "Keep pourin' that syrup up, knowin' it don't help / It's like I got money to please everybody else."

"It's not your fault," Baby's mother told him of the extra burdens. "You can't help that you became great."

"I don't care who's mad, I don't care what you see on Instagram," Lashon went on at brunch. "That man has so much responsibility. First of all, he has two kids. They come first and foremost. Assistants, photographers, security, sound people. 'Oh, he making money,'" she mocked again. "It's not like that—he has people he has to pay. It's a job. He gets up and goes to work.

"'Oh, you can't call for free tickets?' That's how he eats—I can't get you a free ticket every time!" Sometimes, Lashon even bought her own. "He gets mad," she said. "But that's how he eats."

Still, her life was easier than it had ever been—with a retirement she'd never expected and lush trips to exotic locations, not unlike her freewheeling time in Japan, before she had kids or any real responsibilities. Now Lashon cared for her grandchildren as much as she could, and she was mostly delighted when they were all recognized in public—even the toddlers.

"We go to the mall, I have to have him in a hoodie and they still spot him," she said. "'That look like baby Jason! Lil Baby son!' I always have on the same baseball cap. 'You Lil Baby mom?' 'Nuh-uh . . .'"

It happened, she estimated, some twenty times a day in Atlanta, including at that moment, as the table next to us began whispering, craning their necks and eavesdropping harder. "Oh, I heard them," Lashon said, waving it off. She didn't mind the local pride over her son's ascent, the people coming up to her to say how proud they were and to congratulate her for the blessings. As Dominique put it: "I'd rather not have privacy to live like this than to have privacy and live like that."

Besides, not everything had changed from the old days, when Lashon used to send $25 a month to Pat Robertson's *The 700 Club*, despite thinking it was a scam, on the off chance that paid prayer could keep her son safe in the streets. Then, like now, she would've done anything to protect her baby. These days, even with all they had accomplished together, Lashon still liked to start her mornings with an all-purpose plea for Dominique's well-being.

"Only because this world, the jealousy . . . ," she said, trailing off. "But I pray all the evil spirits away. I wake up every day and say, 'Lord, I know you got him. You've had him all this time. I don't think you'd forsake him now.'

"And that's how I start my day."

25.

IMMUNE TO LOSING

THE *ATLANTA JOURNAL-CONSTITUTION* CALLED IT A "LEGAL STUNner." But for Marlo and Lil Baby, the murder trial that never occurred was still more proof that the system worked better when you could afford to keep a close eye on it.

The jury had already been selected. It was the second week of 2020, and the trial that sought to pin a drug deal gone bad on the rappers' loyal partners Head and G-Five was set to begin on a Thursday in a DeKalb County courtroom. Surveillance footage, blasted all over the local news, showed two men who matched the suspects' descriptions at the scene of the crime—a suburban Atlanta apartment complex—both in skinny jeans with hoodies up, a smaller man in white (allegedly Baby's man G-Five) and a bigger guy in black, who was wheeling a substantial rolling suitcase behind him (Marlo's partner Head, supposedly). Neither person's face was fully visible as the men on film tried their hardest not to look up at the security camera as they passed by, but the police thought they had their guys regardless. A third man—initially charged with felony murder in the case, before he was deemed to be a victim, not a perpetrator—was scheduled to be the prosecution's star witness, all set to pin the shooting death of twenty-five-year-old Carthel Johnson on Head and G-Five alone.

But then, without warning, the key witness disappeared. A second person set to testify for the district attorney's office could not be found in time for the trial either. They had both fled to California, according to the last-ditch warrants that sought to force them back, but the courtroom wrangling seemed more hopeless for the government every day. The judge, sick of prosecutors' repeated attempts at stalling, rejected multiple motions to delay the high-profile murder trial. Head and G-Five had already spent thirteen months behind bars awaiting their day in court, the judge reasoned, and she had denied requests for bond at every turn of the case. Finally, on January 9, at the behest of the pair's persistent legal teams, including Drew Findling and Jacoby Hudson, came the surprise verdict from the bench—not guilty. No trial necessary.

In her decision, Judge Shondeana Morris was withering, barely suppressing her contempt for the government attorneys she saw as unprepared and unprofessional despite plentiful resources. She had no choice but to free the accused. "If there are consequences to the community for this acquittal," Judge Morris wrote, "such consequences are attributable solely to the state." Facing life in prison, both men had dodged a legal bullet at point-blank range.

In a jailhouse interview afterward, Head underlined his legal victory. "It wasn't no technicality, it was real facts," he told the local news in his prison blues, a touch of a mustache framing his gold front teeth. He was flanked for the TV spot not just by Jacoby, his and Marlo's old friend from Bowen Homes, but another of the top-tier lawyers Marlo kept on speed dial, Brian Steel. A colleague with a local reputation approaching Findling's—but with less natural flash—Steel was best known in rap circles for his steady work on behalf of Young Thug, and the attorney flaunted his success in "seemingly unwinnable cases."

Head would not be freed right away. Instead, he was transferred from DeKalb to the neighboring Fulton County Jail, both for new minor charges he'd racked up while being held on the murder and because of how this latest arrest complicated his probation for a sex offense from when he was fourteen. But Jacoby and his co-counsel assured that Head would be home soon, and their word usually panned out. The most important thing was the acquittal; everything else was paperwork.

Later, Jacoby insisted they had come by the judge's decision honestly, with the witnesses neither paid off nor intimidated. Head, he said, really was innocent. The lawyers had even hired an expert to analyze the surveillance footage from the apartments and determined that the larger man the authorities believed to be Head was actually someone four inches taller than their client's five feet ten inches.

"There is a killer walking around now that's on video," Head said, nearly taunting the authorities for their investigative and administrative failures.

Marlo, for his part, was pleased, if not totally pacified. He could still tick off a lineup of names from his Bowen Homes and 9th Ward extended family that needed freeing—Fat Steve, Big Bucket, JROC, Larrice, Tay Tay, Tez, ShoutNeck, Kool, Niskie, Black Doc, WoodLeg and more. But Head was like a brother to him, and if Marlo was still going to become a rap star, Head was going to be there by his side. The win was worth celebrating.

In his own victory-lap interview on behalf of G-Five, Drew Findling wore a powder-blue suit and a loud floral tie, seated at his stately desk. He did not mention Baby, but behind him was a copy of Gucci Mane's autobiography and two bags of Rap Snacks potato chips—sour cream with a "dab" of ranch—featuring cartoon likenesses of Migos, always comfortable in their roles as salesmen. Findling, too, seemed right at home on TV, emphasizing another favorable verdict on behalf of a rap-adjacent client. "This judge made a decision that every judge I know of in over thirty years of trying cases in the state of Georgia and throughout the United States would make," the lawyer said. "The state of Georgia needs to now focus on the person that disappeared on them."

Baby, not for the first time, could declare G-Five free for all of the fans who knew his friend's plight only in passing. But with this close call also came something different from the other times G-Five had wriggled out of a jam. In a matter of weeks, Baby's sidekick, who usually hit the studio just to hang out, was teasing his own first single, using as cover art a wicked photo from another murder trial—that indelible image of O. J. Simpson and those ill-fitting leather gloves, a marketing provocation sure to register with the Atlanta prosecutors who already knew him so well. Like Gucci Mane, Offset, JT of City Girls and so many others before him, G-Five was calling his song "First Day Out."

* * *

A few weeks later, with one fewer stressor hanging over him, Marlo was back in the trenches, at least thematically. His new mixtape, and the first release of another year that could be his, was to be called *1st & 3rd*, for the days of the month when those on government assistance, like welfare and social security, typically received their money—and thus, historically, or at least mythically, the busiest time for a drug dealer in the projects.

His commercial experiment from the previous summer, in which Marlo tried his hand at becoming a strip club rapper with "Soakin Wet," had ended up a resounding thud, not really bringing him a new audience, even with Offset and City Girls guesting, and not breaking any new creative ground. The track had failed to chart, and its video had topped out around two million views on YouTube, falling short of even his earliest songs with Baby from two years prior. Straying from the core characteristics of his trap foundation—street business and its attendant darkness over summer vibes and sex appeal—was not a plausible shortcut for Marlo, at least at this point. His new music would be a return to the corner.

Marlo had, however, picked up a new business partner along the way, one from outside of his own tight circle but within the Quality Control family. Lil Coach was, as his nickname advertised, one of Coach K's two adult sons—not to be confused with Baby Coach, Lil Coach's brother—each of whom had decades on the executive's third child and youngest boy, a toddler with a catalog-ready cherub face. Lil Coach had his father's eyes and demeanor, but he had been slower to take up his occupation on the management side of rap, focusing instead for a while on photography, capturing his dad's famous friends and clients. But Marlo needed a real manager, someone to stay on him day-to-day, sort through his business opportunities and politic in and around the industry. The Coach name, meanwhile, had become a brand. So while Jimmy from Bowen Homes had been a suitable pseudo-manager for Marlo in his amateurish fledgling days—and would continue to stick around where he was needed—everyone hoped this new pairing of the young and hungry foretold bigger things.

"Me and you the new Coach and Jeezy," Marlo would tell Lil Coach, calling back to Coach K's breakout client and still Marlo's own best-case scenario for a rap-career blueprint. The title *1st & 3rd* could even be read as a direct reference to the early Young Jeezy hit "My Hood," when the Atlanta forebear rapped about his mutual love affair with the streets: "It's all gravy, still reaching with my words / And make 'em feel good like the first and the third."

The title track of Marlo's forthcoming mixtape had little of the vulnerability he had been experimenting with on his unreleased songs, and he once again opted to push an invincible kingpin persona with backup from his city's most reliable street preachers. The new single featured Future, who had done as much as anyone not named Young Thug to stretch the aural limits of recent trap music, extending its shelf life with croaky hooks, deceptively intricate raps and wily, sin-heavy lyrics. On Marlo's "1st N 3rd," Future was on autopilot but still effective, handling the song's chorus and first verse with as straightforward a premise as he could muster about "finessing and trapping," rattling off the words with Migos-like monomania. Baby, of course, showed up to rap with Marlo, as well.

For the video, the three men took their positions in an exaggerated version of a bando, complete with boards on the windows, and in front of a local corner store. Sandwiched on the second verse in between his nimbler collaborators, Marlo, wearing a sleek white turtleneck under blue workwear, once again traced his origin story in squeaky, almost arhythmic bars: "Eight years old when I jumped off the porch / By the time I was ten, n——s gave me the ropes." Far from stealing the show, lyrically or visually, Marlo blended into his familiar surroundings so well that he risked being swallowed altogether.

Still, even with his own standing as a rapper an open question, Marlo was adamant about pulling up the next generation of talent, ending his verse with a pledge to instill hope in his acolytes. Sure enough, during the music video shoot, Marlo called into the gathered crowd of extras for Check, a junior member of his PFK clique who had lately started taking rap more seriously.

"Where Check at?" Marlo demanded. "Man, give somebody that damn stick, put this chain on and get in front of everybody."

But with Future as the veteran torch-passer and Marlo and Check the eager recipients, Baby was more like the flame itself. His guest verse for Marlo came on the back of two impressive solo singles, "Woah" and "Sum 2 Prove," that were setting the table for Baby's return to releasing music after a booming year of minimal output, and he was no longer positioning himself as an interloper at the top.

Rather than veering toward the pop sound and audience that were now open to him, Baby's rapping had only become more dense and elaborate in structure, like he could never run out of things to say about the differences between his past life and his current one. Yet even while moving at Mach speed, Baby would always gladly slow down and take a moment to assist his original musical partner, despite their divergent roads. "He go his way, I go my way," Baby rapped on his friend's new song.

Because as Marlo was rapping about trapping with the immediacy that came from being within it, Baby found himself progressively at a remove, even if that world could be close enough at hand when he wanted. The hood, he explained, would always be a part of him, even if he had made it out of poverty. But he finished his verse with a rhetorical question that dared anyone to undermine how far he had come: "Is you proud of me?"

On that point, Marlo never wavered. "The whole fuckin' Atlanta better be happy for Lil Baby," he wrote on Instagram, holding his ally's successes over his own career stagnancy. "If not, you a hater."

Years on from their crude beginnings as ambivalent musicians, it was clear by now that Marlo would never match Baby's fluency in writing, rapping or songcraft. But one of the beautiful things about rap was that there were no prerequisites, and any apparent lack in one area could be made up for in another. The ineffable was as valuable as the technical, the practical as important as the natural. Marlo knew he had the background and QC's support. Depending on the hour, the day or the month, he had the drive, too. So on the precipice of another release, he pledged yet again to stay in the studio and off the street, pointing to something Young Thug and P had preached to him, much as they had preached to Baby previously: "God ain't gon' let you do both of 'em."

For a while, it seemed to be working, even if the reward was not yet tangible. Together with Lil Coach, who flogged the run-up to Marlo's mixtape with the hype of a salesman who believed in his product, Marlo appeared more reliably at club nights, where he cheered for his own music and that of his friends; at PFK-sponsored school drives, where he tossed backpacks full of supplies at eager local children; at "Eat & Greet" summits with local DJs, where he schmoozed over wings and seafood; and at profile-building interviews with affable interrogators, who eked out, little by little, the depth of Marlo's experiences, the things that made him more than another Atlanta guy rapping about crack and guns that he may or may not have handled himself.

Opening up to an audience in the way Baby, Thug and Future had done gradually over the years was never going to come easily to Marlo, who was reserved even around those who had known him longest. After all, being the center of attention was exactly what he'd tried to avoid for so long in other arenas. But he understood that fans wanted to know more about the artists they were investing in, and even more so when authenticity was one of the selling points. The most successful modern street rappers had learned to balance their disciplined inclination toward discretion with the demand for intimacy on social media and beyond. Still, even a few years into music, Marlo tended to deflect with generalities when asked about his past, and he could murmur and stammer his way out of almost anything, deploying a sheepish smile as a way to move on.

Yet as with rapping, Marlo was also open to practice through repetition, and his gradual improvement at the art of personal disclosure—important for any celebrity—could be seen in his bettering posture in front of a camera, a place he was finding himself more and more. Telling above all else was that Marlo had started to talk and rap, in bits and pieces, about his late daughter, Rihanna.

Never more self-assured than in his role as a father, Marlo was loose and joyful in discussing his three living kids—Rudy Jr. and Marlo Jr., as well as Tammy's older daughter Kemora, whose name he had tattooed on his arm and whom he treated as his own. But whenever his late baby girl came up, a different, more meditative side of him emerged.

"It hurt, but I'm used to it," Marlo had said at one earlier public therapy session, a designer scarf tied around his shoulders like a superhero's cape. "I been losing people all my life."

He was sitting down on-air with B High, an Atlanta native and radio fixture known for his intimate interviews on Hot 107.9, and the host prodded Marlo, gently but with persistence, about the art of remaining steady in the face of unfathomable loss. The rapper, his skin glowing brighter than his diamond earrings, projected strength, even in a hoarse whisper, and also a sustained base level of despair at the same time, standing in as he was for the traumas of a whole neighborhood, a whole city, a generation of Black men pushed to the brink.

"It's like I'm immune to losing," Marlo said, switching occasionally into the third person, as if he were looking in at his own plight. "It's crazy to see a child immune to losing people—losing his little one, losing people going to jail, losing people dying." Marlo searched for more words and came up mostly empty.

"C'mon," B High injected like a preacher, coaxing on the contemplation.

"I can't even cry no more, you feel me? Because I done lost so much," Marlo said. In the background, Lil Coach filmed the encounter on his iPhone, posting snippets online. ("Monumental," Marlo would write later under the interview clip.)

In the radio station studio, Marlo explained that, above all else, he needed to be a man at all times, regardless of his grief. Every now and then, he would cry in private to let it out, he explained, but those moments had to remain isolated and behind closed doors. "They see me break down, my family gon' break down," Marlo said. "I gotta be the man."

It was a role he ultimately relished, even if it was never really a choice. And like Shawty Lo, Marlo wanted the entire West Side on his shoulders. "I take care of a whole side of town," he told B High.

But even for someone who considered himself a soldier and a boss, well aware of the risks that came with his lifestyle, the death of an innocent child stood apart as a different sort of Purple Heart, one that separated Marlo even from those with whom he shared a struggle. "I tell all my people around me, 'Hey, man, I lost my *child*,'" he said. "I pray we don't never have to lose another child. I did it, I lost mine, so I pray that God don't send nobody else down that road. God, let me be that example. That's it. Don't do it to us no more.

"In my mind I always tell myself, he didn't send me down no road that he think I can't handle," Marlo said. But when asked where he got the strength to continue, Marlo once again found himself stumped. "Just going through stuff on the regular, I guess."

He knew that salvation was now within reach, closer than it had ever been. Fighting for a career in rap, even a middling one, might as well have been a vacation after what he had already been through. B High feted the rapper for his fresh path, and Marlo turned jovial at the thought, the ease of it all.

"You ain't gotta watch over your back, you ain't gotta be looking over your shoulder," he said, grinning that Marlo grin. "Ain't no other feeling than that. I come from where you gotta look over your shoulder two, three times." He mimed being behind the wheel, glancing furtively left and right and then left again.

"I ain't doing none of this," Marlo said with a chuckle. "I'm going *straight*."

26.

EVERYDAY THING

Lil Baby banged on the back door of the Quality Control building like he owned the place.

His manager Rashad was deep in the studio couch scrolling, with only an occasional glance up at ESPN, so it was Baby's assistant, lingering at the ready, who went to let him in. Baby was hours late for an appointment to have his picture taken and preview some of his new music, but that seemed unrelated to his impatience. When he waddled in alone and unapologetic, the butt of a small handgun was poking out atop the waistline of his sagging skinny jeans, revealing itself above the interlocking Fs of his Fendi belt.

As quickly as he'd entered, Baby disappeared into a back room, and when he returned again to the common area, he was about a pound and a half lighter, carrying some Red Hots and a Minute Maid pink lemonade instead. Hungry and anxious about appearing in front of the camera, Baby preferred to fiddle with anything around him rather than have to face his self-consciousness head-on and pose. To go with his snacks, he grabbed an elaborate-looking remote-control car that was parked nearby—a leftover birthday gift from his recent twenty-fifth—and he brought the little vehicle with him into Studio A, although he had no plans to record.

The label building that evening was mostly darkened and empty, the only action prior to the rapper's arrival concerning some possums and a snake that the security guard caught out back. Lately when making music, Baby preferred the more certain quiet of a tucked-away space, his own personal studio—"somewhere real low-key," he said. QC was a hub these days, and as one of its main attractions, Baby found that the constant in-and-outs from hangers-on and other artists could be a bother.

"When I be in my zone, I be in my zone," Baby explained as he commenced rolling a blunt, smoking a Newport as an appetizer. "I don't wanna see people like that."

Within moments, a box of J. R. Crickets wings and fries materialized for him to enjoy post-smoke, with a full glass bottle of Buffalo sauce on the side for personal dousing. The parade of small luxuries resembled the wildest dreams of any college freshman. Even Baby's mobile barber, setting up in the corner, wore Balenciaga.

It was mid-February 2020, and despite his leisurely mien, Baby was in crunch time. His first album in more than a year—and his most anticipated to date—was almost there but not complete, and it was due out in a matter of weeks. Still, any looming pressure had already been accounted for and brushed off by the rapper and his team, the data and fanfare trending too positively to leave any room for real concern about commercial performance. Baby's two warm-up singles had each already charted in the *Billboard* top 20 with little effort, and he knew the album, in flux as it was, contained plenty where those came from.

A mysterious virus that had originated in China and since spread to the United States seemed of no real concern. On the day before it was officially named COVID-19, Baby didn't mention it at all, let alone present a looming pandemic as a potential obstacle for his album to overcome. Instead, the bigger story that evening concerned a viral internet challenge in which—because of something to do with NASA and gravity—a broom could stand up on its own if you positioned it right. In the studio hallway, Baby pulled off the balancing act, and he was bummed when, a Google search later, the whole thing turned out to be a hoax.

P and then Gunna, a friend from before music and a constant collaborator since their career beginnings, called Baby for quick, work-related check-ins via FaceTime. The fellow Atlanta rapper wanted to make sure that his own upcoming album release date did not interfere with Baby's, and both men quickly determined that there was indeed enough space between the two for each to flourish.

"I'mma pull straight up on you when I leave here," Baby said before signing off.

"Man, pull up on me," Gunna replied.

Baby's new album, he had decided recently, would be called *My Turn*, and it was presumptuous on purpose. For him, the title was less a wishful prediction than a foregone conclusion of dominance, his time at the apex of rap all but scheduled to last at least the entirety of 2020 once he provided the appropriate soundtrack. "I forgot what it feels like to drop an album," Baby said with almost conspiratorial excitement. "This is like a whole different me. This a *whoooole* different everything."

Already in the young year, Baby had sat in formal wear and diamonds beside Gunna at the Grammy Awards in Los Angeles, as Sharon and Ozzy Osbourne read their names together on national TV—a surreal moment that lessened the light sting of their song's losing the trophy for Best Rap/Sung Performance to a collaboration starring the late LA rapper Nipsey Hussle.

"I don't really care about shit like that," Baby said. "I just want to put on a suit and take a picture more than anything." He had brought his mother, Lashon, along for the ceremony, telling her that dressing up for something that wasn't a court date or a funeral counted as winning.

Baby admitted to getting a small rush out of imagining who might've cocked their head at hearing an old, famous British woman announce him among the nominees. "For people in prison, stuff like that is probably on nobody's minds until someone like her is saying my name at the Grammys," Baby said. "My old roommate is still in prison, and I've been out for a few years and I done went through all this." It never stopped feeling insane.

In Atlanta, where Baby never stayed for very long but still called home, it was easier to at least pretend that things were normal, and he remained adamant about trying. He insisted on traveling alone, sans security or even an entourage, as often as possible, whether jumping in a random Uber or into a ride of his own for a trip to Chick-fil-A, the gas station or the studio, always with his jewelry on and always with the knowledge that he was now even more of a target—for robbery, humiliation or worse—than he ever had been.

Baby's default defensive posture was even a niche internet meme, communicated through clips of his head always on an overactive swivel in open spaces, his hand clutching at a barely concealed firearm in the pocket of a hoodie or underneath his rolled-down window as eager fans leaned into his car for a selfie. He rapped plenty about always being prepared, both as a boast and a warning—for instance, calling a Glock 45 his "bodyguard"—but the unposed footage that would proliferate across rap websites and WorldStar pages backed Baby up better than any lyrics ever could.

"I don't really got no switch where it's like, *Man, I'm a star*," he said, chomping on wings with his spotless veneers. "I'm careful and shit, but I always would be careful anyway. Sometimes I wonder, like, am I the only person doing this? 'Cause I still be on some regular shit." His barber agreed.

For Baby, regular shit had just always involved carrying a gun and being ready to use it. "Going places by myself in the streets, I already was a target, so I learned how to carry myself, come and go," he said. "In the streets you ain't going to have no security. In the city, I been that lil dude with all that money on me. I've been on a list for the robbers. So it ain't like I'm used to it, but . . ." He was used to it.

Baby's total loss of anonymity happened gradually. At first, he knew there were certain places he couldn't go without being recognized, certain demographics that were early to consider him a celebrity sighting. But then suddenly, he stopped being able to predict who would be onto him out in the wild.

Now the pressures of recognition were constant and all-consuming—"from the bank to church to the doctor, the gas station, anywhere—the weirdest places. Old men, old women. It's serious," Baby said. And if he hadn't noticed, his eldest son, Jason, definitely had, telling his father ahead of various errands and outings, "I don't wanna go in there with my mama because they gonna be like, 'You Lil Baby's son.'" There was, at this point, no denying that.

But even with the extra hurdles of notoriety, Baby was finding much of his life, including fatherhood, smoother and more rewarding as he got older and richer. His son Loyal was about to turn one, and there were plans around Baby's album release for a birthday party at Legoland, one of many elaborate celebrations that he was bankrolling for friends and family at any given moment.

Next, Baby wanted a daughter, but constant headaches with Loyal's mother—not to mention Jason's, his pre-fame girlfriend—were making him think he might need to start fresh. "I think before it's over with, I'll have like four different baby mamas," Baby mused. "I don't see me finding the right one until I'm a little older. But I don't see me stopping trying either. So, four.

"I love my kids to death, but I wish I did it the right way," he said, turning sincere with a dash of dreamy. "Meet a girl and actually settle down. But that ain't my lifestyle. So with this lifestyle, I only see it being a problem when it's a problem, you feel what I'm saying? What a woman has up here already," he explained, pointing to his imagination, "that little fairy tale about having a family, that's going to be hard for me to fulfill that."

Still, as his mother had stressed to him, Baby was intent on continuing to work at being a present father and partner—but mostly father—relationship issues aside. When I asked outright what he still needed to improve at in life, now that he had entered a period of relative stability and nearly mastered his craft, he whistled like a cartoon character.

"My kids," Baby said definitively. "And these hoes.

"That's one of my main things I'm trying to do," he continued, "because I ain't have no dad growing up. My kids already look at me—everything I do to a T."

Jason had even started rapping, calling his father early in the mornings with new freestyles, extra proud when his music really rhymed. At four, he was already itching for studio time. "It's not regular, the way he growing up," Baby sighed, pronouncing both of his sons spoiled rotten.

But he knew the alternative, too, or at least how he'd experienced adolescence. In fact, any downtime Baby did find in his nonstop schedule was spent actively spoiling those around him with frequent, privately chartered tropical vacations for a dozen-plus, flotillas of Jet Skis in various oceans, Lamborghinis swarming the highways of every major island or metropolitan area, not to mention an Atlanta favorite—the muddy off-roading excursions on a fancy fleet of dirt bikes, dune buggies and four-wheelers, Jason almost always in tow.

In this version of the good life, the constant was community—the more the merrier—but also speed and the pursuit of a recreational thrill. Even the $1,000 RC toy car at his feet, Baby bragged, could reach eighty-five miles per hour. "This thing could break your legs," he said, grinning.

It was only recently, at twenty-five with two kids and millions now to his name, that slowing down had even occurred to him. On Christmas Day, Baby and his friends were heading out for one of their off-road adventures in an armada of about twenty when one person in their group was sideswiped on his ATV by a fire truck and killed in a wreck on Dill Avenue.

"And I had my little boy with me," Baby said, recalling the carnage. The incident was enough to warn Baby off of such risk, at least temporarily. "'Cause I got something to lose!" he said.

That sense, not a dominant one throughout his knife's-edge youth, had started to infuse his music, too—Baby literally rapped as much on the chorus of "Sum 2 Prove." But while he was always prone to conversational overlap with his recent lyrics, often quoting his raps directly, whether intentionally or not, it never felt like an arrogant performance or product placement, just further proof that his stream-of-consciousness songwriting style really did plumb his daily preoccupations.

As Baby played his latest tracks aloud, it was hard not to hear a victory lap, his typical minor-key brooding replaced in many instances with songs that sounded like smiles, Baby floating lighter than he ever had. But also present in every song, no matter how specific the flexes—like, say, the $500,000 sports car that Baby bought but didn't even know how to turn on—there was also the wisdom, cut with paranoia, about backsliding and, in some cases, almost wanting to. "My little whodie said he fighting demons, feel like he gotta kill," Baby rapped on one new track, "and I just left the hood to catch a vibe and that shit give me chills."

He remained adamant that he had seen more than enough of prison. "I'd die before I go to jail again," Baby said. His logic wasn't perfect—getting caught with a firearm could, as a convicted felon, send him back, even if he saw carrying a weapon as a necessity and potential lifesaver. But Baby trusted his own willpower and wiliness above all else, and he had convinced himself that swearing off incarceration as a mantra would work, so long as he remembered what it was like in there *before* fame.

"It's different being a celebrity getting in trouble from a regular person getting in trouble," he said. "If I went to prison right now, I'd be lit. I really run the prisons as far as music-wise—number one person they listen to. So me being in prison now, I'd probably have sex and all." That scored some chuckles from the room.

"But in my mind, I ain't even dumb enough to even think like that. I'm smart enough to not even put any bullshit like that in my head. I'm still thinking about prison how it *was*.

"Hell nah," he said, shaking his head. "I'll never go back."

For Baby, the hood was more like an ex-girlfriend. "That feeling you get from 'em," he said, "*and* you all left on bad terms? But you remember the good parts about it. It can never be no more, but you know what I'm saying? It's one of them things. *Ethereal.* Gives me chills.

"Damn," he said. "Reminiscing."

But Baby was also quick to clarify, "I don't miss my old life at all—period." It was simple reverie, nostalgia remaining undefeated. "I get a thrill from my old life sometimes, if I see some stuff, but as far as missing it? Not at all."

I asked Baby whether he ever found himself worrying about the dark fates that had already befallen other young artists of his generation and those surrounding it, from the opioid crisis to the gun violence that touched rambunctious SoundCloud rappers and steely street storytellers alike. In only a few years, there had been accidental overdoses by Juice WRLD, Mac Miller and Lil Peep; fatal shootings of XXXTentacion and Nipsey Hussle; and the cycles of incarceration that had repeatedly ensnared stars like Kodak Black, NBA YoungBoy and so many more.

A week after our conversation, the rising Brooklyn rapper Pop Smoke would also be shot and killed, in a home invasion at an Airbnb in Los Angeles, after he inadvertently revealed his address on Instagram.

But whereas rap may have put these tragedies front and center, making societal problems feel born of or made worse by a genre of music, Baby refused, rightly, to see them as merely hip-hop issues, mirroring as they did the struggles of an entire country.

"At the same time," Baby said, "there's a generation of *people* going through that. It ain't even that deep to me, like, the rappers. I know people who get killed—my personal people. That's what really goes on in life. Rap is just a reflection of real life. I know like ten or twelve people who done died in Atlanta off the fake drugs that's going around. In and out of jail—my family, brothers." He estimated that he knew twenty people serving life sentences. "It's an everyday thing for me," Baby said.

He realized that Atlanta was changing, although not at the same speed for everyone. "A whole 360 since I was a kid—it don't even look the same," Baby said, describing his experience of gentrification the way he knew it most directly—via law enforcement. "Back in the day the police ain't even come like that. But when they did come, they *came*. Now, it's like, they come thirty cars deep about anything. You can hear gunshots back in the day and police don't come. Nowadays you hear gunshots and they automatically come. They got cameras on the poles now.

"Everything done changed," Baby said. "And I'm changing with it."

If gentrification in Atlanta was inevitable, he was going to get in on it. Baby had recently started putting money into various nonmusical businesses around town, claiming seven streams of income in total and more on the horizon, including a potential investment in the $400 million redevelopment of the West End mall, the 1970s shopping center that housed Black-owned mom-and-pop shops and also, as it declined over the years, aspiring drug dealers like Baby himself. Because even as he approached a new peak, Baby knew that a career in rap was almost always fleeting, almost never a forever career.

"If it all stopped today, the money I got right now, I'm going to be set for life," he said. "The businesses that I own, if I had to work with one of them, all right, cool. But as far as me going to get a regular job? Never."

He viewed his 4PF label the same way—a backup plan that might actually be preferable to rapping. For Baby, an advantage of not considering himself a born musician or an *artiste* first and foremost was that he felt no particular fealty to it as a vocation. Despite its being a therapeutic outlet that he was coming to love, it was still a means to an end.

"I want to be on some boss shit," Baby said, like every rapper before him—but, crucially, with much of that plan already in motion and the rest now within reach.

"I don't care about my own music. I really want to own a label—like Def Jam, though. Like Roc Nation. I'd rather go that way, where I manage a Selena Gomez and get ten percent off of it, where I'm not even on the scene no more. That's my mindset. That's what I'd rather do."

He insisted, "I'm telling you, boy, if I can gatdamn pop two artists right now, I'm down to slow up on what I got going on, straight up. Why wouldn't I? I can make the same money and I don't have to be catching all these planes."

But Baby also knew that some of the guys in his circle, like G-Five and Marlo, were evolving more slowly—still closer to the life that he was rapping about having to avoid now that he had reached a new station.

"I ain't going to lie, Marlo getting better and better," Baby put forth optimistically. "Definitely proud of him."

But an uncomfortable aspect of Baby's near-seamless rise to stardom—of the overachieving that had come to be expected from him and the ease with which he had picked up such a specific skill set—was that he had left a lot of his friends, collaborators and heroes in his thick cloud of dust, even as he contorted himself to keep them motivated and included.

Gunna and Marlo, alongside whom Baby had tried some of his first verses, had each stalled somewhat, albeit at different rungs of fame, whereas Baby continued to accelerate around every corner. Much of the Quality Control roster, including Migos and Lil Yachty, had also seen their sheen start to dim as Baby's brightened. Even Atlanta fixtures like Future and Thug were suddenly within reach, artistically and commercially. It was bound to be awkward, because as much as rap could be a brotherhood, or at least presented as one in Atlanta—and as much as QC was portrayed as a family—they were also all striving within the most competitive and individualistic of genres, the one often with the highest stakes.

While sincere, much of Baby's boundless generosity since making it seemed to be equal parts survivor's remorse, inducement and a way to placate any internal dissent that jealousy could bring. Rap families had crumbled for far less. Baby praised P and Coach for setting a great tone, for always insisting that there was more than enough to share. But he also relied on his own savvy ability to politic and manage the personalities that he had known the longest and the deepest. "I'll always have a different bond with people that I had a bond with before rap," he said.

By now, Baby understood how the struggles varied at every level of this strange journey, and he wasn't yet giving up on the ones who weren't entirely out of the gate as entertainers. "You see at first, Marlo ain't making no money for real, he ain't getting booked," Baby rationalized. "So it was hard for him to put in all his effort. But I think seeing me go where I went—it took for him to see his man gatdamn prosper. He know if I can do it, he can do it. He just had to take a different approach."

Baby had seen how quickly things could happen when they finally did. "Almost nothing about me is the same from two years ago," he said, surveying his superstar surroundings. "Nothing. I don't look the same, my jewelry not the same, my car not the same, my money not the same. My mind frame—not the same."

Far from the 2017 days of bringing home $2,500 for a show, Baby was now rapping about getting paid $200,000 per occasion—a line he would be forced to update by the time he started performing it live, because he'd be demanding double that.

But it wasn't all good. "I got into this defensive shell now," Baby acknowledged. "I have so much going, I just get angry. Stressful.

"It's hard to cope with—this person calling, that person calling, they want you to do this, you gotta try to make that person happy, make yourself happy, try to do that, try to do this."

Baby took a breath. Then, like he always did when straying toward darkness or self-pity, he went back to inventorying his blessings. "It's all for the best, though," Baby said.

The next month, as assumed, Lil Baby scored his first number one album, and he did it with oomph, selling the streaming-era equivalent of almost 200,000 copies in the first week, with songs from *My Turn* played a staggering 262 million times in seven days.

Lil Wayne, who appeared on the album and was notorious for listening mostly to his own music, dubbed Baby his favorite rapper, inviting him to Miami to record together in person. No less than LeBron James agreed that Baby was easily the young MVP in his sport. Household-name status was in sight.

On his release day, Baby chose to show up unannounced at the West End mall to celebrate, giving away free CDs, taking photos with fans and signing autographs, the people in his old hood swarming their homegrown champion. That week, Baby also returned to his old high school, Booker T. Washington, with a jumbo check endowing a $150,000 scholarship.

My Turn soon went double platinum, and even more impressively, it didn't disappear, refusing to evaporate into the smog of fugacious art now known as content. Rather than being buoyed by a single smash hit, which could sustain an album and give the misleading impression of a successful body of work, *My Turn*'s popularity was more evenly distributed across all sorts of songs—commercial fare with big-name guests, smooth attempts at romance, tough-talk turn-up tracks and spill-your-guts trap soul—even as it refrained from explicitly addressing most of the competing atrocities (political, social, economic and otherwise) that were now threatening to subsume the country and the world.

Baby, it turned out, had a fix for that, too. At the beginning of May, with much of the globe and the music business locked down or otherwise frozen, and the coronavirus deaths in the US approaching 100,000, Quality Control—under its old credo "more is more"—released *My Turn* all over again, this time with six additional songs and a pile of new music videos, including one called "Social Distancing."

But Baby didn't need topicality to thrive. Instead, his minimalist shit-talk summit "We Paid," a bonus track with Baby's frog-voiced Detroit signee 42 Dugg, became the soundtrack to a nascent coronavirus summer, in which pretending like everything was okay became a national pastime.

Like so many other QC tactics, the deluxe-album trick—more akin to a software update than a new release—quickly became a much-copied trend in rap, eventually trickling up to the pop sphere. After the rerelease of *My Turn*, Baby earned an additional four consecutive weeks atop the *Billboard* albums chart, his February release carrying well into the summer.

When he tripled down with "The Bigger Picture," his surprise song about police brutality—and it debuted at number three on the singles chart in late June, Baby's highest chart position yet, despite its heavy subject matter—it was no longer possible to deny that he was a superstar. Inspired by the murder of George Floyd by the officer Derek Chauvin and the protests that followed, the track was "one of the easiest songs I ever recorded," Baby said. Because like most of his music, "The Bigger Picture," with its perfectly imperfect lyrics about injustice, fear, racism and reconciliation, was autobiography, not polemic.

"I wanted to use a specific situation that would give people an understanding of where I come from," Baby said—the streets of Atlanta, with *Rolling Stone* calling the track "a time capsule for everything the city is, lacks, and can be." As Baby put it, "It's a never-ending saga for the people who really live in it."

But being an advocate, a spokesman or an agitator was not his goal, and Baby didn't plan to linger there. Although, like the professional he had become, Baby embraced the cultural anointments that came with the song—later performing it, amid a scene re-creating the police killing of Atlanta's Rayshard Brooks, at the Grammys in 2021, James Baldwin's words booming in the background—but he also eventually vowed to back off of politics, preferring to keep telling only his own story.

In fact, it wasn't Baby's protest song—or his various upbeat numbers proliferating widely despite the global circumstances—that would come to define the rapper's latest peak. Instead, "Emotionally Scarred," a track buried in the middle of *My Turn*, showcased Baby at his purest and least obviously commercial, and it contained probably the finest rapping of his career to date. Everything Baby's music had ever hinted at in one comprehensive package, the song was a personal waterfall of angst and achievement, his words tumbling into one another like impressionistic shots from a high-speed montage. Over luxe production by Twysted Genius that sounded more like a soul band than a trap beat—with full keyboard chords, stomach-vibrating bass and a mournful guitar riff—Baby was reluctant and preening, humble but proud, turning what began as a breakup ballad into sermonistic uplift. "I don't see nobody but me, who I'm gon' lose to?" he rapped. "I can see me taking the lead over the new school."

Yet even as a conquering hero, Baby offered himself up as a leader only tentatively. His wins were still defined in relation to those around him, and he refused to slip into the too-easy and unrelatable logic of less astute lyricists, whose gloating could often be boiled down to: *I'm rich and you're not, therefore I'm greater*. For Baby, it was never that simple. His friends, he knew, were "still steady trapping," even as he asked them to chill and give him a chance to help. "They see how I made it, I'm the reason they wanna rap now," he offered. But there was always a caveat. Because even as Baby showed his soul, detailing his own winding path to prosperity, he knew the other side of the equation that had created him could only churn on.

27.

"CAN'T SETTLE FOR LESS"

THE SPREE STARTED AROUND 3:30 A.M., AT A WELLS FARGO ATM in the West End. Two nineteen-year-olds, each armed, spotted a white 2020 Jeep Grand Cherokee, and they took it by force, pointing a gun at its owner and then zooming across Ralph David Abernathy Boulevard. At some point after the carjacking, the pair robbed another man, relieving him of a duffel bag, a phone and a camera, pistol-whipping and shooting at their victim.

By the next afternoon, December 4, 2019, Marguell Scott and Emmanuel Fambro were still cruising in the stolen Jeep. Scott, known as Cracker, or Brack around the neighborhood, was driving. Three months earlier, a jury had found him not guilty of murder, aggravated assault and armed robbery in connection with a 2018 home invasion. As solace, the disappointed prosecutors told themselves he had been granted a second chance in life. But around 2:30 p.m., when Atlanta police officers spotted the missing Jeep from the night before and attempted to pull it over, Scott hit the gas.

He managed to lose them for a while. Car chases around the city were controversial because of the potential danger to the innocent and unsuspecting in their path, and the Atlanta Police Department had strict protocols about when they were able to pursue—namely, if the suspects were armed or an immediate violent threat. This one met the criteria.

Sirens wailing and blue lights flashing, the cops finally caught up with the Jeep as it sped northbound on Lee Street toward the Oakland City MARTA stop. As the chase approached the wide, four-way intersection where Campbellton Road turned into Dill Avenue to the east, their light was red. Scott sped through it anyway, and that's when he lost control, swerving slightly to the left and smashing into the driver's side of a dark sedan parked opposite at the light, facing south. The carnage was instant. Airbags in both vehicles deployed, and the nose of the Jeep snarled from ripping through the entire left side of the stopped car.

Scott and his passenger, Fambro, were rushed to Grady Memorial Hospital. The two men in the other car, including the driver, Jermaine Jackson, forty-four—Jay or Jerm to his friends—and Mark Hampton, forty-three, were dead. Hampton had been on his way back from picking up medicine for his disabled eleven-year-old son. The crash was so disturbing, the police said, that they immediately brought in counselors to speak to the reporting officers.

It wasn't until later that night, near Cleveland Ave., that Lil Reek heard news of the accident involving two YSL-affiliated guys he knew from around the neighborhood. But he knew one of the victims, too.

"Daddy please tell me this not true," Reek commented on his estranged father's Instagram account that evening. "Call me please daddy."

Two months later, Reek found himself stopped at the intersection where his father had been killed. He immediately picked up his phone to make a call. "How you doing, Grandma? Would you mind if I just come by and give you a couple kisses on the cheek? I'm coming past Dill. You need anything?"

After they buried Jerm in December, Reek had moved in for a time with his grandmother—with whom he lived as a child—filling the shoes of his late father, who had recently become her primary caretaker while she battled cancer. Her home, not far from his mom's place, provided Reek more space, sans siblings, and some purpose in lieu of much immediate progress in his rap career. But the setup could also be isolating, heaping even more responsibility onto Reek's already overburdened shoulders.

Certain sides of him remained irrepressible. Sometimes, Reek liked to stream live on Instagram from his grandma's house as he smoked and listened to music or while he prepped the Cream of Wheat she ate with her morning pills. He might even hit a few dance moves as it microwaved. A couple dozen people at a time usually tuned in.

"I'm just tired doing the same old shit, y'all, no cap," Reek monologued during one session. "That's why I haven't dropped yet or nothing. I'm trying to really make progress with myself as an artist. Not like these other cap-ass n——s, dropping this same weak-ass music." He tongued a blunt in progress.

"I want you to actually see me getting better at what I'm trying to do with my life," Reek said, promising updates for his fans soon. "For everybody who been rocking with me, who been fucking with me since day one, I promise y'all we finna turn the fuck up."

As we waited in the driveway for Reek to visit with his grandmother, I asked Elijah, his personal A&R and unlikely friend from Wisconsin, if he thought Reek might be depressed. Elijah waffled but did not say no. It was the week Lil Baby's *My Turn* was released to international hype, and the guys who hoped to follow in his footsteps were still bumming around Cleveland Ave., trying to get something going. The next stop was the Donut Shop.

"I'm finna start back up working again," Reek muttered mostly to himself in the driver's seat, after picking up yet another "three-five" of weed from one in the ever-shifting constellation of neighborhood traps. It was a rainy stretch of a mild winter, and the area around Cleveland Ave. felt right on the line between cozy and bleak. The trees were bare and swaying at their tippy tops, dead leaves mingling with dead grass along stretches of woods dotted with soggy trash.

Reek, secure in a puffer jacket, began prepping his afternoon blunt, but he mourned its quality. His Donut Shop compatriots had run out of the top-shelf stuff—the graphically designed packages with brash brand names that most customers expected. But being that Reek was one of them, the purveyors had instead presented his product without ceremony, in a tied-up translucent sandwich baggie like it was the 1970s. Presentation and familiarity aside, there would be no discount—it was $40 for 3.5 grams. Elijah paid, and Reek promised to get him back for half as soon as he could.

Luckily, Reek had scored what sounded like a job offer while buying. "He ain't have to say much," Reek said of his man inside. "Just asked me what's up with it."

Despite being discouraged, Reek refused to consider himself out of options. Selling a little here or there would help with everyday expenses—food, rent, weed and anything else his loved ones might need. "2019 taught me a lot. 2020 I'mma turn up a notch," he promised on Instagram. "Before it's all over I'mma make shit better for my family."

As crucially at the moment, a job could help him get back in the studio. Since his father's death, and even before it, Reek hadn't made or released much music, piggybacking here and there on sessions with friends but not exactly oozing the motivation or financial wherewithal to make recording a regular habit. The sequel to his *Slime Bizness* mixtape, which he had hoped to release by the end of 2019, was still in the works.

Sturdy as ever, Reek refused to blame the guys who had made his life more difficult, hitting and killing his father in the car chase. Marguell Scott was awaiting trial, charged with first-degree murder, among twenty-two other counts, including unlawful participation in criminal street gang activity for his association with what the prosecutors called the Young Slime Life Bloods. His accomplice, Emmanuel Fambro, would soon plead guilty to a concealed weapons charge and receive a year of probation. But Reek knew it had been a freak accident, and he expressed no ill will publicly, instead addressing the unfathomable circumstances the best way he knew how—in his raps. The ongoing sound of his struggle now had a few more layers.

Reek was also newly motivated, having returned refreshed and obviously jet-lagged from a last-minute trip to Los Angeles with his managers Roger and Bird, along with Elijah, who was technically still an intern. There, the professional studio time was paid for, the beats were top-notch, and the hotel had a rooftop pool. Bird was thriving in the business, landing a promising new label deal for his cadre of producers, and he frequently showed the spoils—including seafood, chains, vacations and plaques—on social media. He had planned the LA trip around one of his newer artists, a super-green teenage rapper from Ohio, but the manager came through with a day's notice on flights out for Reek and Elijah, as well.

Reek had come back from California with at least two promising songs, including one called "Walking in the Rain" that addressed his father's death directly. Over a more somber beat than he was typically drawn to, and with a vocal delivery to match, Reek described his current predicament in more detail than ever while also striving for optimism in the face of tragedy. When asking himself outright if he was still ready for fame, Reek's answer seemed to be yes.

I can't settle for less
My grandma always told me that I would be the best
My daddy ain't gotta stress, he in heaven gettin' rest
Who would've thought that my daddy and my two partners would wreck?

This was a different Reek, if not necessarily a more marketable one. In LA, he had experimented with writing out his lyrics ahead of time rather than freestyling all of his verses in the booth, which could lead to falling back on familiar couplets, brands and sentiments. And it seemed to be working, allowing Reek to tap into a new emotional gear. Whenever Elijah put "Walking in the Rain" on in the car, it tended to get quiet.

"Play that one again," Reek said when it finished.

They were hoping to shoot a music video for the song right away upon returning to Atlanta, and the weather was cooperating. But Cam, the director from North Carolina who had previously worked for free or whatever was on offer, had started blowing Reek off in favor of another rapper from his home state who was on the come-up. Elijah surmised that the other rapper's team had seen the videos Cam made for Reek on spec and that they had landed him better-paying work for more eyeballs. "He know he owes you," Elijah said in an roundabout offer of sympathy and solidarity.

Reek was having none of it. "I don't want him to feel like he owe me," he shot back. "If I don't have the money to pay a man for his services at the moment, then he doesn't owe me anything, and I can't expect anything from him."

So instead he drove and drove. The loops of Cleveland Ave. and its side streets were numbingly quiet in the colder months, with even the gas stations and fast-food restaurants that served as hangouts functioning more as places for coming and going than standing and waiting. Boredom made Reek prickly, and he took it out on Elijah in little swipes as they discussed current events and moneymaking schemes—cryptocurrency, forex trading, Fortnite.

With rapping stalled, Reek was considering forming a gaming squad that would stream its play live on Twitch, a newly lucrative online platform. He had some high schoolers in mind as recruits, and so he swung by their campus to check in. But after a quick smoke in a parking lot nearby, he dropped the boys back at school, imploring them to "be safe" and saving the livestreaming talk for another day.

Reek was also on family duty, so he scooped up his little brother after school, letting him ride in the backseat as he tested the engine on my rental car versus Elijah's in little races around the subdivision. As Reek hugged turns, his brother cheered like he was on a roller coaster, squealing, "Rumble tumble! Rumble tumble!" When Reek noticed that the child needed a haircut, he ran him to the barbershop around the corner, offering the guy inside an IOU and rolling another blunt as we waited in the car.

It had been about a month since the World Health Organization declared a global health emergency concerning the virus coming out of China. The United States was still a few days from announcing its first confirmed death from the disease, and most around the neighborhood were paying it no mind. But based on what he had read, Reek was concerned. It didn't help that Elijah was snotty, sniffly and coughing, and Reek chided him for his hygiene, encouraging Elijah to wash his hands more. Still, he passed him the blunt.

Reek was also newly picky about the rental car soundtrack. "Turn that off," he snapped at certain songs by Atlanta artists on his social periphery. "I want to come up with new shit, not the same shit we've been doing."

He mused on the current health of the Atlanta scene, noting that more artists seemed to be sticking to the local independent route, even as the major labels continued to scour the landscape. "If I had one good seed come from this flowerpot, shit, I'mma go back to this flowerpot again next season," he said, imagining the thinking of outside executives. "But some people burn the flowerpots out."

At that moment, no one knew better than Reek how arbitrary the industry could be. Those who made it didn't always deserve it, and neither did all those who fell short. In the mess of variables—talent, timing, drive, luck, looks—the only certainty was that none counted as a sure thing.

At the urging of his grandmother, Reek was once again considering a return to school. He still hoped to study business or tech eventually, and she insisted that he could be a successful entrepreneur, rap career or not. But Reek had other goals to handle first. *Slime Bizness 2* needed to be his strongest release yet, the one that put him back on the radar in his highly trafficked city, he told Elijah. Reek was also diversifying his talents, having landed a role in a feature film about the life of a young rapper. The director planned to take the festival route that summer.

But what Reek didn't know at the time was that there would be no real film festivals in 2020, and not many new rap stars either. Elijah—who had taken a job as an organist and a choir director at a small Manhattan church to continue funding his own music business dreams—would be kept from Atlanta for months, delaying the release of Reek's next mixtape even further. Within weeks, Reek's grandmother would also pass away, leaving him one fewer responsibility and one fewer true believer in his potential.

Yet even before his world shifted again, throwing still more hurdles in his path, Reek knew that he could only ever really count on himself. It wasn't fair, but he had proved his resilience previously and he was confident he could do it again—and again after that, if necessary. He always bounced back.

"With me the whole thing is courage," Reek said that February evening in his neighborhood, "but I'm working on it. I've doubted myself, but I've learned from my mistakes. I know what to do."

When I asked if he still expected to make it as a rapper, given how far he had already come, he did not hesitate. In fact, he acted like it was the stupidest question he had ever heard in his life.

"Duh," Lil Reek replied.

28.

SHARKS

MARLO DID NOT HAVE THE CAREER VELOCITY TO KEEP HIM CAreening forward through a deadly pandemic.

His *1st & 3rd* mixtape, released two weeks before Lil Baby's *My Turn*, on Valentine's Day, was his highest profile to date, and there was plenty of optimism to be found about its prospects at the start of the year. Baby told the world proudly that the project was his partner's best work yet—to which Marlo replied, "I luv u, kiddo"—while P, upon its release, instructed his still-eager pupil, "It's on you to go get it."

And then, just like that, there was nothing much to go get. By late spring, the concert and club bookings that had finally started to materialize for Marlo, even without hits to his name, evaporated almost overnight as Atlanta and the rest of the country attempted a slapdash effort at containing the virus that would go on to kill more than one million Americans, disproportionately affecting Black and Latino people, who were three times as likely to contract the disease and twice as likely to die from it. Most excitement about new regional mixtapes was snuffed out by the dominant talk of aerosol transmissions and freezers full of bodies.

With Baby's album still zooming on every chart, Marlo re-entrenched himself on the West Side, once again living a neighborhood life instead of a nationwide one. The odds of an emerging artist's breaking out with the world on pause had plummeted, and whatever groundwork and marketing he had planned for the year with Lil Coach and the rest of Quality Control was put aside for the time being, Marlo's complete professionalization as a musician still deferred. P promised him that they would catch up when the virus calmed down; in the meantime, the executive told the aspiring rapper, "Keep hustling."

Tammy, in a heart-to-heart, asked Marlo to stay focused. "Even though you feel like things are slowing down, don't get discouraged," his girlfriend said, begging him not to spend too much time on the block. "You can't be hanging around like that anymore. You're trying to go somewhere that they're not trying to go." Together, the couple dreamed of getting out of town as soon as he signed his first major deal. Marlo was thinking Los Angeles, but Tammy imagined a Texas ranch on plenty of land, the kids zooming by on four-wheelers.

On May 1, Marlo turned thirty. His family remained a priority and a bulwark—his little boys, Rudy Jr. and Marlo Jr., had just turned four—but how exactly he would support them in the years to come if rap never panned out remained an open question. He had kicked Percocet altogether, he said, and was even looking for a personal trainer to undo the bloat he'd gained from either aging or opioids. In another move toward self-actualization, Marlo had committed himself further to practicing his West African Ifa religion, adopting as a frequent refrain and sign-off the term "*àse*"—a Yoruba affirmation similar to amen that carried within it the philosophical concept of having the power to make change.

With so much enforced downtime, the studio was also a refuge for Marlo, and he kept working on new music in anticipation of the day he could properly promote it. He even started rapping about the spirituality that he'd previously held close to his chest, mentioning offhandedly on one unreleased track how he spent the entirety of his Sundays with his "chief." Tammy loved to hear him vulnerable. "He believing in himself, breaking out that shell," she said. "Let's go. That's all we wanted was for him to find himself."

Marlo continued to film and release low-budget videos locally, but in place of the Play For Keeps tag that he had been repping for years, he began promoting his immediate circle as Strictly Bout Paper, or SBP, knowing that PFK had been attracting increased attention from local Atlanta police, gang prosecutors and rivals. But for as many times as those around him told Marlo that he needed to fully commit to music before it would pay off and save him—and for as many times as he promised he would, now that he was finally starting to see results—it was hard to blame him for throwing up his hands in frustration at the impossibility of the transition at a moment when so much of the music-industry well had run dry.

Even as everybody understood the stark reality of the situation, Tammy wasn't the only person around Marlo who stressed the wish that he stay far away from the old life that was suddenly summoning him back. "Rudy, wake the fuck up, man," his friend and lawyer Jacoby Hudson implored him on multiple occasions, always using Marlo's real name for intimacy and emphasis.

Jacoby saw clearly that every avenue still connecting his client to the streets was an active hazard. At a recent trial of one of Marlo's alleged underlings, Jacoby had watched from the defense side as a Fulton County prosecutor questioned a top gang investigator and presented a detailed rundown about the dealings of PFK and its associated groups, tying them to a spate of local violence and placing Marlo at the top of the pecking order. Despite the fact that Marlo was not on trial, the government even played one of his music videos for the jury.

"Everyone know Rudy and what he did," Jacoby had said years earlier. "Rudy don't even live that lifestyle anymore. The shit that he was doing—luckily, he done got out the game when they came prosecuting them. Rudy just rapping now. He really with the rap shit. I told him, 'Go on—your albums are selling, you're signed to QC label, you doing good.' And he really done left that shit behind."

But that was before, at a time when things had felt most promising. And even then, celebrating Marlo's complete separation from the streets was probably premature. Now, with nothing sticking musically and nothing likely to, at least for a while, the plentiful risks were once again flashing red. "Bruh, you moving fucked up out here," Jacoby told Marlo as the reality of the pandemic started to set in, bending his ear about both the law-enforcement scrutiny and the street beefs around Bankhead that seemed to be rearing their heads.

Of course, the two dangers were always connected, with the authorities increasingly aware of Marlo's every move since he made himself a public figure in rap—in part by burnishing his real-life reputation. Some of Marlo's old enemies, and even some of his friends, did not approve of his attempts to separate himself and live the cleaner, flashier life of a musician using their shared mythology. So when Marlo started coming around again more often, stale hate hung in the air. "You know your name hot like a motherfucker in these streets—and not on that rap shit," Jacoby cautioned.

But Marlo never took kindly to direction. Rather than fretting all the time, as he plausibly might have, he preferred to think of himself as no less than immortal—Teflon *and* bulletproof. Marlo had also found himself disappointed lately in other ways by Jacoby's counsel, after his friend's trial ended with an unfavorable verdict. On more than one occasion, over text and FaceTime, the two prideful men from Bowen Homes exchanged harsh words, each feeling that they knew better about the other's work and carriage. Things even threatened to boil over one day early that summer, while Marlo was getting a haircut and Jacoby was gambling nearby, with both guys agreeing to hand their pistols to the barber and take it outside, throwback-style—a one-on-one battle among brothers. "I was finna beat his ass," Jacoby said. Instead, the pair ended up hugging it out.

Other simmering disputes Marlo had scattered around Bankhead like land mines were not so easily defused. As the Atlanta air thickened and the asphalt sizzled, it became clear that someone had it out for Marlo in a way that was not likely to be solved with hugs, handshakes or even a cash payoff that signaled respect and retreat—the last-ditch alleviating currency of the realm. The rumor around the neighborhood was that Marlo, in his capacity as a Mafia-like don, had put out, or executed, a successful hit on another man of near-equal standing. The specifics were only whispered about, the details an alphabet soup of micro-crews mixed in a mess of nicknames, Instagram handles and West Side intersections. Like most block-based strife, the ongoing beef was well-known to a few but nearly inscrutable to outsiders, even law enforcement. But regardless of who was in the right or how far back the war between the sides started, a dead man's allies were now out for revenge, and they were adamant. Some of Marlo's people encouraged him to "handle it" before others handled him.

Marlo, in keeping with his intensifying Ifa faith, believed his path had already been set, and he refused to hide. That summer, he reconnected for the first time in years with his father, who sensed a certain peace in him, even as the walls seemed to be closing in. When the two Rudys met up, the younger man gave his dad a bear hug. He also confided in him. *I killed a man*, Marlo said. But his father changed the subject; he didn't want to know, because it didn't change anything.

"I understand how the streets is," Big Rudy said. "Sharks eat sharks. Whatever happened, it had to be justified. But I knew he knew the time was coming."

In the ensuing weeks, the rival factions exchanged gunfire up and down Bankhead in reckless shows of force that may have registered with the local cops assigned to be in the know but did not even make the news. At the same time, Atlanta as a whole was awash in rising gun violence—and thus, the mass PTSD and paranoia that such violence provoked—with more than fifty homicides only halfway through the year and tensions thickening following the Memorial Day police killing of George Floyd in Minneapolis, that heinous footage of a white officer's knee on the neck of a Black man as he pleaded for his life and mother replaying everywhere on a seemingly endless loop. In Atlanta, desperately reinvigorated Black Lives Matter protesters flooded the streets near Centennial Olympic Park, with some smashing windows, burning cars and saving a special ire for the CNN statue outside of the network's headquarters. "FUCK 12"—the now-nationalized Atlanta rap slang for disrespecting the police—was spray-painted enough times to sound like a Quavo hook.

Desperate to lower the city's temperature, Mayor Keisha Lance Bottoms recruited the rap legends TI and Killer Mike, who had been members of her transition team, to flank her at a news conference as she begged those taking over the streets to go home. "You're not protesting anything, running out with brown liquor in your hands, breaking windows in this city," Bottoms said. "TI, Killer Mike own half the West Side, so when you burn down this city, you are burning down our community." TI, whose presence as a community paragon was controversial even before the sexual abuse allegations against him surfaced, called the city Wakanda, to plentiful mockery from those who knew the more complicated reality. "It's sacred," he said in his capacity as elder. "It must be protected."

Less than two weeks later, on June 12, Atlanta police shot and killed Rayshard Brooks at the Wendy's near what had once been Brownsville, a thriving Black community. In 1906, white mobs had stormed the area, killing dozens and destroying homes and businesses, a massacre largely lost to history. But Brooks's killing, like Floyd's, was on camera, and when the fast-food restaurant was burned to the ground the next day, the city was only further inflamed. Over Fourth of July weekend, at least eleven shootings were reported around Atlanta, injuring twenty-six people and killing five, including an eight-year-old girl, Secoriea Turner, whose family's car was shot up near the Wendy's that had become ground zero for the angst, protests and ensuing chaos.

"Enough is enough," Mayor Bottoms said at another news conference. "We are doing each other more harm than any police officer on this force." She cited a stomach-dropping statistic—there had been more than seventy-five shootings in the city over the span of only a few weeks.

In her pleas during those anguished days, Bottoms was referring in part to Bankhead and neighborhoods like it, even if those areas were rarely part of the picture on CNN, their internal strife too unwieldy to stuff into any existing national narrative. But even as the city leaders begged for peace, there were shots fired during the filming of a music video at a Bankhead barbershop, and then again at Continental Seafood, right near the old Bowen Homes, when some men jumped out of the woods behind the restaurant and started spraying. Blue Flame, the strip club down Donald Lee Hollowell Parkway, was hit up, too. Doors were kicked in. In each incident, Marlo was the common denominator and, many believed, the likely mark.

Somehow, untouchable as ever, he escaped them all without a scratch. And so the next time Jacoby saw Marlo, at the annual Bowen Homes Day block party in late June, the lawyer gave his favorite client another meaningful embrace meant to smooth over whatever static remained between them.

Marlo was surrounded that night on Bankhead by his PFK family, and they were strapped—a reality that could be as worrying as it was heartening for those who knew the score. *Live by the gun, die by the gun*, as Marlo had explained to me more than two years earlier. As he always did, Jacoby urged the rapper to stay safe, and he left the man he would always call Rudy with a kiss on the cheek.

Two weeks later, Marlo was back on Bankhead for another block party. The night prior, he had been up late at the Quality Control compound, recording a song with Lil Yachty and hanging with some of the 4PF guys until around 4 a.m., as Tammy curled up on the studio couch, happy to watch her man working. But the next night, as she tried to track Marlo down amid the West Side revelry, he was nowhere to be found. Tammy's calls rang and rang.

Marlo had just pulled off, driving away over the protestations of Head, his loyal muscle, who told him repeatedly not to go anywhere alone, given the state of things. "Can't nobody hurt you if you with me," Head said. Still, Marlo took Bankhead past the Flame and hopped on the highway, tracing a route he had known his whole life and heading south on I-285. When Tammy finally reached him after a few more missed calls, he promised he would be right back. She was annoyed and confused, but Marlo was never one to owe anybody an explanation.

That weekend, Marlo's two sons were with their grandfather, across the state line in Alabama. "I'm so glad you got the boys," Marlo had told Big Rudy when they'd checked in the night prior. It even got a little mushy as the two grown men exchanged *I love you*s, continuing their attempts to put a lifetime of baggage behind them, to heal for the next generation. "I'm grateful for the relationship you have with my sons," Marlo said.

His father knew the words were loaded. "I never took him swimming, never went fishing, we never did none of that, because he was in the jungle—that's not what he needed," Big Rudy said later. "But with my grandsons, I'm trying to raise them differently."

As Marlo was speeding down 285, destination unknown, the kids and Big Rudy were at a drive-in movie. But Rudy Jr. was agitated. "Somebody touching on me!" the child yelled at one point, to the confusion of the adults around him. "Somebody's pulling on me, Granddad!" Startled and confused, Big Rudy even whipped out his pistol. But nothing, and no one, was there.

At the same time, word was starting to get around on Bankhead: Marlo had been shot on the expressway. There was no clarity about his condition, and Tammy immediately jumped in the car with her sister to start heading that way. He couldn't have made it far. But as they were backing out, an unmistakable ache hit Tammy in the heart. It was the same certain pain she'd felt the night Rihanna died. She knew Marlo was gone.

When they made it to the highway, the traffic backed up for several exits seemed to confirm Tammy's worst fears. But she had to be certain, so she leapt from the car, running for miles on the side of the road, crying and screaming all the way. As she arrived at the convoy of flashing emergency vehicles, the paramedics tried to comfort her. But Tammy knew by the way the woman touched her back that it was Marlo and he was dead.

Even after Tammy correctly confirmed the details on Marlo's license, the authorities would not let her see him right there at the crime scene. She didn't want to see him like that, they said. But the authorities further verified Marlo's identity using the tattoo of Tammy's oldest daughter's name on his arm.

Police had been dispatched at 11:37 p.m. to what looked like a single-vehicle wreck near the Benjamin E. Mays Drive overpass, less than two miles from where Shawty Lo had died four years earlier. There, they found a black Cadillac CTS that had quickly become a casket, Swiss-cheesed with bullet holes, at rest on the far left shoulder. Marlo was slumped over in the driver's seat, with two shots to his legs and one to his head, just behind his left ear. His killers had likely tracked him the whole way from Bankhead, itching and bloodthirsty at the realization that they had at last gotten him alone and otherwise occupied. Investigators promptly dubbed Marlo the intended target. Those would be among the last words they ever said about the case in public.

Later, at the Willie A. Watkins Funeral Home, a community staple in Southwest Atlanta for decades, Tammy asked to visit with Marlo's untreated body. But instead of the nightmare she feared, Tammy saw serenity, the face of someone who could now exhale. "He just looked like he was at peace," she said. "Like, *It's over. I don't have to look over my back.* It was okay. Like he just didn't have to worry anymore."

They finally got me, his face told Tammy.

THE MORNING AFTER the shooting, amid the tributes pouring out online and around the city of Atlanta, it was Marlo's extended Bowen Homes family—those who knew him before rap—who were taking it hardest, even if they had seen the outcome approaching with varying immediacy for years. Jimmy was distraught, bawling and unable to eat. Only the sorrow of losing his mother and Lo, a death roundly echoed by Marlo's in so many ways, could compare. Gouch, though floored, tried to make himself useful. But Jacoby, who had received the call he'd long been dreading around 3 a.m., was shattered.

The lawyer thanked God that he and Marlo had managed to clear the air in time. Yet his frustrations remained, too. "It's heartbreaking, because I told Rudy it would end like this if he didn't change the people he was around," Jacoby said that Sunday morning, as the news started to travel.

On Instagram, he posted a photograph showing the two of them together at baby Rihanna's funeral, arms around each other's shoulders, the glow of a setting sun illuminating their weighty embrace. Jacoby was in black and Rudy in white, his index figure aimed at his lawyer's chest as if to say, *This man right here—I know he's got me.* And he did, for as long as he could. "Now," Jacoby wrote in tribute underneath, "you are back with RiRi."

29.

STAY DANGEROUS

Lil Baby, who ceded the number one album in the country to the late Pop Smoke the weekend Marlo was killed, took his time responding to his friend's death. It was a private matter that the public felt entitled to speculate about, given Marlo's proximity to fame—to Baby—but in the absence of real information, baseless gossip festered, including the idea that Baby was somehow the intended target of the shooting, with a rumored $50,000 bounty on his head.

In reality, despite their bond as rappers and as men, the pair were on mostly parallel tracks that only occasionally overlapped, even at the beginning, coming as they did from two different neighborhoods with different groups of friends and different grudges. What happened on Bankhead had nothing to do with Baby. "We'd go a week or two without talking," Baby told *GQ* a few weeks after Marlo's murder. "It just feels like he's somewhere handling his business."

The news had made him cry for the first time in eight years, Baby said later—a claim that felt true, if nothing else, for its needless specificity. Yet even at his most vulnerable, Baby was deliberate with his words and at least partially hardened. "It's like don't too much good come out this street shit," Baby wrote directly to his fans, knowing that millions of followers would take in the reaction and, he hoped, take it to heart. "Few n——s get away but you don't hear about them that often. Streets a stepping stool to the next level! I say that to say I'm fucced up bout Yung Ru, but at the same time I'm so familiar with this shit I find myself numb." He nodded to his own ongoing struggle with "straddling the fence."

"Marlo was a gangster," Baby continued, "and sometimes death comes with that. I want all the people who look up to me or even admire what I'm doing to understand and know what come with this 'gangster shit.'" He ended his message with an aphorism aimed as much at himself as anyone else—the inverse of telling somebody to *stay safe*, which was a largely passive, or defensive, act, and which hadn't been enough so many times in his universe. "Stay dangerous," Baby wrote.

Coach and P mourned, too, but in limited ways that resisted much public consumption or performance. There was no grand lesson in Marlo's death that they didn't already know, that they hadn't already experienced—no teachable moment worth underlining that might diminish or paper over the realities of the life Marlo had lived, and almost lived. "So much potential that the world didn't get a chance to see," P posted, ever succinct. "It's really hard for me to say RIP." Coach remembered that Marlo smile. "Àse," he added.

But the outwardly muted reactions from most were counter to the prevailing feelings that boiled closer to the Bankhead nucleus, where one PFK associate said the whole of Atlanta would be flipped upside down in response to the shooting. Even Young Thug warned ominously, "Something gotta happen 'bout this one." Few were expecting justice in any official sense, something that went without saying in a part of town where the police had been viewed skeptically long before 2020, with crimes rarely solved and their underlying causes even less likely to be addressed. But more violence seemed certain.

At a candlelight vigil off Bankhead a few days after Marlo's death, in front of the chain-link fence where Bowen Homes once stood, dozens gathered to pay tribute to the neighborhood hero. Votives spelled RIP MARLO PFK on the ground, while balloons in black and purple, the Play For Keeps colors, filled the air. *Can't let this one go* was the refrain on everybody's tongue. Jacoby, pouring sweat, noted the prevalence of guns in waistbands. "Them folks strapped up," he said. Three Black police officers surveyed the scene from the overflowing Texaco parking lot.

Across the street, one of Marlo's aunts addressed the mourners, encouraging them to give money to his kids whenever they could. "Because guess what, he did a lot for the community," she said. "Helped a lot of children." But at that moment, a phone chimed in the crowd, and a few seconds later, its owner piped up with a warning. "Excuse me," the young woman said, raising her quavering voice above the murmurs and the eulogizing. "My friend just called, and she said they finna come shoot it up."

Before she could finish, people scattered and balloons were let loose, with women and children taking off for the other side of Bankhead. Men with guns drawn, held low near their right knees, moved toward the center of the action as if in formation. A little boy ducked behind a car.

"They shooting over there?" he asked the adults streaming past.

"Boy, you better get up out of here," one man responded. "You not grown." The cops had disappeared.

Marlo's funeral service, on a sweltering July day, was another all-white affair, just like Rihanna's, but with his traditional Ifa faith front and center—a request he had made sure to leave with both Tammy and his mother. Purple and black, for PFK, popped up in the masks required by the coronavirus, some spruced up with screen-printed pictures of Marlo, as well as in bunches of balloons and the flowers that sat atop his shining white casket. In a small miracle for the grieving, Marlo was able to appear asleep and at peace, despite his gruesome end. To Tammy, he resembled an African king.

She wore a floor-length white fishtail gown with ruffles and a matching headdress. A horse-drawn carriage, like the one that had transported their late daughter, brought the body of Rudolph Simmons Johnson IV to its final resting place in a West Side cemetery. Rudy Jr. and Marlo Jr., in coordinated West Africa–inspired outfits, cried out for their father, but they also danced together in a drum circle led by older men in traditional garb. In the spirit of an African American homegoing, the mood was largely celebratory. And although a program for the funeral had the QC logo printed on its cover, the label lay low in the intimate setting, drawing no attention to itself as Marlo's family farewell foregrounded him as a man, not a rapper—a father of four always with two in his arms, giving squeezes and smirks and kisses.

Printed alongside a photo of Tammy planting a big one on a stoic Marlo was a poem. "He was my very world, my ever guiding star," the final lines said. "Just kiss me softly on the cheek and tell me where you are." Marlo was remembered by those present as fearless and talented, a Bankhead legend and a good listener—shy, reckless and savvy. "The streets don't love nobody," Marlo Jr.'s mother said in her own social-media eulogy. "They only make us single parents."

But the rawest response to Marlo's murder may have come from behind bars, from a man who knew him better than anyone—the one who put Marlo on his little-heard, first-ever song as a featured artist but was otherwise absent from his too-brief journey through the music business. Terrell Davis, better known as Ralo, was another local legend in that classic Atlanta mode—a rapper from the Bluff who signed with Gucci Mane (who else?), collaborated with Future (of course) and seemed to already have the respect of every artist and manager in the city when he started making music in 2015, not long after converting to Islam. Ralo's mixtapes, like Marlo's, were boiled-down trap essentials from a non-natural, with pain in the marrow and titles like *Diary of the Streets* and *Plugged in with the Cartel*. But before all that, Ralo was Marlo's cousin, another person who knew him first and foremost as Rudy and who was there at Rihanna's funeral, again demonstrating how deep the familial connections were, even behind the rap façade, across the city of Atlanta.

In 2018, Ralo had been arrested as part of an alleged criminal conspiracy and charged with possession of marijuana with intent to distribute, after he and a group of others were caught traveling back to Atlanta from Northern California on a private jet with hundreds of pounds of weed—twice. The first major seizure, three days before Christmas of 2017, turned up 37 gift-wrapped packages weighing in at about 520 pounds, or a million dollars' worth. Four months later, according to a federal indictment, Ralo, who had somehow avoided arrest the first go-around, took a similar voyage, this time bringing back 444 pounds worth another $840,000. The feds painted Ralo as the leader of Famerica—a "criminal street gang" that also happened to be the name of his record label—and they alleged that at his direction "gang members sell drugs and firearms and engage in other traditional street gang activities."

Only in the years that followed, with marijuana legalization spreading rapidly across the country, did Ralo's case start to be framed by supporters and his lawyers as a political issue, even drawing the attention of Drake. "At a time where so many young white people and others are capitalizing off marijuana's new legitimacy to see this brother sit and suffer is sickening," Killer Mike wrote on Twitter as Ralo fought for bail ahead of an oft-delayed trial. "He is a real one and helped his community, and now he is hostage of the state." Ralo was later granted a $250,000 bond in the case. But it was promptly revoked after authorities argued that Ralo was continuing to arrange drug deals from prison using an Apple Watch.

Ralo had missed most of Rudy's life as a rapper, locked up as he was for the majority of the Marlo years. But when news of his cousin's death reached prison, Ralo was clear-eyed about where they had come from, what they had endured together and where they had ended up. He reminisced on Instagram about their shared dream, as young men calling themselves Double R (for Ralo and Rudy), to "take over the streets"—fantasies that had started small enough, like buying SUVs for their girlfriends.

"WHEN WE SIGNED UP FOR THIS SHIT WE ACCEPTED RISKING OUR LIVES TO BECOME GREAT AMERICAN GANGSTERS, BUT TO ACTUALLY FEEL THE SACRIFICE HIT DIFFERENT, CUZ," Ralo wrote. "WE SIGNED THE DUMBEST FUCKIN CONTRACT IN THE WORLD WHEN WE SIGNED UP FOR THESE STREETS."

Music had not come easy to either man, even as it teased redemption. "THEY SAID WE COULDN'T RAP," Ralo went on. "WE AINT NEVER CATCH AH BILLBOARD HIT. WE OUTCHA THUGGIN FR CUZ NO RAP CAP. QC P TOLD US BOTH TO CHOOSE BETWEEN THE STREETS AN THE INDUSTRY. WE PICKED THE STREETS AN LOOK AT OUR RESULTS."

Ralo mourned for their kids and for their women, vowing to one day buy a house big enough for all of them. But despite a brief moment where it looked like he might be out of prison in time to offer his condolences in person, Ralo was not allowed to attend the funeral. "FROM THE SAND BOX, TO WEST FULTON MIDDLE, TO FREDERICK DOUGLAS HIGH SCHOOL, TO OUR CAREER IN THESE STREETS," Ralo wrote instead, in his long-distance remembrance. "THESE BULLET HOLES IN OUR BODIES IS OUR CERTIFICATES, THESE INDICTMENTS IS OUR TROPHIES, WE DON'T GET NO GRAMMYS, THE ONLY AWARDS WE GET OUT THIS SHIT IS DEATH AN PRISON."

To a broader audience, the fact that Marlo's murder happened in his own backyard—the place he used to define his identity for three decades and the one he documented in detail, in hopes of getting far away—brought home a reality that had become a hip-hop truism, even as it continued to occur: "Most rappers die in their own city," as the Baton Rouge legend and troubled provocateur Boosie famously put it. "It's a fact."

In recent years, this arc had shortened and intensified as more and more individuals could conceivably identify as a rapper, and thus, die as one. The barriers to entry for a self-described musician had all but disappeared, and rap's middle class had swelled as a result. Like Hollywood character actors, these street-level regional favorites may still have been less visible and less glamorous than the hip-hop one percent, the ones who hogged a majority of the streams and cultural headspace. But it was a boom time for this in-between tier of artist, including those from beyond the rap strongholds of Atlanta, Chicago, New York and Los Angeles, as artists from previously overlooked cities like Charlotte, Sacramento and Pompano Beach started to develop and sustain large national followings.

Atlanta, having had a longer history with it, knew this archetype better than most. But that didn't mean the city's local heroes weren't also at risk. In 2016, the rapper Bankroll Fresh, another West Side up-and-comer, was killed in a shootout with No Plug, his childhood friend and a

9th Ward ally of Marlo and 21 Savage. The situation was later chalked up to some combination of territorial jealousy, women, an overabundance of firearms and miscommunication. Plug, who claimed self-defense, was never charged. But Bankroll's death outside of Street Execs Studios had haunted the city and its rap talent ever since.

Three years after Bankroll and a year before Marlo's murder, a similar killing reverberated somewhat unexpectedly around the world when Nipsey Hussle was shot in front of the clothing store he owned in the South Los Angeles neighborhood where he had grown up and invested his winnings. A well-respected and connected member of the Rollin' 60s Neighborhood Crips who became a bigger entrepreneur and motivational figure than he ever was a rapper, Hussle grabbed headlines and the attention of no less than Barack Obama in death, due in part to the Shakespearean tragedy of being gunned down by a longtime acquaintance in the place he'd devoted his adult life to uplifting.

"Everything about Nipsey was Crenshaw and Slauson," the LA rapper the Game said in the days that followed. "Those are the two streets that ended up taking his life." The same could be said for Marlo and Bankhead. Because while the residual mainstream understanding of hip-hop beef came mostly from the East Coast–vs.–West Coast war of nineties gangster rap—with the deaths of Tupac and Biggie remaining the genre's deepest wounds—most rap politics were local, or not rap-based at all. With an eye toward understanding the systemic disadvantages facing young Black men in America, some diagnosed the problem as a "crabs in a barrel" mindset, comparing it to *The Hunger Games* or just chalking it up to the way of the wild. "It's like putting a bunch of lions in one zoo and telling them to share a piece of the food," CyHi the Prynce, a rapper and songwriter from Stone Mountain, Georgia, said after his car was shot up in Atlanta, not even a year after Marlo's death. "There's always going to be tension in those scenarios, so no, I'm not surprised."

But following a spate of deaths and close calls in and around the genre, some rappers took to calling their profession the most dangerous job in the world. The dice-roll of reaching for fame, they pointed out, could be its own kind of gamble. "Every day you're taking one of the biggest risks of your life by being a rapper and living in your community, or continuing to pull up there," Mozzy, a Sacramento artist who hadn't entirely made it out with his music about gang ties and their consequences, said after Hussle was murdered. "But you take that risk out of a love for the people." This dynamic was echoed every hood over each time a Bankroll Fresh, a Nipsey, a Marlo, a FBG Duck, a Young Dolph or a Drakeo the Ruler was killed.

Jacoby Hudson could only shake his head. "He still wanted to be in the neighborhood," Marlo's lawyer said. "He cared about people and he took care of people. And his loyalty is probably what got him killed.

"He didn't let the music save him," Jacoby said. Stacked up against everything else, it may have never really stood a chance.

30.

THE CYCLE

By the turbulent end of 2020, Lil Baby was on top of not only his world but the wider one. *My Turn*, his latest album, might have called its shot with that title, but even Baby and Quality Control at their most assured would not have dared to divine its ultimate achievement, one announced after the release had already gone double platinum. When all was said and done, *My Turn* was crowned the most popular, most listened-to album of the year by anyone in any genre, topping even Taylor Swift.

Even more impressively, Baby had sacrificed nothing to reach this summit of culture. His most intimate thoughts, dreams, regrets, fantasies, friendships and rivalries—the ones that poured out of him in late-night and early-morning recording sessions around Atlanta and the world—were heard, over and over again, more than any other lyrics in the country, a once-marginalized Black Southern existence and subgenre now inarguably a ubiquitous story and sound.

The sheer numbers—including nearly four *billion* streams of songs from the album—spoke volumes. This was today's pop music, and anyone who had ever questioned Baby's inextinguishable accent, his refusal to pander, his commitment to weighing down danceability with bruising realities and unpredictable rhyme schemes, was left behind as he and his Atlanta rap cohort continued to drag the mainstream deeper into its vortex, where a folk tradition and the avant-garde swirled together nonstop. As a genre, this strain of hip-hop—Atlanta trap and its spinoffs—had outlasted fad status, adapting too many times over and burrowing its influence too resolutely in too many places, from electronic dance music to the default African American vernacular of everyday social-media speak.

Yet for the individuals behind the sounds, the words and the ideas, the breakneck success couldn't last. It never did. A young man's game played in an underdog's arena, rap never had cared much for its well-established elders, beyond maybe two handfuls of lucky individuals who turned street currency into boardroom status. Musically, songs about wanting to make it had a sell-by date for their creators, who eventually either did or didn't, and music about having made it could get stale even quicker. Becoming successful enough to be out of touch with the realities of the block was always the point of rapping, but the further those artists tended to get from their old lives, the less their enduring subject matter made urgent sense to its core base, the audiences who decided what music would trickle up and outward.

Lil Baby would face this conundrum soon enough, if he was lucky. The cycle was always starting over again, the machine always hungry for more Black exuberance, more Black pain. And thanks in part to the ongoing realities of the American underclass, the churn of fresher faces and voices with more urgent stories and pressing problems—not to mention updated packaging, slang and sounds—was constant, in line with the desire from listeners for whatever came next.

It's not that the music or the personalities that reigned for a time, only to be replaced, were disposable—though some certainly treated them as such—but rather that they could serve their purpose for a period, a moment, and then the formula could be tweaked enough to work for somebody else entirely. This iterating, while punishing on a human level, was what kept rap fresher than many of the genres it had since surpassed in popularity. In the best-case scenario, the exchange between the industry and the individuals who made it work would be mutually beneficial, leaving those who gave so much of themselves to the rap world deposited safely in higher realms that were also worth conquering—Hollywood, tech, fashion, fine art, or anything wholly ownable.

By 2020, Migos embodied all the risks and the upsides of hip-hop transcendence in an iced-out, world-beating, three-headed package. Following *My Turn* and the diminishing impact of the group's own musical onslaught, no one in the QC universe was under any illusions about who the label's biggest breadwinner was at the moment—and who still had new heights to climb. Dealing with Baby, an individual who leaned constitutionally toward diligent low-key-ness, was always going to be simpler than juggling the demands of a trio potentially approaching a period of decline in a fickle business. No rap empire—Death Row, Bad Boy, No Limit, Cash Money, Roc-A-Fella, Ruff Ryders, G-Unit, Dipset, GOOD Music, ASAP Mob or anyone else—had ever completely avoided the internal clashes that arose from the unavoidable existence of a natural and evolving pecking order. And there were steady rumblings that hinted at dissension within the QC ranks.

In March 2020, grainy video and wobbly witness accounts surfaced, fueling reports that Offset had been jumped by Baby's 4PF crew outside of an Atlanta nightclub, leaving him begging in his boxer shorts, possibly due to some gambling gone wrong. Offset never commented on the speculation that surrounded the incident, and Baby did the honorable thing by calling it "fake news." But P may have shown his hand when he posted an image online the day the gossip started circulating that paraphrased a Jay-Z and Beyoncé song: "No one wins when the family feuds."

Already, collaborations between Baby and Migos had dried up, and the stars and their respective teams were rarely, if ever, seen together. A few months later, when Migos was asked in an interview about Baby's runaway success, the group went stone-faced and monosyllabic.

But the real fissures in the family were revealing themselves in court documents. Days after the fatal shooting of Marlo, Migos sued its label's lawyer. The timing could not have been worse.

In the lawsuit—which was not technically a direct attack on the trio's longtime backers, Coach K and P, but was broadly interpreted as one—Quavo, Offset and Takeoff alleged that they had been "robbed and cheated out of millions of dollars," due to the fact that their legal representative in negotiating entertainment contracts also represented QC and had all along. The three rappers claimed that their business attorney, Damien Granderson, failed to get the proper waiver to cover this glaring conflict of interest, dubbing him "the personification of a self-absorbed shyster lawyer who saw his clients as a mechanism to get rich by any means necessary."

Painting Migos as "easy targets" for the lawyer's manipulations, the suit noted that the members were "in their late teens and early twenties" when they signed their original label contracts "and had nothing more than a high school education." Granderson was therefore free to pursue one-sided deals that benefited his "higher-priority client"—Quality Control Music.

This wasn't outright war, but it hinted openly at the possibility. And although years of commercial domination and flaunted financial success made it difficult to paint QC's stewardship of Migos' career as a hindrance, the idea of artists' being underpaid because of allegedly shady contracts was basically an industry-wide assumption. But while a contract fight between a midcareer artist and a day-one label was all but a music-business inevitability, it was also a development that rarely happened while things were going well.

P, of course, was allergic by nature to litigating such matters in court, and when news of the lawsuit went wide, he was livid and lashed out. QC had long studiously avoided most outward signs of messiness when it came to business, but all of a sudden that reputation for aboveboard dealings was at risk thanks to the label's foundational act.

"It is unfortunate that the same people that we have worked hard, provided opportunities for, and championed for are now alleging that we have participated in any kind of immoral or unfair business practices or took advantage of them and their careers, especially while we are dealing with the death of an artist on our label that was dear to us," P wrote on Instagram. "We built this business on family values, which has been so hard to do when you are dealing with so much pride and ego."

He seemed to hint at nefarious—and racialized—business forces that may have planted seeds of doubt, or greed, in the ears of Migos, and he urged direct communication while flat-out daring the group to actually walk away.

"It is hard enough to be fighting and battling with corporations and the powers that be, I am not doing it with those who I consider family.

I understand in this business that you are not always going to end with the people you started with. I say that to say, I am not forcing anybody to be in business with us that has a problem and cannot communicate and does not want to work as a unit.

"Everything," P added, "is negotiable."

Then, in August, Takeoff, the youngest and calmest of the trio, was sued for sexual battery, assault and more. An anonymous woman said she had been invited to a house party in Los Angeles by Migos' DJ and producer Durel, only for Takeoff to take an aggressive interest in her, and eventually force himself on her in a darkened bedroom. The next morning, the woman went to the hospital, where her lawyer said an exam found "physical evidence of forceful rape." The Los Angeles Police Department opened an investigation and Drew Findling went to work, citing Takeoff's reputation as "quiet, reserved and peaceful" and claiming "an obvious exploitative money grab."

In line with Takeoff's level of individual fame, the alleged horror story did not become a widespread scandal. But the tensions were compounding, and the coronavirus pandemic was not helping. In time, Migos' contract lawsuit with its label's lawyer would be settled out of court, and the parties put on a good face, with everyone involved swearing that *Culture III* would represent a return to form for the group. Criminal charges in the Takeoff case were never filed and the civil lawsuit, too, went away with a whisper.

Amid the tempestuousness, QC's rappers were diversifying according to plan. Offset invested in an E-sports team, voted for the first time in a presidential election and encouraged others to do the same, reinventing himself as a budding activist. He almost got dumped for the umpteenth time by Cardi B, who went as far as to officially file for divorce and custody of the couple's daughter Kulture, but they reconciled once again, announcing to the world at the BET Awards in 2021 that they were expecting a second child. After hosting an ill-fated, ten-minute streaming show about cars on something called Quibi, the soon-to-be father of five was cast as a computer engineer in a Pete Davidson movie, while also producing and judging a fashion competition under the HBO umbrella.

Early one summer morning, Offset rang the opening bell at the New York Stock Exchange.

Quavo, meanwhile, found a Cardi of his own for a time, posing in fashion editorials with his rapper girlfriend Saweetie—until she accused him of cheating and an old video of the couple tussling in an elevator leaked, leading to public speculation of abuse. But Quavo now had additional industry power in his corner, having signed as a solo act with Scooter Braun, Justin Bieber's power manager, and his growing stature as a celebrity continued apace. In his own role as an aspiring actor, Quavo even one-upped Offset in the costar contest, getting cast in a film starring John Malkovich and Robert De Niro. Of course, he rapped about it, rhyming De Niro with "dinero."

Along the way, QC resumed its role as the trio's most steadfast backers, only now there were more Hollywood talent agencies and individualized functionaries in the mix, as well. But new, fairer contracts or not, something had shifted in the family, and the path they had traveled together was irreversible, as everyone involved always hoped it would be, but perhaps without fully grasping what might be lost in the process.

P knew these conundrums, but like Baby, he would take how far they had come and the comfort it afforded every time. Still, the executive had not lost his itchy palms or hustler's mentality, and he remained eager to start from scratch and break a new artist or two at every turn—to make a couple more millionaires, as he always said. *Keep flipping* remained his motto. "Don't nobody stay on top forever," P declared online. "Plan for the future."

But no longer would any legacy industry executive have the gall to brush off P or Coach when they said they had one in hand, and proving people wrong had always been part of the fun. Nonetheless, the QC duo picked up new trappers-turned-rappers from Florida and Arkansas, and now, female artists from Milwaukee and East Saint Louis, too. They invested in vintage cars, car washes, fast-food franchises and gentlemen's clubs; in gaming, like Offset; and in film, like everyone who ever made a little bit of money. Nearly three decades after he dropped out, Coach finished his bachelor's degree at his old HBCU, and he gave a talk at Harvard for good measure. Atlanta's High Museum of Art even welcomed him to its board.

Quality Control kept expanding. Thanks to the company's diversification, a semi-biographical City Girls show was in the works, as was a Lil Yachty "action heist comedy" based on the card game Uno, made in association with Mattel. In an unlikely move given his early days of bubblegum trap, Yachty made a second home for himself in Michigan, spinning the earlier slights about his rap skills into motivation and developing a mutually beneficial relationship with new sects of lyrical street rappers from cities like Detroit and Flint. Then he tried other places and styles on with an enduring and contagious good attitude. More than anything, Yachty became what Coach had promised: a brand, appearing on a box of Reese's cereal and launching a cryptocurrency coin, a nail polish line and a venture capital fund.

Baby, in a sly twist, went back to weed. This time, however, it was legal—and his investment in The Holding Company LLC (THC, for short) came with the title of president, as the company promised to provide "medical and recreational markets in the USA with access to the best possible cannabis." Along with playlists' worth of new songs where he was the A-list guest that Drake once had been—from the soundtrack to the new *Space Jam* to the latest from Kanye West—Baby's name now also adorned the pristine, bright blue public basketball courts, sponsored by Foot Locker, in his old Oakland City neighborhood.

Atlanta had changed along with him and his friends. Condos popped up along the Beltline, the former railway corridor around the city perimeter, and neighborhoods like the West End and Bankhead were being "revitalized" in the form of $500,000 town houses. The Dungeon, once the Southeast Atlanta headquarters for Organized Noize and OutKast, was bought by Big Boi and briefly became an Airbnb. But as crime continued to spike in the city, Buckhead threatened to secede, potentially taking almost 20 percent of Atlanta's population and more than 40 percent of its property value in the process. Mayor Keisha Lance Bottoms declined to seek a second term, citing the litany of challenges she faced in office, including the pandemic, the protests against police and the "madman in the White House."

On the fringes of success, guys like Ced and Gouch had bigger roles to play, as labels begat other labels and beauty shops and dog kennels and fashion lines and shopping centers. G-Five went back to jail on outstanding warrants, discovered by cops under the bed in a Buckhead penthouse, alongside $20,000 in cash and $11,000 in sneakers. His fledgling rap career would have to wait. But Drew Findling was always around for more business, and Jacoby Hudson could never run out of clients either—the state would see to that. A man like Jimmy from Bowen Homes was always going to figure something out.

As usual in Atlanta, those left struggling were pushed deeper down, out of sight. Because for every kid like Baby, there was a Reek; for every Reek, a Marlo; and for each of them, thousands more still fighting their way out of a problem they didn't create. Even at the heights some had reached, the ones who made it could never bring everyone. It wasn't on them, anyway. Rap couldn't be expected to save a city or its sons, but that wouldn't stop the trying.

A clean break from one's old life, however, felt increasingly like a fantasy. In May of 2022, Fulton County District Attorney Fani Willis, a Democrat and Black woman, unveiled an eighty-eight-page RICO indictment accusing Young Thug's YSL crew—twenty-eight people in all, including Thug, Gunna and other rappers from the label—of operating as a criminal street gang with ties to the national Bloods. Among the fifty-six counts were allegations of drug dealing, armed robbery, assault and murder, the events spanning nearly a decade, back to the start of Thug's ascent as a rapper in 2013.

The investigation cited jailhouse calls, Instagram captions, emoji use, hoodie logos, face tattoos and plentiful song lyrics, all alleged to be "in furtherance of the conspiracy," with Willis calling social media "a wonderful tool" for prosecutors. She claimed that gangs accounted for up to 80 percent of the city's violent crime and promised more cases to come.

Barely six months earlier, Thug had been celebrating *Punk*, his second number one album of the year—the first being YSL's label compilation *Slime Language 2*—and performing on *Saturday Night Live*. Now, the lawyer Brian Steel was promising to fight until his "last drop of blood to clear him." Young Thug was potentially facing life in prison.

Years earlier, in her Atlanta-area office, the industry executive and Thug whisperer Amina Diop had warned me about the "human toll" of this world. She praised those she'd watched improve their circumstances, and the lives of those around them, through rap music—from Gucci Mane and Young Thug to P and Baby—but had already seen too much to ever be free of anxiety, or of caveats. "I'm happy for all of their maturity and hope they don't get dragged down," she said. "Because they're up, but they're not so far up that the fucking bullshit . . ." She trailed off.

"Atlanta is love, Atlanta is light, Atlanta is prosperity, Atlanta is productivity," Diop said. "But with all of those words, there is a counterpart. There's hands raising up and there's hands pulling you down."

"I always hope for them to be able to keep looking up and not looking back," she said. "Because when you look back, that's when you turn to a pillar of salt. 'Cause Atlanta is that, too."

Yet there had been too many flukes across too many decades for the music industry to keep the city at arm's length any longer. The chip on Atlanta's shoulder had turned to a stage. At Motown Records, Ethiopia Habtemariam, the Atlanta-raised executive who brought Quality Control in, was named chairman and CEO, vowing to open even more doors for those who looked like her, who came from where she came from. Their formula was now a trusted one, and more lives could be changed as a result, though never as many as needed it.

At its gleaming new Atlanta headquarters for music, sports, film and tech—one with boardrooms of their own—Quality Control could lead the way for the city, at least until someone hungrier came along to supplant them. That was the idea, after all. Soon, it would be somebody else's turn.

ACKNOWLEDGMENTS

Thank you to the city of Atlanta for having me. Thank you to my family for supporting me—Mom, Dad, Alyssa, Carrie, Curi, Gerard, Miles, Lita, Papi, Frankie, Vida. Thank you to my friends for putting me up and putting up with me—Alice, Beau, Bryan, Camilla, David, Justin, Leon, Matthew, Sophie, Zara. Thank you to my coworkers, readers and colleagues, who I also consider friends, for making me better—Ben, Caryn, Jon, Jon, Wesley, Avi, Ben, Dan, Naomi, Naomi, Marc, Zeke, Christina, Christopher, Francis, Jack, Jayson, Natalie, Teddy. Thank you to William and Stuart for making this happen. And all the rest.

A NOTE ON SOURCING

This book is the result of countless hours of observation, listening, research and reporting, including more than 100 firsthand interviews over the course of four-plus years. Some were dedicated, extended sit-downs, some were in the course of my work for *The New York Times* and others were less formal conversations in passing, but I always made a point to identify myself as a journalist working on a book about Atlanta rap. These exchanges were recorded digitally, or else rendered in contemporaneous notes. I am beyond grateful to everyone who spoke with me and shared their opinions and experiences.

I also relied on those writers who came before me. In rendering Atlanta's history, I depended heavily on work from W. E. B. Du Bois, James Baldwin, Maurice J. Hobson, Frederick Allen and Mark Pendergrast, whose books informed my thinking and led me back to primary sources. While the legacy of Southern hip-hop is thus far woefully underrepresented in books, the information in those sections was influenced especially by *Third Coast* by Roni Sarig, *Chronicling Stankonia* by Regina N. Bradley, *Dirty South* by Ben Westhoff, *The Autobiography of Gucci Mane* and *Atlanta* by Michael Schmelling, Kelefa Sanneh and Will Welch, along with the journalism and criticism of Rodney Carmichael, Mara Shalhoup, Christina Lee, Jon Caramanica and more cited below.

I referred often to local news reports, court records, trial transcripts and other public records. Chart positions and sales totals are from *Billboard* and MRC Data (formerly Nielsen SoundScan) unless otherwise noted; sales certifications are via the RIAA.

Less traditional sources were crucial, as well. Because so much these days happens online, especially in rap, I pored over blogs, message boards, YouTube channels and social media accounts, especially Instagram and Twitter, to more fully understand my subjects' actions, reactions, emotions and relationships. By nature, much of this was ephemeral, making it tougher to cite, but I kept extensive archives of posts, hoping to preserve in these pages their information and essence for the historical record.

Introduction

xv *"To be an ATLien":* Rodney Carmichael, "ATLieNation," Creative Loafing, October 5, 2016, https://creativeloafing.com/content-267264-atlienation.

xvii *ended the year with 157 homicides:* Shaddi Abusaid and Christian Boone, "Atlanta's Deadliest Year in Decades Has City on Edge and Demanding Change," *Atlanta Journal-Constitution,* January 15, 2021, https://www.ajc.com/news/atlantas-deadliest-year-in-decades-has-city-on-edge-and-demanding-change/WAF3MV7AVBD2BO2RZVANXDI6E4/.

xvii *"south of the North, yet north of the South":* W. E. B. Du Bois, *The Souls of Black Folk* (Oxford: Oxford University Press, 2007), 54.

xviii *"vulgar money-getters":* Ibid., 56.

xviii *"a bastion of both white supremacy":* William A. Link, *Atlanta, Cradle of the New South: Race and Remembering in the Civil War's Aftermath* (Chapel Hill: University of North Carolina Press, 2015), 90.

xviii *"on the brink of either":* Mark Pendergrast, *City on the Verge: Atlanta and the Fight for America's Urban Future* (New York: Basic Books, 2017), ix.

xviii *"a 60 percent Black city":* Robert Scheer, "Blacks Increasingly Isolated in Atlanta," *Los Angeles Times,* November 20, 1978.

xviii *a white minority keeps:* Pendergrast, *City on the Verge,* 82.

xix Forbes *called Atlanta the best city:* Joel Kotkin, "The Cities Where African-Americans Are Doing the Best Economically 2018," *Forbes,* January 15, 2018, https://www.forbes.com/sites/joelkotkin/2018/01/15/the-cities-where-african-americans-are-doing-the-best-economically-2018/?sh=5d0fb6041abe.

xx *"an impulse to keep the painful details":* Ralph Ellison, "Richard Wright's Blues," *Antioch Review* 50, no. 1/2 (1992): 62, https://doi.org/10.2307/4612492.

xx *"the paradoxical, almost surreal image":* Ibid., 63.

xx *"basically the same as Miami's":* Bob Mack, "Hip Hop Map of America," *Spin,* June 1990.

xxi *"Tell them we are rising":* Oliver Otis Howard, *Autobiography of Oliver Otis Howard, Major-General, United States Army: Pt. 2.* (Franklin Classics Trade Press, 1907), 414.

xxv *represents more than 80 percent:* Joshua P. Friedlander, "Mid-Year 2021 RIAA Revenue Statistics," RIAA, 2021, https://www.riaa.com/wp-content/uploads/2021/09/Mid-Year-2021-RIAA-Music-Revenue-Report.pdf.

xxv *$12.2 billion in revenue:* Joshua P. Friedlander, "Year-End 2020 RIAA Revenue Statistics," RIAA, 2021, https://www.riaa.com/wp-content/uploads/2021/02/2020-Year-End-Music-Industry-Revenue-Report.pdf.

Chapter One

3 *A self-proclaimed studio hand:* Reginald Stuart, "Suspect in Atlanta: Young, Big Ideas, but a Career of Limited Achievements," *New York Times*, June 22, 1981, https://www.nytimes.com/1981/06/22/us/suspect-in-atlanta-young-big-ideas-but-a-career-of-limited-achievements.html.

3 *he worked for years:* Ibid.

3 *Born on May 27, 1958:* Ibid.

4 *Near 3 a.m. on a Friday:* Ken Willis and Tony Cooper, "Wayne Williams Is Charged in Nathaniel Cater's Slaying," *Atlanta Journal-Constitution*, November 10, 1981, https://www.ajc.com/news/crime—law/wayne-williams-charged-nathaniel-cater-slaying/l11zKO68bhhQsA9ce1C6UJ/.

4 *his family's white 1970 Chevrolet:* "Atlanta Child Murders," FBI Records: The Vault, FBI, November 30, 2010, https://vault.fbi.gov/Atlanta%20Child%20Murders.

5 *as an "odd creature":* James Baldwin, *The Evidence of Things Not Seen* (New York: Henry Holt, 1985), 9.

5 *"a spoiled, lost and vindictive child":* Ibid., 112.

5 *Baldwin described as "terrifying":* Ibid., 111.

5 *"Whether he's guilty of these crimes":* Stuart, "Suspect in Atlanta."

6 *the fifth boy and sixth child:* "Atlanta Child Murders," FBI Records: The Vault.

6 *was ten when he disappeared:* Dan Collins, "Atlanta Mother Mourns Dead Son," UPI, March 13, 1981, https://www.upi.com/Archives/1981/03/13/Atlanta-mother-mourns-dead-son/6697353307600/.

6 *four feet eight inches and seventy-one pounds:* Walter Leavy, "The Mystery of the Disappearing Blacks," *Ebony*, December 1980.

6 *discovered by FBI agents:* Bernard D. Headley, *The Atlanta Youth Murders and the Politics of Race* (Carbondale: Southern Illinois University Press, 1998), 91.

6 *Mathis's mother, Willie Mae:* Ibid., 44.

6 *His father, William, a security guard:* Maurice J. Hobson, *The Legend of the Black Mecca: Politics and Class in the Making of Modern Atlanta* (Chapel Hill: University of North Carolina Press, 2017), 253.

6 *or "drop shots," in the suspect's:* "CNN Live Event/Special: Atlanta Child Murders," CNN, July 4, 2011, https://transcripts.cnn.com/show/se/date/2011-07-04/segment/02.

7 *an explosion occurred:* "Bowen Homes Records," Atlanta Housing, 2015, https://www.atlantahousing.org/wp-content/uploads/2019/05/2015.0017-Bowen-Homes-records.pdf.

7 *"Let's Keep Pulling Together, Atlanta":* Hobson, *The Legend of the Black Mecca*, 108.

7 *Mayor Jackson's "silly press statements":* E. R. Shipp, "3 Atlanta Mothers Visit Harlem Group," *New York Times*, March 15, 1981, https://www.nytimes.com/1981/03/15/nyregion/3-atlanta-mothers-visit-harlem-group.html.

7 *threatened with criminal and civil misconduct:* Hobson, *The Legend of the Black Mecca*, 116–17.

7 *"cultural and commercial haven":* Ibid., 111.

7 *spurred neighborhood vigilantes to mobilize:* Bob Keating and Barry Michael Cooper, "A Question of Justice," *Spin*, September 1986, https://www.spin.com/2015/12/atlanta-child-murders-wayne-williams-1986-feature/.

7 *"left the city bewildered":* Hobson, *The Legend of the Black Mecca*, 120.

8 *"resembled Boss Hog counting his money":* Ibid., 108.

8 *Muhammad Ali, outraged at the ongoing emergency:* Ibid., 112.

8 *Frank Sinatra and Sammy Davis Jr. headlined*: Reginald Stuart, "Top Entertainers, in a Benefit Concert, Joint Outpouring of Support for Atlanta," *New York Times,* March 11, 1981, https://www.nytimes.com/1981/03/11/us/top-entertainers-in-a-benefit-concert-join-outpouring-of-support-for-atlanta.html.

8 *"We use humor, music and talent":* Ibid.

8 *"buck-dancing on the graves":* Baldwin, *The Evidence of Things Not Seen*, 11.

8 *"a kind of grotesque Disneyland":* Ibid.

8 *"The parents don't know what happened":* Associated Press, "Police Files in Atlanta Child Slayings Unsealed," August 7, 1987, https://apnews.com/article/e4140f728338dfb42bf26054a0490e75.

8 *"are also the heirs":* James Baldwin, "Atlanta: The Evidence of Things Not Seen," *Playboy,* December 1981.

9 *"The music, storytelling, folklore":* Dr. Joycelyn Wilson, "The Music of the Murders," Bitter Southerner, April 18, 2019, https://bittersoutherner.com/from-the-southern-perspective/the-music-of-the-atlanta-child-murders-joycelyn-wilson.

9 *She, too, has recalled the constant warnings*: Audra D. S. Burch, "Who Killed Atlanta's Children?" *New York Times,* April 30, 2019, https://www.nytimes.com/2019/04/30/us/atlanta-child-murders.html.

9 *"help bring some peace to the families":* Ibid.

9 *an Atlanta white supremacist with ties:* Robert Byrd, "Police Informant Says Klan Had Role in Killings," Associated Press, October 8, 1991, https://apnews.com/1967cb17be5e0937c6767e4951af92bb; Robert Byrd, "Investigator Says Suspected KKK Link in Killings Was Kept Secret," Associated Press, October 9, 1991, https://apnews.com/0b214e5727b614b276b02bbfbbf18638.

9 *"wiped out a thousand future generations":* Harry R. Weber, "Tapes May Link White Supremacist to Slayings," LJWorld.com, Associated Press, August 6, 2005, https://www2.ljworld.com/news/2005/aug/06/tapes_may_link_white_supremacist_slayings/.

10 *with the FBI noting:* "FBI Records: The Vault," FBI, November 30, 2010, https://vault.fbi.gov/Atlanta%20Child%20Murders.

10 *Around 7 p.m. that Monday*: Dan Collins, "Atlanta Mother Mourns Dead Son," UPI, March 13, 1981, https://www.upi.com/Archives/1981/03/13/Atlanta-mother-mourns-dead-son/6697353307600/.

Chapter Three

17 *more esoteric forms of dance music:* Kelefa Sanneh, "How Coach K Guides Atlanta's Hip-Hop Stars," *New Yorker,* December 11, 2017, https://www.newyorker.com/magazine/2017/12/18/how-coach-k-guides-atlantas-hip-hop-stars.

18 *for the party known as Tracks:* Tony Greene, "The A-Team," *Spin,* August 1998.

18 *It began near the Atlanta University Center*: Errin Haines Whack and Rebecca Burns, "Freaknik: The Rise and Fall of Atlanta's Most Infamous Street Party," *Atlanta Magazine,* March 18, 2015, https://www.atlantamagazine.com/90s/freaknik-the-rise-and-fall-of-atlantas-most-infamous-street-party/.

18 *"It was very innocent":* Ernie Suggs, "Street Party Became Its Own Undoing," *Atlanta Journal-Constitution,* April 14, 2008, https://web.archive.org/web/20080420055026/http://www.ajc.com/metro/content/metro/atlanta/stories/2008/04/13/whatever_0414.html.

18 *began in Midtown's Piedmont Park:* Ibid.

19 *In 1994, attendance at the loosely organized event:* Ibid.

19 *claims of looting, indecent exposure, sexual assault:* Ibid.

19 *In 1973, Georgia governor Jimmy Carter:* "Bill Thompson Named Director of Georgia's Film, Video and Music Office," Georgia.org, November 1, 2006, https://www.georgia.org/newsroom/press-releases/bill-thompson-named-director-of-georgias-film-video-and-music-office.

19 *Mayor Jackson's Bureau of Cultural Affairs:* Maurice J. Hobson, *The Legend of the Black Mecca: Politics and Class in the Making of Modern Atlanta* (Chapel Hill: University of North Carolina Press, 2017), 204–5.

19 *wanted to start a public relations firm:* Ibid., 205–6.

20 *Bunnie would become a go-to promoter:* Ibid., 213.

20 *Bunnie and Maynard divorced in 1976:* Ibid., 206–7, 211.

20 *Bunnie quickly stretched beyond PR and promotion:* Ibid., 208.

20 *She also crossed paths:* Ibid., 211.

20 *the former First Lady married:* Ibid., 213.

20 *Mauldin had a son who was known:* Michael A. Gonzales, "Song of the South," *Vibe,* September 1996.

20 *the teenager dropped his dad's name:* Ibid.

21 *Dallas Austin—who would help:* Roni Sarig, *Third Coast: Outkast, Timbaland, and How Hip-Hop Became a Southern Thing* (Cambridge, MA: Da Capo Press, 2007), 104.

21 *"They didn't sing, they didn't rap":* Ibid., 105.

23 *"Black city with strong Black politicians":* Lynn Norment, "Pebbles' Southern Hideaway," *Ebony,* April 1991.

23 *his not-quite-blood-cousin:* Will Stephenson, "Rapp Will Never Die," *Oxford American,* January 29, 2016, https://main.oxfordamerican.org/magazine/item/757-rapp-will-never-die.

24 *"Even today, my records don't":* Sarig, *Third Coast,* 104.

25 *a local DJ turned A&R executive:* Ibid., 188.

25 *André Benjamin and Antwan Patton met:* Ibid., 120.

25 *In 1992, Rico Wade invited:* Ibid., 122–23.

25 *in a storage room at Jellybeans:* Ibid., 117.

25 *was a family friend of the Wades:* Ibid., 118.

26 *"ain't no Christmas in the ghetto":* Hobson, *The Legend of the Black Mecca,* 224.

26 *"It represented all our asses":* Ibid., 133.

27 *"We made these packets":* Ibid.

27 *"It was the beginning of 'flexing'":* Haines Whack and Burns, "Freaknik."

28 *including about forty functioning strip clubs:* Ben Brasch, "Atlanta's Legendary Strip Clubs Ready for Super Bowl Guests," *Atlanta Journal-Constitution,* January 31, 2019, https://www.ajc.com/news/local/atlanta-legendary-strip-clubs-ready-for-super-bowl-guests/csEbBMF1bMYhiIOPDy3NYN/.

29 *Lee was visiting with some drug dealer friends:* Sanneh, "How Coach K Guides Atlanta's Hip-Hop Stars"; "Quality Control Music Founders Kevin 'Coach K' Lee and Pierre 'P' Thomas," *Empower Atlanta Magazine,* October 22, 2021, https://empoweratlantamagazine.com/2021/10/22/kevin-coach-k-lee-and-pierre-p-thomas/.

29 *His late-night "two-to-sixes":* Sanneh, "How Coach K Guides Atlanta's Hip-Hop Stars."

29 *he would create his first record label:* David Lindquist, "Hip-Hop Mogul Kevin 'Coach K' Lee Aims to Help an Indianapolis Act Break Through," *Indianapolis Star,* July 22, 2018, https://www.indystar.com/story/entertainment/music/2018/07/22/hip-hop-mogul-kevin-coach-k-lee-seeks-breakthrough-indianapolis-act/787132002/.

Chapter Four

34 *He was still prepubescent:* "Lil Baby—PREACHERMAN Official Documentary," YouTube, Lil Baby Official 4PF, 2018, https://www.youtube.com/watch?v=VS0utODCw2E.

35 *wear coveralls just like the old man:* Ibid.

36 *"typical little baby shit":* Charles Holmes, "The Remarkable Rise of Lil Baby," *Rolling Stone,* July 20, 2020, https://www.rollingstone.com/music/music-features/atlanta-rapper-lil-baby-bigger-picture-song-1027815/.

37 *some government assistance:* "Lil Baby Reflects On Dropping Out of High School in the 10th Grade, Working at Zaxby's for 1 Day," YouTube, DJ Smallz Eyes 2, 2017, https://www.youtube.com/watch?v=D96ltApN3SQ.

Chapter Five

40 *The many homeless people locked up:* Maurice J. Hobson, *The Legend of the Black Mecca: Politics and Class in the Making of Modern Atlanta* (Chapel Hill: University of North Carolina Press, 2017), 196.

40 *as a special education teacher:* Kelefa Sanneh, "How Coach K Guides Atlanta's Hip-Hop Stars," *New Yorker,* December 11, 2017, https://www.newyorker.com/magazine/2017/12/18/how-coach-k-guides-atlantas-hip-hop-stars.

41 *"They rapped about substance":* Aron A., "QC's Co-Founder Coach K Has Plans to Preserve the Culture on All Fronts," HotNewHipHop, November 11, 2019, https://www.hotnewhiphop.com/qcs-co-founder-coach-k-has-plans-to-preserve-the-culture-on-all-fronts-news.95397.html.

41 *"the Blackest city in America":* Ibid.

41 *"It was a moment that can't":* Ibid.

43 *"Pastor Troy really introduced street music":* Thomas Morton, "Trap Mastermind, Part Two: Coach K on Young Jeezy, Gucci Mane, and the Rise of Modern Atlanta," VICE, January 25, 2015, https://www.vice.com/en/article/rjxqx7/coach-k-interview-part-2-young-jeezy-gucci-mane-pastor-troy-the-rise-of-modern-atlanta.

43 *"crazy-ass, wild energy":* Ibid.

44 *"This is a lick for you":* Ibid.

44 *he had a 2001 Lexus LS 400:* Ibid.

45 *"One day he was just like":* Ibid.

45 *"I was like":* Ibid.

46 *"I remember it was like six a.m":* Ibid.

46 *shot at one of the two luxury Miami:* Ibid.

46 *faced a crushing federal indictment:* "Black Mafia Family Members Sentenced to 30 Years," Drug Enforcement Administration, September 12, 2008, https://www.dea.gov/sites/default/files/divisions/det/2008/detroit091208ap.html.

47 *Federal prosecutors later estimated:* Mara Shalhoup, *Black Mafia Family: The Rise and Fall of a Cocaine Empire* (Milo Books, 2010), 112.

47 *There was a $500,000 music video:* Mara Shalhoup, "BMF—Hip-Hop's Shadowy Empire—Part 1," Creative Loafing, December 6, 2006, https://creativeloafing.com/content-196219-bmf—-hip-hop-s-shadowy-empire—-part.

47 *For Meech's mythic thirty-sixth birthday:* Ibid.

47 *"Whenever there's drugs in the street":* Morton, "Trap Mastermind, Part Two."

48 *Jermaine Dupri's company announced itself:* Ben Westhoff, "Jermaine Dupri's Free Fall,"

Creative Loafing, July 20, 2010, https://creativeloafing.com/content-160957-jermaine-dupri-s-free-fall.

48 *On I-75 and even Peachtree Road:* Mara Shalhoup, "BMF—Hip-Hop's Shadowy Empire—Part 3," Creative Loafing, December 20, 2006, https://creativeloafing.com/content-196221-bmf—-hip-hop-s-shadowy-empire—-part.

48 *murder, kidnapping, money laundering:* Shalhoup, *Black Mafia Family,* 112.

49 *Drama's studio would be raided:* Christina Lee, "How DJ Drama Became the King of Mixtapes," Red Bull Music Academy Daily, August 15, 2016, https://daily.redbullmusicacademy.com/2016/08/dj-drama-mixtape-feature; Samantha M. Shapiro, "Hip-Hop Outlaw (Industry Version)," *New York Times,* February 18, 2007, https://www.nytimes.com/2007/02/18/magazine/18djdrama.t.html.

49 *"Man, when the rapper's rapping":* Thomas Morton, "Trap Mastermind: Coach K on Gucci Mane, Migos, and The Sound of Modern Atlanta," VICE, January 22, 2015, https://www.vice.com/en/article/ryzgb5/coach-k-interview-noisey-atlanta-gucci-mane-migos-qc.

49 *"Crack-baby beats":* Ibid.

50 *"buoyant and melodic, with light comedic flourishes":* Jon Caramanica, "Gucci Mane, Buff, Sober, out of the Pen and Ready to Flow," *New York Times,* July 20, 2016, https://www.nytimes.com/2016/07/24/arts/music/gucci-mane-everybody-looking-interview.html.

51 *Gucci was another hustler:* Gucci Mane and Neil Martinez-Belkin, *The Autobiography of Gucci Mane* (New York: Simon & Schuster, 2017), 87–93.

51 *promoted the song via unpaid performances:* Ibid., 129–30.

51 *the rapper had already fallen out:* Ibid., 130.

51 *a Gucci look-alike pretend to rap:* Ibid., 131.

51 *Gucci met Coach at Walter's:* Morton, "Trap Mastermind, Part Two."

52 *it immediately took off in clubs:* Benjamin Meadows-Ingram, "Hard to Kill: The Oral History of Gucci Mane," The FADER, October 25, 2017, https://www.thefader.com/2015/10/01/gucci-mane-oral-history-hard-to-kill.

52 *he turned down $100,000:* Mane and Martinez-Belkin, *The Autobiography of Gucci Mane,* 147.

52 *DJs start cutting off "Icy":* Ibid., 150.

52 *Gucci said he fired in self-defense:* "Murder Charges against Gucci Mane Dropped," *Billboard,* January 3, 2006, https://www.billboard.com/articles/news/60214/murder-charges-against-gucci-mane-dropped.

53 *left the Blazin' Saddles strip club:* Shalhoup, "BMF—Hip-Hop's Shadowy Empire—Part 1"; Mane and Neil Martinez-Belkin, *The Autobiography of Gucci Mane,* 157.

53 *Pookie had reportedly been close to signing:* Ibid.

54 *clubs that played house music were "Kevin's world":* Sanneh, "How Coach K Guides Atlanta's Hip-Hop Stars."

54 *referred to as "hipster-hop":* "Music Issue—Chasing the Cool," Creative Loafing, April 23, 2008, https://creativeloafing.com/content-196149-music-issue—-chasing-the-cool.

55 *bringing the world a man dubbed Future:* Yoh Phillips, "Brothers Turned Adversaries: The History of Future & Rocko," DJBooth, February 23, 2017, https://djbooth.net/features/2017-02-23-history-of-future-and-rocko.

55 *a much smaller, street-level deal:* Dan Rys, "Future Sued for $10 Million over Alleged Breach of Contract," *Billboard,* June 9, 2016, https://www.billboard.com/articles/columns/hip-hop/7401044/future-sued-10-million-breach-contract-rocko.

55 *"The money came from out the black market":* Sanneh, "How Coach K Guides Atlanta's Hip-Hop Stars."

56 *Antney convinced her unruly charge:* Mane and Martinez-Belkin, *The Autobiography of Gucci Mane*, 251.

56 *Coach checked with his friends and partners:* Morton, "Trap Mastermind, Part Two."

56 *the rapper would offer his new ally a bonus:* Ibid.

56 *"We'd go into the city":* Ibid.

56 *"He's really good at keeping the process moving":* Sanneh, "How Coach K Guides Atlanta's Hip-Hop Stars."

57 *Gucci had also violated his probation:* Mane and Martinez-Belkin, *The Autobiography of Gucci Mane*, 255–56.

57 *he was sentenced to a year in jail:* Ibid., 270.

57 *even renegotiating Gucci's deal with Warner:* Meadows-Ingram, "Hard to Kill."

57 *"He had a couple more stints in jail":* Ibid.

57 *allegedly pushing a woman:* Mane and Martinez-Belkin, *The Autobiography of Gucci Mane*, 315–16.

57 *"gangbangers, hipster kids, Blacks, Mexicans, whites":* Meadows-Ingram, "Hard to Kill."

58 *"Gucci was the epitome":* Ibid.

58 *Coach and Gucci would part ways:* Ibid.

58 *Gucci was fit, sober and seemingly rehabilitated*: Caramanica, "Gucci Mane, Buff, Sober, out of the Pen and Ready to Flow."

58 *"He's such a free spirit":* Thomas Morton, "Trap Mastermind: Coach K on Gucci Mane, Migos, and The Sound of Modern Atlanta," VICE, January 22, 2015, https://www.vice.com/en/article/ryzgb5/coach-k-interview-noisey-atlanta-gucci-mane-migos-qc.

59 *a total stranger to Mr. East Atlanta:* Mane and Martinez-Belkin, *The Autobiography of Gucci Mane*, 353.

59 *"There's some boys here":* Ibid., 355.

60 *"fake-ass jewelry":* Ibid.

60 *$45,000 in cash for the rappers:* Ibid.

60 *Gucci says he noticed the necklaces:* Ibid., 357.

60 *"some hippie commune shit":* Ibid., 359.

60 *"We locked in":* Meadows-Ingram, "Hard to Kill."

61 *"I remember hollering at some of the little hipster cats":* Morton, "Trap Mastermind."

61 *"I'm going after these boys":* Ibid.

Chapter Six

62 *Pierre Thomas sold his first crack rock:* "Lil Baby—PREACHERMAN Official Documentary," YouTube, Lil Baby Official 4PF, 2018, https://www.youtube.com/watch?v=VS0utODCw2E.

62 *delivered newspapers or sold chewing gum:* Zack Guzman and Mary Stevens, "Here's How Warren Buffett Hustled to Make $53,000 as a Teenager," CNBC, June 27, 2017, https://www.cnbc.com/2017/01/31/heres-how-warren-buffett-hustled-to-make-53000-as-a-teenager.html.

63 *Sometimes he and his brother had to go:* Kelefa Sanneh, "How Coach K Guides Atlanta's Hip-Hop Stars," *New Yorker*, December 11, 2017, https://www.newyorker.com/magazine/2017/12/18/how-coach-k-guides-atlantas-hip-hop-stars.

63 *Thirty off a hundred:* "Lil Baby—PREACHERMAN Official Documentary."

63 *You gotta go sell the ten crack rocks:* Ibid.

64 *Thomas was first locked up at age fourteen:* Ibid.

64 *"N——s go to jail every day out here":* Ibid.

64 *"Do you know what I had to do":* Sanneh, "How Coach K Guides Atlanta's Hip-Hop Stars."

64 *"hardworkin' money":* Leon Neyfakh, "Who Will Survive When Migos Meets Big Data?" The FADER, April 16, 2020, https://www.thefader.com/2014/11/04/cover-story-migos-definitively-better-than-the-beatles.

66 *P bought some buildings and even a daycare center:* Sanneh, "How Coach K Guides Atlanta's Hip-Hop Stars."

66 *But he also kept getting arrested:* "Case Records—Pierre Thomas," justice.fultoncountyga.gov, accessed November 14, 2021, https://justice.fultoncountyga.gov/PASupCrstCM/search.aspx?ID=100.

66 *"a real situation":* "Rap Radar: Quality Control," YouTube, Tidal, 2017, https://www.youtube.com/watch?v=h-YHj5LkCOI&list=PLTzbgTLLMTmc01ClgyZ-MTHH9wLiuXF7b&index=10.

66 *"I survived," P said:* Ibid.

67 *Metropolitan Parkway, formerly known as Stewart Avenue:* Bill Montgomery, "Evolution of a Road: It's Fact; Sleaze, Crime Yield to Hope, Gentrification," *Atlanta Journal-Constitution*, January 12, 2006, sec. Metro News, 1C.

67 *"the last of the redneck biker bars":* Scott Henry, "Cover Story: Dive in—The Beauty of Atlanta's Shabby Bars," Creative Loafing, March 18, 2004, https://creativeloafing.com/content-184800-cover-story-dive-in.

67 *a hot-pillow joint with the unofficial slogan:* Montgomery, "Evolution of a Road."

67 *By 1997, the street had a new name:* Ibid.

67 *"bricked up all the windows":* Sanneh, "How Coach K Guides Atlanta's Hip-Hop Stars."

68 *P spent about $300,000:* "Quality Control Music," Motown Records, accessed November 13, 2021, https://www.motownrecords.com/artists/quality-control-music/.

68 *P's first attempt at a record company:* Kate Bein, "Management Group Quality Control Is Aiming for Total Media Domination," Gotham, September 15, 2021, https://gothammag.com/quality-control-management-group-interview?utm_source=pocket_mylist.

68 *He considered renting out the studio:* "Rap Radar: Quality Control."

69 *"Man, help me get out these streets":* Ibid.

69 *the center of drug trafficking in the Southeast:* Andria Simmons, "Drug War Hits Home for Gwinnett Residents," *Atlanta Journal-Constitution,* December 26, 2009, https://www.ajc.com/news/local/drug-war-hits-home-for-gwinnett-residents/m5GiOLzJNQ93Shl9EAX2uI/.

70 *When Coach visited Migos at the Bando:* Neyfakh, "Who Will Survive When Migos Meets Big Data?"

70 *with a little computer propped precariously:* "Rap Radar: Quality Control."

Chapter Seven

71 *his team won only one of its ten games:* "Berkmar Football (2009) Schedule," Berkmar Patriots (Lilburn, GA), Varsity Football 2009–10, accessed November 13, 2021, https://www.maxpreps.com/high-schools/berkmar-patriots-(lilburn,ga)/football-fall-09/schedule.htm.

71 *its "spindly" quarterback ran a no-huddle:* Guy Curtright, "Berkmar 33, Meadowcreek 6," *Gwinnett Daily Post,* January 25, 2016, https://www.gwinnettdailypost.com/archive/berkmar-meadowcreek/article_597373ba-cc4c-5bea-bf59-3342dacf678e.html.

71 *liked to throw the ball deep:* Natalie Weiner, "Migos Hit-Maker Quavo Was Actually a Record-Setting High School Quarterback," Bleacher Report, October 3, 2017, https://

bleacherreport.com/articles/2703342-migos-hit-maker-quavo-was-actually-a-record-setting-high-school-quarterback.

71 *Quavious dropped out before graduating:* Simon Vozick-Levinson, "Migos: Young, Rich and Outrunning Trouble," *Rolling Stone,* June 24, 2015, https://www.rollingstone.com/music/music-news/migos-young-rich-and-outrunning-trouble-61658/.

71 *the pair grew up more like brothers:* Naomi Zeichner, "Interview: Migos," The FADER, July 18, 2013, https://www.thefader.com/2013/07/18/interview-migos.

71 *"She had a house full of n——s":* Jonah Weiner, "Migos' Wild World: One Night in the Studio with 'Bad and Boujee' Trio," *Rolling Stone,* February 8, 2017, https://www.rollingstone.com/music/music-features/migos-wild-world-one-night-in-the-studio-with-bad-and-boujee-trio-123122/.

71 *whose father died when he was a child:* Touré, "Migos: High Times and Heartache with the Three Kings of Hip-Hop," *Rolling Stone,* January 23, 2018, https://www.rollingstone.com/music/music-features/migos-high-times-and-heartache-with-the-three-kings-of-hip-hop-122262/.

71 *Rap was mostly Takeoff's thing at first:* Zeichner, "Interview: Migos."

72 *As a child, Kirsnick loved wrestling:* Weiner, "Migos' Wild World."

72 *the boys grew up buying albums:* Christina Lee, "Bando Brothers: Migos Makes Their Move," *Spin,* July 12, 2013, https://www.spin.com/2013/07/migos-interview-versace-drake-2013/.

75 *Offset and Quavo were arrested:* Weiner, "Migos' Wild World."

75 *Quavo said later that the arrest was "just for show":* Ibid.

75 *"We cliqued together, called ourselves Migos":* Ibid.

75 *first felony conviction for possessing stolen property*: *State of Georgia v. KIARI CEPHUS,* Case No. 11-B-06188-4 (Division Court, November 16, 2011).

75 *about $4,000 worth from the local Guitar Center:* Vozick-Levinson, "Migos: Young, Rich and Outrunning Trouble."

76 *But Coach knew that P could be slow:* "Rap Radar: Quality Control."

76 *"You need to ride to this shit":* Ibid.

77 *"Man, these n——s are crazy":* Ibid.

77 *"Bro, go get 'em,":* Ibid.

77 *"What's the history of groups?":* Neyfakh, "Who Will Survive When Migos Meets Big Data?"

77 *"If you give me ten years of your life":* Ibid.

77 *"The music was crazy":* Weiner, "Migos' Wild World."

78 *"It all came together":* Sanneh, "How Coach K Guides Atlanta's Hip-Hop Stars."

79 *P felt that Dirty Dollar had been a bad fit:* "Rap Radar: Quality Control."

80 *But Quavo had his heart set:* Lee, "Bando Brothers."

80 *was considering who he could invite:* "DJ Drama 'Atl Birthday Bash Weekend' Vlog Feat. Drake, Migos, Rich Homie Quan, J Cole & More," WorldStarHipHop, June 28, 2013, https://worldstarhiphop.com/videos/video.php?v=wshhFF6X9Fsp27aSTIJa.

81 *the first time that the group ever rehearsed:* Zeichner, "Interview: Migos."

81 *Quavo was eating wings:* Lee, "Bando Brothers."

81 *"We're looking at him like, You Drake!":* Zeichner, "Interview: Migos."

82 *Coach and P assumed that Drake:* "Rap Radar: Quality Control."

82 *Yung LA, the Atlanta rapper who showed it:* Aaron Dodson, "Superproducer Zaytoven's Gospel Truth about Trap Music: It Needs to Be 'Spontaneous and Unorthodox,'" The

Undefeated, April 27, 2018, https://theundefeated.com/features/zaytoven-trap-music-rap-red-bull-documentary/.

83 *In 2012, there was a glimmer of hope:* "Global Music Report 2021," IFPI, 6, accessed November 14, 2021, https://www.ifpi.org/wp-content/uploads/2020/03/GMR2021_STATE_OF_THE_INDUSTRY.pdf.

83 *But 2013 saw another dip:* Richard Smirke, "IFPI Music Report 2014: Global Recorded Music Revenues Fall 4%, Streaming and Subs Hit $1 Billion," *Billboard,* March 18, 2014, https://www.billboard.com/articles/business/5937645/ifpi-music-report-2014-global-recorded-music-revenues-fall-4.

84 *"I've been through it before":* Naomi Zeichner, "Interview: Offset of Migos," The FADER, October 15, 2013, https://www.thefader.com/2013/10/15/interview-offset-of-migos.

84 *"He can just jump right in":* Lee, "Bando Brothers."

84 *"I wanna go to the studio":* Zeichner, "Interview: Offset of Migos."

Chapter Eight

87 *Offset had basically given:* Charles Holmes, "The Remarkable Rise of Lil Baby," *Rolling Stone,* July 20, 2020, https://www.rollingstone.com/music/music-features/atlanta-rapper-lil-baby-bigger-picture-song-1027815/.

89 *Dominique's various looming offenses:* "Jones, Dominique—Find an Offender," Find an Offender, Georgia Department of Corrections, accessed November 15, 2021, http://www.dcor.state.ga.us/GDC/Offender/Query.

Chapter Nine

95 *Findling played baseball:* Lateef Mungin, "High-Powered in Court, on Field; Attorney Uses All His Skills to Help Team Get Scholarships," *Atlanta Journal-Constitution,* November 24, 2006.

95 *choked, stabbed and decapitated:* Bill Torpy, "Ga. Juries Rarely Buy Insanity; Nichols Team's Choice of Defense Used in Less than 1 Percent of Trials," *Atlanta Journal-Constitution,* September 28, 2008, Main edition, sec. Metro News.

96 *about one hundred liquor licenses existed:* Rick Maese, "Atlanta Was a Nightlife 'Mecca.' Then the Super Bowl Murders Involving Ray Lewis Happened," *Washington Post,* January 29, 2019, https://www.washingtonpost.com/sports/2019/01/28/atlanta-was-nightlife-mecca-then-super-bowl-murders-involving-ray-lewis-happened/.

96 *Baltimore Ravens star Ray Lewis was charged:* Ibid.

97 *One BMF associate caught:* Mara Shalhoup, *BMF: The Rise and Fall of Big Meech and the Black Mafia Family* (New York: St. Martin's Press, 2010), 56.

97 *witnesses from the parking lot weren't talking:* Ibid., 54.

97 *the cops received an anonymous call:* Ibid., 55.

97 *She identified the shooter as "Meechie":* Ibid., 56.

97 *Flenory denied his involvement:* Ibid., 57.

97 *"All over":* Ibid., 57.

97 *"just comical":* Ibid., 57; Mara Shalhoup, "BMF—Hip-Hop's Shadowy Empire—Part 3," Creative Loafing, December 20, 2006, https://creativeloafing.com/content-196221-bmf---hip-hop-s-shadowy-empire---part.

98 *known as the White House:* Shalhoup, *BMF,* 49–50.

98 *turn up a notebook:* Ibid., 59.

98 *the authorities had nothing:* Ibid., 64.

98 *opted to plead guilty:* "Black Mafia Family Members Sentenced to 30 Years," Drug Enforcement Administration, September 12, 2008, https://www.dea.gov/sites/default/files/divisions/det/2008/detroit091208ap.html.

98 *taking thirty years each in prison:* Shalhoup, *BMF*, 554–55.

98 *More than one hundred people with ties:* "Black Mafia Family Members Sentenced to 30 Years," Drug Enforcement Administration.

99 *he stormed into the lawyer's office:* Gucci Mane and Neil Martinez-Belkin, *The Autobiography of Gucci Mane* (New York: Simon & Schuster, 2017), 377.

100 *"I told them it wasn't mine":* Ibid.

101 *Migos had moved—at P and Coach K's urging:* Leon Neyfakh, "Who Will Survive When Migos Meets Big Data?" The FADER, April 16, 2020, https://www.thefader.com/2014/11/04/cover-story-migos-definitively-better-than-the-beatles.

101 *In an online Vice documentary:* "Meet the Migos. Noisey Atlanta," VICE, 2015, https://video.vice.com/en_us/video/meet-the-migos/55d1fc771ce00c683baee839?popular=1.

101 *forced to live at a separate apartment:* Neyfakh, "Who Will Survive When Migos Meets Big Data?"

102 *"I wanted five million dollars":* Ibid.

102 *$40,000 per show:* Ibid.

102 *"to import the essence of Atlanta to the world":* Ibid.

102 *neighbors complaining about a shooting*: Kelefa Sanneh, "How Coach K Guides Atlanta's Hip-Hop Stars," *New Yorker*, December 11, 2017, https://www.newyorker.com/magazine/2017/12/18/how-coach-k-guides-atlantas-hip-hop-stars.

102 *Coach and P spent a year and more than:* David Peisner, "Why the Rap Veterans behind Atlanta Indie Label Quality Control Music Are the Smartest Guys in Hip-Hop," *Billboard*, January 20, 2015, https://www.billboard.com/articles/news/6443743/quality-control-smartest-guys-in-hip-hop.

103 *Mercedes Sprinter van carrying the group:* Liane Morejon and Amanda Batchelor, "At Least 1 Member of Rap Group Migos Involved in Shooting on I-95," WPLG Local 10, March 29, 2014, https://www.local10.com/news/2014/03/29/at-least-1-member-of-rap-group-migos-involved-in-shooting-on-i-95/.

103 *News reports said a Migos bodyguard:* "Migos Shooting—Rap Group Involved in 'Scarface' Style Shootout in Miami," TMZ, June 17, 2020, https://www.tmz.com/2014/03/28/migos-rappers-shootout-miami-highway/.

103 *"advised and encouraged":* Lauren Gorla, "Migos Arrested Following Delayed Spring Concert," George-Anne Media Group, April 21, 2015, https://thegeorgeanne.com/8118/news/migos-arrested-following-delayed-spring-concert/.

103 *a forty-five-minute set for $33,000:* Holli Deal Saxon, "Migos Rapper Charged in Bulloch County Jail Fight," *Statesboro Herald*, May 4, 2015, https://www.statesboroherald.com/local/migos-rapper-charged-in-bulloch-county-jail-fight/.

104 *using the smell of marijuana as pretense:* "Members of Hip-Hop Group Migos Arrested after Georgia Show," Associated Press, April 20, 2015, https://apnews.com/1aa7804de7d34c6d9545ec23f32913ce/members-hip-hop-group-migos-arrested-after-georgia-show.

104 *Police discovered less than an ounce:* Holli Deal Saxon, "Migos Rapper Offset Freed after Sentencing," *Statesboro Herald*, December 4, 2015, https://www.statesboroherald.com/local/migos-rapper-offset-freed-after-sentencing/; "Exclusive: Migos Rapper Offset Speaks Out Following Release from Jail," WSB-TV Channel 2–Atlanta, December 14, 2015,

https://www.wsbtv.com/news/local/exclusive-migos-rapper-offset-speaks-out-following_npjfw/17248976/.

104 *Fifteen people present were arrested:* Lauren Gorla, "Migos Arrested Following Delayed Spring Concert," George-Anne Media Group, April 21, 2015, https://thegeorgeanne.com/8118/news/migos-arrested-following-delayed-spring-concert/.

104 *Offset was being accused of violating: State of Georgia v. Kiara Cephus* (Indictment no. SU 15-CR-254T, SU 15-CR-285T, December 3, 2015).

105 *Offset picked up another set of charges:* Holli Deal Saxon, "Migos Rapper Charged in Bulloch County Jail Fight," *Statesboro Herald*, May 4, 2015, https://www.statesboroherald.com/local/migos-rapper-charged-in-bulloch-county-jail-fight/.

105 *the prosecutors failed to link: State of Georgia v. Kiara Cephus.*

105 *"make some money off of this rapper":* Ibid.

105 *the days in jail started at 5 a.m.:* Zara Golden, "Offset Speaks on Jail Stint and His Return to Music," The FADER, January 18, 2016, https://www.thefader.com/2016/01/18/offset-migos-jail-interview.

105 *took plea deals:* "Exclusive: Migos Rapper Offset Speaks Out Following Release from Jail," WSB-TV Channel 2–Atlanta.

106 *he could be off again in two: State of Georgia v. Kiara Cephus.*

106 *"generically opportunistic and endearingly jolly":* Robert Christgau, "Future Is the Proof We Need That Money Doesn't Buy Happiness: Expert Witness with Robert Christgau," VICE, October 2, 2015, https://www.vice.com/en/article/r3z5vy/expert-witness-with-robert-christgau-future-young-thug.

107 *"I don't belong in there":* Golden, "Offset Speaks on Jail Stint and His Return to Music."

Chapter Ten

110 *"They ain't really inspiration":* "Lil Baby—PREACHERMAN Official Documentary," YouTube, Lil Baby Official 4PF, 2018, https://www.youtube.com/watch?v=VS0utODCw2E.

110 *like Yo Gotti and Starlito:* Christina Lee, "Lil Baby Isn't Leaving Anything to Chance," Complex, May 18, 2018, https://www.complex.com/music/2018/05/lil-baby-harder-than-ever-interview.

110 *"He looked at us, trying to get in where he fit in":* "Lil Baby—PREACHERMAN Official Documentary."

111 *"He hopped out dead fresh":* Ibid.

112 *"In two years, probably caught five cases":* Ibid.

113 *"I ain't trying to go through that":* Ibid.

116 *"Let Lil Baby go":* Brian Hiatt, interview with Coach K and Pee, *Rolling Stone Music Now*, podcast audio, August 27, 2019, https://podcasts.apple.com/us/podcast/how-migos-lil-baby-and-atlanta-hip-hop-conquered-the-world/id1078431985?i=1000447396981.

Chapter Eleven

120 *officers from Atlanta reportedly attended:* Gary Young, "US Police Put Hip-Hop under Surveillance," *The Guardian*, March 11, 2004, https://www.theguardian.com/world/2004/mar/11/arts.usa.

127 *leading to more than a year of litigation:* Brandon "Jinx" Jenkins, "Quality Control Talks the Rise of Migos & Lil Yachty, Leaking 'Bad & Boujee,' & Building an Empire," Com-

plex, February 2018, https://www.complex.com/music/quality-control-music-interview-2018-cover-story.

127 *"For eighteen months, we couldn't sell no product":* Ibid.

128 *A week after they reached a detente:* "Rap Radar: Quality Control," YouTube, Tidal, 2017, https://www.youtube.com/watch?v=h-YHj5LkCOI&list=PLTzbgTLLMTmc01ClgyZ-MTHH9wLiuXF7b&index=10.

129 *the day the song was finished:* "Tag Team (Cecil Glenn and Steve Gibson) on the Dan Patrick Show (Full Interview) 1/22/21. Dan Patrick Show," YouTube, 2021, https://www.youtube.com/watch?v=I1jjL6PP4l0&t=2s.

130 *in the early 1970s after a judge ruled:* Bill Torpy, "For This Lawyer, Naughty Is Nice," *Atlanta Journal-Constitution*, July 5, 2013, https://www.ajc.com/news/crime—law/for-this-lawyer-naughty-nice/dRI5ejnIZCBaZEM14IsUJJ/.

130 *barely more than a dozen such clubs remained:* Ben Brasch, "Atlanta's Legendary Strip Clubs Ready for Super Bowl Guests," *Atlanta Journal-Constitution*, January 31, 2019, https://www.ajc.com/news/local/atlanta-legendary-strip-clubs-ready-for-super-bowl-guests/csEbBMF1bMYhiIOPDy3NYN/.

132 *"My-gos," correcting the pronunciation:* "Donald Glover—Golden Globes 2017—Full Backstage Speech," YouTube, *Variety*, 2017, https://www.youtube.com/watch?v=-PxkbXeMe50.

Chapter Twelve

136 *"It happened so fast":* Brian Hiatt, interview with Coach K and Pee, *Rolling Stone Music Now*, podcast audio, August 27, 2019, https://podcasts.apple.com/us/podcast/how-migos-lil-baby-and-atlanta-hip-hop-conquered-the-world/id1078431985?i=1000447396981.

137 *He was also direct about his self-medicating:* "Lil Baby on Quitting $20K Per Month Lean Habit After Getting on Probation (Part 3)," YouTube, djvlad, 2017, https://www.youtube.com/watch?v=8mska4zHf94.

137 *sent Baby deeper toward opiates:* "Lil Baby: I Spend $4000 or $5000 A Week On Lean Addiction," YouTube, DJ Smallz Eyes 2, 2017, https://www.youtube.com/watch?v=kKD3Bc-avkY.

137 *"We're going to freeze on whatever":* Hiatt, interview with Coach K and Pee.

137 *"If I can just get Baby to listen to me":* Ibid.

137 *"Whatever you was doing in the streets":* Ibid.

138 *"Did somebody write these for you?":* Ibid.

139 *"Everything that define a street cat":* Ibid.

143 *moved to Atlanta from Tuskegee, Alabama:* Gail Mitchell, "How Ethiopia Habtemariam Became Universal Music Group's Most Powerful African-American Woman: 'I Love Proving People Wrong,'" *Billboard*, June 28, 2018, https://www.billboard.com/articles/news/magazine-feature/8463016/ethiopia-habtemariam-interview-billboard-cover-story-2018.

144 *the industry grew its revenue to $8.7 billion:* Joshua P. Friedlander, "News and Notes on 2017 Revenue Statistics," RIAA, 2018, https://www.riaa.com/wp-content/uploads/2021/02/2020-Year-End-Music-Industry-Revenue-Report.pdf.

144 *dethroning rock in 2017 for the first time:* Hugh McIntyre, "Report: Hip-Hop/R&B Is the Dominant Genre in the U.S. for the First Time," *Forbes*, July 17, 2017, https://www.forbes.com/sites/hughmcintyre/2017/07/17/hip-hoprb-has-now-become-the-dominant-genre-in-the-u-s-for-the-first-time/?sh=55447f615383.

144 *accounting for more than 30 percent:* Keith Caulfield, "Lil Baby's 'My Turn' Is MRC Data's Top Album of 2020, Roddy Ricch's 'the Box' Most-Streamed Song," *Billboard,* January 7, 2021, https://www.billboard.com/articles/business/chart-beat/9508037/mrc-data-2020-recap/.

145 *Greatness was shot and killed at a Waffle House:* WWL staff, "Rapper 'Young Greatness' Fatally Shot Outside New Orleans Waffle House," wwltv.com, October 30, 2018, https://www.wwltv.com/article/news/crime/rapper-young-greatness-fatally-shot-outside-new-orleans-waffle-house/289-609057238.

146 *he and a friend were shopping at the hat store Lids:* Adam Sacasa, "Two Men Accused of Having Dozens of Fake Credit Cards at Mall in Palm Beach Gardens," *South Florida Sun-Sentinel,* June 15, 2018, https://www.sun-sentinel.com/local/palm-beach/fl-palm-beach-gardens-mall-fraud-20150901-story.html.

147 *"I hadn't talked to Shannon in a minute":* Hiatt, interview with Coach K and Pee.

148 *"I like weird":* Ibid.

148 *"I'm Yachty man I'm 18 and i rap":* Kelefa Sanneh, "How Coach K Guides Atlanta's Hip-Hop Stars," *New Yorker,* December 11, 2017, https://www.newyorker.com/magazine/2017/12/18/how-coach-k-guides-atlantas-hip-hop-stars.

149 *"It was a pivotal time to do that":* "Quality Control Music," Motown Records, accessed November 13, 2021, https://www.motownrecords.com/artists/quality-control-music/.

150 *"Brands last longer than songs":* "Rap Radar: Quality Control," YouTube, Tidal, 2017, https://www.youtube.com/watch?v=h-YHj5LkCOI&list=PLTzbgTLLMTmc01ClgyZ-MTHH9wLiuXF7b&index=10.

Chapter Thirteen

158 *"it taught me to really be humble":* "Are Lil Reek and Young Thug Biologically Related? Find Out Here," YouTube, DJ Smallz Eyes 2, 2018, https://www.youtube.com/watch?v=dkyHDfMYNes.

162 *"unlawfully present United Kingdom national":* J. D. Capelouto, "ICE Arrests Rapper 21 Savage, Says He Is Actually British and Overstayed Visa," *Atlanta Journal-Constitution,* February 5, 2019, https://www.ajc.com/news/breaking-ice-arrests-rapper-savage-says-actually-british-and-overstayed-visa/HgORJxcJCckHjlMdzlqwKM/ .

162 *"I'm here to try to build something":* Nick Sylvester, "Meet Brodinski, the French Producer Finding New Life in Atlanta Rap," The FADER, June 19, 2018, https://www.thefader.com/2017/01/19/brodinski-gen-f-interview.

162 *"I didn't know who the hell Brodinski was":* "Lil Reek Breaks Down New 'Slime Bizness' EP; Talks Cleveland Ave, Brodinski, Lil Keed & More," YouTube, Dirty Glove Bastard, 2019, https://www.youtube.com/watch?v=p6vmslZ6_Xw.

163 *"used to come through the hood":* Ibid.

163 *"I'm like, 'Shit, boy'":* "Are Lil Reek and Young Thug Biologically Related? Find Out Here."

163 *"I ain't finna go down there":* "Lil Reek Breaks Down New 'Slime Bizness' EP; Talks Cleveland Ave, Brodinski, Lil Keed & More."

163 *Reek had even taken some French in school:* Reed Jackson, "Meet Lil Reek, the Teenage Rapper Punching above His Weight," Pitchfork, August 15, 2018, https://pitchfork.com/features/rising/meet-lil-reek-the-teenage-rapper-punching-above-his-weight/.

163 *Drug Money described the music as:* Max Mertens, "Hear Bromance Records and Drug Money USA's Venomous New Mixtape with Atlanta Rap Crew Young Slime Life," VICE, November 22, 2016, https://www.vice.com/en/article/4x8bqj/slime-life-mixtape.

163 *"He developed my sound":* "Lil Reek Breaks Down New 'Slime Bizness' EP; Talks Cleveland Ave, Brodinski, Lil Keed & More."

165 *"I was out here going with the flow":* "Are Lil Reek and Young Thug Biologically Related? Find Out Here."

165 *"I wasn't fucking with that working-no-job":* Ibid.

165 *"I'm the boss":* Ibid.

166 *"I just felt like I was worth a million":* "Lil Reek Breaks Down New 'Slime Bizness' EP; Talks Cleveland Ave, Brodinski, Lil Keed & More."

Chapter Fourteen

172 *A month earlier, the couple had gotten legally married:* "Cardi B and Offset Secretly Married Last Year," TMZ, May 14, 2019, https://www.tmz.com/2018/06/25/cardi-b-offset-married-marriage-license-wife/.

175 *Billions of dollars had recently been pledged:* J. Scott Trubey, "Atlanta Mayor, CIM Alter Gulch Financing Deal," *Atlanta Journal-Constitution,* October 15, 2018, https://www.ajc.com/news/local-govt—politics/mayor-bottoms-cim-alter-gulch-financing-deal/KSfK61gLqgWehSOHjZmnmI/.

178 *Bank spent about a week straight pestering Marlo:* "Lil Marlo Talks About Leaving the Streets, Encouraging Lil Baby to Rap, Spending $100k in a Day," YouTube, Dirty Glove Bastard, 2019, https://www.youtube.com/watch?v=9wVg_w8YW94.

178 *"If he would've said, Bro":* Ibid.

Chapter Fifteen

186 *With most "sales" now coming in streams:* Joshua P. Friedlander, "News and Notes on 2017 Revenue Statistics," RIAA, 2018, https://www.riaa.com/wp-content/uploads/2021/02/2020-Year-End-Music-Industry-Revenue-Report.pdf.

186 *In 2017, the three major record companies signed 658 acts:* Larry S. Miller, "Same Heart, New Beat: How Record Labels Amplify Talent in the Modern Music Marketplace," NYU Steinhardt School of Culture, Education, and Human Development, Music Business Program, https://s3.amazonaws.com/cache.transmissionmedia.com/musonomics/MusonomicsModernLabelReport.pdf.

187 *Spotify was seeing 20,000 tracks uploaded:* G. C. Stein, "Highlights from Spotify Investor Day (March 2018)," Streaming Machinery, July 20, 2020, https://streamingmachinery.wordpress.com/2020/07/19/highlights-from-spotify-investor-day-march-2018/.

187 *By 2020, only about 870 artists:* Ashley Carman, "Spotify Says over 13,000 Artists' Catalogs Earned at Least $50k in Royalties Last Year," The Verge, March 18, 2021, https://www.theverge.com/2021/3/18/22336087/spotify-loud-clear-website-launch-pay-artists-streaming-royalities.

193 *a deal worth more than $3 million:* "Juice Wrld Signs with Interscope," *Billboard,* accessed November 17, 2021, https://www.billboard.com/articles/columns/hip-hop/8244598/juice-wrld-signs-interscope-3-million-joint-venture.

Chapter Sixteen

196 *a street rebranded in the late nineties:* Ernie Suggs, "Atlanta Street Fight: Who Was Donald Lee Hollowell?" *Atlanta Journal-Constitution,* October 4, 2016, https://www.ajc.com/news/local/atlanta-street-fight-who-was-donald-lee-hollowell/Im7bpTT8q8DoANz13dnJYP/.

197 *Bowen Homes projects were constructed in 1964:* "Bowen Homes Records," Atlanta Housing,

2015, https://www.atlantahousing.org/wp-content/uploads/2019/05/2015.0017-Bowen-Homes-records.pdf.

198 *Bowen Homes was made up of 650 units:* Ibid.; Renee Lewis Glover, "Bowen Homes Targeted for Demolition," Bizjournals.com, June 23, 2008, https://www.bizjournals.com/atlanta/stories/2008/06/23/daily12.html.

198 *once stalked by an indiscriminate serial killer:* Rodney Carmichael, "Straight Outta Stankonia—Bowen Homes and 'The Atlanta Model,'" Creative Loafing, April 10, 2014, https://creativeloafing.com/content-232561-straight-outta-stankonia—-bowen-homes-and-the-atlanta.

198 *168 violent crimes in seven months:* Lewis Glover, "Bowen Homes Targeted for Demolition."

198 *Atlanta had the highest number of public housing residents:* Julie B. Hairston and Michael Hinkelman, "Good Money after Bad," *Atlanta Business Chronicle*, December 16, 1994.

198 *Some 93 percent of the families:* Ibid.

198 *constructed the nation's first prominent projects:* "Techwood-Clark Howell Homes and Centennial Place Records," Atlanta Housing, 2014, https://www.atlantahousing.org/wp-content/uploads/2021/05/Techwood-Clark-Howell-Homes-and-Centennial-Place-records.pdf.

199 *30 percent of their adjusted gross income in rent:* Hairston and Hinkelman, "Good Money after Bad"; Michelle E. Shaw, "Bulldozers Begin Razing Bowen Homes Housing Project," *Atlanta Journal-Constitution,* June 9, 2009, https://www.ajc.com/news/local/bulldozers-begin-razing-bowen-homes-housing-project/QjEyV2jJqNlLdu4iWDVgBL/.

199 *"warehousing families in concentrated poverty":* Shaw, "Bulldozers Begin Razing Bowen Homes Housing Project."

199 *typically relocating within three miles:* Gwynedd Stuart, "Life after the Projects," Creative Loafing, August 25, 2011, https://creativeloafing.com/content-170626-life-after-the-projects.

199 *Atlanta had one of the highest eviction rates:* Brian Goldstone, "The New American Homeless," *New Republic,* August 21, 2019, https://newrepublic.com/article/154618/new-american-homeless-housing-insecurity-richest-cities.

199 *the city's stock of low-income housing declined:* Ibid.

199 *Atlanta's income inequality among the worst:* Ibid.

199 *Eighty-five percent of the local unhoused:* Ibid.

199 *"I know how to survive in the jungle":* "Lil Marlo Talks About Leaving the Streets, Encouraging Lil Baby to Rap, Spending $100k in a Day," YouTube, Dirty Glove Bastard, 2019, https://www.youtube.com/watch?v=9wVg_w8YW94.

202 *consisted of only six officers:* Steve Visser and Bill Torpy, "Specific Numbers on Gangs Sketchy," *Atlanta Journal-Constitution,* August 21, 2009, https://www.ajc.com/news/local/specific-numbers-gangs-sketchy/eGjemSnssWRAh1JvGxO8JI/.

202 *when an influx of refugees from Louisiana:* Gwynedd Stuart, "Cover Story: Gang Mentality," Creative Loafing, June 17, 2010, https://creativeloafing.com/content-185559-Cover-Story%3A-Gang-mentality.

203 *"get them off the street":* Visser and Torpy, "Specific Numbers on Gangs Sketchy."

203 *more parochial groups "hybrid" gangs*: "State Gang Task Force Leader Reflects on First Month on the Job," CBS46 News Atlanta, May 15, 2019, https://www.cbs46.com/news/state-gang-task-force-leader-reflects-on-first-month-on-the-job/article_3316bf26-775f-11e9-8dad-b3aa3218c2b2.html.

204 *GoodFellas, also known as GF or the Mobb: State of Georgia v. Eric Steven Kendrick* (Indictment no. 19SC170379 February 19, 2019).

204 *"This isn't Iraq. This isn't Afghanistan":* Ibid.

204 *seizing more than twenty guns:* Ibid.

204 *raze the twenty-eight-building Sierra Ridge:* Jaclyn Schultz, "'Crime-Ridden' Apartments Ordered Torn Down," FOX 5 Atlanta, May 2, 2018, https://www.fox5atlanta.com/news/crime-ridden-apartments-ordered-torn-down.

205 *quadrupling its staff to twenty-six officers:* Visser and Torpy, "Specific Numbers on Gangs Sketchy."

205 *somewhere between fifty and one hundred: State of Georgia v. Eric Steven Kendrick.*

205 *"From a law-enforcement standpoint":* Ibid.

206 *She died when he was seventeen:* S. Samuel, "'What [50 Cent] Is to New York, I Am to Atlanta,'" SOHH.com, July 28, 2011, https://www.sohh.com/what-50-cent-is-to-new-york-i-am-to-atlanta/.

210 *the FBI's High Intensity Drug Trafficking task force:* Lynn Zinser, "Jamal Lewis Charged in Drug Case," *New York Times,* February 26, 2004, https://www.nytimes.com/2004/02/26/sports/pro-football-jamal-lewis-charged-in-drug-case.html.

210 *Lo was facing twenty to forty years on three different cases:* CNN Wire, "Rapper Shawty Lo Dead at 40," WTVR, September 21, 2016, https://www.wtvr.com/2016/09/21/shawty-lo-dead-at-40/.

212 *Lo had left the strip club around 2 a.m.:* Lauren Foreman, "Atlanta Rapper Shawty Lo Killed in Fiery Crash," *Atlanta Journal-Constitution,* September 21, 2016, https://www.ajc.com/news/local/atlanta-rapper-shawty-killed-fiery-crash/Q2JV2yaXiAtWBG1IpxGcKN/.

213 *police blocked off Bankhead as cars blared:* Rodney Carmichael, "ATLieNation," Creative Loafing, October 5, 2016, https://creativeloafing.com/content-267264-atlienation.

Chapter Seventeen

216 *Baby's sister Deja had told of the time:* "Lil Baby—PREACHERMAN Official Documentary," YouTube, Lil Baby Official 4PF, 2018, https://www.youtube.com/watch?v=VS0utODCw2E.

216 *Drake let the young rapper know:* "How Lil Baby Connected with Drake on 'Yes Indeed' & His Upcoming Project with Gunna," YouTube, Power 106 Los Angeles, 2018, https://www.youtube.com/watch?v=4zPxmlW4-8A.

219 XXL *released its annual Freshman Class issue:* "XXL 2018 Freshman Class Revealed," XXL Mag, June 12, 2018, https://www.xxlmag.com/2018-xxl-freshman-cover/.

219 *forcing Baby to visit the XXL offices:* Michael Saponara, "Lil Baby Talks Crafting His Debut Album 'Harder than Ever,' Working with Drake & His Decision to Quit Lean," *Billboard,* May 18, 2018, https://www.billboard.com/music/rb-hip-hop/lil-baby-interview-harder-than-ever-album-drake-8456473/.

Chapter Eighteen

224 *"I ain't tripping":* "Lil Marlo Talks About Leaving the Streets, Encouraging Lil Baby to Rap, Spending $100k in a Day," YouTube, Dirty Glove Bastard, 2019, https://www.youtube.com/watch?v=9wVg_w8YW94.

225 *The twenty-year-old born Christopher Copeland: State of Georgia v. Eric Steven Kendrick* (Indictment no. 19SC170379, February 19, 2019).

229 *An ancient spiritual system:* Jonathan M. Pitts, "West African Religions Are on the Rise in Maryland as Practitioners Connect with Roots," *Washington Post,* April 6, 2019, https://www.washingtonpost.com/religion/west-african-religions-are-on-the-rise-in-maryland-as-practitioners-connect-with-roots/2019/04/06/024827a0-562f-11e9-9136-f8e636f1f6df_story.html.

Chapter Nineteen

238 *"I'm just trying to handle my business":* Reed Jackson, "Meet Lil Reek, the Teenage Rapper Punching above His Weight," Pitchfork, August 15, 2018, https://pitchfork.com/features/rising/meet-lil-reek-the-teenage-rapper-punching-above-his-weight/.

Chapter Twenty

244 *"If* Culture *marked the very peak":* Meaghan Garvey, "Migos: Culture II," Pitchfork, January 30, 2018, https://pitchfork.com/reviews/albums/migos-culture-ii/.

244 *"If they really want to take their time":* Eric Skelton, "In Search of Exotic New Sounds: How DJ Durel and Quavo Constructed 'Culture II,'" Complex, February 1, 2018, https://www.complex.com/pigeons-and-planes/2018/02/dj-durel-interview-migos-culture-ii.

246 *"It's all about market share":* Eric Diep, "'It's All about Market Share': Behind Quality Control's Plan to Dominate the 4th Quarter," Complex, November 15, 2018, https://www.complex.com/music/2018/11/quality-control-plan-dominate-fourth-quarter-coach-k-pee-interview.

246 *at least four women accused TI:* Melena Ryzik and Joe Coscarelli, "Lawyer Seeks Criminal Investigation of T.I. and Tiny on Behalf of Multiple Women," *New York Times,* February 28, 2021, https://www.nytimes.com/2021/02/28/arts/music/ti-tiny-allegations-sexual-assault.html.

247 *could have been "misinterpreted":* Joe Coscarelli and Melena Ryzik, "Music Mogul Russell Simmons Is Accused of Rape by 3 Women," *New York Times,* December 13, 2017, https://www.nytimes.com/2017/12/13/arts/music/russell-simmons-rape.html.

247 *P said he first heard about the group:* Meaghan Garvey, "City Girls Open Up about JT's Jail Time—and Why They're Ready to Conquer 2020," *Billboard,* January 10, 2020, https://www.billboard.com/music/rb-hip-hop/city-girls-billboard-cover-story-interview-2020-8547638/.

248 *banking two albums' worth of songs:* Ibid.

249 *"conceived, arranged and orchestrated Cardi B's rise": Worldstar Marketing Group, Inc., KSR : Group, LLC, and Klenord Raphael, : : 18-cv- Plaintiffs, : : Complaint v. : : Demand for Jury Trial Belcalis Almanzar p/k/a Cardi B, : Patientce Foster, Quality Control : Management, LLC, Kevin "Coach K" Lee, : and Pierre "Pee" Thomas, :* (United States District Court for the Southern District of New York, April 26, 2018).

250 *Cardi B countersued Shaft for $30 million:* Ryan Naumann, "Cardi B Now Demanding $30 Million from Ex-Manager Shaft in Nasty Court Battle," Yahoo!, June 25, 2019, https://www.yahoo.com/now/cardi-b-now-demanding-30-160205365.html.

255 *pulled over in the rapper's:* "Migos' Offset Arrested on Felony Gun Charges in Clayton County," CBS Atlanta, July 23, 2018, https://atlanta.cbslocal.com/2018/07/23/migos-offset-arrested-on-felony-gun-charges-in-clayton-county/; Gil Kaufman, "Offset Lawyer Calls Gun & Drug Charges 'Utter Ridiculousness,' 'an Embarrassment,'" *Billboard,* August 15, 2018, https://www.billboard.com/pro/offset-lawyer-gun-drug-charges-interview/; Zachary Hansen, "Charges against Migos Rapper Offset Dropped in Clayton County Due to Federal Probe," *Atlanta Journal-Constitution,* July 9, 2019, https://www.ajc.com/news

/crime—law/charges-against-migos-rapper-offset-dropped-clayton-county-due-federal-probe/DN8J0u87QirIyWCcRor73I/.

255 *"driving while Black":* Kaufman, "Offset Lawyer Calls Gun & Drug Charges 'Utter Ridiculousness,' 'an Embarrassment.'"

256 *"There's a tremendous amount of money":* Natelege Whaley, "Meet Drew Findling, the Go-to Lawyer for Some of Atlanta's Biggest Rappers," Mic, October 5, 2018, https://www.mic.com/articles/191299/drew-findling-atlanta-lawyer-gucci-mane-waka-flocka-flame.

256 *"much larger" "ongoing federal investigation" :* Hansen, "Charges against Migos Rapper Offset Dropped in Clayton County Due to Federal Probe."

257 *selling more than half a million tickets:* "Pollstar: 2018 Year End Top 200 North American Tours," Pollstar, 2018, https://www.pollstar.com/Chart/2018/12/2018YearEndTop200NorthAmericanTours_698.pdf.

260 *"It wasn't anyone's team":* Michael Saponara, "Offset on Genies Partnership, Plans for Keeping His Solo Album Feature-Free & Dominating 2018: 'I Been Eating N-as,'" *Billboard,* November 20, 2018, https://www.billboard.com/music/rb-hip-hop/offset-solo-album-migos-cardi-b-genies-interview-8485866/.

Chapter Twenty-One

266 *"serious like a motherfucker now":* "LIL MARLO: REP MY CITY [ATLANTA SEASON 1] EPISODE 4," YouTube, Hood Affairs, 2019, https://www.youtube.com/watch?v=Dlx7aqpKzjQ.

266 *"Me and Lil Baby call him Pop":* Ibid.

266 *"Streets like crack to me":* Ibid.

270 *"chain gang"—was "for suckers":* "Lil Marlo Talks About Leaving the Streets, Encouraging Lil Baby to Rap, Spending $100k in a Day," YouTube, Dirty Glove Bastard, 2019, https://www.youtube.com/watch?v=9wVg_w8YW94.

271 *"Hell nah, I ain't going":* Ibid.

275 *a splurge he'd made the very day:* "Lil Baby—Global," verified annotation, Genius, accessed November 18, 2021, https://genius.com/15964637.

275 *"I got a couple of homies rapping":* Ibid.

275 *"I let them know what we doing":* Ibid.

278 *wanted on twenty-four simultaneous warrants:* "Police Say Man Is Responsible for 100+ Car Break-Ins," WSB-TV Channel 2–Atlanta, July 25, 2014, https://www.wsbtv.com/news/local/police-say-man-responsible-100-car-break-ins/137490778/.

278 *"Baby made a way for everybody":* Kyle Kramer, "Lil Baby Is Destined for Rap Greatness," VICE, May 16, 2018, https://www.vice.com/en/article/9k8yy3/lil-baby-harder-than-ever-interview-2018.

278 *G-Five was taken back into custody:* Neighbor Staff, "Brookhaven Police Arrest Two More Suspects in Double Shooting," MDJOnline.com, December 11, 2018, https://www.mdjonline.com/neighbor_newspapers/brookhaven-police-arrest-two-more-suspects-in-double-shooting/article_992c5692-fd96-11e8-ab82-fbf88b374226.html.

280 *Baby was pulled over:* "Lil Baby Arrested, Accused of Reckless Driving in a Corvette," Associated Press, February 8, 2019, https://apnews.com/1894bdf52787462a8f54da1eef4a96a2.

Chapter Twenty-Two

283 *The single had actually been sitting around:* "Lil Marlo Talks About Leaving the Streets, Encouraging Lil Baby to Rap, Spending $100k in a Day," YouTube, Dirty Glove Bastard, 2019, https://www.youtube.com/watch?v=9wVg_w8YW94.

283 *"Boy, you been had this?":* Ibid.

283 *"You ain't my daddy":* Ibid.

284 *"Whose song is this?":* Ibid.

Chapter Twenty-Three

291 *"odd, pre-pubescent but also slightly raspy":* Alphonse Pierre, "Lil Reek: The Graduation," Pitchfork, July 5, 2018, https://pitchfork.com/reviews/albums/lil-reek-the-graduation/.

Chapter Twenty-Four

300 *the real estate equivalent of a Big Gulp:* Bill Torpy, "Bill Torpy at Large: Got a Beef with the McMansion Next Door?" *Atlanta Journal-Constitution,* January 10, 2017, https://www.ajc.com/news/local/bill-torpy-large-got-beef-with-the-mcmansion-next-door/9IlFghWYOJalRdPuRAKqwJ/.

303 *P was engaged in a brutal custody battle: Pierre Thomas v. Tylira Mercer* (Civil Action File No. 2019CV321645 May 29, 2019).

303 *"consistently demonstrated physically violent":* Ibid.

303 *Galore sought at least $15 million in damages:* Ibid.

305 *"If I would have stayed there":* Josh Eells, "Lil Nas X: Inside the Rise of a Hip-Hop Cowboy," *Rolling Stone,* May 20, 2019, https://www.rollingstone.com/music/music-features/lil-nas-x-old-town-road-interview-new-album-836393/.

305 *recorded in under an hour:* "Lil Nas X Takes Gayle King inside the Studio Where He Recorded 'Old Town Road,'" CBS News, September 30, 2019, https://www.cbsnews.com/news/lil-nas-x-inside-the-recording-studio-where-rapper-made-old-town-road/.

307 *"an attempt at crowd control":* Sheldon Pearce, "Various Artists: Control the Streets, Volume 2," Pitchfork, August 21, 2019, https://pitchfork.com/reviews/albums/various-artists-control-the-streets-volume-2/.

308 *five or six ounces of prescription opioid:* "Lil Baby on Kicking Lean, Falling Into the Rap Game, His Debut Album + More," YouTube, Breakfast Club Power 105.1 FM, 2018, https://www.youtube.com/watch?v=9s0KmG1a5ds&t=3s.

308 *"That shit started fucking with me":* Ibid.

310 *Living in "dental professional shortage areas":* "Dentists," County Health Rankings & Roadmaps, accessed November 18, 2021, https://www.countyhealthrankings.org/explore-health-rankings/measures-data-sources/county-health-rankings-model/health-factors/clinical-care/access-to-care/dentists.

310 *one-third of white children:* Mary Otto, *Teeth: The Untold Story of Beauty, Inequality, and the Struggle for Oral Health in America* (New York: New Press, 2017).

314 *"I'd rather not have privacy":* "Lil Baby Speaks on Fatherhood, Young Thug as a Mentor, New Music + More," YouTube, Breakfast Club Power 105.1 FM, 2020, https://www.youtube.com/watch?v=HtaTL_qQo8c.

Chapter Twenty-Five

315 *a "legal stunner":* Joshua Sharpe, "A Tossed Murder Case Leads to Discord in DeKalb," *Atlanta Journal-Constitution,* January 15, 2020, https://www.ajc.com/news/local/legal-stunner-dekalb-judge-tosses-murder-case-after-witnesses-don-show/xv2koaBNudnsVUC3DVMlzJ/.

315 *Surveillance footage, blasted all over the local news:* "Murder Charges Dropped against Man in Jail for More Than a Year," WSB-TV Channel 2–Atlanta, January 23, 2020, https://www.wsbtv.com/news/local/dekalb-county/murder-charges-dropped-against-man-jail-more-than-year/BREVIOWXY5DCTMUOZOFOBI44RE/.

315 *A third man—initially charged with felony:* Sharpe, "A Tossed Murder Case Leads to Discord in DeKalb."

316 *"If there are consequences to the community": State of Georgia v. Quintez Griffin and Stephen McAllister* (Criminal Indictment No. 19CR1559-4, January 10, 2020).

316 *"It wasn't no technicality":* "Murder Charges Dropped against Man in Jail for More than a Year," WSB-TV Channel 2–Atlanta.

316 *"seemingly unwinnable cases":* Steel law firm, accessed November 18, 2021, https://thesteellawfirm.com/brian.html.

316 *neighboring Fulton County Jail:* "Murder Charges Dropped against Man in Jail for More Than a Year," WSB-TV Channel 2–Atlanta.

317 *"There is a killer walking around":* Ibid.

317 *"This judge made a decision":* Portia Bruner, "Defense Attorney Says Judge Was in the Right Acquitting 2 Murder Suspects," FOX 5 Atlanta, January 11, 2020, https://www.fox5atlanta.com/news/defense-attorney-says-judge-was-in-the-right-by-acquitting-2-murder-suspects.

322 *"It hurt, but I'm used to it":* "Marlo: 'I'm Immune To Death,' Soakin Wet, New Mixtape and More," YouTube, B High Atl, 2019, https://www.youtube.com/watch?v=Ag6o1Bowdmk&list=LL1x3dT5BogTFnTAFGnsJ1Lg&index=197.

322 *"It's like I'm immune to losing":* Ibid.

Chapter Twenty-Six

329 *Baby and his friends were heading out:* Donesha Aldridge, "'We Lost a Good Person': Friends Honor Man Killed in Tragic Christmas Day Crash Involving Fire Truck, ATV," 11Alive.com, December 30, 2019, https://www.11alive.com/article/news/local/sadiki-madden-vigil/85-978b9f29-2bac-47f0-92ee-b713981a4953.

331 *twenty people serving life sentences:* Charles Holmes, "The Remarkable Rise of Lil Baby," *Rolling Stone,* July 20, 2020, https://www.rollingstone.com/music/music-features/atlanta-rapper-lil-baby-bigger-picture-song-1027815/.

331 *$400 million redevelopment:* Raisa Habersham, "New Renderings Released in Mall West End Redevelopment," *Atlanta Journal-Constitution,* January 27, 2020, https://www.ajc.com/news/local/new-renderings-released-mall-west-end-redevelopment/DTRvSQc4PU5BCWviUjBEEM/.

334 *Lil Wayne . . . dubbed Baby his favorite rapper:* "Lil Wayne | Ep 24 | ALL THE SMOKE Full Episode," YouTube, SHOWTIME Basketball, 2020.

335 *"one of the easiest songs I ever recorded":* Shirley Ju, "Voice of Impact: Hitmaker Lil Baby Blends Sound and Vision for 'Bigger Picture,'" *Variety,* December 3, 2020, https://variety.com/2020/music/news/lil-baby-hitmakers-voice-of-impact-award-1234845059/.

335 *"I wanted to use a specific situation":* Jason Lipshutz, "Lil Baby Wanted His 'Bigger Picture' Grammys Performance to Remind Us That America Hasn't Been Fixed," *Billboard,* March 16, 2021, https://www.billboard.com/music/rb-hip-hop/lil-baby-grammys-performance-interview-bigger-picture-9541642/.

335 *"a time capsule for everything the city is":* Charles Holmes, "Lil Baby Always Had a Lot to Say—You Just Weren't Paying Attention," *Rolling Stone,* June 12, 2020, https://www.rollingstone.com/music/music-news/lil-baby-the-bigger-picture-1014126/.

335 *"It's a never-ending saga":* Lipshutz, "Lil Baby Wanted His 'Bigger Picture' Grammys Performance to Remind Us That America Hasn't Been Fixed."

Chapter Twenty-Seven

337 *The spree started around 3:30 a.m.:* "2 Killed after Suspects Crash Head-on into Another Car during Police Chase: Officials," 11Alive.com, December 4, 2019, https://www.11alive.com/article/news/local/campbellton-road-lee-street-dill-avenue-deadly-crash/85-fb6cec55-08f1-4a55-a5a7-5787e055e177; Michael King, "Teen Charged with Murder in Deadly Police Chase to Face Judge," 11Alive.com, December 6, 2019, https://www.11alive.com/article/news/crime/teen-charged-in-deadly-police-chase-to-face-judge/85-9b3d5534-4332-4f52-a740-9ad5a2d5aef9.

337 *the pair robbed another man: The State of Georgia v. Marguell Scott a.k.a "Cracker," Emmanuel Fambro* (Indictment No. 19CP188309, December 22, 2020).

337 *a jury had found him not guilty of murder:* Shaddi Abusaid, "2 Charged with Murder after Chase, Crash in SW Atlanta," *Atlanta Journal-Constitution,* December 6, 2019, https://www.ajc.com/news/crime—law/new-details-charged-with-murder-after-chase-crash-atlanta/vo9BhrB9k0VayhacMxx2WJ/.

Chapter Twenty-Eight

345 *disproportionately affecting Black and Latino people:* Richard A. Oppel, Robert Gebeloff, K. K. Rebecca, Will Wright, and Mitch Smith, "The Fullest Look Yet at the Racial Inequity of Coronavirus," *New York Times,* July 5, 2020, https://www.nytimes.com/interactive/2020/07/05/us/coronavirus-latinos-african-americans-cdc-data.html.

349 *fifty homicides only halfway through the year:* Ryan Young, Melissa Alonso, and Amir Vera, "Atlanta Homicides Are the Highest They've Been in 30 Years, Police Say," CNN, November 25, 2020, https://www.cnn.com/2020/11/25/us/atlanta-homicide-increase-2020/index.html.

Chapter Twenty-Nine

354 *"We'd go a week or two without talking":* Jewel Wicker, "Lil Baby on Success, Death, and the D.A. Who Locked Him Away—and Then Suddenly Sought His Endorsement," *GQ,* September 28, 2020, https://www.gq.com/story/lil-baby-success-death-and-the-da.

357 *Ralo had been arrested:* Adrianne Haney, "'He Has a Good Heart': Friends Says [*sic*] of Atlanta Rapper Ralo Arrested on Conspiracy Charges," 11Alive.com, April 19, 2018, https://www.11alive.com/article/news/crime/atalanta-rapper-ralo-arrested-on-conspiracy-charges/85-542785028; Raisa Habersham, "Officials: Rapper Flew Drugs across U.S., Sold Them from Apartments He Rented," *Atlanta Journal-Constitution,* April 24, 2018, https://www.ajc.com/news/crime—law/officials-rapper-flew-drugs-across-sold-them-from-apartments-rented/NyJV5yHMGRk2Cnmnw52FIJ/.

358 *Ralo was later granted a $250,000 bond:* Aleia Woods, "Ralo Granted $250,000 Bond, Ex-

pected to Sign Paperwork Friday," XXL Mag, July 8, 2020, https://www.xxlmag.com/ralo-granted-250000-dollar-bond/.

358 *But it was promptly revoked:* Aleia Woods, "Judge Revokes Ralo's Bond after He Made Drug Deals in Prison Using an Apple Watch," XXL Mag, December 21, 2020, https://www.xxlmag.com/ralo-bond-drug-deals-prison-apple-watch/.

359 *"Most rappers die in their own city":* "Flashback: Boosie—Most Rappers Die in Their Own City, Hypnotized with Hatred," YouTube, djvlad, 2018, https://www.youtube.com/watch?v=61sTLramFEM.

360 *Plug, who claimed self-defense:* Adrianne Haney, "Bankroll Fresh Case File: Beef between Rappers Escalated to a Chaotic Fight, Deadly Hail of Gunfire," 11Alive.com, July 18, 2018, https://www.11alive.com/article/news/bankroll-fresh-case-file-beef-between-rappers-escalated-to-a-chaotic-fight-deadly-hail-of-gunfire/85-574894166.

360 *"Everything about Nipsey was Crenshaw and Slauson":* Joe Coscarelli, "For Nipsey Hussle and Rap's Thriving Middle Class, Staying Close to Home Can Have a Price," *New York Times*, April 4, 2019, https://www.nytimes.com/2019/04/04/arts/music/nipsey-hussle-shooting-death.html.

360 *comparing it to* The Hunger Games*:* Bill Torpy, "Opinion: Street Violence a Bad Rap for Atlanta's Music Industry," *Atlanta Journal-Constitution*, February 24, 2021, https://www.ajc.com/opinion/columnists/opinion-street-violence-a-hard-rap-for-atlantas-music-industry/IJA6AF5PMZG5JAQNTFNUWDTDOA/.

360 *"putting a bunch of lions in one zoo":* Ibid.

360 *"taking one of the biggest risks":* Coscarelli, "For Nipsey Hussle and Rap's Thriving Middle Class, Staying Close to Home Can Have a Price."

Chapter Thirty

362 My Turn *was crowned the most popular:* Keith Caulfield, "Lil Baby's 'My Turn' Is MRC Data's Top Album of 2020, Roddy Ricch's 'the Box' Most-Streamed Song," *Billboard*, January 7, 2021, https://www.billboard.com/articles/business/chart-beat/9508037/mrc-data-2020-recap/.

362 *nearly four billion streams*: Ibid.

364 *"robbed and cheated out of millions of dollars": MIGOS, LLC, a Delaware limited liability company; QUAVIOUS MARSHALL PIK/A QUAVO, an individual; KIARI CEPHUS PIK/A OFFSET, an individual; KIRSNICK BALL PIK/A TAKEOFF, an individual; MIGOS TOURING, INC., a Georgia 14 corporation, v. DAMIEN GRANDERSON, an individual; DA VIS SHAPIRO LEWIT GRABEL & LEVEN, LLP, a New York limited liability partnership; GRANDERSON DES 20 ROCHERS, LLP, a California limited liability partnership; and DOES 1 through 100, inclusive* (Case No. 20STCV26508, July 15, 2020).

364 *"the personification of a self-absorbed shyster lawyer":* Ibid.

365 *"easy targets":* Ibid.

366 *Takeoff, the youngest and calmest of the trio, was sued for sexual battery: JANE DOE, an individual, Plaintiff, v. KIRSHNIK KHARI BALL a.k.a. TAKEOFF, an individual; and DOES 1 through 25, inclusive, Defendants* (Superior Court of the State of California for the County of Los Angeles).

366 *"physical evidence of forceful rape":* Ibid.

368 *G-Five went back to jail on outstanding warrants:* Morse Diggs, "Convicted Felon Released by Mistake Taken Back into Custody during Drag, Sneaker Bust," FOX 5 Atlanta, Au-

gust 8, 2020, https://www.fox5atlanta.com/news/convicted-felon-released-by-mistake-taken-back-into-custody-during-drag-sneaker-bust.

369 *Buckhead threatened to secede:* Jennifer Peebles and J. D. Capelouto, "What Would 'Buckhead City' Look Like? We Crunched the Numbers," *Atlanta Journal-Constitution*, April 25, 2021, https://www.ajc.com/news/atlanta-news/what-would-buckhead-city-look-like-we-crunched-the-numbers/WRIYJBY2PBCEJFKWTFK2YDWXYA/.

369 *"madman in the White House":* Richard Fausset, "'It Is Time to Pass the Baton': Keisha Lance Bottoms Won't Seek Second Term as Atlanta Mayor," *New York Times*, May 7, 2021, https://www.nytimes.com/2021/05/06/us/keisha-lance-bottoms-atlanta-mayor.html.

369 *The Dungeon . . . was bought by Big Boi:* Nancy Clanton, "Big Boi Buys the 'Dungeon' Where OutKast Got Its Start in Atlanta," *Atlanta Journal-Constitution*, January 17, 2019, https://www.ajc.com/entertainment/big-boi-buys-the-dungeon-where-outkast-got-its-start-atlanta/hMARdHf8HfidF7FDXQovwK/.

369 *briefly became an Airbnb:* "Big Boi Invites Music Fans to Stay at the Iconic Dungeon Family House," Airbnb, June 17, 2021, https://news.airbnb.com/dungeon-family/.

INDEX

ABOUT THE AUTHOR

Joe Coscarelli is a culture reporter for *The New York Times* with a focus on music, and the host of the video series *Diary of a Song*. He previously worked at *New York* magazine and *The Village Voice*. *Rap Capital* is his first book.